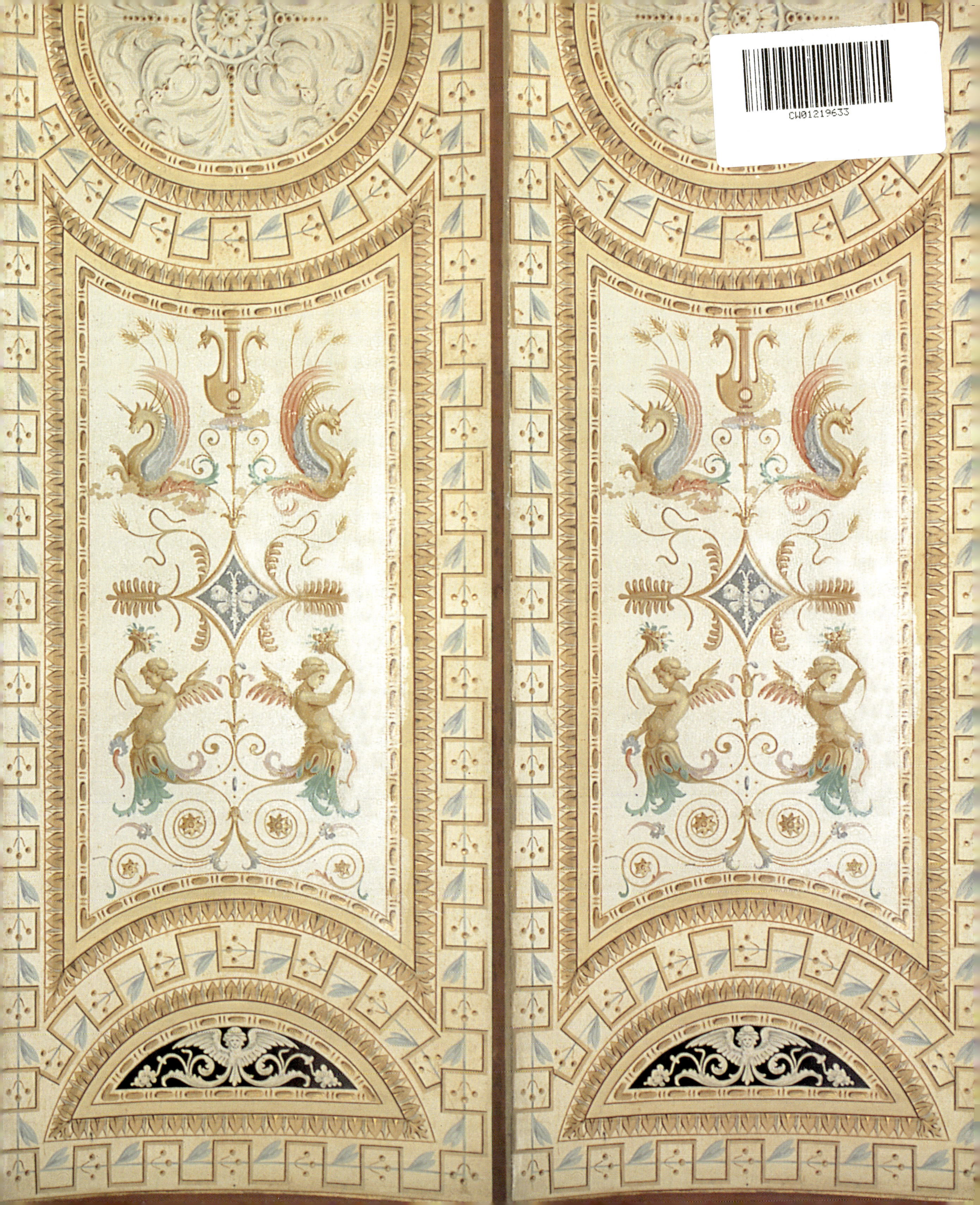

Neoclassical Architecture in Greece

Greek edition © 2001 Melissa Publishing House
English translation © 2004 Melissa Publishing House
Athens, Greece
www.melissabooks.com

Athina Ragia, *General Editor*
Katerina Logotheti, *Text Editor*
David Hardy, *Translator*
K. Adam, *Reproduction of Illustrations*

First published in the United States of America in 2004 by
Getty Publications
1200 Getty Center Drive, Suite 500
Los Angeles, California 90049-1682
www.getty.edu

Christopher Hudson, *Publisher*
Mark Greenberg, *Editor in Chief*

Ann Lucke, *Managing Editor*
Mollie Holtman, *Editor*
Pamela Heath, *Production Coordinator*

Library of Congress Cataloging-in-Publication Data
Birēs, Manos G.
  [Neoklasikē architektonikē stēn Hellada. English]
  Neoclassical architecture in Greece / Manos Biris, Maro Kardamitsi-Adami;
translated by David Hardy.
    p. cm.
  Includes bibliographical references and index.
  ISBN 0-89236-775-X (hardcover)
1. Architecture—Greece—19th century. 2. Neoclassicism (Architecture)--
Greece. I. Kardamitsē-Adamē, Marō. II. Title.
NA1097.B5713 2004
720'.9495'09034—dc22
                        2004013770

Printed and bound in Greece

The reprinting, republication, or reproduction in whole or in part of
the text or illustrations of this book is forbidden without the written permission
of the publisher.

Manos Biris
Maro Kardamitsi-Adami

Neoclassical Architecture in Greece

The J. Paul Getty Museum, Los Angeles

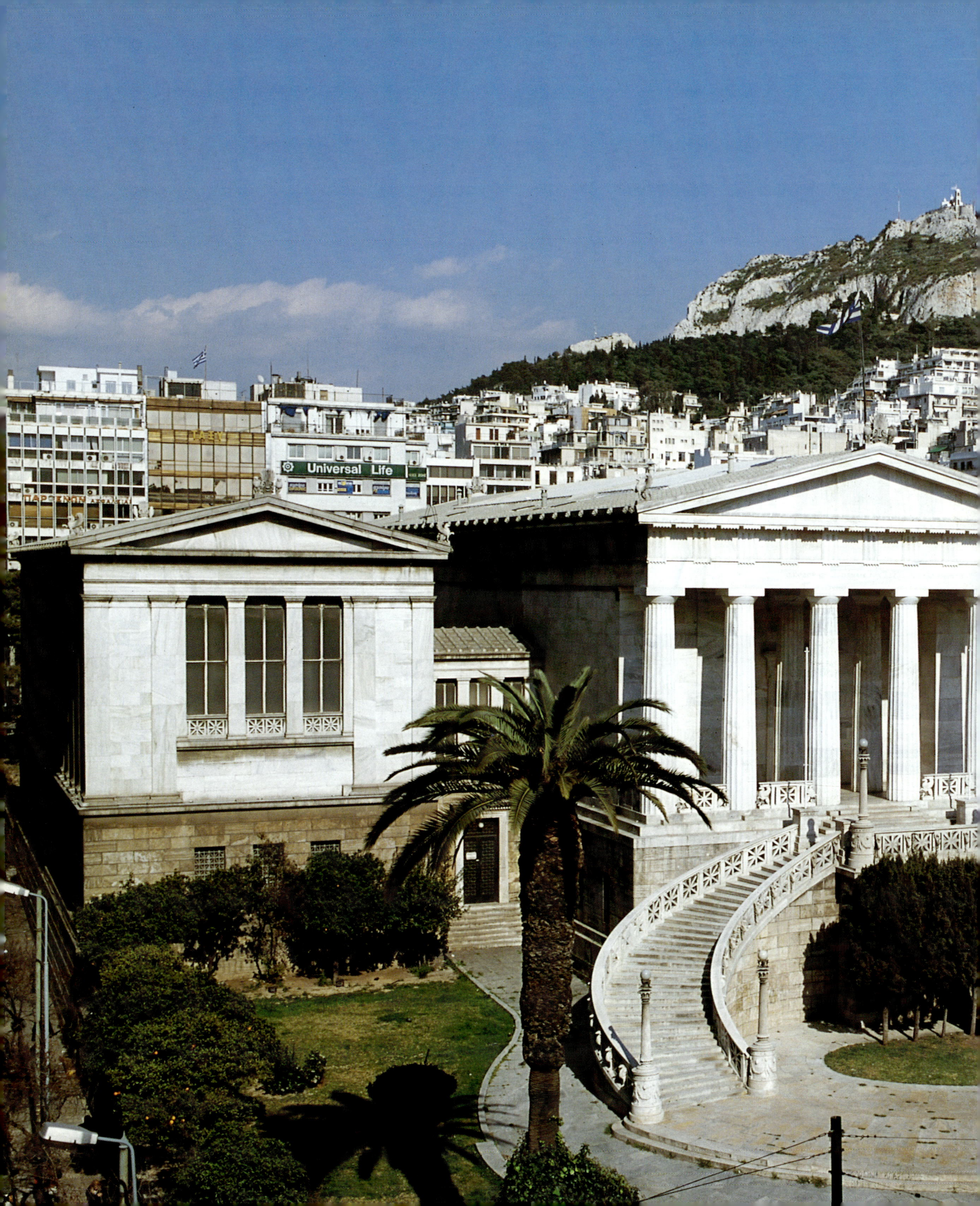
Universal Life

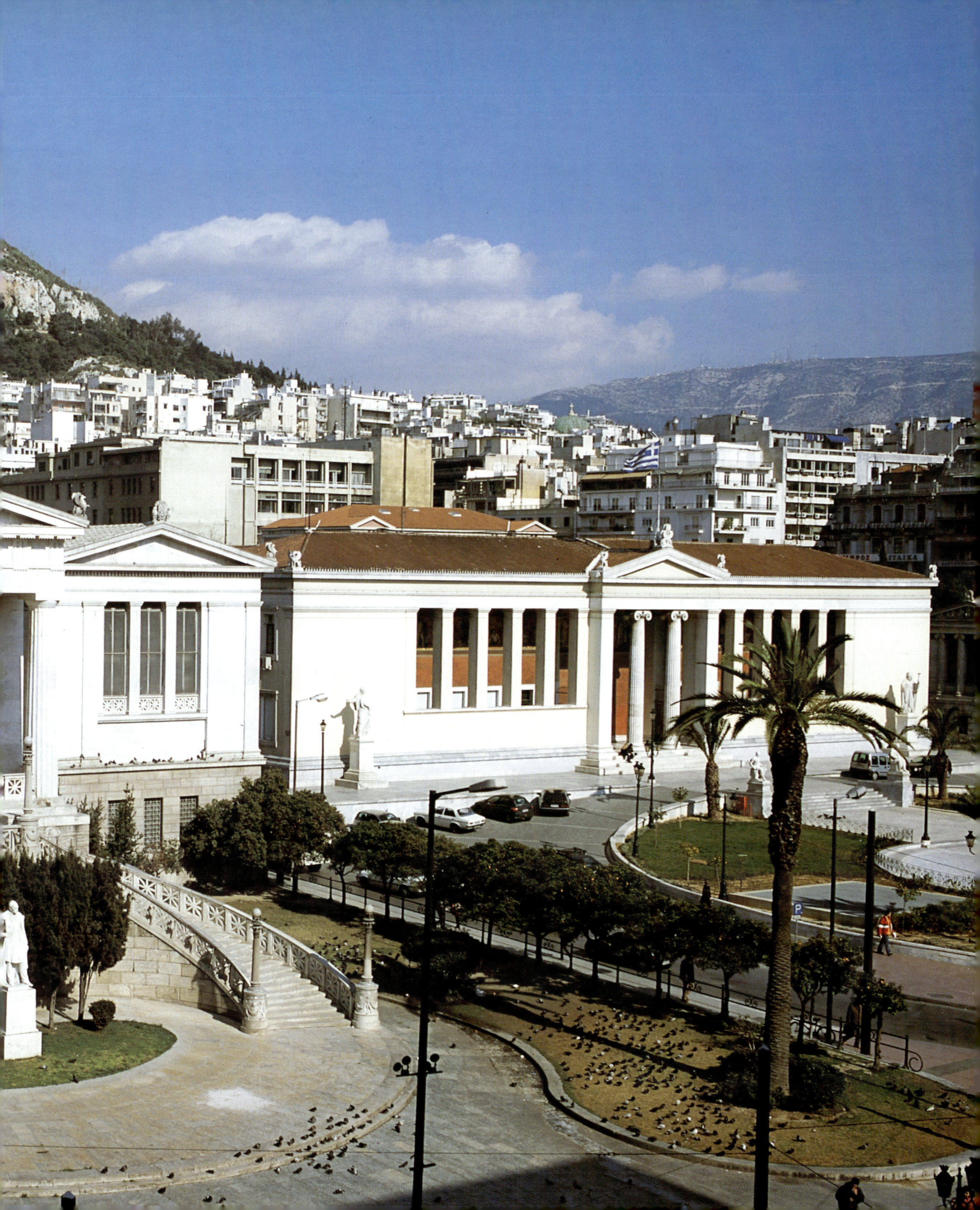

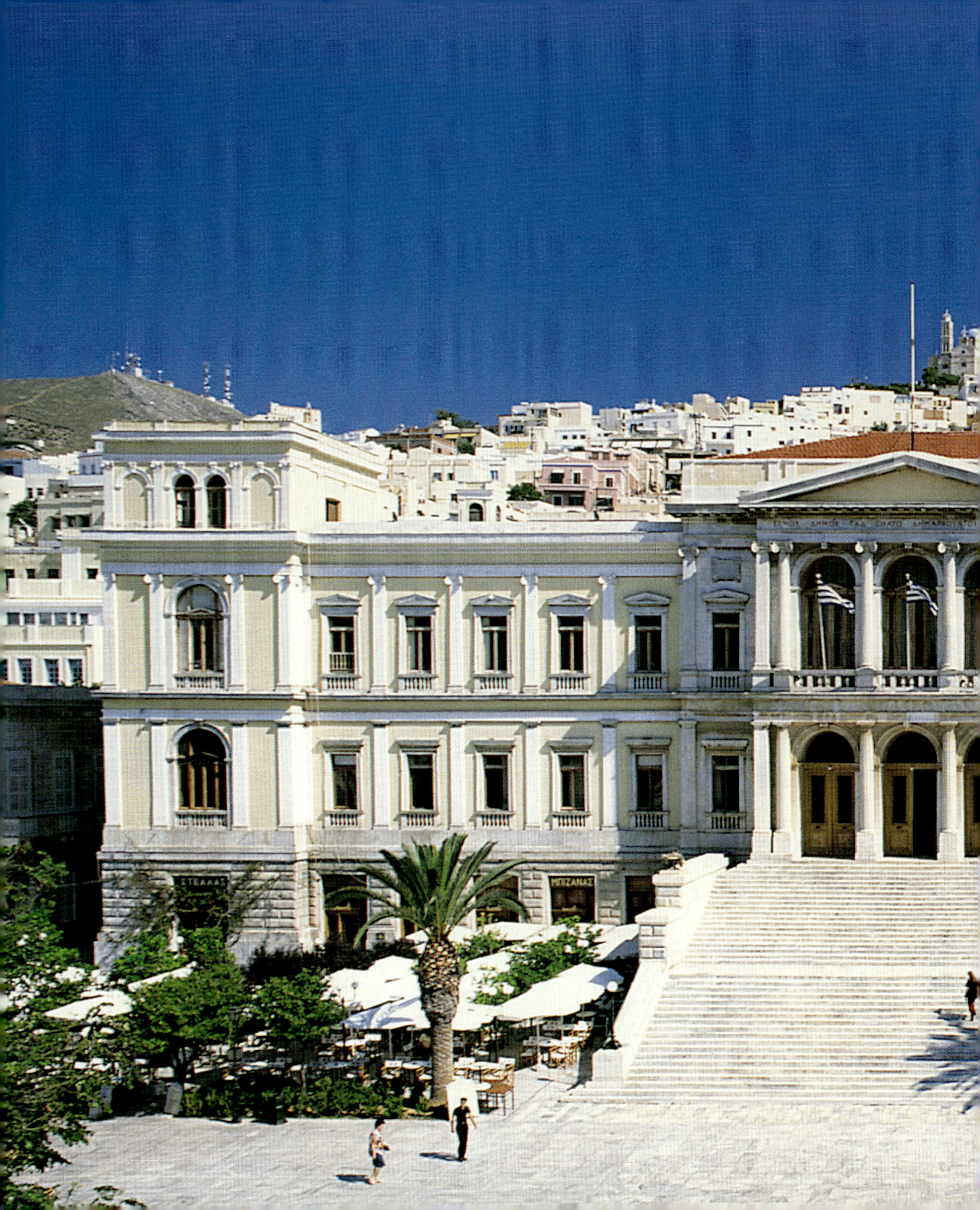
ΣΤΕΛΛΑΣ
ΜΠΙΖΑΝΑΣ

ACKNOWLEDGMENTS 10

INTRODUCTION 13

THE MODELS 15
The Reappraisal of Antiquity
The Urban Character
Classical Order as a Means of Expression

TRADITION AND WESTERN INFLUENCES 27
Transmutations of the "Classical"
Ideological and Aesthetic Openings

THE NEW GREEK STATE 51
The Imposition of Planning under Kapodistrias

ATHENS THE CAPITAL 69
Reconstructing the City
The Consolidation of Monumentality

THE REGENERATION OF THE TOWNS 103
Social and Architectural Transformation
The Mediating Role of Classicism

THE ZENITH OF ATHENIAN CLASSICISM 133
Urban Society Matures
Public Buildings
Athenian Residences

THE UNREDEEMED TERRITORIES 171
The Period of Modernization
Epiros
Central and Northern Greece
The Islands

MASS CLASSICISM 211
The Late-Nineteenth-Century Aesthetic
The Work of Ernst Ziller
Decentralized Classicism
The Symbolism of Style
The Byzantine Revival

THE TRANSITION TO MODERNISM 261
The Centers That Received the New Styles
Between Academism and "Greekness"

EPILOGUE 297

BIBLIOGRAPHY 305

INDEX 308

SOURCES OF ILLUSTRATIONS 312

ABBREVIATIONS 312

ACKNOWLEDGMENTS

We embarked on this book fully aware of the difficulties of studying modern Greek architecture, which is geographically and culturally extensive, as well as morphologically multifaceted. As we made our visits, we experienced both the charm and the painful deterioration of Greek towns and buildings. Having gleaned substantial historical testimony, we are now prepared to confirm or refute earlier views, add new evidence, and make the case for our own conclusions. We leave it to our readers to judge whether we have achieved our objectives.

We would like to thank all those who have assisted us. People from every corner of Greece provided information on their birthplaces, and their contributions have been crucial to our research. Our thanks also go to Velis Voutsas, Yorgis Yerolympos, Ilias Georgouleas, and Stelios Synodis, who accompanied our travels and used their lenses to capture the images that illustrate the text. The heads of the archives of ELIA (Hellenic Literary and Historical Archive), KTNA (Documentation Centre for Neo-Hellenic Architecture), and State General Archives have unstintingly provided us with rare, frequently unpublished, documentation from their invaluable collections. Above all, however, we express our gratitude to Yorgos Ragias, who provided us with the occasion and the opportunity to rise to the challenge of this project, and to his daughters, Annie and Athina, whose professionalism and perfectionism have made this book possible.

---

page 6–7. Athens. View of part of the "Neoclassical Trilogy," with the National Library on the left and the University of Athens on the right. The harmonious relationship between the elements of the complex, and the individual scale of the monumental buildings, integrates the group into the built and natural environment of Athens.

page 8. Ermoupolis. View of the Town Hall. A mansion of impressive appearance designed by the German architect Ernst Ziller, it exhibits imposing scale and surprising quality of morphology. This important architectural expression was inextricably linked with the town's then-flourishing bourgeois society.

page 11. Athens. The central Ionic porch of the Academy of Athens. This supreme architectural composition by Theophil Hansen is without question one of the outstanding creations of European classicism.

page 12. Patras. Typical town house with two residences. Elements associated with the ancient orders are combined in a facade that has been given a rationalist design. The unavoidable reduction in size of the ground-floor entrance is a distinctive feature.

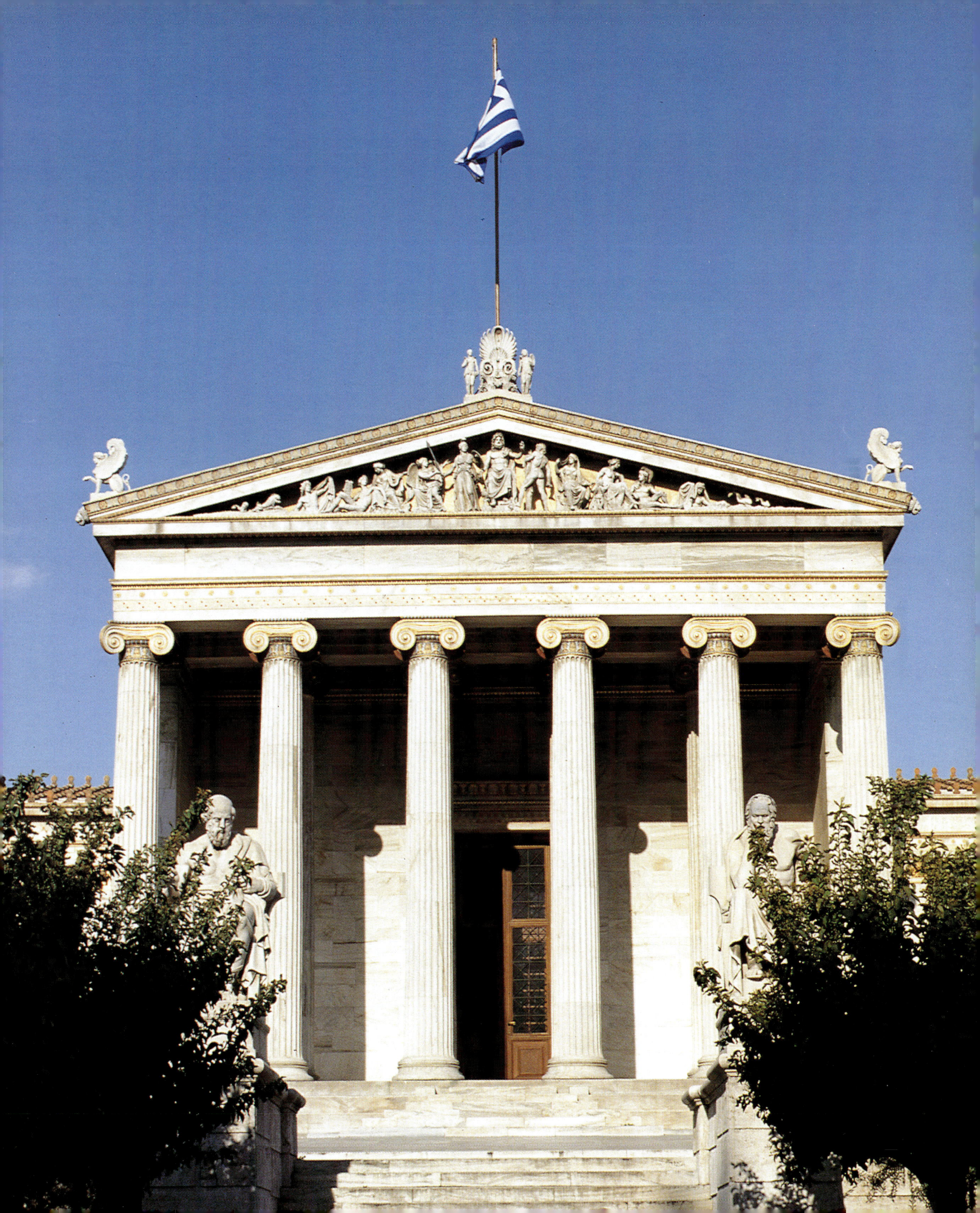

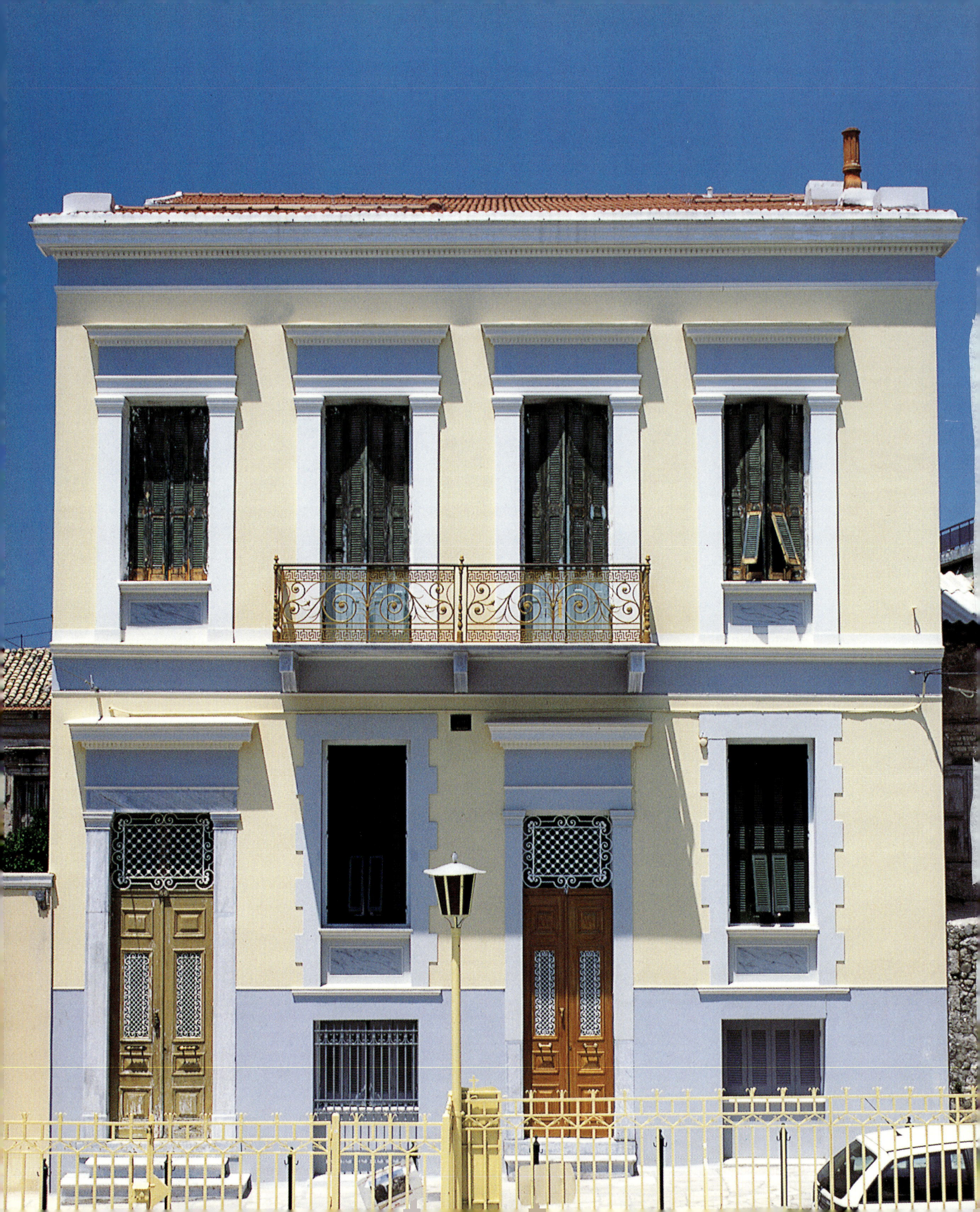

INTRODUCTION

Neoclassical architecture's introduction to Greece after that country's War of Independence (1821–31) and the style's dominance for at least eight decades constitute a phenomenon unique in the history of European art and civilization. Neoclassical architecture exhibits significant local variations in its morphology and was prevalent until the beginning of the twentieth century, in some cases evolving into the mature expression of eclecticism. Its distant roots, however, are to be found in the Enlightenment and in the general climate of Western humanism, which extended to the spheres of art, culture, and politics with the eighteenth-century urban revolution.

Within both the restricted geographic borders of the newly founded Greek state and the wider areas of unredeemed Greece, ideal forms were revived and old-fashioned ideas reappeared, though as a whole these were associated with progressive ideas and reflected the aesthetic models of the urban culture of Europe. Inevitably, these models were juxtaposed with the rich, inexhaustible post-Byzantine tradition of roughly four centuries—a tradition that, by its very nature, was far removed from the restless theories of Western Romanticism and even more remote from the love of the ancient world cultivated by the pioneers of classicism.

On the other hand, there can be no doubt that these ideological changes took place long before 1800, as they were consciously adopted by large segments of the Greek diaspora.

According to current views of modern Greek architecture, the emergence of classicism coincided with King Otto's arrival in Greece and its cultural repercussions. The reality, however, appears to be different. Classicism, in other respects a uniform aesthetic movement, had different starting points and traveled along a variety of routes.

In the present study, we attempt to provide, as far as possible, an overall picture of Neoclassical architecture in Greece, introducing a number of factors and criteria that lead to a more penetrating examination of its distinctive forms, the background against which it was created, and its models, which are associated with this background.

In our judgment, the kind of fullness of essential components that represents the Greek architectural expression of the nineteenth and early twentieth centuries, particularly with regard to general ideological and artistic criteria, is exhibited mainly by public or private urban buildings, and only to a lesser extent by religious ones. Although the historical context to which this architecture belongs and in which it developed does not permit the definition of a clear, constant, corresponding "ethnic space," reference must be made also to those architectural structures that express an inclination or devotion to the national ideal, even though these fall within the sphere of urban Romanticism and, later, historicism.

The material in this book is presented historically (by successive chronological phases) and geographically (by areas within Greece). This dual approach is dictated not so much by the need to emphasize the contextual character of forms and types as by the need to investigate various architectural perceptions in the dimensions of place and time. We are also concerned to identify any likely coincidence between them in different contexts and social environments.

It should be recognized that, despite recent progress made in individual research subjects, significant gaps in documentation exist, and a very high proportion of Neoclassical buildings has unfortunately disappeared as a result of the reconstruction of towns, particularly in the postwar period.

Regarding the critical approach adopted for the phenomena under examination, certain adjustments have been made. The distinctive character of the nineteenth century in Greece, as indeed in Europe, lies in the circumstance that its urban architecture cannot be classified according to a charter of typological, stylistic, and morphological systems defined on the basis of immutable prescriptions and perceptions regarding the conditions under which they were produced. Such a classification system is a necessary prerequisite of the methodology usually applied to the study of the history of architecture, but the phenomena of the period in question are not associated with homogeneous types and styles. Instead, they exhibit attributes reflecting the provincial consciousness of the societies that created them. There are, of course, exceptions, such as in the case of Athenian Neoclassicism, in which an independent and autonomous cultural consciousness can be identified that formed the substructure for the purity of design and authenticity of forms used in architecture.

For each case, it is therefore necessary to examine the context in which the architectural phenomena were created and to describe the forms' specific typologies and stylistic idioms in order to identify the intrinsic features and their internal gradations. By so doing, it becomes possible to understand the relationships and dialectical effects of creative influences. The specific aesthetic views and the potentialities of the morphological expressions of this period impose their own rules of qualitative analysis and interpretation, which define a new stance on the researcher's part toward the history of architecture.

The Models

F. 6.   F. 7.

2 Mod.= 0,658 m.

THE MODELS

The Reappraisal of Antiquity

The creation of the modern Greek state in the wake of the national liberation struggle of 1821 took place many years after the events in eighteenth-century Europe that led to a fundamental readjustment of its social structures, contributed to the formation of a new bourgeois class, and defined its progressive attitude to the components of production and knowledge, of intellectual activity and aesthetics, and, finally, of life itself.

Until the time of liberation, the overwhelming majority of people in the new state had never enjoyed, in their own land, certain important elements that often antedate the acquisition of independence itself. These were the natural development, step by step, of an infrastructure of innovative ideas, the undistracted quest for historical roots and models, a practical experience of research and knowledge, and the emotional approach to the perception of the beautiful: in other words, all the elements that had been created in Europe by bourgeois liberalism (figs. 3, 4).

By good fortune, however, the Greeks of the diaspora had experienced some aspects of this movement as early as the late eighteenth century, which to some extent moderated the more absolute stance adopted by the Enlightenment. They were therefore in a position to transmit to Greece essential ingredients of this cultural change, the immediate result being the incubation of a broader climate of romantic nationalism.

It should be noted, however, that in Greece this climate did not coincide with the Romanticism of those European thinkers who viewed the turn to the past through an appreciation of a popular, native element. The Greek version was aimed rather at the idealized reconstruction of the values of antiquity: the values of literature, language, and aesthetics in the arts and, of course, in architecture. It was thus identified with the concurrent trend of European Romanticism, which added an ideological dimension to the perceived superiority of the "classical," which it regarded as unique and unparalleled. To this extent, the principles of Roman architecture and the Renaissance were reimbued by the Europeans with the spirit of an ecumenical aesthetic that is today generally called romantic classicism.

In nineteenth-century Greece, then, the reappraisal of antiquity proceeded mainly along two paths: one characterized by a predilection for the ancient world that pervaded eighteenth-century thought, in contact with the European heritage of the revival of Roman architecture during the Italian Renaissance; the other a new aesthetic orientation—Greek classicism—which was governed primarily by the use of the Greek orders (figs. 1, 2).

In the former case, that of the predilection for the ancient world, Western influences were various and independent of their historical and geographical source. By contrast, the introduction of the ancient Greek orders into architecture is inextricably bound up with the official promotion of nationalism, through its own historical and ideological roots, from as early as the time of Ioannis Kapodistrias (1776–1831), Greece's first governor from 1827 to 1831. And it was consolidated

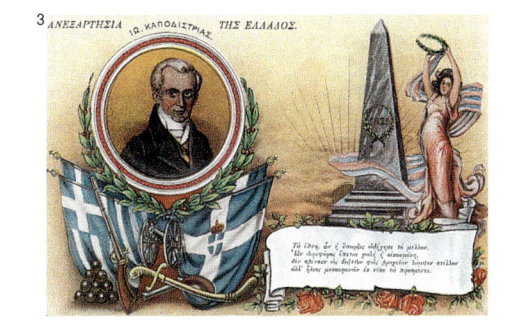

2. Seventeenth-century landscape illustration of the Athenian Acropolis, one of the earliest European depictions of ancient Greece. (Source: Marcian Library, Venice.)

1. Internal frieze, Ionic capital, and base from the cella of the temple of Apollo Epikourios at Bassai. This drawing accurately depicts the ancient original.

3, 4. Popular depictions of the leaders of the Greek struggle for independence: Ioannis Kapodistrias, founder of the modern Greek state, and Adamantios Koraïs, herald of the Greek Enlightenment. Postcards.

with the establishment of the rule of King Otto and the attendant imposition of the German morphological models of classicism.

On the one hand, therefore, we have the long and potentially classicizing history of Western architecture, which made its mark on the built environment in Greece—sometimes transiently and sometimes more permanently—either through Renaissance archetypes or through the idiosyncratic manifestations of Romanticism and, later, historicism (figs. 5, 6).

On the other hand, we are faced from 1830 onward with the complete predominance of a standard view of the design of urban buildings, perceived through specific ideological references and aesthetic theories. The classical models are now clearly organized in a hierarchy that determines the style, the quality of the adaptation of the forms, and the fidelity of the rendering of the ancient order. It is mainly during this phase that the Greek nation was reborn, as a result of important state reforms that established in people's consciousness new connections and ideas about the models. The goal of these reforms was to secure recognition of the relics of the classical past as essential elements in any form of creative art, especially urban architecture itself.

The Urban Character

The morphology of Greek classicism arrived in Greece through circumstantial ideological and artistic processes directly connected with German influence. Nevertheless, the aesthetic styles and trends related to classicism that were, in the end, cultivated in the context of urban transformation developed indisputably into a native expression of the waning Romantic and flourishing Neoclassical aesthetic. This reveals a corresponding relationship between nineteenth-century Greek society and the morphological examples of post-Romantic historicism that it had itself adopted. In the case of architecture, this relationship disturbed the "natural" and anticipated changes to a long tradition, one that had matured preeminently in popular culture.

This comprehensive transformation demonstrated that the ability of a rapidly changing society to adopt and assimilate aesthetic models depends almost exclusively on the way guiding principles are assigned to a hierarchy in place and time. "Guiding principles" are those that make a substantial contribution to the formation of a specific, socially acceptable cultural identity. Without doubt, one of the factors contributing to the establishment of national independence was the idea of a Greek architectural identity that was consciously sought and found an ideal home in the ideological dictates of romantic classicism.

On the other hand, within the climate of nineteenth-century liberalism, the acquisition of an urban character—the most important achievement of the transformation of Greek society—should have been strongly projected, in contrast with the underdevelopment and marginalization of the years of subjection, oppression, and enslavement.

In a way, then, the "national" architecture destroyed the traditional forms of the past, which were inextricably linked with the years of subjugation, through new associations of ideas identified with individual dignity and collective modernization. Its morphology provided the figurative codes through which the symbolic view of the new urban life could be expressed.

The classical ideal in the context of pre-Romantic academism.

5. The five architectural orders, according to Claude Perrault, 1683.

6. Model for a Corinthian capital, according to Claude Perrault, 1684.

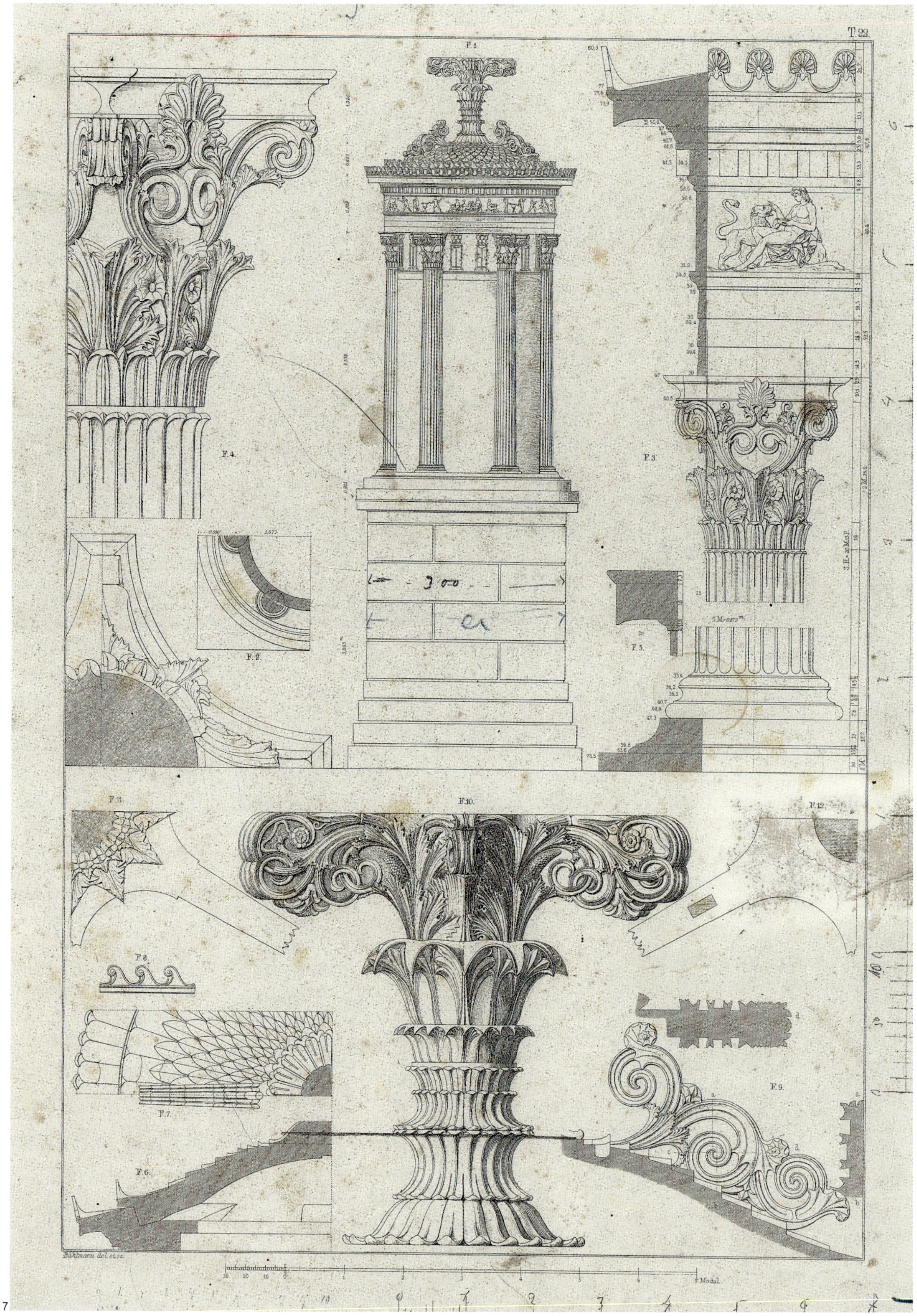

The archaeological approach to the Greek models revealed three fundamental virtues of classical morphology: authenticity and accuracy of detail; harmony and aesthetic self-sufficiency of the whole; and high-quality application of the order in pentelic marble.

7. Athens. Lysikrates Monument.

8. Athens. Temple of Wingless Victory.

Classical Order as a Means of Expression

Vernacular architecture as a whole may be defined as the result of a spontaneous creative act; that is, as something produced not by standardized rules, but by tried and tested experiences, in which form is an expression of function, moderation, and the human scale.

The demand for "Greekness" was presumably not, in itself, of interest to the agents of vernacular architecture; it was a dimension inherent in the spirit and component principles of the creative act. Even the Westernizing "learned" elements of vernacular architecture — for example, individual features from the Italian Renaissance — enjoyed unimpeded access to the Greek tradition, to the extent that the structure did not depart from the principles mentioned above.

In the period under examination, however, which saw a rapid transformation of the modern Greek urban consciousness and an attendant assimilative influence of the planned urban environment, architecture changed radically. Its role now was to respond to selective values, both symbolic and mnemonic, which, to some extent, made the introduction of a monumental expression necessary. This expression was the product of an ideological approach to historical time and was capable of giving prominence to the supreme achievements of the national past. In the case of the modern Greek state, the achievements that enshrined the most exciting and idealized view of Greek creative architecture were none other than the monuments of classical antiquity.

However, contact between Greece and the outstanding models of its architecture had been severed for about four centuries. The liberated Greece of 1828 had not forged any direct links with monumental architecture since the Byzantine period, with a few exceptions, such as important monastery churches. By contrast, the West had for centuries enjoyed countless transubstantiations of its medieval and Renaissance past, in association, of course, with the historical circumstances and cultural variety of the individual regions.

Until about 1760, Europe maintained contact with the "classical" solely through the Italian Renaissance. After the middle of the eighteenth century, the descriptions and illustrations published by foreign travelers led to increased European interest in Greek antiquities. Two impressive books played a leading role in this change: *Les ruines des plus beaux monuments de la Grèce* (The ruins of the most beautiful monuments of Greece, 1770), by the French architect Julien-David Le Roy, and *The Antiquities of Athens Measured and Delineated* (2 vols., 1762, 1789), by the British painters and architects James Stuart and Nicholas Revett. At the same time, a critical assessment of the "Greek miracle" was propounded by the brilliant German antiquarian and aesthete Johann Joachim Winckelmann in his essay *Gedanken über die Nachahmung der griechischen Werke* (Thoughts on the imitation of Greek works, 1755) and was later supported by the leading German exponents of Hellenocentric philosophy and speculation, such as the philosopher and theologian Johann Gottfried von Herder, the poet, playwright, and critic Johann Christoph Friedrich von Schiller, and the prolific poet and sage Goethe (figs. 7–11).

Greece itself, still subject to foreign rule, naturally played no part in these significant changes. Until about 1750, the post-Byzantine architectural tradition underwent gentle changes that no doubt reflected an authenticity associated with specific living and working conditions. Only in rare cases did anonymous architecture partake of what might be called the official or learned rendering of forms.

In any event, it is possible to identify in Greek architectural expression, especially in decoration from the period before the War of Independence, a

9. German historian and critic Johann Joachim Winckelmann. His essays, written just after the middle of the eighteenth century, had a catalytic influence on the recognition of ancient Greek art throughout Europe. Winckelmann extolled "the noble simplicity and the tranquil grandeur of its historical models." (Source: *Berlin und die Antike* catalogue, Berlin, 1979.)

10, 11. James Stuart and Nicholas Revett, British architects and painters and emissaries of the Society of Dilettanti, which was interested in the ancient world. On their visit to Athens in 1751, Stuart and Revett drew the most faithful illustrations of the classical orders up to that time. Their famous albums made a major contribution to acquainting the European public with Greek antiquities. (Source: Stuart and Revett, *The Antiquities of Athens Measured and Delineated*, London, 1762–1816.)

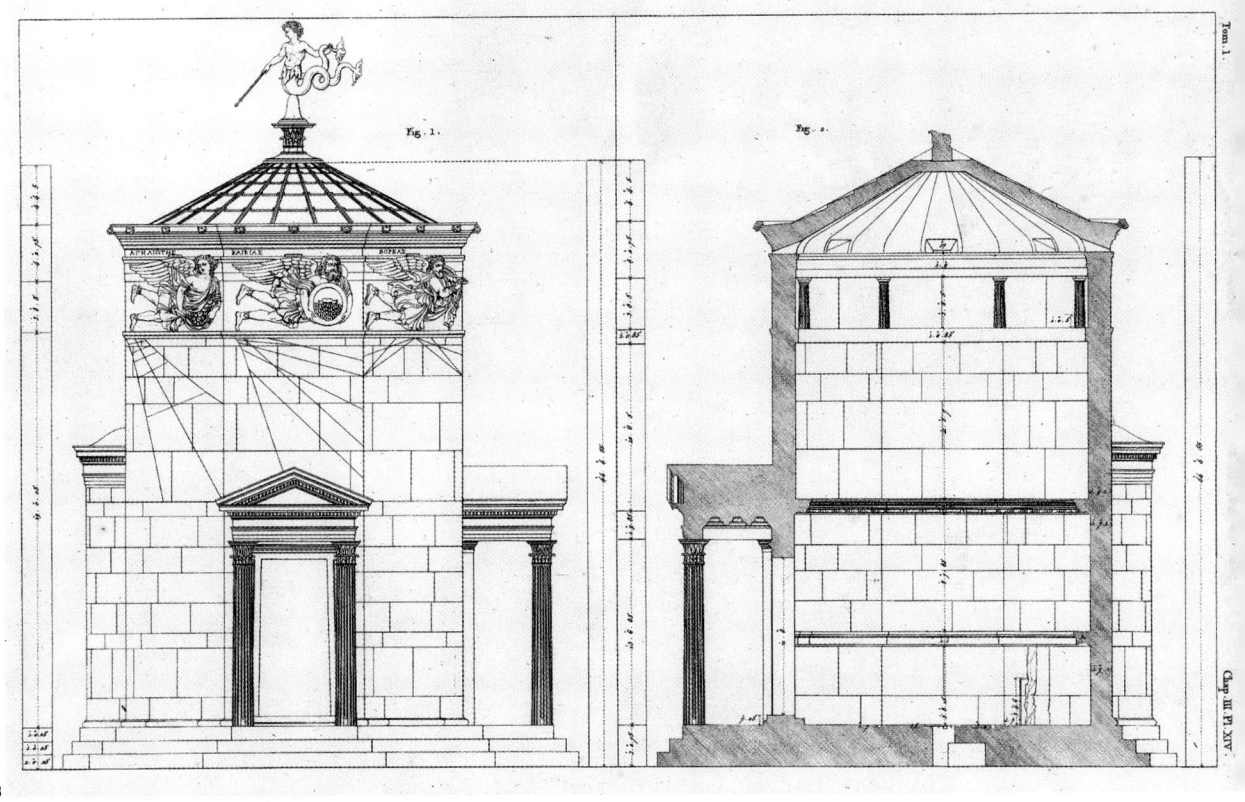

12. Athens. Tower of the Winds (Clock of Andronikos Kyrrhestes): elevation and ground plan. This early drawing of the monument departs significantly from reality. (Source: R. Pococke, *A Description of the East and Some Other Countries*, London, 1743, 1745.)

13. Reconstruction drawing of an elevation and section of the Tower of the Winds. This accurate reconstruction reflects an archaeological approach to the monuments. (Source: Stuart and Revett, *The Antiquities of Athens Measured and Delineated*, London, 1762–1816.)

14. Depiction of the Tower of the Winds among ruins and houses of the late Ottoman period. The Tower's romantic style is characteristic of the middle of the eighteenth century. (Source: Julien-David Le Roy, *Les ruines des plus beaux monuments de la Grèce*, Paris, 1770.)

15. General view of the area around the Tower of the Winds, with the Acropolis in the background. This rendering of the subject is more realistic than the one in figure 14. (Source: Stuart and Revett, *The Antiquities of Athens Measured and Delineated*, London, 1762–1816.)

variety of elements drawn from the classicizing, or at least the Westernizing tradition, normally admirably incorporated into the native forms. Their presence, however, does not contribute to a pure monumental style; it is rather an older foreign influence and has a pictorial, grafted character, and it usually reflects the local development of the art. By contrast, in the free Greek state of the nineteenth century, and here and there in the territories occupied by the unredeemed populations, "official" architecture made a systematic appearance. Despite its stylistic differences (whether classical or not), it abandoned the hitherto undefined, spontaneous, and intermediate forms and strongly projected a perception of monumental style. Its basic ingredients are the design canon and classical order. These not only represent the essential hallmarks of urban architecture; both also reveal profound changes in creative thought—that is, in the ability to achieve a unified conception of a monument and its historical environment (figs. 12–15).

Classical order, in particular, should be perceived not simply as the reproduction of monumental form but as a sufficient and necessary condition for the internal structure of architectural style. It should render—in addition to the canonical, the essential, the ideal aesthetic character—a fundamental and indisputable ethos as the basic content of the critical perception of the edifice.

The question that arises, of course, is whether the product of the creative act examined here represents a homogeneous, immutable order, so that intermediate categories and deviations (of typology and form) may be ruled out. The fact that a new social group with specific demands was emerging does not automatically preclude the variety of forms that inevitably results from the interweaving of existing heterogeneous factors. Moreover, variety is inherent in the spirit of Romanticism, while nineteenth-century historicism soon went beyond its theory to be diverted into morphological aspirations and stylistic differentiation, particularly in its late phase. And the empiricism and spontaneous creativity of ordinary people that inform a significant proportion of anonymous works should not be ignored. It is to some extent accepted that popular art, through its reducing filter, treated academic forms with unprecedented imagination and a naïve intent. In this case, the result, deprived of the precision of the authentic canon, nevertheless contains the characteristic and recognizable morphological codes. These stem from the predominant aesthetic beliefs, from the existing stylistic systems and their mutations, and, in general, from whatever distinguishes the qualities and principles of the new urban architecture.

Tradition and Western Influences

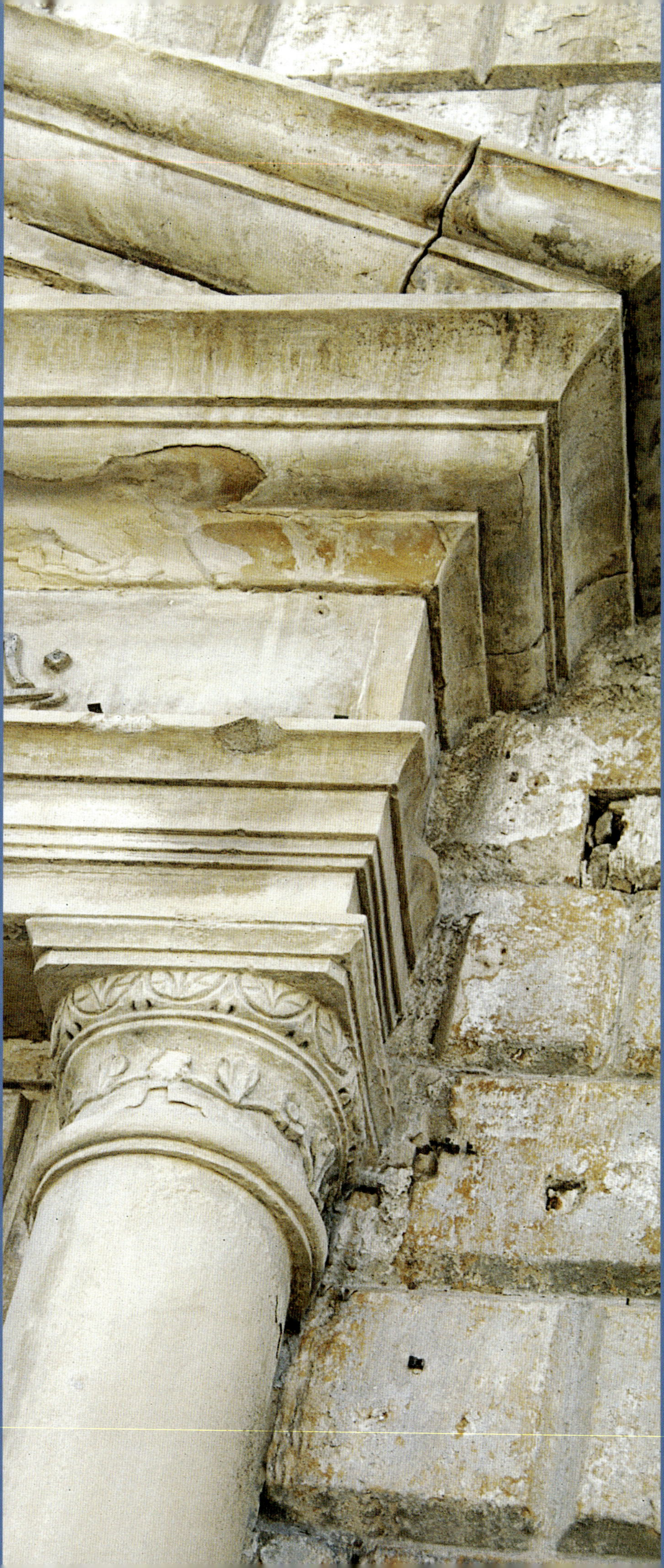

TRADITION AND WESTERN INFLUENCES

Transmutations of the "Classical"

The dawn of the nineteenth century found the whole of Greece under foreign occupation. The larger part of Asia Minor, Thrace, Macedonia, Epiros, Central Greece, the Aegean islands, Crete, and other areas were ruled by the Ottoman Empire.

The Ionian islands, however, continued to be Venetian possessions until the end of the nineteenth century, offering a hospitable welcome to Cretan artists and craftsmen who sought refuge and asylum there after the Ottoman conquest of Crete. The Ionian islands are perhaps the only region in which Western influences are predominant (fig. 17).

The architecture of Greece in the period before the national uprising exhibited a wide range of expression, depending on historical circumstances, cultural variety, and customs of each individual geographic area. The struggle for liberation and its grand objective, the creation of a nation state, inevitably made its mark on the integration and rehabilitation of Hellenism (with significant borrowings from Western culture), at least down to the critical early decades of the nineteenth century. However, this standardization of individual features and expressive means of the vernacular tradition was not yet visible.

As a whole, the forms of traditional architecture still spontaneously blended local elements with borrowings characteristic of a given historical and social reality. The aesthetic result, however, cannot easily be classified into clearly defined chronological periods. In this architecture, even when borrowed elements whose distant origins going back to the historical architectural orders can be identified, they are given a timeless quality and transformed by popular craftsmen in an endless process of trial-and-error and imitation. They are also subjected to remodeling, as, for example, with forms corresponding with Western models (Renaissance and Baroque), which survived mainly in the former Venetian possessions such as the Aegean islands. Despite the so-called learned approaches adopted for them, these remodelings certainly did not display harmony and balance, or the classical order and aesthetic—in short, they did not display the morphological values later given prominence by the ideology that underpinned free urban life. These forms are thus more properly included among the general manifestations of popular perception, and they should not be regarded as an early turn to classicism by traditional architecture. For, in practice, it was impossible for local societies under a regime of

16. Rethymnon. Detail of a doorway on Arkadiou Street showing the end of the entablature and pediment. High-quality application of the details of the orders are accurately carved in local stone.

17. Zakynthos. Street scene, about 1800, in a painting of the period. (Source: National Library, Paris.)

foreign occupation (regardless of whether this was of Eastern or Western origin) to have conscious access to an "official," much less a monumental, architecture. Moreover, in regions where people were not theoretically or ideologically predisposed to faithfully reproduce historical models of any kind, architecture, despite its detailed learned references, was governed and molded mainly by the collective memories and cultural affinities inherent in popular culture.

Setting aside prejudices and dilemmas, the spontaneous development of pre-revolutionary Greek architecture in the direction of the classical should be

18. Venice. Drawings of expanded facades. An impressive variety of form and scale and the use of different styles in the facades, ranging from Gothic and Renaissance to Mannerist, were the main source of inspiration for the urban architecture of the Ionian islands. Postcards.

recognized only where the historically evolving environment was capable of cultivating in the populace an intense experience of the relevant morphological models' values and qualities. In modern Greece, this relationship can be identified in close association with the emergence of comparatively independent urban societies and the concomitant creation of towns such as Corfu, Nafplion, Chania, and others, whose architecture is discussed below.

In the towns of the Ionian islands, in particular, the prevailing historical conditions offered no obstacle to transplanting flourishing Venetian urban traditions there. As a result, the local societies had scarcely any contact with the crude administrative regime of the Ottoman Empire and, along with the prospering Greeks of the diaspora, became the most privileged branch of Hellenism. The *Provveditore Generale* of the East, who exercised supreme authority in the Ionian islands, applied the social and administrative system imposed by the *Serenissima Repubblica* on all its colonies. Desirous of maintaining good relations with the Orthodox inhabitants of the islands and true to the principle "Venetians first and Christians second," Venice left the islanders free to perform their religious duties and recognized the rights of the Orthodox clergy (fig. 18).

19. Corfu. Ayion Panton Street. Multi-story residential buildings with related architectural elements show the discreet influence of the Venetian tradition and the later renewal of forms in the direction of British classicism.

20. Corfu. Nikiphorou Lytra Street. This cohesive urban complex is still preserved in its authentic style. Postcard.

21. Zakynthos. Rouga Square as it was before the earthquake in 1953. An imposing juxtaposition of multi-story facades reveals discreetly projecting cornices and balconies and rhythmical openings in the arcaded porticoes on the ground floor.

22. Zakynthos. Nikolaos Kyvetos villa at Akrotiri. The harmonious composition of the facade, with an arched porch and a Baroque element over the central section, was characteristic of the morphological perceptions of the architect Bocher. The villa was built at the end of the eighteenth century. (Source: *Neoclassical Villas of Zakynthos* [in Greek], Athens, 1987.)

The Greek society of the Ionian islands, divided on the model of Venice into three classes, the nobles (*nobili*), the bourgeoisie (*civili*), and the ordinary people (*populari*), was a vigorous, dynamic community, fully aware that, although it was under a foreign yoke, its yoke was very different from that borne by fellow Greeks and fellow Christians in the rest of Greece. They were left in no doubt about this by the inhabitants of the Peloponnese, Nafpaktos, Methoni, Monemvasia, and Nafplion, and the Cretans, Maniots, and Athenians who sought refuge in the islands after the capture of their own towns by the Ottomans. Alongside the Greek refugees, a significant number of earlier colonists remained or resettled in the Ionian islands.

Caught between West and East, the people of the Ionian islands gathered together memories, traditions, and experiences and created their own distinctive architecture. In the mansions and bourgeois residences of the towns and the mansions of the countryside, and also in the churches and, of course, the public buildings, Western influences are evident in the layout of the ground plan and the design and treatment of the facades (figs. 19–21).

Here, the Italian Middle Ages, the Renaissance, and Baroque found a new, perhaps more austere and spare, means of expression and were adapted to the local situation. The climate, the local materials, the different way of life, and the scale together created a distinctive architecture.

The mansions of Zakynthos, Corfu, Kephallonia, and Kythira are not Venetian *palazzi*, of course, but neither are they merely humble copies of *palazzi*. Richly and meticulously built, the mansions serve and express the economic ease, social status, and cultural life of their occupants.

Although differing from island to island, especially with regard to their internal layout, the mansions exhibit many features in common. Two- or three-story structures built in terraces, they obey laws of symmetry in their facades, which are usually flat and divided into parallel horizontal zones, with ground-floor arcades, larger or smaller balconies with railings, imposing entrance doors and gateways, and an abundance of windows to admit sunlight. The interior of such a mansion is divided into a zone with reception rooms and a zone with the living quarters. On Zakynthos, the first floor consists of a *piano nobile* (main room) dominated by sitting rooms, a dining room, and often a two-level ballroom with interior balconies. The large, imposing rooms—richly decorated with painted coffered ceilings, pillars, and colonnettes, curving and indented cornices, and elaborate doorways—add an air of grace and gentility. The feeling is intensified by the luxurious furniture, heavy tapestries, chandeliers, mirrors, paintings, silverware, crystal, and porcelain that supplement the decoration. Some furnishings were made in local workshops, which abounded in the Ionian islands, while others were imported directly from Europe.

The consequences of the devastating earthquake of 1953 were truly irreparable. Zakynthos and Kephallonia were razed to the ground, and superb architecture vanished forever; today we can only form an idea of it from descriptions, drawings, and photographs (figs. 23, 24).

If the mansions of the town are typical examples of European urban architecture, those of the countryside, built on conspicuous sites—usually on the crest of a hill amid acres of vineyards, farmland, olive groves, and gardens—frequently reveal the clear influence of corresponding Venetian complexes in the Italian countryside (figs. 22–25).

The mansion, the residence of the lord, was a large, imposing structure forming the core of a large complex that included ancillary buildings (rooms for

23–25. Local architecture of the countryside and the emergence of urban classicism in the Ionian islands incorporated an overall design in which the openings, entrances, and building line were harmonized.

Kephallonia. Aninos mansion at Argostoli. The facade follows the fluid lines of Italian Baroque.

Kephallonia. Metaxas residence at Argostoli. The robust facade dates from 1755 and embodies the morphological spirit of Italian modernism.

Kephallonia. Two-story country house at Pessada, with an arched portico on the ground floor and a roofed veranda on the upper story. (Source: K. P. Kosma-Kosmetatou, *Kephalliniaka, II Architecture* [in Greek], Athens, 1962.)

personnel, storerooms, stables, presses, and so on). The complex dominated the surrounding area and was developed either in a straight line, as on Zakynthos, with the ancillary rooms spreading to right and left in two rectangular wings, or around a central courtyard, as on Corfu. The maistra, the longitudinal pathway that led to the mansion through symmetrically designed gardens or drying floors for currants, lent it a greater sense of authority and power. The individual elements — gateways, wells, and paved courts — followed Western forms.

The urban houses of the middle and lower classes, though simpler, also reflected Venetian influences. On Corfu they are typically multistory structures, taking the form of an apartment building with a portico on the ground floor to house shops and storerooms. The facades are adorned by stone balconies with sculpted corbels and with elaborate door frames and an abundance of windows (figs. 26–28).

The monumental public buildings, usually designed by Venetian architects, were obviously intended for self-promotion, and their individual forms are clearly derived from Venetian models (figs. 29, 30). Characteristic elements include *loggias* (meeting places for the nobles), official residences, fountains, and entrance gates.

In contrast, the churches, despite having Renaissance forms and Baroque features on the exterior, followed strict Orthodox conventions in the interior.

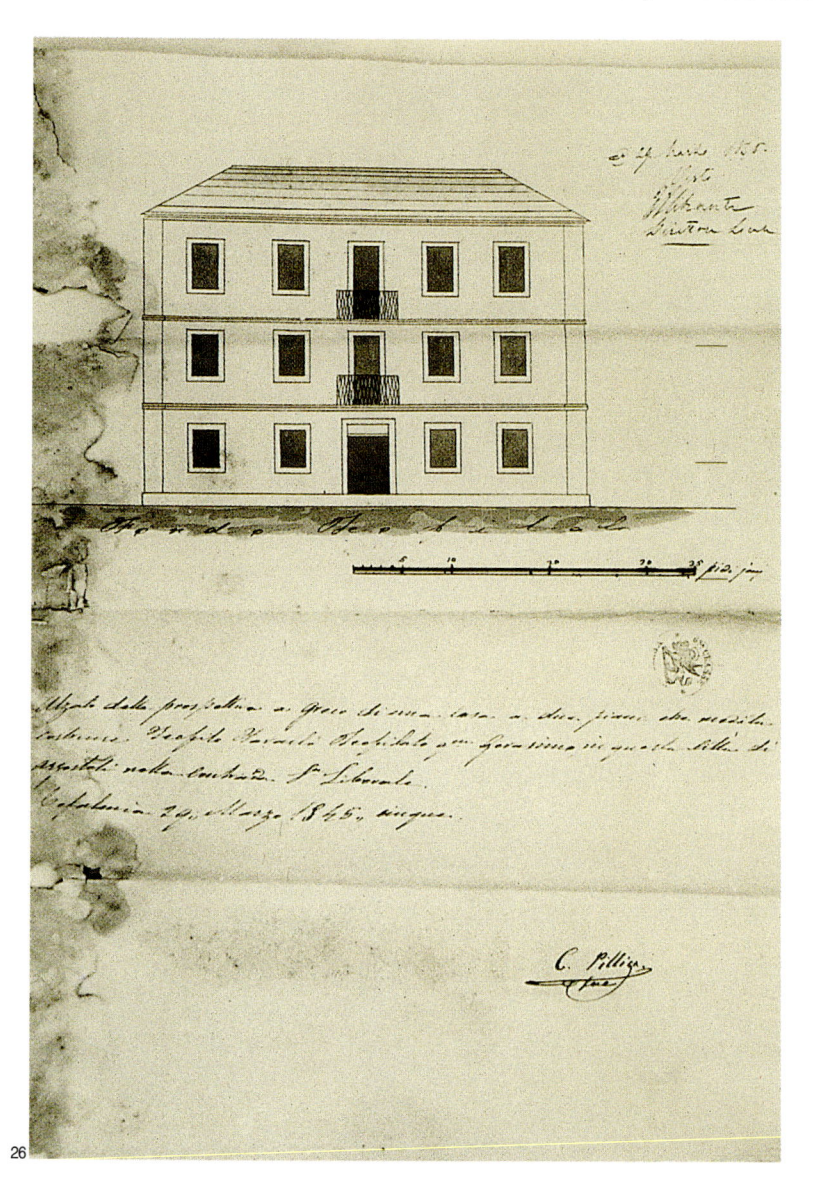

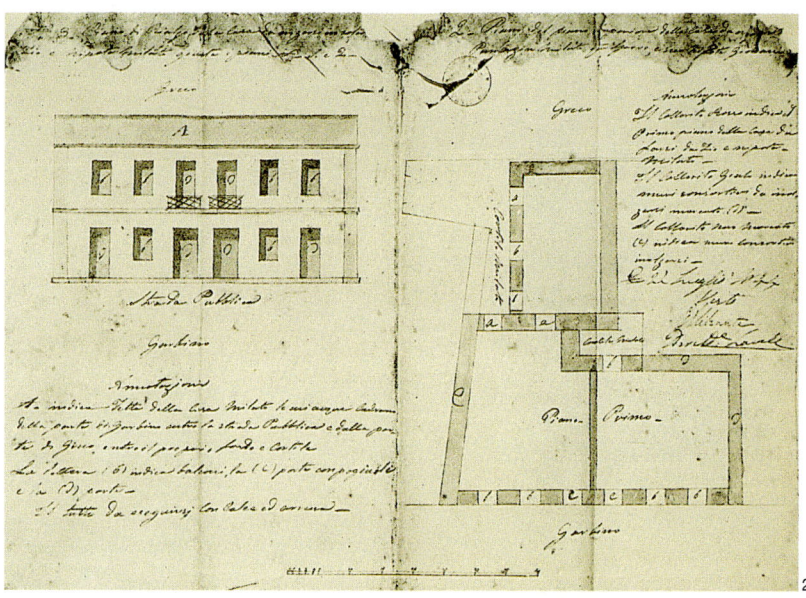

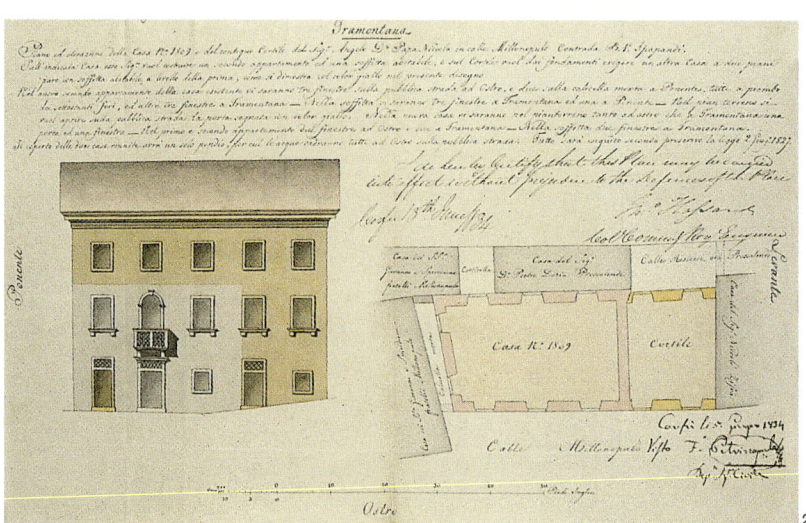

26. Kephallonia. Elevation of a three-story house. (Source: Kephallonia Town-planning Archive.)

27. Kephallonia. Elevation and ground-floor plan of a double residence. (Source: Kephallonia Town-planning Archive.)

28. Corfu. Elevation and ground-floor plan of a three-story residence. (Source: State General Archives, Ionian Archive, Corfu.)

29. Corfu. The gate of the New Fortress facing the harbor reflects a purely Venetian design.

30. Corfu. Paschaligos or Grimani Barracks. Home of the Ionian Academy after 1840. The facade exhibits Italian influence and has a classical frugality of expression, dictated, in this case, by the building's purpose.

Superb wood-carved *templa* divide the sanctuary from the nave, and there is often also a women's gallery. The morphological elements of the ceiling (*ourania*), *templon*, bishop's throne, pews, and campaniles, whether in the form of a tower or a simpler double arch, are again borrowed from the West, though remodeled by the Greek craftsmen who created them.

In the monasteries and the houses of ordinary people, local influences clearly dominate: construction and function are considerably simplified, and decorative elements are minimized. However, traces of the long foreign occupation can still be discerned (fig. 31).

After the liberation of Greece, a densely flowing "cultural river" between the communities of the Ionian islands and some of Old Greece's urban centers was restored, through which certain elements were transferred to the latter. This communication was particularly important to the developing cultural life of the new capital, Athens.

Crete, the largest of the Greek islands, shares many features in common with the Ionian islands. Over the centuries, it was occupied in turn by Arabs, Venetians, and Ottoman Turks, all of whom influenced its architecture. The Venetian period saw large-scale building activity, mainly in urban centers. Once again, Italian Renaissance elements either remained uncontaminated (figs. 16, 32, 33) or were blended with local traditions to create a distinctive architectural type (figs. 34–36).

In Crete, the risk of earthquakes prevented the construction of multistory apartment buildings like those found in Zakynthos and Kephallonia. The one- or two-story houses usually had two courtyards: one facing the street and another at the back of the plot. Here, too, storerooms, shops, and workshops were on the ground floor, while residential areas occupied the upper stories. The main family living room (*portego*) was located on the first floor. Directly above it, in three-story houses, was the *piano nobile* (main story).

A particularly interesting feature of Cretan houses is the presence, invariably on the upper story, of a long, wholly or partly roofed area that faces the street

31. Kephallonia. An old depiction of the Monastery of Ayios Gerasimos. The building complex follows the Orthodox design, though forms associated with Italian influence can be seen in the tall campanile above the entrance.

32. Rethymnon. Monumental facade of the house at 60 Arkadiou Street. High-quality Renaissance design is evident in this proposed reconstruction. (Source: I. Dimakopoulos, *Anthology of Greek Architecture* [in Greek], 1981.)

33. Rethymnon. Door frame of an urban residence in Arkadiou Street. Venetian tradition is formulated with a blend of early modern decorative features.

34. Rethymnon. Characteristic arched doorway of the Venetian period. This rendering of distinguished models betrays a rather local, popular intent.

35. Rethymnon. Impost block carved with decoration inspired by Venetian models. (Detail of fig. 34.)

36. Chania. Simplified form of impost block. Popular rendering recalling Italian examples.

37. Siteia. Lintel above a doorway, worked in the popular style, as remodeled from the Venetian period to the end of the nineteenth century.

38. Patmos. Arched fanlight with a characteristic early Neoclassical design.

39. Patmos. Detail of a window frame. Double pilaster is surmounted by an architrave with a straight cornice. The sculpted details (cavetto and ovolo moldings) attest to the Italian origins of the forms.

through a large archway. This room, the *iliakos*, or *liago* as it was called by the Venetians, has purely Byzantine origins. A similar room is to be found in the medieval houses of Chios.

In earlier buildings, the roofs of ground-floor rooms are often vaults in the shape of a pointed arch in cross-section, signaling the influence of Gothic architecture. The private urban residences of Crete, most of them carefully built, narrow-fronted structures with typical Venetian door frames and more or less richly decorated windows, provide much evidence for the period when architecture and other, allied arts were at their zenith on the island. Western influences, though not entirely absent from the countryside, are undoubtedly rarer here.

The Ottoman Turks, who gradually occupied Crete between the last decades of the 1600s and 1771, did change the appearance of urban centers. In the years of the island's struggle for liberation, the Ottoman Turks retained in their possession only the fortresses, while the Greeks controlled the entire countryside. In the following period, until 1898, when Crete acquired its independence, continual struggles between the Cretans and the Egyptians and Ottomans led to the island's devastation. A large part of the population migrated to the Ionian islands, the Peloponnese, and the Cyclades. It could be said that from an architectural point of view the nineteenth century found Heraklion, Rethymnon, Chania, and other towns of Crete more or less as the Venetians had left them; after each war and act of destruction, the inhabitants were not discouraged but repaired and rebuilt their houses and settlements (fig. 37).

The Aegean islands were less influenced than the Ionian islands by Westerners, who consisted of mainly Franks but also Venetians. Generally speaking, this influence was exercised on a much smaller scale. The architectural character of the islands remained largely true to local popular traditions; only a few isolated examples of Renaissance and Baroque elements can be found, and these did not define the image of a particular island. The larger of the Dodecanese islands, which remained under Italian rule up to the Second World War, are exceptions here, as are Chios and Lesvos. On these, Frankish memories remained alive and fertile until almost the end of the eighteenth century (figs. 38–46).

About 1800, foreign aesthetic elements began to be seen in mainland Greece and some of the eastern Aegean islands, but these took an overtly different form from those in the Ionian islands and Crete. They were indirect and derived not merely from the West but also from a variety of centers of cultural influence.

The fine mansions of these regions reveal the progress, prosperity, and cultural aspirations of their inhabitants. Under specific historical circumstances,

40. Andros. The Stylianidis *archontiko*. A blend of architectural features are drawn from Western tradition: on the ground floor, the door frame exhibits a frugal classicism; on the upper story, a light two-arched loggia recalls the Italian Renaissance tradition.

41. Tinos. Elegant arcaded porch in a two-and-a-half story house, clearly earlier than its neighbor, expresses the approach of mature urban classicism. Photograph taken at the beginning of the twentieth century. (Source: ELIA, Ar. Zachos Archive.)

42. Naxos. Palaiologos Tower at Sangri. Most of the towers on Naxos were built by the Venetians, from as early as the beginning of the seventeenth century. They were gradually incorporated into the local style, forming the nuclei of rural complexes.

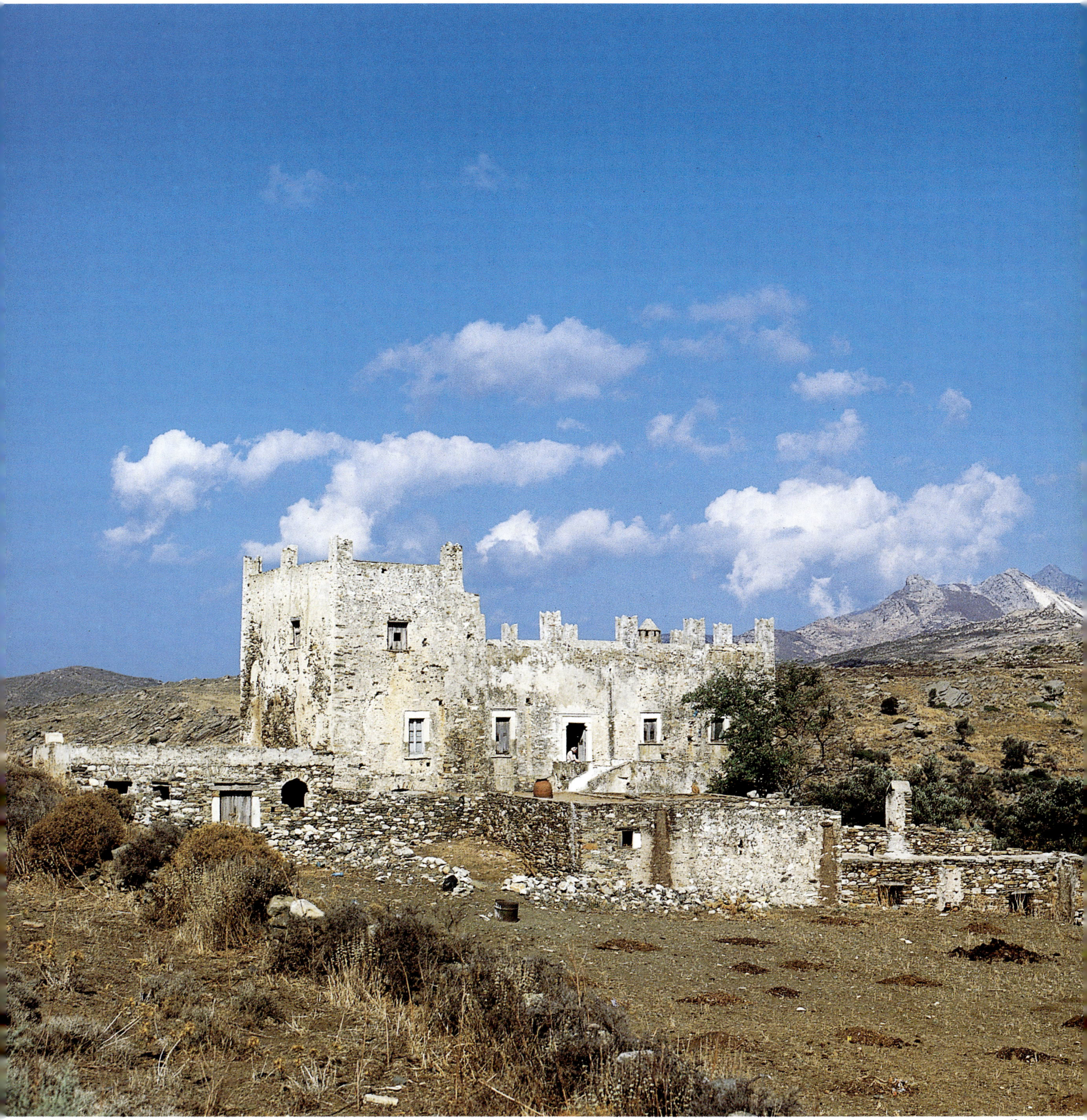

42

43. Chios. Gate of the Giustiniani mansion at Kambos. Carved entirely of stone, it exhibits the malleable forms of Baroque, while the strong color contrasts between the alternating masonry courses emphasize the building's tectonic style. Photograph taken in 1920. (Source: ELIA, Ar. Zachos Archive.)

44. Siphnos. Carved marble frame of an outer door. It provides an outstanding example of the blending of the popular artistic tradition with the classical order system. The use of corbels at the corners of the doorway is common in the Aegean islands and elsewhere. Photograph taken at the beginning of the twentieth century. (Source: ELIA, Ar. Zachos Archive.)

45. Mytilini. Learned architecture of a transitional nature. Ottoman Baroque elements are combined with more rationalist structures, as in the openings on the first story. Photograph taken at the beginning of the twentieth century. (Source: ELIA, Ar. Zachos Archive.)

46. Chios. Carved door frame at Kalamoti. Its striking sculptural elements recall the Genoese culture of the eastern Aegean. Photograph taken at the beginning of the twentieth century. (Source: ELIA, Ar. Zachos Archive.)

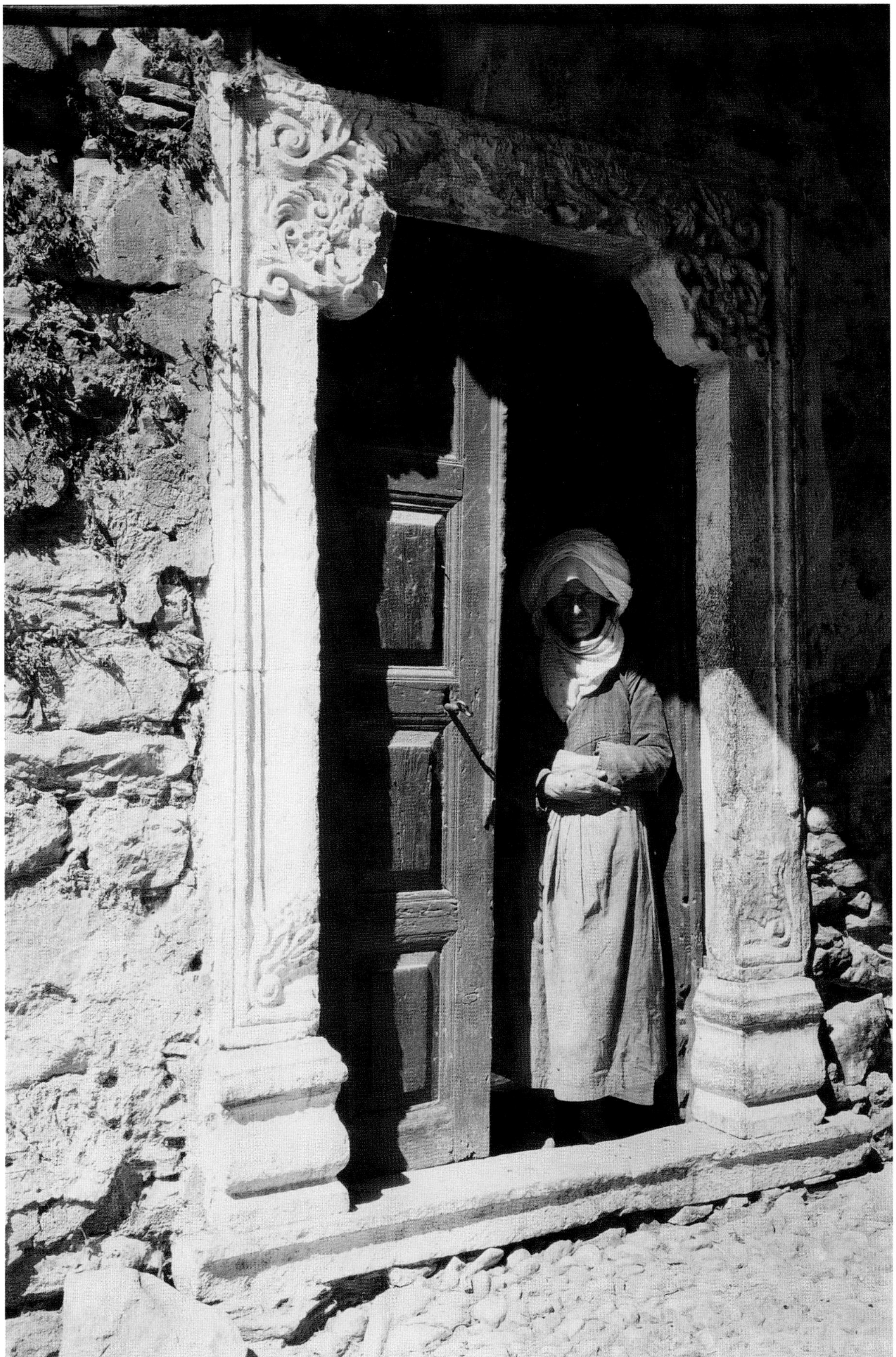
46

47. Kozani. Courtyard of a house during the tobacco-drying season. The sources of these architectural forms were common throughout the entire Balkans about 1800. Photograph taken at the beginning of the twentieth century. (Source: ELIA, Ar. Zachos Archive.)

48. Portaria. *Archontiko* executed in the expressive architecture of Thessaly during the period before liberation. The volumes are arranged in a U shape. Photograph taken at the beginning of the twentieth century. (Source: ELIA, Ar. Zachos Archive.)

49. Ioannina. Interesting expanse of a house facade with *sachnisia* set in a stepped arrangement and cornices undulating above the rows of windows. Photograph taken at the beginning of the twentieth century. (Source: ELIA, Ar. Zachos Archive.)

50. Arta. House with an elegant wooden *chayati* and porch. In the Ottoman tradition, arches open onto the stone substructure and the main staircase. Provides an example of form and material combined in a deterministic expression. Photograph taken at the beginning of the twentieth century. (Source: ELIA, Ar. Zachos Archive.)

51. Ambelakia in Thessaly. The Schwartz *archontiko*. This outstanding work of architecture was created during the period when the Greek communities under Turkish rule were flourishing. Photograph taken in 1921. (Source: ELIA, Ar. Zachos Archive.)

52. Ambelakia in Thessaly. Rare depiction of the formal rooms (*ontades*) of the Schwartz *archontiko*, during a period when they were used for silk production. The cocoons spread on the floors provide a striking contrast with the luxury of the interior decoration. Photograph taken in 1921. (Source: ELIA, Ar. Zachos Archive.)

and despite subjection to Ottoman sovereignty, a ruling class emerged that was composed of men engaged in advanced craft-industrial and retail activities on a more than local scale (from Asia Minor to Russia, the Danubian regions, and Central Europe). These men had experienced a cosmopolitan world, and they responded—directly or indirectly—to the European Enlightenment's call. The private architecture that sprang from these conditions was not purely urban—like that of Corfu, for example—but continued to be the product of the dynamism of the popular tradition, albeit distinctly transformed by the ecumenical consciousness that informed the privileged communities of Greece.

In contrast with the situation in the islands, the type of buildings found in the rest of Greece, from Macedonia and Thrace to the Peloponnese, are quite similar to one another, exhibiting only slight differences between them. They are types that, according to Aristotelis Zachos, share a common origin in the Byzantine house. These large two- or three-story *archontika* (mansions) had stone ground floors and lighter timber-and-brick structures on the upper stories. This arrangement not only made sense structurally but also gave craftsmen greater flexibility, allowing them to create more and larger openings, to use projecting timber structures (*sachnisia*) and large balconies (*chayatia*)—forms encountered throughout the entire Balkans. Most of the mansions were L- or U-shaped, though they were often simply quadrilateral at the ground-floor level (figs. 47–52). They retained a fortress-like character in the small-windowed stone core, which is where the storerooms, workshops, and ancillary rooms were located.

In contrast, the windows were larger on the upper stories, where family sitting rooms and reception rooms were placed, and balconies facing the interior courtyard effectively extended life into the open air.

The morphological choices available to the master craftsmen of the traveling guilds who built these imposing *archontika* included not only native elements but a large number of foreign borrowings, taken either from the ubiquitous Baroque and Rococo examples throughout Central Europe or from the "official" mirror image of these idioms in the Baroque-influenced Turkish forms of the East, and also incorporating a number of isolated classicizing motifs—all combined in a superb unified expression (figs. 53, 54). Here the Eastern influences are evident: special rooms for the women, separated by latticework partitions (*kafasota*); the lack of furniture; low sofas in the sitting rooms (*ontades*), on which the men of the house sat cross-legged or half-reclining to drink coffee and rose-flavored liqueur and smoke their hookah. The lavish wood-carved decoration of the rooms (built-in cupboards, ceilings, paneled partitions) is supplemented by vibrant painted decoration and fanlights with brightly colored glass panes that, together with the

53. Nafplion. Detail of a cornice. Common application of the popular tradition to the exteriors of houses of the early nineteenth century.

54. Nafplion. Detail of a decorated cornice.

rest of the movable furnishings (textiles, embroidered hangings, copperware, glass), gave the room a distinctive, magical quality.

Wealthy merchants frequently traveled to the West (fig. 55) and to Constantinople, which led to Baroque and Rococo features—as well as landscapes, such as views of Constantinople and the Western cities visited by the owners—gradually becoming incorporated into the decoration. In this way, the decoration became a permanent record of memories and experiences.

In the mountainous regions of the Peloponnese, Arkadia, Mani, and Monemvasia, the residences are more austere: stone two- and three-story towers, with harsh volumes and small windows. In coastal towns like Nafplion, in contrast, Ottoman and Venetian elements are woven into a distinctive and unique visual amalgam with its own characteristic features.

Ideological and Aesthetic Openings

After 1800, more purely classical models began to be increasingly preferred by progressive Greeks in the occupied territories, and certainly by those who lived in Greek communities abroad. The distinct classicizing trend of architecture not only in houses but also in welfare buildings (such as schools, for example, which were usually financed by private benefactors) still attests most clearly to the spirit of Greek humanism and its ramifications in the sphere of ideas. These ideas planted in men's minds the anticipation of the liberation of their fatherland.

It is perhaps hazardous and an oversimplification to regard this pre-revolutionary Greek architecture, so rich in heterogeneous stylistic idioms, as a note on the scale of Western bourgeois values. It might better be described as a half-tone—one that emerged toward the end of the 1700s, derived from the experience of long centuries of subjugation and signaling the hope and prospect of the birth of a new socio-cultural system. This system maintained an ambivalent attitude toward the "national" and "ecumenical" ideal, but undoubtedly distanced itself from its fundamental dependence on popular culture.

From the closing decades of the eighteenth century, moreover, the French Revolution, the current of the Enlightenment that pervaded the whole of Europe, and the turn to the ancient world that had begun much earlier all affected the Greek world in regions where conditions were now ripe.

The major centers in which Greek communities flourished, both within and outside of strict national borders (Venice, Trieste, Smyrna, Vienna, Ioannina, the Aegean islands, and the Ionian islands), were more or less ready to receive the new messages. Many wealthy merchants, scholars, and merchant-scholars played a leading role in this process. The ideas of the Enlightenment naturally elicited a response in all forms of art. Varying degrees of influence and transformation may be observed, mainly in the printed word but also in poetry, music, decoration, painting, and architecture, as they were exposed to and came into contact with the new ideas. Above all, there were changes in the way of life, in relations between individuals and the sexes, in culture, and in education. The Enlightenment was at once ideology and fashion.

The nineteenth century opened with brilliant prospects for the future of subjugated Greeks. Contact with the new predominant currents of the West and political events in the East, including successive Russo-Turkish wars, encouraged the Greek people and intensified economic and intellectual fermentation within their ranks.

The Greek bourgeoisie living outside Greece were now free to declare their opposition to tyranny and to promote the swift currents of liberalism and the ideas of the French Revolution, having as their allies the European bourgeoisie and representatives of the arts and intellectual life.

Greece, in an initial impulsive move, turned its back on the East and opened up to the West. The East symbolized slavery, the West, liberty; Europe was wise, cultured, enlightened. But was all this true? Many years were to pass before Greece came to appreciate that her position lay between East and West, and that her role was to act as a link between the two. Despite the strenuous efforts of many, these dual features could not be effaced from the Greek people: the appropriate symbol here is the double-headed eagle of Byzantium, with one head facing West and the other East.

This was the feature that made Greece so unique, but so isolated.

55. Wealthy Greek merchants in the West. A group of friends socialize on a street in Leipzig in a depiction of the period (about 1800).

The New Greek State

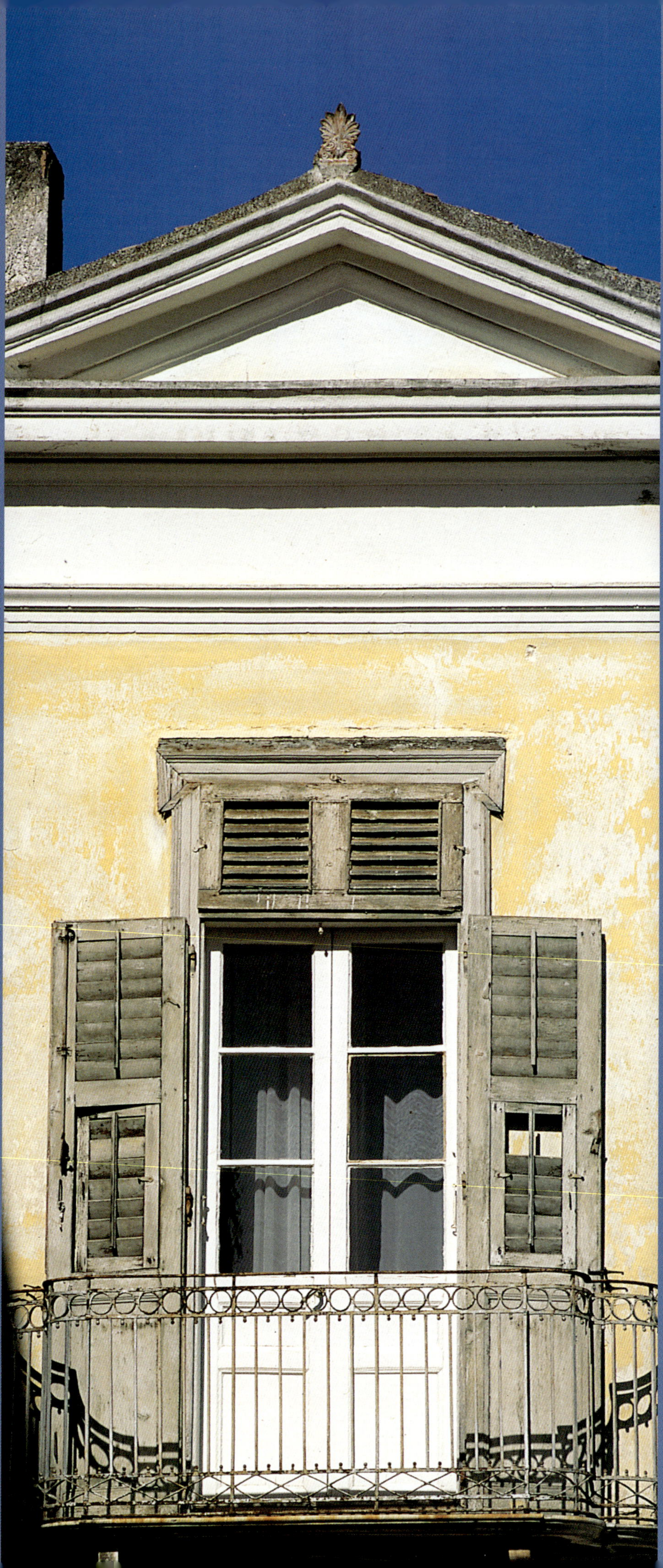

THE NEW GREEK STATE

The Imposition of Planning under Kapodistrias

Contrary to the general belief, Neoclassicism did not make its first appearance in Greece with the arrival of the Bavarians. The construction of the first buildings in a Neoclassical style began as early as 1815, when the British captured Corfu and thus completed their occupation of the Ionian islands. The largest and most important monuments were executed, as would be expected, in the capital of the Septinsular Republic, Corfu itself. Moreover, intensive reconstruction of the island had already started during the period of the French occupation. The arches of the Liston Arcade, the well-known portico on the Spianada, work of the French architect Lesseps, were clearly under the influence of the work of Charles Percier and Pierre-François-Léonard Fontaine, who had built the arcade in the rue de Rivoli in Paris.

In Corfu, which was still under French rule, the first School of Fine Arts was founded in 1811 and was worthy of comparison with corresponding European schools. Gerasimos Pisamanos of Kephallonia, who had studied at the San Luca Academy of Fine Arts in Rome and then in Paris, was appointed professor of civil architecture (1782–25). In 1817, a private School of Architecture was founded by Antonio Villa, though it does not appear to have functioned for very long.

The first qualified Greek architects studied at these schools, and they were subsequently employed both by the British in the Ionian islands and by Kapodistrias in the new Greek state he was in the process of reconstructing (fig. 57). Ioannis Chronis, perhaps the most important Greek architect of Corfu and the designer of many of the island's best-known buildings (the Ionian Bank, the Ionian Parliament Building, the Kapodistrias mansion, and others), seems to have studied for a time at Villa's school. After completing his studies in Italy, Chronis returned in 1831 to work in his native island (fig. 58).

Equally important work was carried out by foreign, mainly British, engineers in the Ionian islands. In Corfu examples include the palace of St. Michael and St. George, by Sir George Whitmore, with its elegant Doric peristyle; the church of St. George, also in the Doric style; the *monopteros* (a circular Ionic monument), built in honor of the first High Commissioner, Thomas Maitland; and Mon Repos, a typical example of a British country house based on the models of Robert Adam and Thomas Jefferson. The courthouse and its market by P. H. Kennedy at Argostoli and Lixouri, respectively, and the lighthouse of the Ayioi Theodoroi by Charles-Philippe de Bosset, also on Kephallonia, are other public buildings in the Neoclassical style constructed at this period in the Ionian islands. The British architects and engineers were followed by their young Greek colleagues, who transferred the style from public to private edifices. Old Venetian buildings, mainly military barracks, sometimes had their facades converted to reflect the new trends. Thus, when Kapodistrias arrived in Greece in 1828, the architecture of classicism had already spread to the Ionian islands (figs. 59–62).

The long struggle for liberation, which was, indeed, still in progress, left the country torched, devastated, and plundered. The scale of the damage and the extent of the ruins was horrific. Amid the chaos, Kapodistrias set about the difficult task of creating a state. The period of his government, though brief, exerted a significant impact on the course of modern Greek architecture and town planning, which was informed by an austerity and severity very different from the spirit that prevailed after the arrival of King Otto and the Bavarians.

The policy pursued by Kapodistrias may perhaps be summed up in a single phrase: "a Greek remedy for Greek ills." From the very first days after his arrival, this general attitude permeated Kapodistrias's efforts to reconstruct Greece. His

56. Nafplion. Detail of a house facade with a characteristic balcony and pediment (see also fig. 172).

57. Portrait of Ioannis Kapodistrias. Detail of a painted ceiling.

58. Direct Renaissance influence on the morphological details of early classicism. Characteristic use of cyma reversa moldings with a plain geometrical tracing. Plate from a handbook by the fine Corfiot architect I. Chronis. (Source: I. Chronis, *Manual of Urban Architecture* [in Greek], Corfu, 1862).

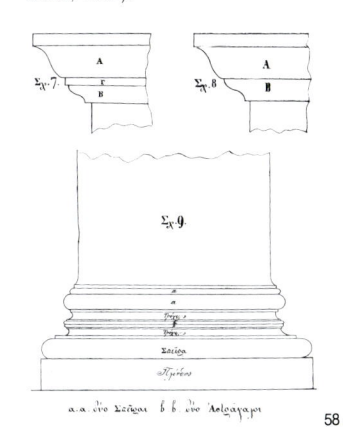

59. Kephallonia. The *Markato*, the building on the seafront at Lixouri housing the market, law courts, and town hall. Built by Napier and Kennedy in 1828. Typical early classical public building, integrated into the urban environment by a portico supported on columns. Postcard.

60. Corfu. The country house Mon Repos. Built for the young Corfiot wife of the high commissioner, Maitland, by the architect Whitmore. Typical application of the English early-nineteenth-century classical tradition, with Greek and Palladian features. Postcard.

61. Corfu. The uncluttered Ionic monument erected in honor of Thomas Maitland in the Spianada. This ancient type (*monopteros*) was quite popular. It had previously been applied in the lighthouse of Ayioi Theodoroi at Argostoli on Kephallonia, by the Swiss architect de Bosset (1800). Postcard.

closest colleague, Stamatis Voulgaris—Corfiot engineer, officer in the French army, and personal friend—was one of the few included in Kapodistrias's entourage aboard the ship that brought him to Greece in January 1828. Voulgaris was accompanied by a staff of specially trained town planners, land surveyors, architects, and military and civil engineers, both Greeks and foreigners. Some already had experience in civil and defensive works, among them Theodoros Vallianos and Baron C. de Schaumbourg, both of whom were officers in the Russian engineer corps; A. T. Garnot, Pauzié, E. Peytier, and Audoy, members of the French army under Maison; and A. Devaud and P. Ippoliti, from Switzerland and Italy respectively. Others, notably the Greeks S. Kleanthis, D. Stavridis, S. Isaias, I. Kallergis, and E. Manitakis, had just graduated from military schools or academies of architecture in Europe (Austria, France, and Italy) and came to offer their services to their native country. Among their ranks were many from the Ionian islands: in addition to T. Vallianos and I. Kallergis, mentioned above, there were Lambros Zavos and Andreas Gasparis-Kalandros from Lefkada, Antonios

62. Corfu. The palace of St. Michael and St. George. Work on it began in 1819, as a residence for the British high commissioner. Its form emphasized in the most solemn manner the consolidation of British romantic classicism in the Ionian islands.

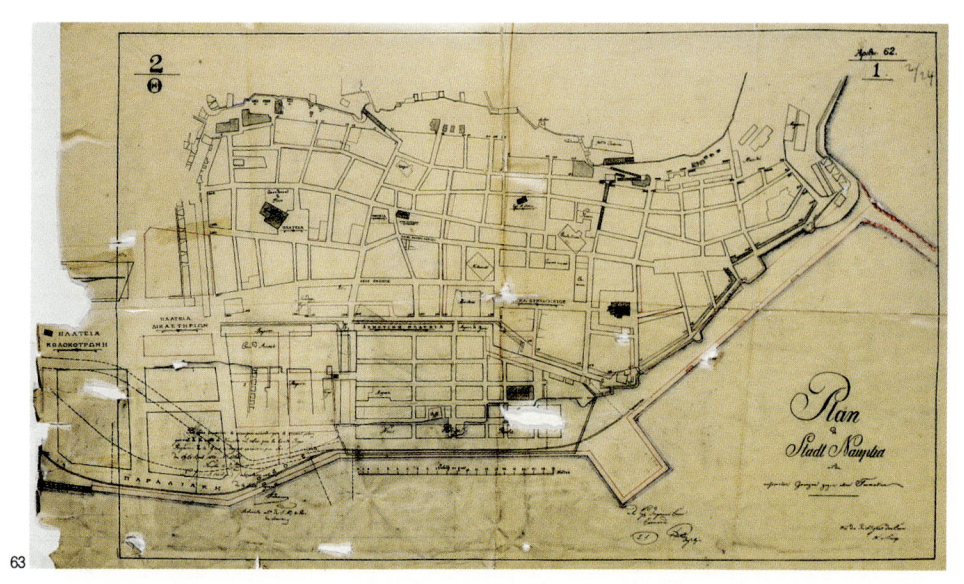

63. Nafplion. Town plan, by Stamatis Voulgaris, drawn up by King Otto's Bavarian engineers in 1834. It clearly shows the rationalist design of the extension of the town outside the walls in the direction of the sea, and the creation of a quay and harbor. (Source: Ministry for the Environment, Town Planning and Public Works Archive.)

64. Argos. Town plan, by A. Devaud (1823). It attempts to achieve a functional articulation of the old and new urban environments. (Source: Ministry for the Environment, Town Planning and Public Works Archive.)

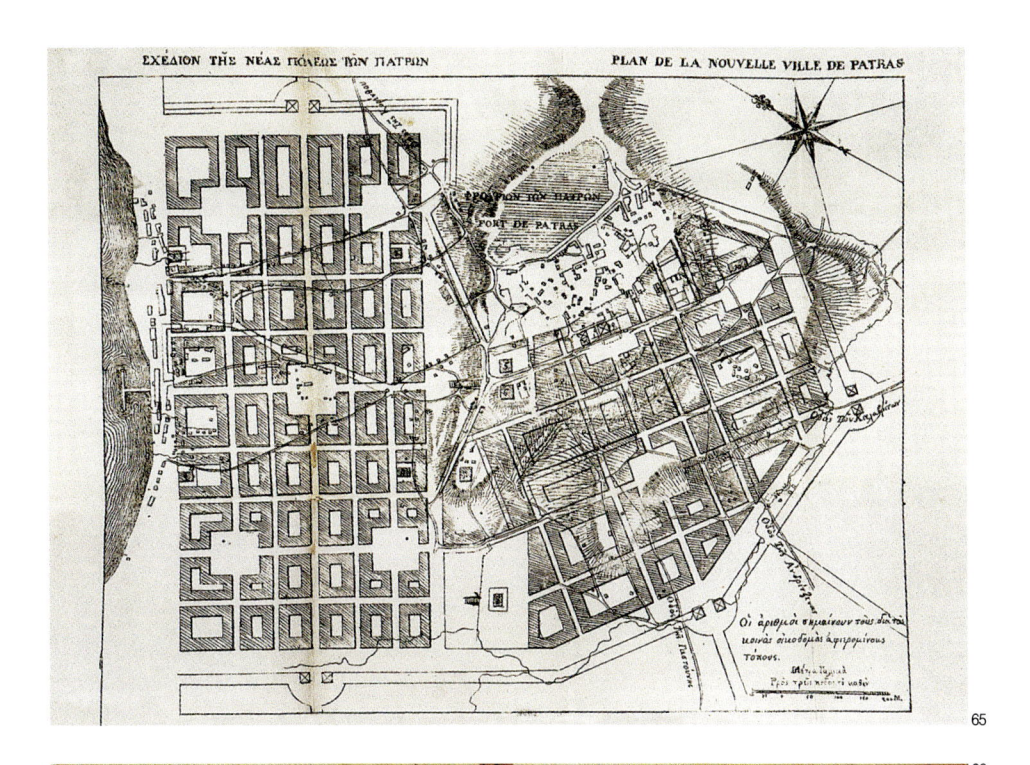

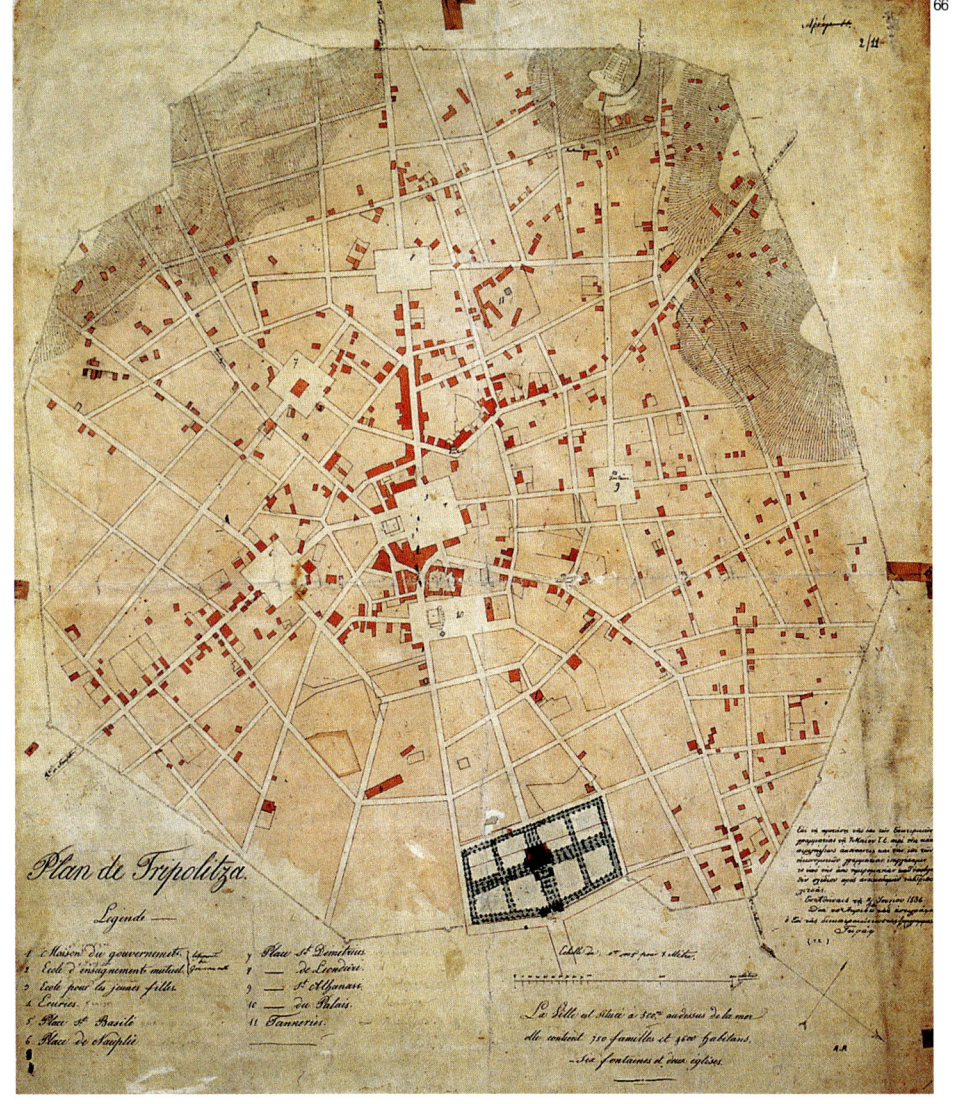

65. Patras. Town plan of the Upper and Lower Town (1830). This plan represents the most important work of the military engineer Stamatis Voulgaris. The two sectors of the town are designed separately. The plan clearly shows the integration of the relevant historical landmarks and features of the terrain. In the Lower Town, in particular, the rationalist design is developed without any restraints. The plan underwent several amendments during its implementation. (Source: S. Voulgaris, *Memoirs* [in Greek], Paris, 1835.)

66. Tripolis. Town plan. Street layout by Garnot and Voulgaris, redrawn by Bavarian engineers (1836). Straight axes and rectilinear public squares are applied within the traditional design. (Source: Ministry for the Environment, Town Planning and Public Works Archive.)

Tseroulis and Stylianos Lykoudis from Corfu, Dionysis Valsamakis and, toward the end of the period, Gerasimos Metaxas from Kephallonia.

According to the available evidence, the three and a half years that Kapodistrias governed Greece saw the finalization of the town plan for nine Greek towns: Nafplion, Argos, Tripolis, Itea, Corinth, Lidoriki, Vostitza (Aigion), Patras, and Pylos. At the same time, the plans for seven more were in hand, and the necessary preparations had been made for the revision of the town plan of a few others. In total, there were twenty-two towns and nineteen plans, some complete and some not, many of which were still in force for decades afterward. Several of them, such as the town plan of Nafplion, which covers what is now the historical center of the town, and that of the suburb of Pronoia, are still in force today, with very few modifications (figs. 63–66).

Special decrees regulated all the details associated with reconstructing towns based on a town plan, including financial provisions and other aspects. An entire series of decrees regulated the reconstruction of specific towns, such as Nafplion, Argos, Patras, Itea, and others. Only in the case of Athens was no such decree promulgated, because that city had not been formally annexed to the modern state. It is now certain, however, that instructions and guidelines to map Athens had been given to Kleanthis and Schaubert by Kapodistrias himself in the spring of 1831.

The characteristic features of planning new towns were rationalism and the pursuit of functionality. The influence of French models, as composed during the first years of the French Revolution and the First Empire, is evident, since the majority of the engineers were educated in France.

At the same time, the first building regulations were published. Clear directions defined the heights of buildings, the building materials to be used, and the nature of the masonry, which had to be "secure and solid" (and not of straw, which is highly flammable). The regulations also made it obligatory to construct a toilet, with the associated sewers and chimneys.

It was also stated clearly that every building under construction was to be supervised by the civil engineer. (The term is used in contradistinction with military engineer, not with architect. The distinction between civil engineer and architect in the modern sense arises later.) This supervision related to the stability and hygienic conditions of the construction, and also to morphological matters, such as the form of the facades and the proportions of the volumes.

The first towns to benefit from Kapodistrias's policy were, of course, Aigina, the temporary seat of government, where the governor first made his home (figs. 67–69), and Nafplion.

The first and possibly the largest building of the Kapodistrias period, a clear example of "artistic" architecture, was erected on Aigina: this was the orphanage, a charity founded by the Governor with the aim of providing a home for the orphans of Aigina. Known as the adopted children of the soldiers, these youngsters followed the army from place to place, with all the obvious consequences.

The study for and construction of the orphanage was assigned to Theodoros Vallianos, a graduate of the Military Academy of St. Petersburg and an officer in the tsar's engineer corps. The orphanage was a large complex measuring 140 by 80 meters and designed around a closed inner courtyard. The basic principles of the design recall those of similar European colleges of the eighteenth century. The strict symmetry of its floor plan and the simplicity and clarity of its organization point to its having been designed by a military engineer. The same symmetry, austerity, and severity characterize its facades, which exhibit typical features of

67. Aigina. The building that housed the first printing press in free Greece bears a discreet typological resemblance to Aigina's government building (see fig. 69). Postcard.

68. Aigina. *Archontiko* of the early nineteenth century. Sketch by the Danish architect Christian Hansen (1835). The European architect was clearly interested in the forms of private architecture in modern Greece. (Source: Kunstakademie, Copenhagen.)

69. Aigina. The historic Government Building. This older building, renovated by T. Vallianos, displays the frugal, economical approach to architecture typical of the Kapodistrias period. Postcard.

70. Aigina. The orphanage in its present condition. View of the largest building complex of the Kapodistrias period, designed by T. Vallianos (1829).

71. Aigina. Part of the main facade of the orphanage. Row of windows in which the forms of the frames and crowning elements alternate. Though of a classical style, the forms clearly go back to the earlier Italian tradition.

72. Aigina. View of the main doorway of the orphanage with an oval fanlight above it and an inscription, in Greek, on the lintel: "The Governor erected this orphanage in the year 1829."

73. Aigina. The Eynardeion Main School. View of the large portico on the north side. The Neoclassical style is evident, appearing here for the first time in a public building in free Greece.

classicism. Vallianos had become acquainted with classicism in tsarist Russia, where it had embodied the ideals of absolute monarchy, though transformed by the personal taste of a series of tsars and tsarinas (figs. 70–72).

The orphanage's typology follows that of buildings with similar functions in both Europe and the East; it is an excellent example of the encounter between the Greek architectural tradition and early romantic classicism.

The orphanage also served as a school, so to speak, for a large number of workmen. More than two thousand unskilled laborers helped build it. In addition to specialized craftsmen, there were also foremen, builders, carpenters, explosives experts, stonecutters, marbleworkers, clay-makers, woodworkers, sawyers, and others.

The lack of engineer-architects and also of specialist master craftsmen was a matter of concern to Kapodistrias and his colleagues. They were obliged to bring master builders to Greece from Italy and France in order to teach their art, and to send craftsmen to these countries to learn and teach others upon their return.

One can readily understand, therefore, the warm welcome that both Kapodistrias and the well-known scholar and archaeologist Andreas Moustoxydis accorded to Stamatis Kleanthis and Eduard Schaubert when these two came to Greece at the end of 1829, particularly because they brought with them a letter of recommendation from the Bavarian philhellene Karl Wilhelm Freiherr von Heideck. Graduates of the School of Architecture in Berlin and pupils of Karl Friedrich von Schinkel and Wilhelm Stier, Kleanthis and Schaubert were the first to bring to Greece the Berlin School's spirit of the Greek Neoclassicism—a spirit of measure and balance like that of classical Greece.

The text of the decree appointing the two architects (no. 1658, June 15, 1830) indicates the far-ranging prestige and reputation acquired by Schinkel's school, particularly in Greece:

The Greek State.

The Governor of Greece.

Wishing to make the knowledge and competence of MM. S. Kleanthis and E. Schaubert, students of the Berlin Academy and distinguished architects, beneficial to our country, and desiring to demonstrate how much we appreciate the noble lack of self-interest that has moved them to serve Greece,

We ordain that

A) MM. S. Kleanthis and Eduard Schaubert are appointed architects to the Government, and will receive from the Government Secretariat instructions relating to the works that will be entrusted to them

B) The Secretary of State is to communicate the present decree

In Nafplion, 15 June 1830

The Governor

I.A. Kapodistrias

The Secretary of State

N. Spiliadis

No other appointment of this kind, accompanied by so warm a recommendation, was published during the Kapodistrias period.

Meanwhile, Moustoxydis had made contact with the two architects, who had established their home on Aigina and had undertaken the study for a large composition to consist of three buildings (the main school, a museum, and a library), a small trilogy similar to the one that would be built a few years later in Athens by the Hansen brothers, Theophil and Christian. Although the designs for this composition have not been found, its budget, the first of the period drawn up by a Greek engineer, clearly indicates that the composition was Neoclassical (State General Archives, Kapodistrias Archive, Secretariat of Education, file 24).

The project was beyond the financial means of the new state and was not carried out, though it did establish the status of Schinkel's students. Moustoxydis recommended that "whereas the Government has other architects in the employ of the state, it would be good to introduce everywhere the courtesy of always inviting Kleanthis and Schaubert to give their opinion on the plans put forward by others for these buildings" (State General Archives, Kapodistrias Archive, General Secretariat, June 17, 1830).

The first project built by the two architects in Greece was inaugurated shortly afterward. This was the Eynardeion on Aigina, a building designed to house the main school. A structure of pure Neoclassical morphology, it was the most important work of the Kapodistrias period, not only on Aigina but in the whole of Greece at that time. "Through the contribution of Mr. Eynardos," wrote Moustoxydis in March 1831, in a report published in the first issue of the newspaper *Aiginaia,* "a new building has been erected in plain Doric architecture, the facade of which is formed of a stoa, while the sides are adorned with pediments" (fig. 73).

Kleanthis's view that "similar public buildings should be erected as far as possible in the most conspicuous parts of the towns, to be an embellishment to them and to be in view of all" (State General Archives, Kapodistrias Archive, Secretariat of Education, file 30B) was to prevail for almost a century. The large number of Neoclassical school buildings erected both in free Greece and in the unredeemed territories reflect that impulse.

At the same time, the reconstruction of the towns proceeded, beginning, naturally, with Nafplion, where the government and the governor had taken up residence. New buildings were erected in a simple Neoclassical style, while older buildings constructed during the period of Venetian rule were repaired and adorned with a variety of Neoclassical features, such as cornices and pediments, though they retained their marble Venetian door frames. Typical examples include the Koliopoulos and Kallergis residences (better known as the Armansberg and Mauer residences, after the names of Otto's regents, who resided there for the first few years after the prince's arrival in Greece) and the old Town Hall on the main street. Other elements of an early Neoclassicism include the cornice with the phoenix being reborn from the ashes at the corners, the balcony railings, and the forms of the windows on the upper story. In contrast, the heavy marble door frame on the side attests to the Venetian origins of the buildings (figs. 56, 74–77).

On Kapodistrias's orders, *sachnisia* (timber structures) were abolished on the grounds that they were an Ottoman element, and the town began to assume a European form. Nevertheless, there was still a lack of specialist craftsmen and materials.

The situation in Nafplion is described in a written report by Ludwig Thiersch to the Royal Court of Bavaria. The newly built residences were more carefully constructed than the old ones. According to Thiersch, however, they were, in general, a century behind in this matter, and all the essentials—locks, building work, and so on—were still in the infancy of the art. The floors were very poorly constructed and very thin, and, although the walls might be decorated with paintings, a painter had to be summoned especially for the purpose because there were none in Nafplion. No hangings, whether of paper or fabric, were used, because insects would make their homes there. Similar problems are noted with regard to equipping houses with furniture, porcelain, mirrors, glassware, and textiles. However, these needs were quickly met by imports, and the first craft-industry units were beginning to be founded. The first specialist craftsmen came from the Ionian islands and neighboring Italy, and they quickly passed on their art to others. Nafplion and Aigina were followed by Argos, Tripolis, Patras, and Corinth. Officers of the military engineers corps and civil architects undertook the construction of public buildings, government houses, schools, lazarettos, and the like (figs. 78–86).

For Patras, Baron C. de Schaumbourg designed three types of residences "of differing architecture," to which the building facades of the new town were to be

74. Nafplion. The historic Armansberg residence. In the Kapdostrias period, the third story, with the characteristic phoenix at the angle of the cornice, was added to an existing building of Venetian date.

75. Nafplion. The Venetian doorway of the old Town Hall. Kapodistrias's coat-of-arms has been added above the frugal Renaissance frame.

76. Nafplion. Large building of the Venetian period with additions from the Ottoman period. At the time of Kapodistrias, this building was enriched with early Neoclassical elements and the projecting *sachnisi* was removed from the upper story on the instructions of the government.

77. Nafplion. The Cadet School building. The building's severe lines are in keeping with a spirit of economy and rationalism.

77

78–81. Nafplion. The architecture of these facades is fully formulated in a classical style, but distinct details are drawn from the Venetian tradition.

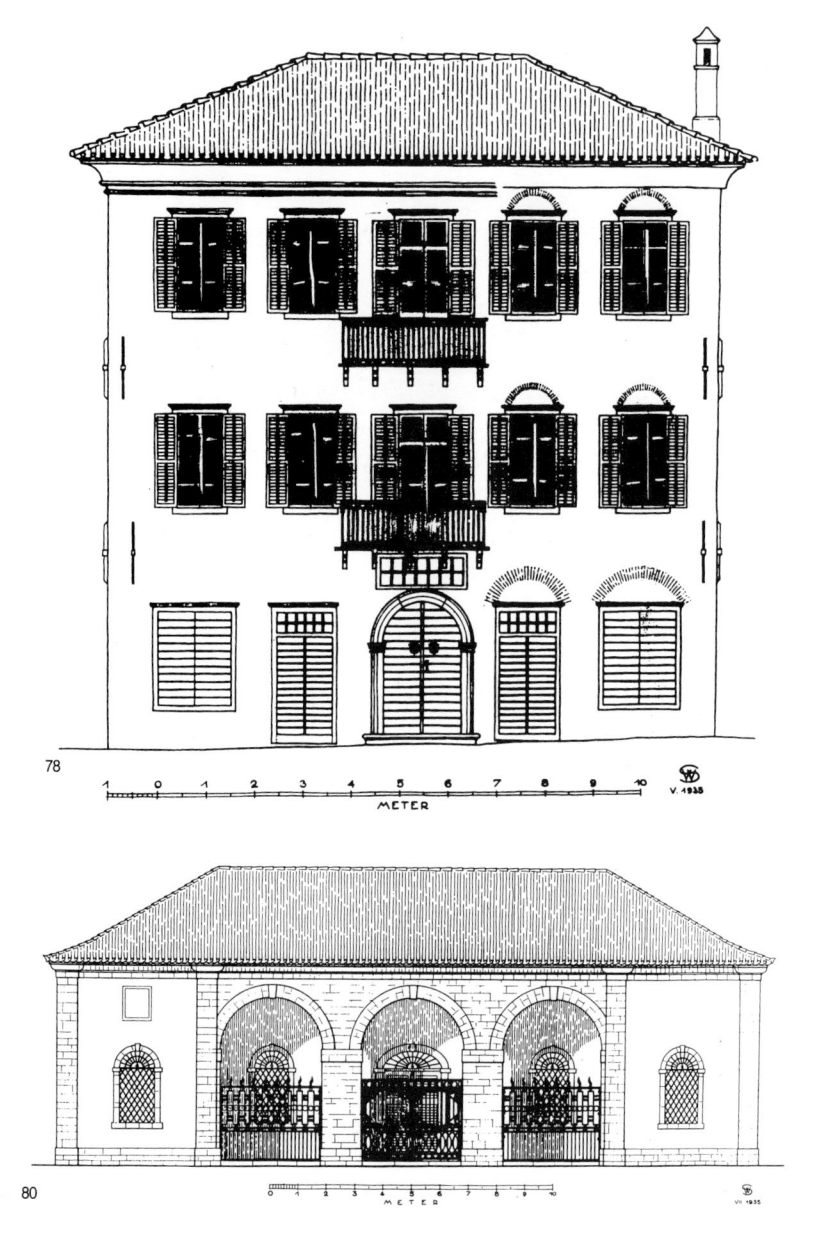

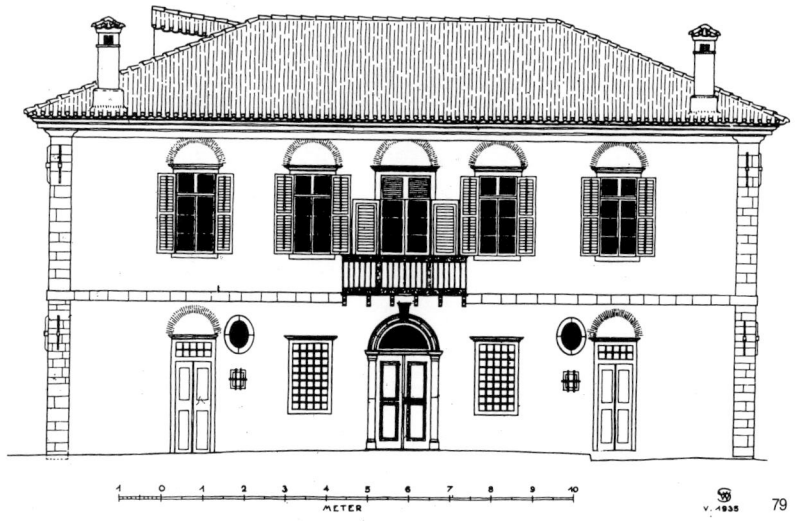

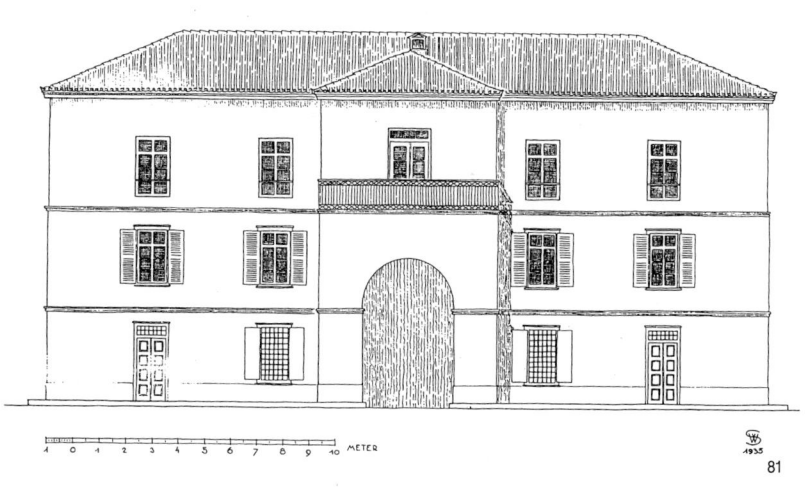

82. Aigina. Lazaretto complex, built by T. Vallianos on the ruins of an ancient theater. It represents a successful functional installation of modern facilities on an existing historical substructure. (Source: measured drawing by L. A. Winstrup, Kunstakademie, Copenhagen.)

83. Syros. The Lazaretto at Ermoupolis in the first, naïve design by Garnot. (Source: State General Archives, Kapodistrias Archive.)

84. Syros. W. Weiler's treatment of the ground-floor plan of the Lazaretto at Ermoupolis. In its final form, the building was distinguished by its functionality. (Source: State General Archives, Ermoupolis Archive, Othonian period.)

85. Patras. Proposal for the market by the engineer A. Tseroulis. Ground plan showing geometrical arrangement. (Source: State General Archives, Kapodistrias Archive.)

86. Patras. Proposal, in the form of a sketch, for the government building by the engineer A. Tseroulis. The lines of the facade display the clear canon of early classicism: symmetry and rationality, emphasis on the horizontal, economy of expressive means. (Source: State General Archives, Kapodistrias Archive.)

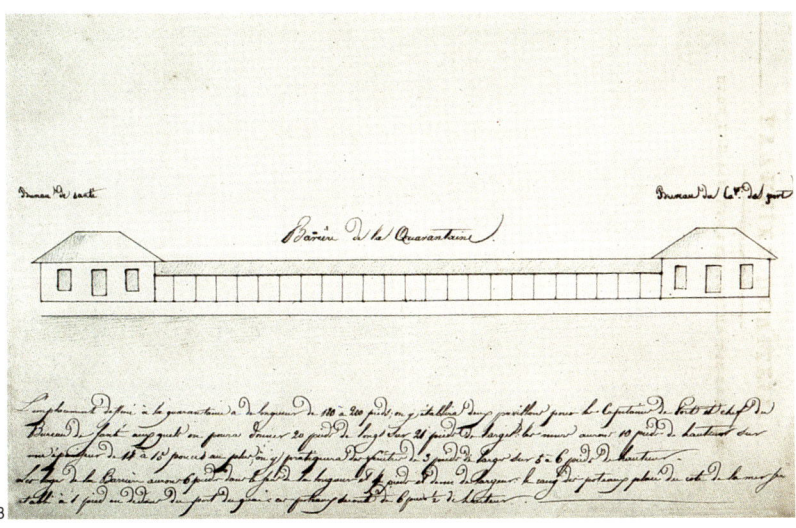

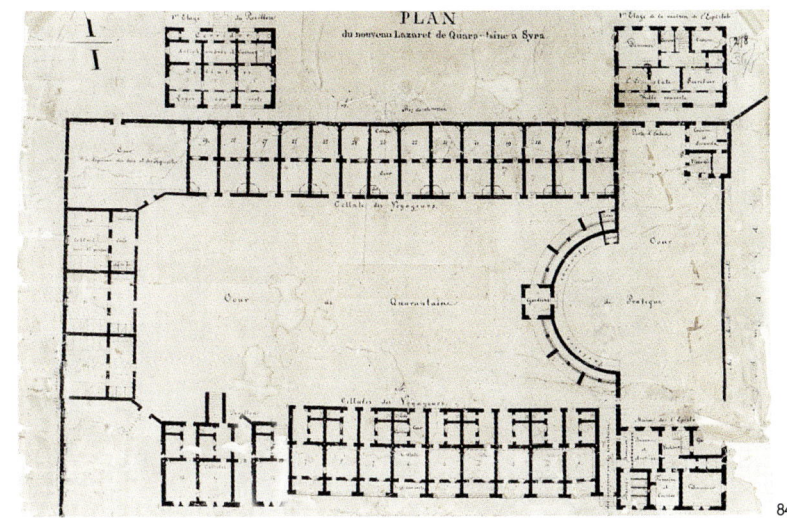

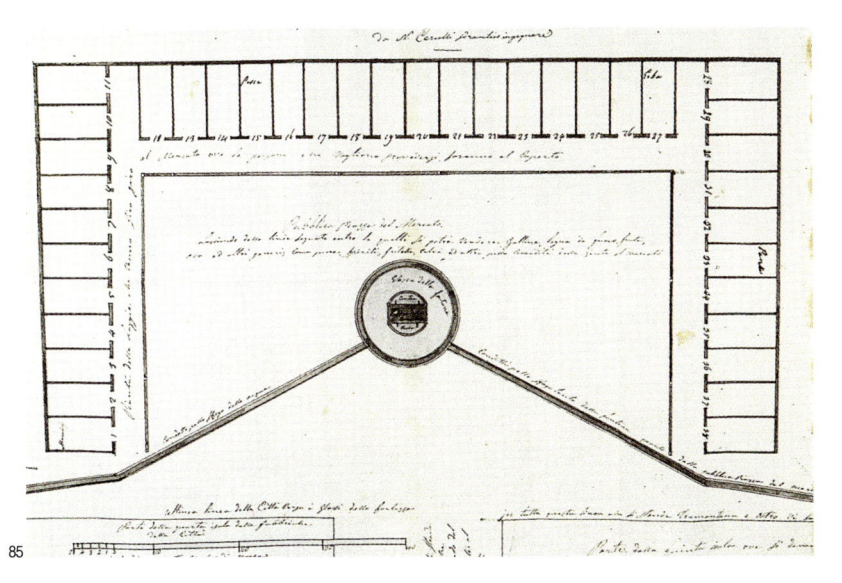

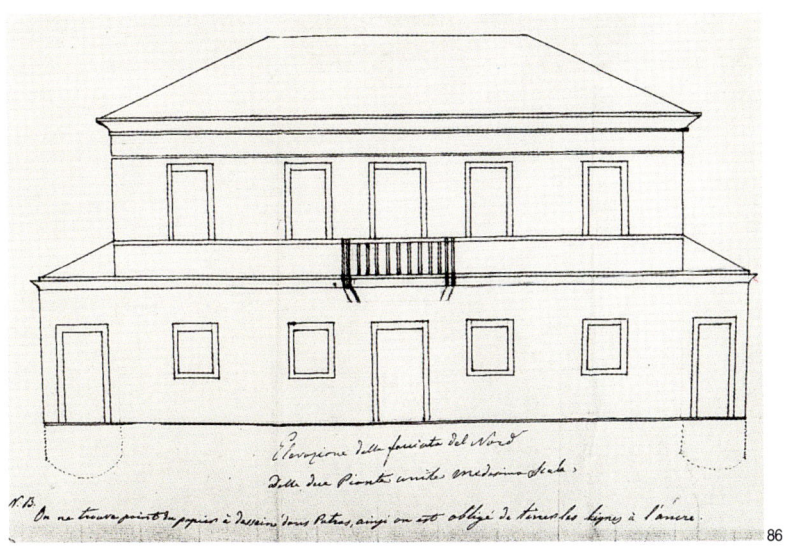

accommodated. The first type was intended for the avenue along the seafront and the first few streets parallel with it and involved three-story buildings with a luxurious portico on the ground floor. The second type involved a two-story structure, again with a portico. The third consisted of simple ground-floor buildings. Because most inhabitants did not possess the necessary capital, these types were not represented over a wide area, though some examples (reflecting to some extent the forms used on Corfu) can be found in the Lower Town of Patras (figs. 87–90).

87. Corfu. Potamos. The house in which S. Voulgaris died. The Italian memories of the architecture in the architect's birthplace clearly influenced the form of his later proposals for the town of Patras.

88. Corfu. The naïve form of the house on the river at Lefkimi in which S. Voulgaris was born. Though frugal, its local character stands forth robustly.

89, 90. Patras. The introduction in the Lower Town of elements of ordered Neoclassicism in their simplest expression. Porticoes with either colonnades or arcades were an essential feature. The two-story houses normally corresponded with the type of "buildings with a portico on the ground floor" proposed by Voulgaris and Schaumbourg.

Athens the Capital

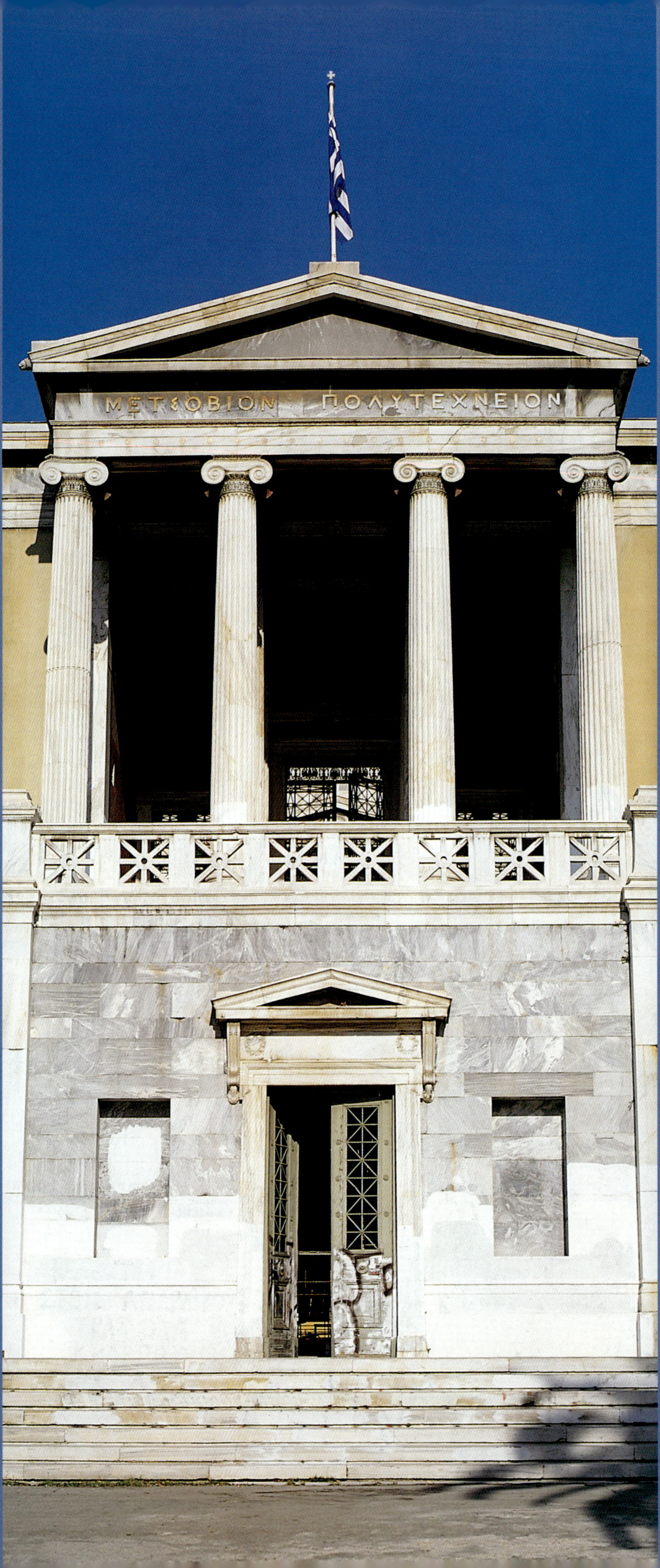
ΜΕΤΣΟΒΙΟΝ ΠΟΛΥΤΕΧΝΕΙΟΝ

ATHENS THE CAPITAL

Reconstructing the City

In January 1831, after the Greek government's response to the London Protocol (in which Kapodistrias demonstrated considerable flexibility in negotiating the evacuation of Ottoman Turks from Attica) had been communicated to the representatives of the three Great Powers, the Athenians began to leave Aigina and other regions and gradually return to Athens.

Along with the indigenous Greeks came others from the unredeemed areas as well as Greeks of the diaspora—including princes, rulers, and bourgeoisie from the Danubian Principalities, Moldavia and Wallachia. The Turks leaving the city sold their houses and land, and the work of rebuilding began. In the summer of 1831, and possibly even earlier, the architects Kleanthis and Schaubert took up residence in Athens, having undertaken to "measure and delineate the town." They bought a large two-story residence in Rizokastro from the Ottoman Turk Sante Hanuk. This was an old Frankish building that they repaired and converted into an atelier and two independent apartments. Many of the foreign architects who visited Athens were given hospitality and worked in this building, which was later home to the first high school of Greece and after that the first university. A number of Neoclassical morphological elements that can be seen in its facades were probably added when the building was repaired and converted to serve the needs of the two architects (figs. 92–94).

The first early Neoclassical buildings erected in the city should probably be attributed to Kleanthis and Schaubert. These include the school of the missionaries King and Hill, or "Academy Branch of the brotherhood of New York, America," near the entrance to the Ancient Agora in Plaka, the Kontostavlos residence on the site of the present Old Parliament Building, and others (figs. 95, 96).

A decree issued in 1834 transferred the royal seat from Nafplion to Athens on December 1. "The city shall from that day be called the royal seat and capital." This act undoubtedly had European as well as local significance. The nineteenth century was the century of urbanization, technological advance, steady industrialization, and (as a consequence of these changes) the redrawing of social structures. It was also the century of urban expansion and the reconstruction of the modern national capitals.

91. Athens. The main Averoff building of the National Technical University (Metsovion Polytechnic), the crowning achievement of L. Kaftantzoglou. The imposing composition of the Ionic porch stands on the "base" of the marble exterior staircase, with the main entrance leading into the ground floor.

92. The arrival of the marquis de Nointel in seventeenth-century Athens. The house in Rizokastro, in which S. Kleanthis, the designer of the modern capital, took up residence about a century and a half later, can be seen beneath the tower, to the right of the Parthenon. Painting by J. Carrey (1674). Athens, National Art Gallery.

93. Athens. The house on Tholou Street, known as the Old University, in which S. Kleanthis and E. Schaubert lived. Its rooms housed the first "architectural workshop" in Athens. On the surface of the end wing can be seen the interventions by the two architects (narrow horizontal cornices). (Source: *The First Greek Craftsmen* [in Greek], Athens.)

94. Athens. Interior courtyard of the house on Tholou Street, with its open *chayatia*. (Source: *The First Greek Craftsmen* [in Greek], Athens.)

Diplomatic treaties and conferences had determined the distribution of territories in Europe. The same nationalist feeling that caused Greece to revolt against Ottoman rule and caused Belgium to break from Holland in the first half of the century also led to the unification of groups of "statelets" into unified states, such as the Kingdom of Italy (1870) and the Federal German State (1871).

New capital cities were created: Brussels, Athens, Rome, Berlin. The proclamation of Brussels, Rome, and Berlin as capitals naturally led to a new expansion of these cities, though without any radical modification of their urban character.

95. Athens. Lithograph of the Kontostavlos residence on the site now occupied by the Old Parliament Building. The polygonal annex was the ballroom dating from the time the building was used as Otto's Palace, when it was probably modified by Christian Hansen. (Source: National Bank of Greece, Photographic Archive.)

96. Athens. The Hill School near the gate of Athena Archegetis in the Roman Forum. It was inaugurated in 1833 and is one of the few noteworthy buildings erected in Athens before that city became Greece's capital.

In the case of Athens, by contrast, we are faced with an act of re-creation and the planning of a city *de novo*. Classical Athens, the city whose reputation extended to the boundaries of the then known world, had declined over the centuries. Her monuments had been plundered, deformed, distorted, and in many cases comprehensively destroyed.

After the Ottoman capture of the city in 1456, Athens was gradually converted into a Turkish province. Mosques, hammams, and public buildings were erected among the ancient monuments that stood as irrefutable testimony to the city's ancient glory. In the final period of Ottoman rule, during the second half of the

97. The Athens market in the late Ottoman period. Buildings of different periods are integrated into the hub of the town's life. (Source: Dodwell, London, 1819.)

98. Athens. The Roman Forum in the middle of the nineteenth century, with the headquarters of the Ottoman *voevod* in the background, on the fringe of Hadrian's Library. (Source: ELIA, Photographic Archive.)

99. Athens. The house of Mrs. Masson in Plaka. It was also used as a residence by the architects C. Cockerell and H. von Hallerstein during their stay in Athens. (Measured drawing by H. von Hallerstein, 1814.)

100. Athenian house of the early nineteenth century (Mertud's residence in Plaka). Plans of the ground floor and first floor. The overall form clearly echoes that of ancient houses. It is shown incorporated into an old church and hammam. (Measured drawing by H. von Hallerstein, 1814.)

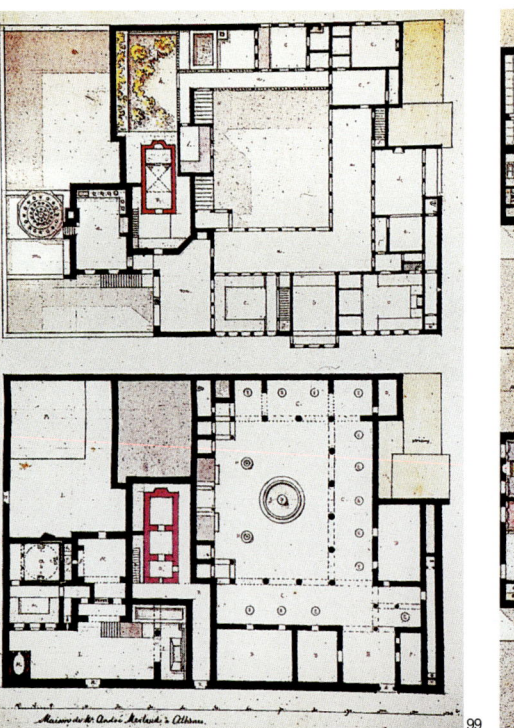

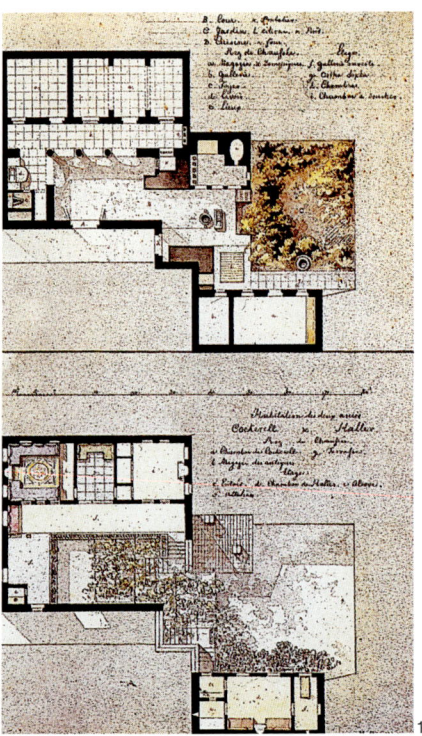

eighteenth century and the early nineteenth century, Athens began to be transformed into a flourishing provincial town of about twelve thousand inhabitants. Structures were densely built in the fortress on the Acropolis and the surrounding north fringes of the rock (figs. 97, 98).

Among the Greek, Ottoman, and Albanian houses, with their closed inner courtyards (a modification of the atrium of the ancient Greek Athenian house, now assimilated into the Ottoman way of life), a few Frankish and Venetian ruins and a large number of Byzantine and post-Byzantine monuments could be seen. Some of these were in ruins and others were still in use, incorporated into modern buildings (figs. 99–102).

As we have already seen, Athenians began to return in the winter of 1830, even before the city had officially been liberated. In May 1831, a provisional Council of Elders was elected. The work of reconstruction began and proceeded steadily. Its rate intensified after March 1833, when the Turkish garrison finally left the Acropolis and Athens — a free town — was handed over to its inhabitants, who could not have been more than five thousand in number. The larger part of the town presented a grievous spectacle, with its ruined houses and narrow, dirty streets.

The architects Kleanthis and Schaubert, who had taken up residence in Athens in the spring of 1831, devoted themselves to the task of making measured drawings of the town and devising a new plan "to rival its glory and brilliance, and worthy of the century in which we live" (State General Archives, Othonian Archive, Ministry of Foreign Affairs, file 220).

The two young architects planned the new capital as a Neoclassical garden city, in keeping with the design principles predominant in early-nineteenth-century cities: a right-angled isosceles triangle with the palace placed at the right angle, from which radiated three main axes-avenues (the two equal sides and the perpendicular of the triangle). These basic axes were ingeniously combined with much older directions and links, and the architects took into account the site's perspective views, geomorphology, and existing settlement.

101. Athens. Church tower on Scholeiou Street, Plaka. Building surviving from the Turkish period and probably of Frankish origins, shown at a time when it was still occupied. Photograph taken at the beginning of the twentieth century.

102. The conversion of open Athenian *chayatia* into glassed-in functional rooms during the Ottoman period. (Source: Johannes – Biris, 1939.)

The new town spread over the north slopes of the sacred rock ". . . distancing itself from the Acropolis, it was freed of the mist that enveloped the city of Theseus and Hadrian, and was exposed to the batis wind, with its fresh sea-breath; people in former times built their houses beneath the Acropolis for reasons of security and proximity to the Kalliroi fountain and the sacred precincts there," explained Kleanthis one moonlit evening, sitting among the arches of the ancient aqueduct on the Kiphisos and conversing with Panayiotis Soutsos, an old friend and fellow pupil at the school on Voukourestiou Street. Kleanthis went on: "Since all the towns in Greece are being rebuilt, the Government has a duty to provide all of them with Greek, elegant designs" (*Ilios*, June 18, 1833, issue 8).

The choice of Athens as capital was undoubtedly well received outside the narrow borders of Greece. One of the most fervent supporters of the idea, as we have already seen, was Ludwig I, the king of Bavaria and father of Otto. His support for the regeneration of Athens was not only ideological, but also took the form of direct intervention in the urban design and the architecture of the buildings, in some cases involving financial support for large-scale projects. Ludwig also intervened at the crucial phase of implementation of the new town plan. Leo von Klenze (1784–1864), royal architect and privy councilor, arrived in Athens in 1834 on the orders of his ruler and employer; his main objective was to revise the town plan drawn up by Kleanthis and Schaubert (even though it had already been approved), in order to overcome the unfortunate circumstances that had arisen during its implementation. "Abruptly, a new order invalidated everything and assigned to Mr. Klenze, the king of Bavaria's architect, the creation of a new plan . . . and a third is expected from Mr. Klenze," noted the Athenian press (*Athina*, August 2, 1837, issue 171) (figs. 103, 104).

Klenze, who was acknowledged in his day as one of the finest exponents of Greek classicism, reduced those aspects in the plan that he considered excessive for what, in his view, constituted Athens's moderate prospects for development. He also proceeded to mitigate the effects of the extremely symmetrical design and,

104

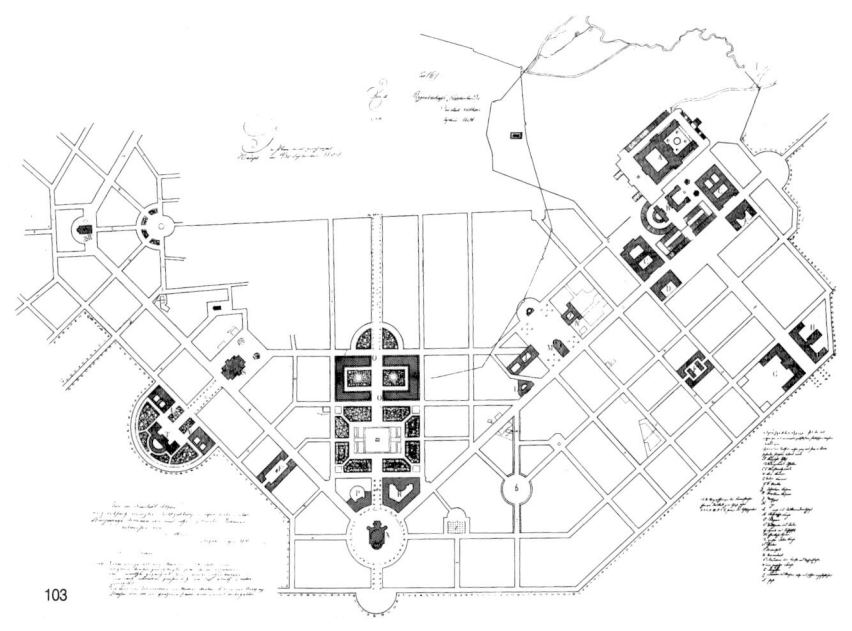

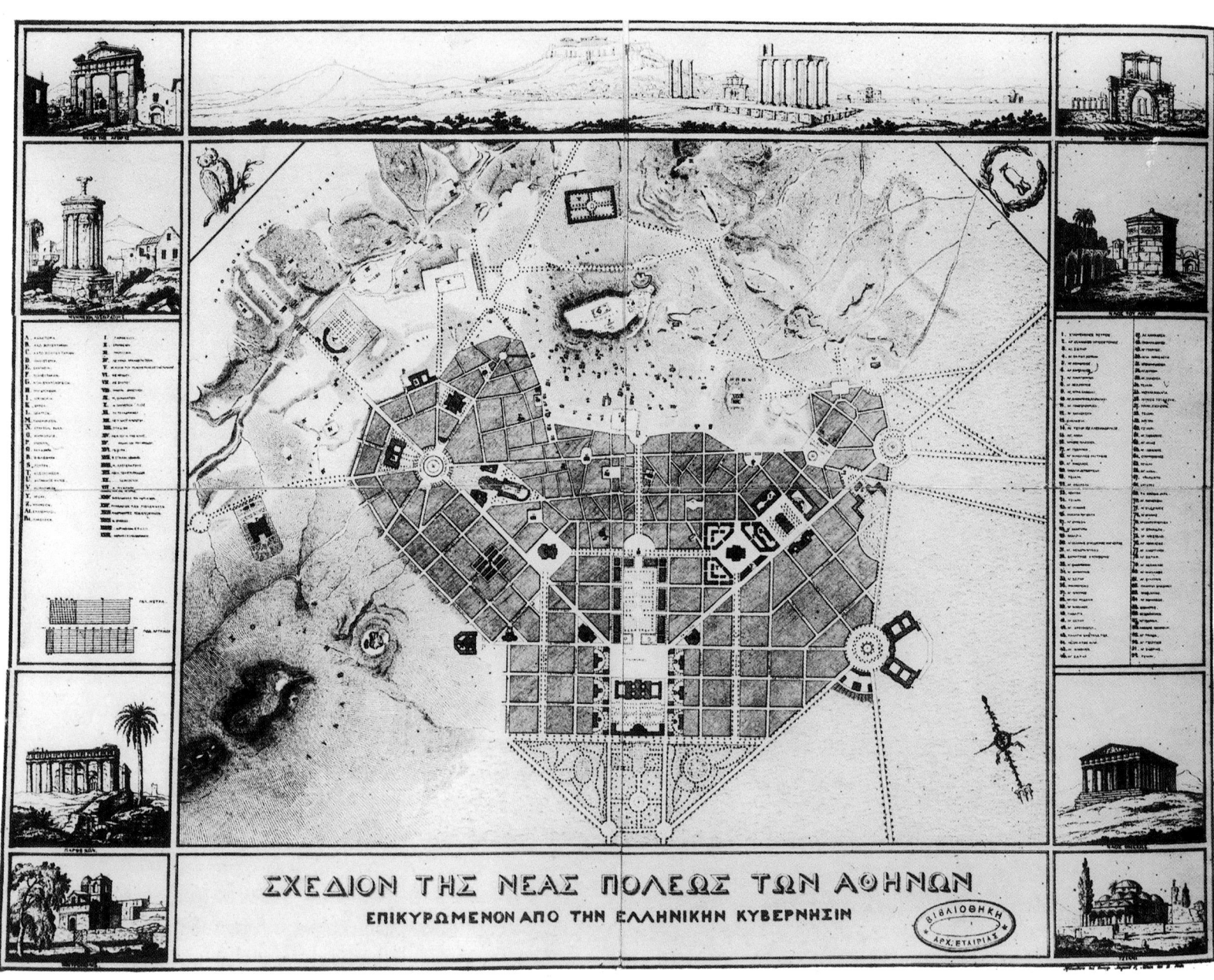

ΣΧΕΔΙΟΝ ΤΗΣ ΝΕΑΣ ΠΟΛΕΩΣ ΤΩΝ ΑΘΗΝΩΝ
ΕΠΙΚΥΡΩΜΕΝΟΝ ΑΠΟ ΤΗΝ ΕΛΛΗΝΙΚΗΝ ΚΥΒΕΡΝΗΣΙΝ

more generally, the inflexible geometric provisions of the plan; he believed that they served no essential purpose and were not in keeping with the ancient Greek approach to composition.

However, despite the modifications made to the original plan, first by Klenze and later by Friedrich von Gaertner, the present form of the urban design of Athens generally follows the original plan created by Kleanthis and Schaubert.

On the basis of the approved plan, new buildings had already begun to be designed and erected, and, according to the press of the time, expropriating these would have required inflated sums in compensation (figs. 105, 106). "Greek interests are the rights possessed by all Greeks for Athens to be designed in such a way that everyone is able to take up residence easily. Athenian interests are divided into the interests of native Athenians and those of Athenians from elsewhere. These different interests found themselves in conflict. They therefore had to compromise and to conform with the limited revenues of our country, and the town plan of Athens had to emerge from this combination" (*Athina*, August 2, 1837, issue 171).

103. Klenze's revision of the town plan of Athens (copy from 1853).

104. Kleanthis and Schaubert's town plan of Athens (copy from 1836).

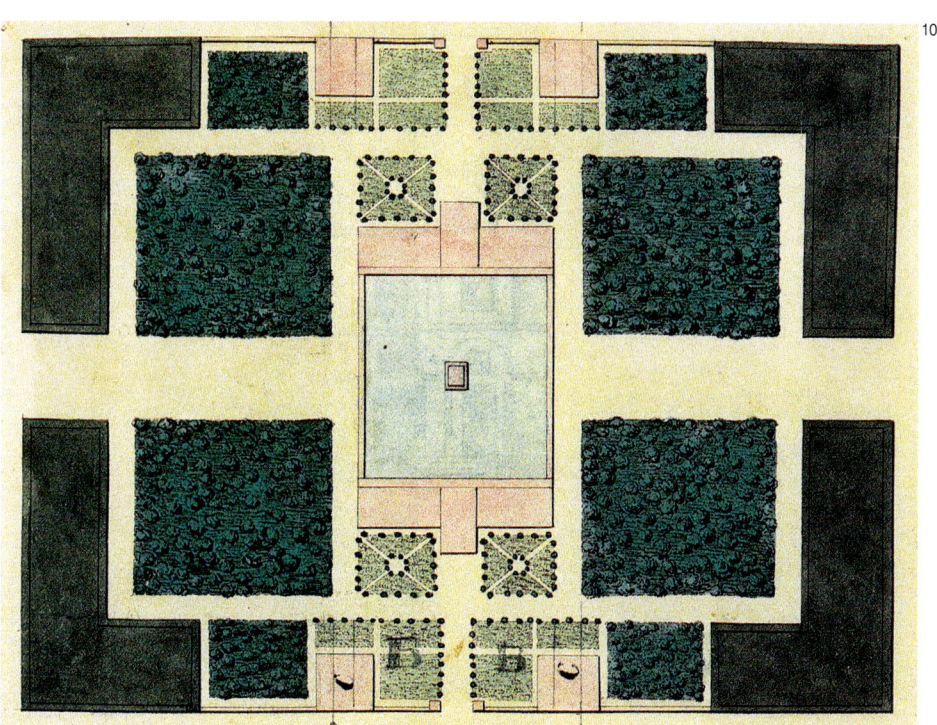

105. Spread of the facades in Feraldi's proposal for the Athens Market. (Source: State General Archives, Othonian Archive.)

106. The Athens Central Market on Laou Square, according to the proposal by the businessman Feraldi. It was a first attempt at private intervention in a public space. (Source: State General Archives, Othonian Archive.)

107. Athens. Drawing of the Vlachoutsis house on Pireos Street. The tripartite symmetrical arrangement dictated by rationalist design as early as the first phase of classicism is clearly evident. In addition to the original design, the proposed annex can be seen that was intended to enable the building to function as an art school. (Source: State General Archives, Othonian Archive.)

108. Athens. The Vlachoutsis house today.

109. Athens. The Paparigopoulos house on Kydatheneon Street. The unbroken surfaces dominate the linear decoration: the corbels and marble slab of the balcony are thin, and the window sills are wooden. By S. Kleanthis.

110. Athens. The Aiolos Hotel near the Roman Forum. By S. Kleanthis.

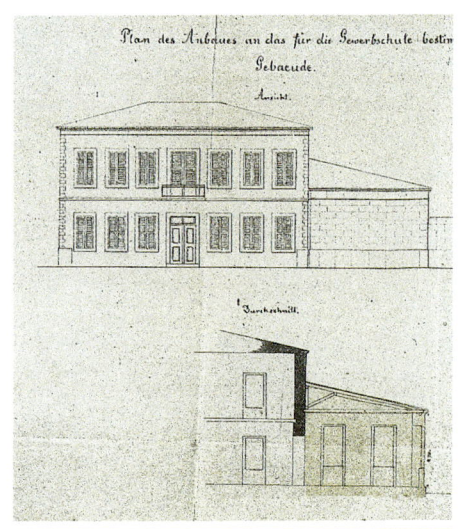

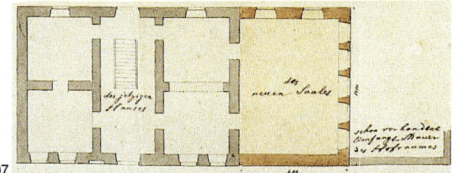

111. Athens. The D. Soutsos house at the corner of Panepistimiou and Korai Streets. One of the first buildings erected in accordance with the lines of the new plan. Two-story building with emphasis on the horizontal features. (Source: National Bank of Greece, Photographic Archive.)

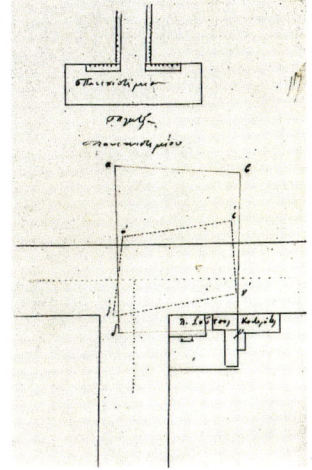

112. Athens. Part of a town plan showing the junction of Panepistimiou and Korai Streets (1844). The site of the D. Soutsos house can be seen, as well as the finished west wing of the University. (Source: State General Archives, Othonian Archive.)

113. Athens. Sloping alley in Plaka, near the Metochi of the Church of the Holy Sepulchre. The aesthetic expressed in this typical picturesque settlement of the Othonian period differs from the monumental style of urban classicism.

114. Athens. Residential building (probably a hostel) at 13 Thoukydidou Street. Windows are arranged rhythmically on the unarticulated facade. (Source: National Bank of Greece, Photographic Archive.)

A list of houses available in Athens that could be placed at the disposal of the government and its employees in 1834 refers to a mere 73 buildings (see "Old expropriations for the excavation of Ancient Athens," [in Greek], Arch. Delt. appendix, 1929). The majority of them had only two or three rooms. They were simple two-story structures with courtyards, gardens, wells, scented shrubs, and small trees, covered balconies, and rooms on the ground floor with a raised wooden platform reached by way of a small wooden ladder, with storage space beneath it.

The same list also mentions a few larger houses, with twelve or sixteen rooms. These were mainly new houses built according to European models. The influence of European architecture begins to become apparent in the residences of the families of Kontostavlos, Vlachoutsis, Finlay, Count Botsaris, and Ydriotis (figs. 107, 108).

"Architects should not forget that they are working in classical Greece, and should embrace the form of Greek architecture" observed Kleanthis, "or that the houses of Greece should have only two stories (apart from the basement), and

115. The Propylaia of the Royal Square in Munich were the monumental expression of Ludwig I's vision of Greece's rebirth. Painting by L. von Klenze (1848).

should not be set too close to each other, so that they are airy" (*Ilios*, June 18, 1833, issue 8). The pioneering architect's statement clearly suggests that Neoclassicism, the architectural style that appeared in Europe in the second half of the eighteenth century in reaction to the excesses of Baroque and Rococo, offering a way out of the impasse in which architecture found itself, was now arriving in Athens.

The first public architecture erected in Greece during the initial phase of the country's freedom (that is, at the time of Kapodistrias) took place in highly unfavorable circumstances in terms of the economy and the general organization of the newly founded state. As was to be expected, the buildings that were absolutely essential to the program of reconstruction displayed no particular morphological aspirations, but reflected the direct functionalism of the period. At the beginning of the 1830s, architects and builders could not afford the luxury of expressing themselves through a higher aesthetic model that projected a distinctive ideological content. On the contrary, their buildings were simple structures whose form provided a note of "good order" through some fundamental rules of composition.

The buildings' discreet, reliable style was completely in keeping with their functionalism. In the best examples, their aesthetic had a "classicizing" tone, though in practice their style — if it can be called such — reflected the more austere rendering of the Italian and French post-Romantic schools (figs. 109–14).

More specifically, in about 1800, France had supplied a substantial impetus to the education of the architects of central Europe, in the spirit of a well-rounded, comprehensive approach to the task of building in both its functional and morphological expression and in the rationality of its structures. The romantic spirit of the late eighteenth century and the free recourse to the forms of the past associated with it naturally had their place here. However, the outcome of this architecture — at least as demanded by the rationalist approach — shunned strong ideological associations and sentimental caprice and had recourse to making the entire process of composition objective, and to aesthetic self-sufficiency and "readable" forms. And it was the "classical" element — at that time modeled on the revival of Roman architecture — that most convincingly satisfied the above principles.

116. Idealized view of Athens, showing the Acropolis and the Areopagos. This imaginary depiction of the monumental group expresses the German ideology of capturing the "beautiful" through classical antiquity. Painting by L. von Klenze (1846).

This kind of classical expression was preferred by the famous professor at the École Polytechnique, J. N. L. Durand, whose teaching was a major factor in establishing the foundations of the German architectural tradition about 1800. The creative architects in the major centers of classicism, Berlin, Munich, and Karlsruhe, were directly or indirectly beneficiaries of this architectural education. This circumstance acquired special significance when these architects abandoned Roman models and embraced Greek ones. For it was precisely at this time — the beginning of the nineteenth century — that the architecture of Germany, while not departing from entrenched views on the composition of urban buildings, was nevertheless re-baptized in a completely new spirit with regard to the hierarchy of forms, which would be called upon to express a more profound aesthetic and ideological content (figs. 115, 116).

German idealism thus breathed life into the discreet academic classicism of the period about 1800, bringing it closer to an introspective approach toward achieving aesthetic perfection and transcending both the cohesive canons of morphological rationalism and the imponderable stylistic repertoire and impulsive choices of Romanticism. This basic ideological acknowledgment of the formal models, whether these were "classical Greek" or derived from other historical styles (at the beginnings, that is, of a spirit of eclecticism) was characteristic of the generation of Karl Friedrich von Schinkel (1781–1841) in Berlin and Leo von Klenze (1784–1864) in Munich. In the Bavarian capital, indeed, Ludwig I's influence, founded on the spirit of an idealized approach to the archaeological models, was paramount. His vision of the rebirth of Athens was critically important not only in the selection of the town as the capital of free Greece but also in the decision to erect monumental structures in the center of Munich, such as the Glyptothek (1816) and, later, the Propylaia (1846), which were modeled by the architect Klenze in the spirit of Greek classicism.

The first Greek engineers who settled and worked in free Greece during the Kapodistrias period were, as we have seen, students at the schools of Munich, Vienna, and Paris. In 1829, a military school modeled on the corresponding French polytechnic school was founded in Nafplion. The first engineers to study in the new state as military and civil engineers, and also as freelance professionals, graduated from Nafplion's Military Cadet School. These were the men who, along with the Bavarians and other foreign engineers of the following period, formulated the style of the modern Greek towns (fig. 117).

The procedure for executing technical projects of all kinds and implementing town planning regulations now included planning, which was applied from the time of Kapodistrias onward and marked a boundary between the traditional and the modern periods. With regard to architecture, the buildings' generally reliable appearance included, in the best cases, simplified elements drawn from the Italian and French post-Romantic schools, on which the early German technique and the artistic tradition of the nineteenth century were based.

After about 1815, however, German classicism began to mature and to become firmly oriented toward the now idealized objectives defined by the ancient Greek heritage. The way had, of course, been smoothed by the initial critique of Greek art, the foundations of which had been laid somewhat earlier by J. J. Winckelmann, to whom reference has already been made. His pronouncements had been confirmed beyond doubt by later discoveries of classical monuments, such as those presented in the numerous albums published by early foreign travelers to Greece.

In connection with the German turn to ancient Greece, however, it should be stressed once more that a major contribution was made by the aesthetic views and, above all, the philosophical theories that came to prominence in the creative climate of German nineteenth-century idealism. That strong conceptual framework developed into a central philosophy of art, according to which the highest form of creative art is a direct product of the most advanced intellect. According to its exponents (from Goethe to Schelling and Hegel), this supreme theory of knowledge and the spirit emerges only through the predominant aesthetic reality.

At the theory's inner core lie the same forces that transformed the earlier romantic classicism of architecture into an expression of more demanding symbolic content. In an ideal reciprocal relationship, an expression of this nature had to achieve a complete balance between form (that is, the visual entity) and the dominating intellectual value.

117. Proposal for the official uniform of geometricians and architects in the employ of the Ministry of the Interior (1840). (Source: State General Archives, Othonian Archive.)

The Consolidation of Monumentality

The general spirit of classicism, particularly of its Greek revival and the ideological bases that contributed to its consolidation and widespread acceptance in the Western world, constitutes an enormous subject with many factors and variations.

The fact that the Greek War of Independence began precisely at the time when the ideal of ancient Greek civilization held sway over the people of Europe and America (which was, of course, not unconnected with the general ideological climate) evoked great enthusiasm and emotion throughout the world. The vision of a revival of the ancient classical models was on the verge of becoming a reality. After the proclamation of Athens as capital, the town became a pilgrimage site for archaeologists, architects, and artists, each aspiring to make his own mark next to the immortal ruins of classical Greece.

Thus, an architectural style born in the West under the influence of the austere moderation and harmony of classical Greek antiquity returned to the land in which it had been nurtured. It is fascinating to observe the way it was incorporated into and assimilated by Greek society and life. The new form of design was introduced, initially at least, under prescriptive conditions—that is, within a strong institutional framework for the implementation of town planning and urban architecture.

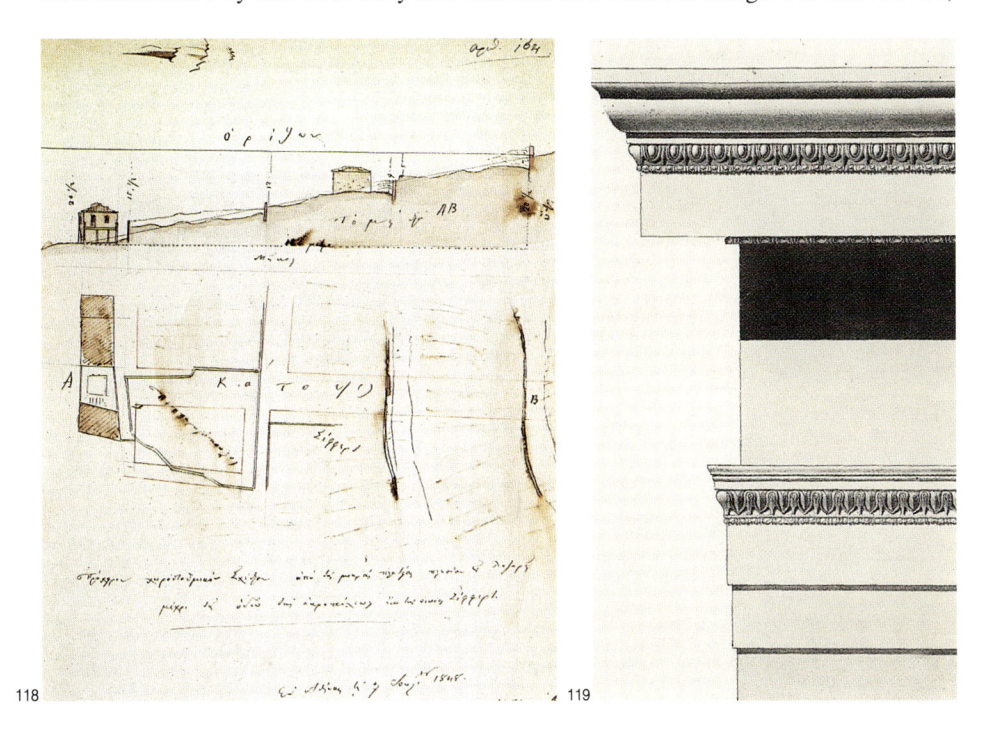

In 1835, a decree "Concerning the hygiene of towns and buildings" was published. This was followed by two more decrees: "Concerning the execution of the town plan of the city of Athens," the extensive clauses of which laid down the basic planning specifications for the capital (the minimum area and shape of building plots, the heights of buildings on the main streets, and so on); and "Concerning the management of political public buildings," promulgated in May and December 1836 respectively (fig. 118). The fifty-four clauses of the latter provide a detailed analysis of everything connected with public buildings: budget, design, auctioning out of the work, construction, materials, supervision, maintenance, repair, and more. "All new buildings and repairs to buildings belonging to political Secretariats shall be carried out by civil architects and in the absence of these by county-engineers." The series of building plans was required to include a topographical plan "and when the site does not have horizontal surfaces, a plan at

118. Introduction of planning into the control of the built environment. The town plan regulated the establishment of heights, in order to preserve the line of the horizon and the view of the historical landscape. By the engineer D. Zezos (1848). (Source: State General Archives, Othonian Archive.)

119. Model Ionic entablature. Drawn by a student at the School of Arts in Athens, it demonstrates a high-quality graphic approach to the archaeology and the aesthetic virtues of classical models.

120. Extract from a handbook of architecture by Stamatis Kleanthis (undated). In a simplistic educational sketch with annotations, it indicates the structural approach to ordinary building work. (Source: Gennadios Library.)

121. Athens. First Primary School, at Athinas and Voreou Streets, known as the Karamanos School. Drawing of the facade by Fr. Stauffert (1840). (Source: State General Archives, Othonian Archive.)

122. Athens. First Primary School. Side elevation. (Source: State General Archives, Othonian Archive.)

123. Athens. Designs (not implemented) by Ludwig Lange for the town's high school (1836). The influence of the Berlin school's severe style of classicism is clear. (Source: State General Archives, Othonian Archive.)

124. Design by Eduard Schaubert for a custodian's box at the entrance to an archaeological site. (Source: State General Archives, Othonian Archive.)

125. Design by Eduard Schaubert for a monument dedicated to the archaeologist O. Mueller. (Source: State General Archives, Othonian Archive.)

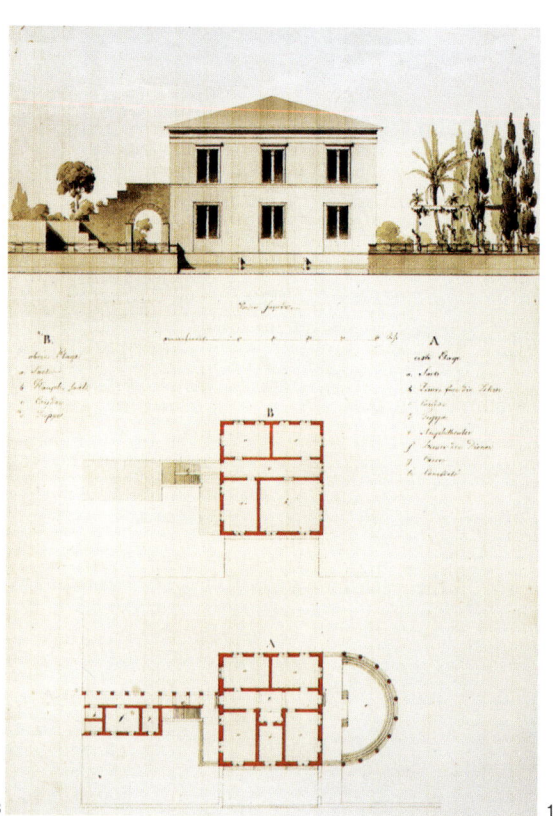

two levels, a cross-section and elevations, all drawn up according to the accepted measures, that is the metric system."

According to Article 52 of the same decree, "no architect may enjoy a permanent appointment until he provides reasonable proof of his knowledge and competence through an examination set by the buildings department of the Secretariat." These three royal decrees defined fully the legislative framework for the construction and reconstruction of Greek towns.

Later in 1836, a decree was published creating a school of architecture. Its objective was to educate all those who "wish to be instructed as master-craftsmen in architecture." The school came under the jurisdiction of the Architecture Department, of which Eduard Schaubert had been appointed head, in the Directorate of Public Works in the Ministry of the Interior. Teaching began in 1837, under the direction of the Bavarian engineer Friedrich von Zentner (the inspiration behind the school). At first, the Polytechnic School, as it was called, was open only on Sundays. In 1847, under Lysandros Kaftantzoglou, it began to open on a daily basis, and its name was changed to Royal Polytechnic University or School of Arts (figs. 119, 120).

The institution was staffed by a team of select architects, sculptors and painters and was, in effect, the forerunner of the National Technical University (Metsovion Polytechnic). In addition to Zentner, those who taught there included the Danish brothers Christian and Theophil Hansen; the French architect C. Laurent; the sculptors Karl Heller, Rafaello Ceccoli, and C. Siegel; the painter Pierre Bonirote (who came to Athens with a recommendation from the famous classicist Jean-Auguste-Dominique Ingres and received a salary from the duchesse de Plaisance); the architects T. Komninos and M. Georgiadis, from Constantinople; a hieromonk from Mount Athos, Agathangelos Triantaphyllos; Ludwig Thiersch, son of the great philhellene and archaeologist Frédéric von Thiersch; and others.

126. Design for a palace on the Acropolis by Karl F. Schinkel. (Source: Gennadios Library.)

In theory, the first graduates of the School of Arts built the new Athens. Among them were some fine nineteenth-century artists, several of whom went on to study abroad. Both the government and King Ludwig I of Bavaria personally gave financial support to the most competent and talented, in the form of scholarships to study in Vienna, Berlin, and, above all, Munich.

The construction of the large private residences and mansions, as well as of the public buildings, was undertaken by well-known Greek and foreign architects. During the first period of King Otto's reign, public buildings, in particular, were almost invariably designed by architects connected with the Architecture Department, where the head of the department, Schaubert, who sat on committees and councils, usually recommended that the projects be assigned to the Hansen brothers or to German architects (figs. 121–25).

The fact that the most important positions in the public sector were occupied by foreigners, mainly Bavarians, and that the major projects were assigned to them, combined with the general colonial policy pursued by the Regency, eventually led to the uprising of 1843 and the constitutional reform of 1844, which provided for the dismissal of all foreigners from public services. Even so, many monumental buildings continued to be assigned to foreign architects, sometimes justifiably, as in the cases of Klenze, Gaertner, and the Hansen brothers (especially Theophil), whose prestige transcended the borders of their native lands, and sometimes out of an indefensible worship of things foreign—a phenomenon that still afflicts Greece today.

The first important public project to be assigned to a foreign architect was, of course, Otto's Palace. Klenze, following the general spirit of Kleanthis and Schaubert's modification of the town plan, was the first to move the palace from the north-south axis of symmetry (Athinas Street, according to Kleanthis's proposed plan) to an off-center location at the west, near the Kerameikos. Indeed, he drew up a preliminary design for a highly interesting complex of ancient-style buildings set in gardens and arranged in irregular formations—thus demonstrating his romantic disposition, but also revealing a sound knowledge of the ancient Greek approach to composition. At the same time, the great Schinkel, prompted by Otto's brother, Maximilian, put forward a bold study for a palace set among the classical monuments on the Acropolis. This design, though clearly not destined to be implemented, was unrivaled in its compositional skill and was a fine example of artistic sensitivity and beauty (fig. 126).

Ludwig, however, who visited Athens the following year (1835), decided, on the advice of his councilors and particularly of the architect Friedrich von Gaertner (1792–1847), who accompanied him, to assign the study and building of the palace to Gaertner himself. Accordingly, the building was sited, as Gaertner recommended, at the east end of Ermou Street (it is the modern Greek Parliament building), while Syntagma Square and the axis of Amalias Avenue opposite Stadiou Street were created in front of it, to a design by the military engineer Hoch (fig. 127).

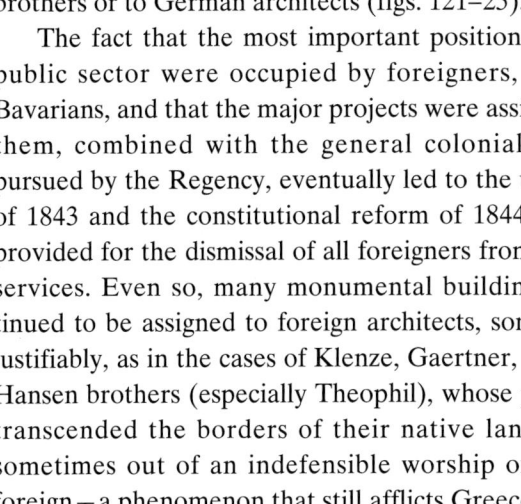

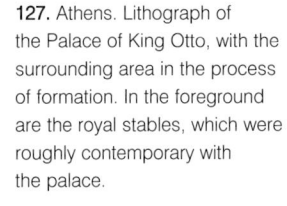

127. Athens. Lithograph of the Palace of King Otto, with the surrounding area in the process of formation. In the foreground are the royal stables, which were roughly contemporary with the palace.

128. Athens. The Palace of King Otto in the already formed urban environment, toward the end of the Othonian period. The large square (modern Syntagma Square) has been laid out, defining the east edge of the old town at the end of Ermou Street, where the Koromilas house and a large number of Neoclassical buildings of the first period can be seen. The Dimitriou mansion can be seen in the background, in the then-deserted slopes of Lykavittos Hill, on the site of the later Grande Bretagne Hotel. (Source: Benaki Museum, Photographic Archive.)

129. Athens. The Palace of King Otto, now the Greek Parliament building, erected from 1836 to 1843. The structure was a monumental reference point for the later development of Athenian classicism. It was incorporated into the moderated aesthetic and structural approach adopted toward important public buildings of the time. By F. von Gaertner.

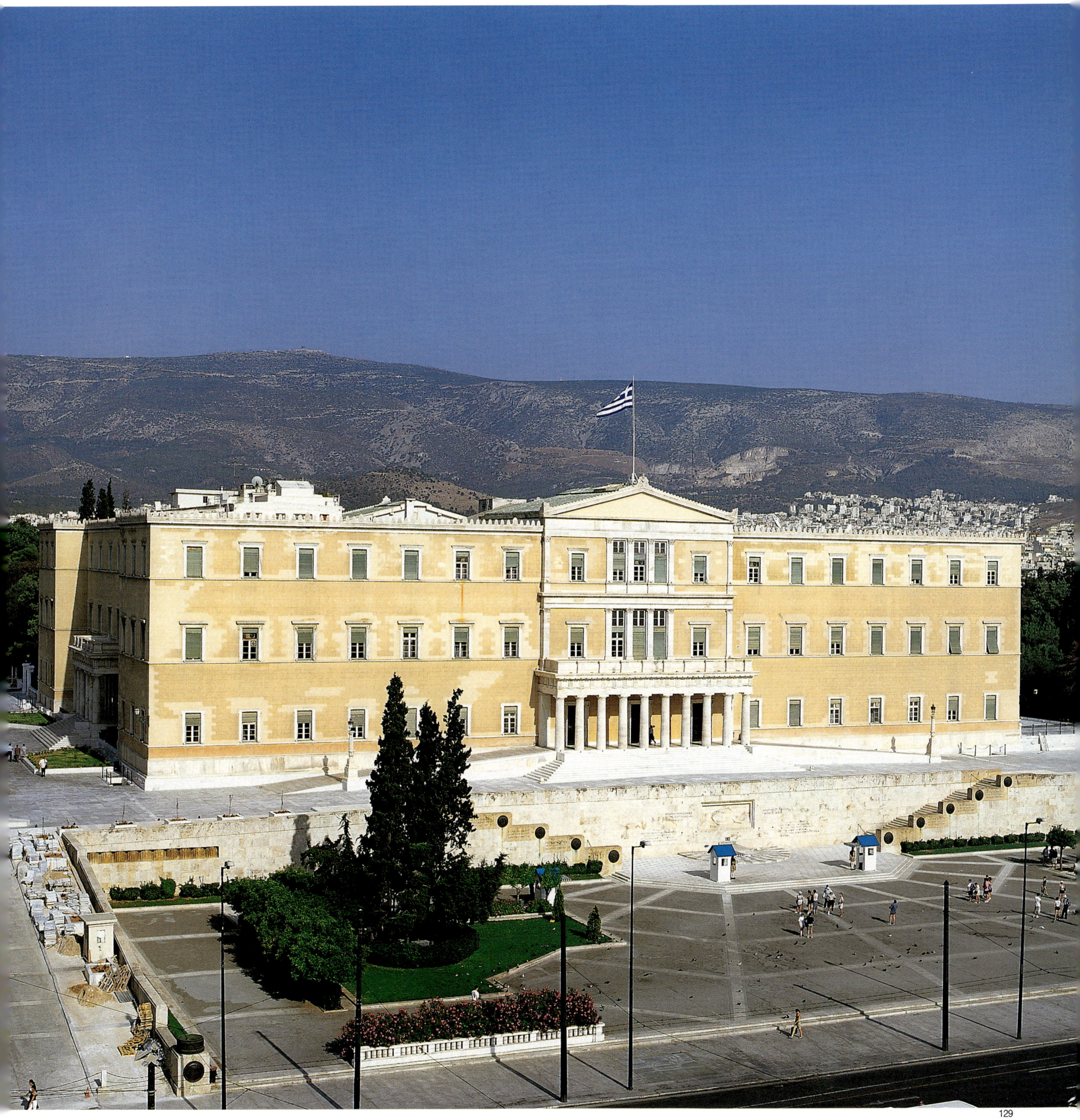

129

The Palace (1836–43) was the first building of monumental scale in the new capital. It introduced the style of official classicism into the architecture of the town. Just as important, it served during its construction as a training school for Greek craftsmen in the builder's arts. For the first time in many centuries, marble-carvers once again sculpted ancient pieces in their authentic form, and craftsmen created one-piece columns and entablatures of the various orders in the ancient-style porches of the structure.

When complete, the monument's robust rectangular volumes dominated the then-virgin landscape between the old town and Lykavittos Hill. Gaertner, presumably following Ludwig's instructions, gave it the imposing tranquillity and morphological autonomy of a large classical composition. The flat expanses of the walls, with their plain windows, clearly emphasize the sense of the horizontal. The central part of the west facade, near the official entrance, projects slightly and is emphasized at ground-floor level by a marble Doric porch and crowned by a striking classical pediment. The cornices are adorned by a dense row of antefixes, also carved from pentelic marble. Indeed, the ancient quarries on Mount Penteli were reopened for the purpose (figs. 128, 129).

130. Athens. The Royal Mint (about 1835). A building of rather austere form, with a square ground plan and a central courtyard. It stood in Klafthmonos Square, precisely on the axis of Korai Street. Before it was demolished in 1939, it housed the Ministry of Economic Affairs.

In contrast with the austere appearance of the exterior, luster was added to the interior of the building by fine color murals and painted ceilings of classical, Pompeian, and Renaissance inspiration. Unfortunately, most of these were lost during the great fire of 1909, and about twenty years later the entire core of the building was drastically remodeled by the architect Andreas Kriezis to enable it to serve as a parliament building.

In the meantime, during the early part of Otto's reign, other, functional, buildings — such as the mint and the press — were erected. These were mostly the work of foreign architects who, for primarily economic reasons, gave them a very simple appearance. Architects such as Christian Hansen, Roser, J. Hoffer, Fr. Stauffert, and others undertook to construct buildings of this kind, as we have already seen, on behalf of the administration and the Architecture Department of the Ministry of the Interior, at that time headed by Eduard Schaubert (figs. 130, 131).

Apart from Hansen, Kleanthis, and a few others, the architects of this period were military engineers. One of them was W. von Weiler, who in 1834 constructed the most interesting building in this category, the Military Hospital on Makriyanni Street, which now houses the Centre for the Acropolis Studies (fig. 132).

131. Athens. The Royal Press and Lithographic Workshop (about 1835). Its symmetrical design opens mainly toward Stadiou Street. The building's frugal appearance is rendered in a classical style, with walls articulated by elements based on the ancient orders. Earlier Athenians knew it as the main building of the law courts.

This long, rectangular, two-story structure is characterized by its rather anti-classical form, with exposed masonry, arched windows on the ground floor, visible brickwork in the arches above the doors and windows, and austere brick decoration. It is certainly a departure from academic architecture, though it is not a clear example of a romantic trend. However, the building is rendered with great candor, and the absence of superfluous decoration emphasizes its functionality. In all probability, this building represents the transition that occurred in Germany about 1830 to a materialist architecture (*Materialstil*) that was patently emancipated from classical and Renaissance models. Because arched openings (*rundbogen*) were commonly used in this style of architecture, it became known as the *Rundbogenstil*. Moreover, some impressive applications of this morphology were to be found in other developing urban centers in Greece, as, for example, about 1840, in the important infrastructure buildings of the harbor in the then-flourishing town of Ermoupolis on Syros, to which we shall return below.

Aesthetic departures of this kind, of course, were sporadic and certainly did not indicate an intent to enfeeble the classical spirit at birth, particularly in the city that was home to classicism's ancient models. On the contrary, private buildings had begun to be erected whose form stressed the consolidation of the classical canon. One example is the house of Alexandros Kontostavlos on Stadiou Street, in which King Otto resided until 1836. The preserved measured drawings made by Christian Hansen provided clear evidence for the characteristic symmetrical, tripartite articulation of a typical Neoclassical building (fig. 133).

There was also the neighboring house of Stamatios Dekozis-Vouros (1833, by G. Lueders and J. Hoffer), on the south side of Klafthmonos Square, in which Otto lived from 1836 until 1843 (fig. 134). The building has been preserved, and today houses the Museum of the City of Athens. It offers direct testimony to the form of early Athenian classicism: a plain, horizontally organized facade, a dominance of wall surfaces (in which the order is established by the simple pilasters on the upper story), a few windows placed symmetrically, and a main entrance on the ground floor with a marble balcony above it. This composition heralds the tranquility and aesthetic self-sufficiency that were to be applied on a monumental scale a few years later by Gaertner in the palace building that we have already examined. At this stage of urban classicism, austerity was not the product of diffidence or introspection in composition but rather the outcome of classicism's inherent creative principles and ideology. The personality of the architect, however, also played a

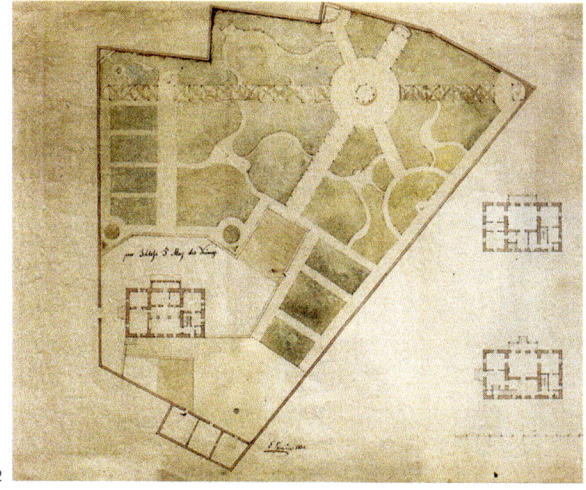

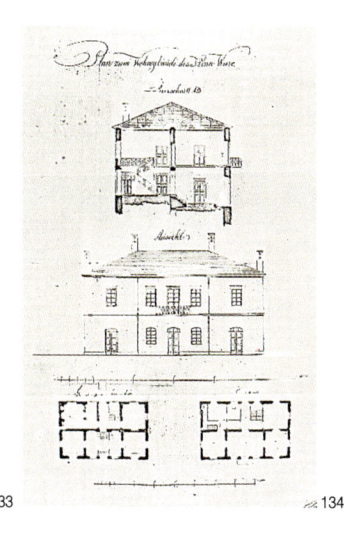

132. Athens. Military Hospital in the Makriyanni neighborhood. This robust building's morphological expression represents a move toward functionality and the creative use of construction material (*Materialstil*), though here it is executed with a generally romantic style. The arches (*rundbogen*) above the ground-floor windows are typical, as is the decorative frieze of ceramic tiles. By W. Weiler.

133. Athens. Measured drawing of the Kontostavlos house (see also fig. 95), by Christian Hansen. The drawing affords evidence for the classicizing design of the rooms of this very early structure, as well as the typically romantic layout of the garden. (Source: National Sculpture Collection, Munich.)

134. Athens. The Dekozis-Vouros house on Klafthmonos Square. As early as the 1830s, this building established the simplicity and geometrical clarity of urban architecture as applied in Greece's new capital by the Bavarians. It now houses the Museum of the City of Athens. (Source: Vourou-Eftaxia Museum of the City of Athens.)

135. Athens. The A. Rallis house (now demolished), opposite the Vouros house (see fig. 164) in Klafthmonos Square, by the architect Stamatis Kleanthis. It exhibits striking classical style, aesthetic quality, and proportions, and, above all, a free morphological formulation of details (the balcony railings and decorative brick frieze). The stone-carving technique used in the sculpted details is notable.

136. Athens. The Ilissia palace of the duchesse de Plaisance. This imposing romantic structure recalls medieval models and includes features of the Italian villa. It is now the Byzantine and Christian Museum. By S. Kleanthis.

137. Mount Penteli. The Rododaphne villa. Its romantic style incorporates Gothic morphology. The facades are roughly articulated with dressed stonework. By S. Kleanthis.

137

dominating role with regard to the manner in which these principles were assimilated. In the slightly later mansion of A. Rallis (fig. 135), for example, which was built directly opposite the Vouros house (fig. 134) by Kleanthis (and unfortunately demolished in 1938), the style is richly rendered: the facade was articulated into side wings and a projecting central section emphasized by a classical pediment. The large balcony on the upper story, with its wonderful metal railing; the pilasters, with their Corinthian-style impost blocks; the carved window and door frames; and the distinctive decorative brickwork embellishing the crowning element (the "frieze," as it was called at the time) all gave the building an unrivaled expressivity and lent a rather romantic impression that transcended the established submission to the classical canon.

In the 1840s, Kleanthis had the opportunity to develop these trends, which may be described as being unfettered by academism, when he built the villas of Sophie de Marbois, duchesse de Plaisance: the imposing Ilissia mansion—now the Byzantine and Christian Museum—and the picturesque residences Tourelle, Maisonette, and the little palace of Rododaphne on the pine-clad slopes of Mount Penteli. All of these, which had dressed masonry and featured rough lines in the medieval picturesque style, constituted a notable departure from the established classical morphology (figs. 136, 137).

Kleanthis, in fact, was among those architects working during the Othonian period who apparently sought a freedom and maturity of composition that was capable of liberating them from the existing confines of the classicizing Munich School. However, because the administration was under German control he was prevented from undertaking any important public buildings. Although Kleanthis submitted a proposal, he lost the opportunity to build the Arsakeion Girl's School, and a similar fate befell his study for the present University building, which was, in the end, designed by Christian Hansen.

Construction of the University (figs. 138–40) began in 1839 and was completed in 1864, after countless difficulties, most of them financial, had been overcome. The project was funded by a large number of benefactors, including King Otto himself, who supported it from his personal wealth.

The Palace, with its robust appearance, conveyed the formal expression, impressive tranquility, and reliability that are the hallmarks of a ruler's residence; in contrast, the University—with its human scale, elegant classical lines, and light sculptured and painted decoration—projected the superiority of uncorrupted intellectual and aesthetic activity, cultivated through the free urban consciousness.

Christian Hansen emphasized the entrance on the west front of the building by designing an Ionic distyle porch modeled on the unrivaled proportions of the Propylaia on the Acropolis. The side wings of the facade were given porticoes, the

138. Athens. Drawing of a lateral section through the University building, clearly showing the arrangement of courtyards at the sides and the portico supported on plain pillars.

139. Athens. The University (construction started in 1839). This building is exemplary in terms of not only the inspired handling of the order but also the functional design of the rooms. By C. Hansen.

140. Athens. The central Ionic porch of the University, with a color frieze on the wall at the back, above the main entrance.

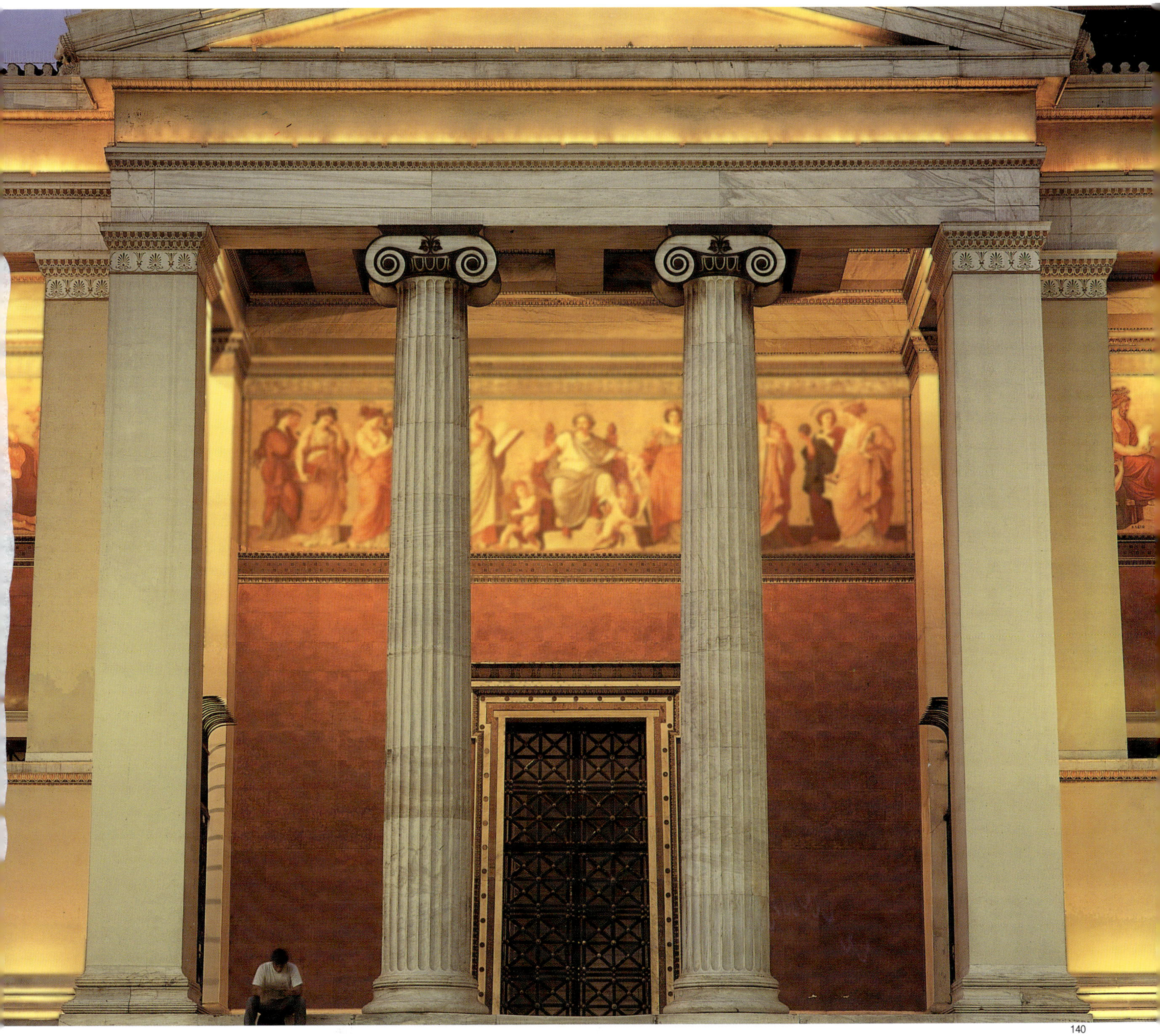

140

141. Athens. The Dimitriou mansion (1842), by T. Hansen, at the period when it presented an authentic appearance. The monumental structure incorporates discrete deviations from the austere classical school of the Bavarians. It was intended that marble arcades be widely used on Syntagma Square, but this did not occur. Photograph taken before 1940. (Source: KTNA, P. Mylonas Archive.)

142. Athens. The Dimitriou mansion, as drawn by T. Hansen.

143. The Eye Hospital in its present form. The entrance was remodeled by L. Kaftantzoglou, and a story was later added by G. Metaxas. This work revealed Christian Hansen to be an expert handler of Byzantine morphology, a skill he also applied to buildings in Copenhagen.

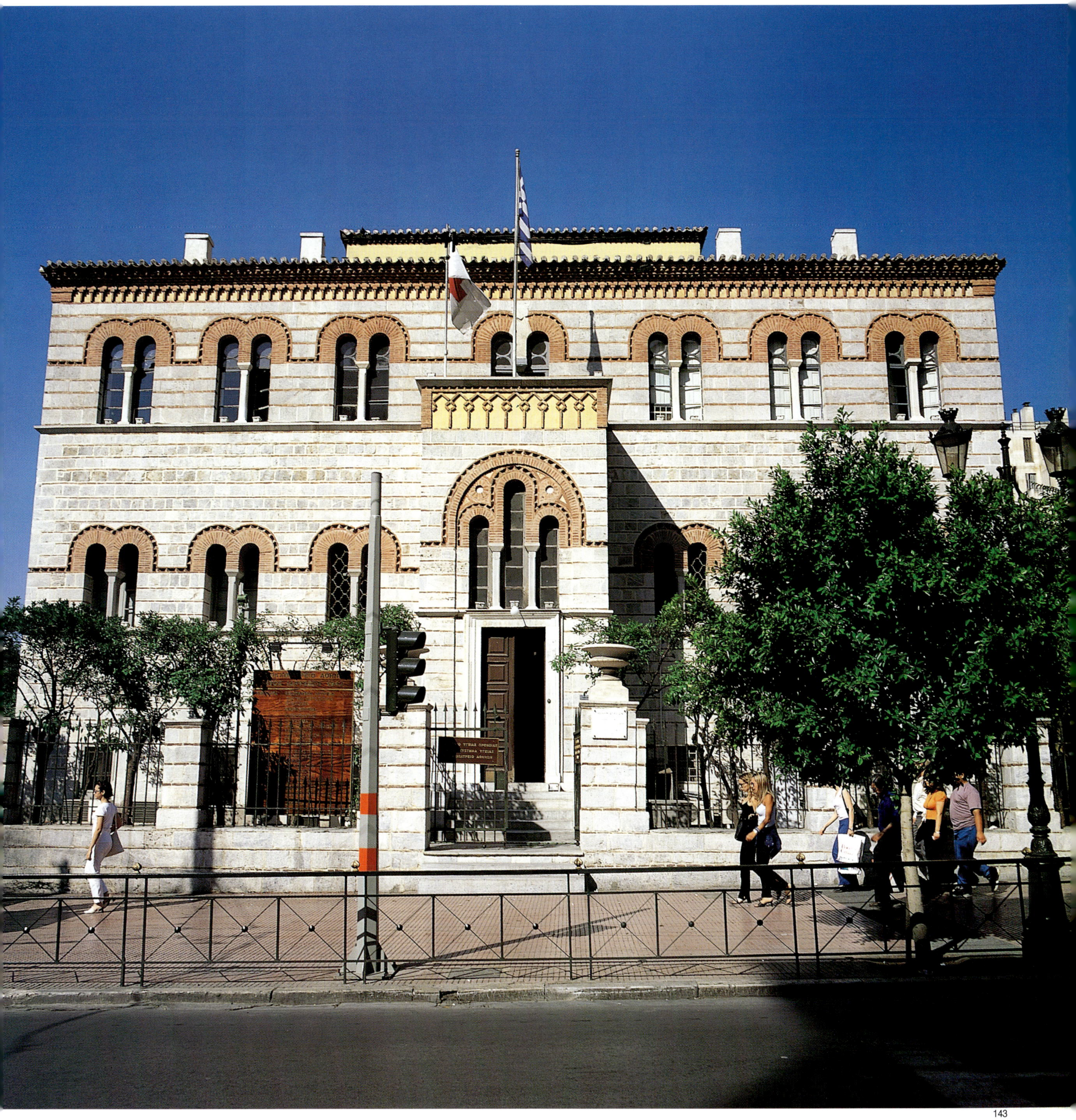

143

rear walls of which were decorated by the painter Karl Rahl with a broad, multi-colored frieze depicting the rebirth of the Sciences. The tranquil horizontality of the west facade, in which the entrance is set, almost conceals the fact that the building has two stories. The vestibule of the entrance includes an interior marble staircase leading to the main ceremonial hall above, which is adorned by a superb painted ceiling, while the other rooms are devoted to the lecture theaters and offices. Hansen, like other foreigners, was obliged to leave Greece after the constitutional reform of 1843, and the work was completed by Lysandros Kaftantzoglou, A. Georgantas, Anastasios Theophilas, and other engineers, while the financing was resumed with the support of the Greek expatriate D. Bernardakis.

The finished monumental structure was, and remains, a supremely Athenian building. Its image, incorporated as a self-contained aesthetic unit in the Attic landscape, embodied the sensual rather than the imposing essence of monumentality. This quality was warmly embraced by the Athenians and the building was certainly the model that set its seal on urban classicism in the new capital throughout the following period, down to the end of the nineteenth century.

144. Athens. The Eye Hospital. Christian Hansen's original design. Paradoxically, this classical approach was revised in favor of the Byzantine-revival style at the wishes of King Ludwig of Bavaria. (Source: Eye Hospital Archive.)

145. Athens. The Church of St. Dionysios of the Catholics on Panepistimiou Street. This Christian basilica was designed in accordance with trends in nineteenth-century European church-building. During the execution of the project, L. Kaftantzoglou made a number of changes to the style of the west porch, in the interests of simplification. By Leo von Klenze. Postcard.

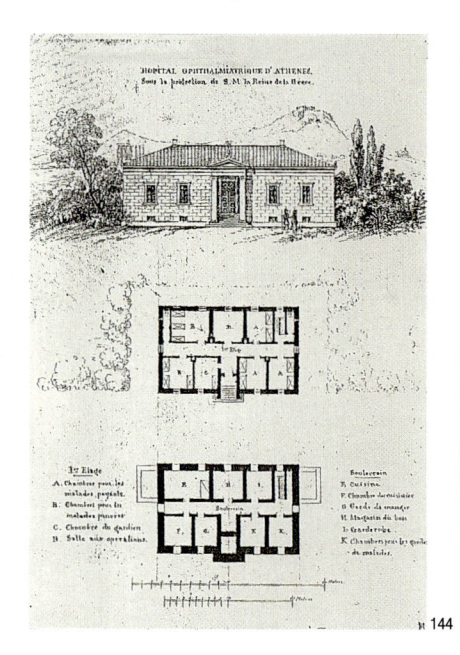

Meanwhile, Athens had the good fortune to extend its hospitality to Theophil Hansen (1813–1891), younger brother of the architect of the University and the inspiration behind late-Viennese classicism, and without doubt one of the most distinguished architects of his day. Like his brother Christian, Theophil had been employed as a professor at the School of Arts and had an excellent knowledge of the historical monuments of Athens. When he built the mansion of A. Dimitriou on Syntagma Square, Theophil Hansen provided Athens with a benchmark for refined academic architecture, with mild eclectic departures, which turned to the fruitful aesthetic heritage of Schinkel's school in Berlin. He did not hesitate to embellish the main facade of the building with two-story arcaded loggias that formed a charming contrast with the Doric strength of the forms of the Palace nearby (figs. 141, 142).

Theophil Hansen derived his self-confidence not only from his talent, which was generally recognized, but also from the powerful commissioner of the work, Baron Georgios Sinas, an expatriate Greek resident in Vienna, and, after him, from the baron's son Simon Sinas. The former funded one of the most original works of European classicism, the Athens Observatory on the Hill of the Nymphs (1842–46). The plain spaces of this building, designed, of course, by Hansen, were arranged in the shape of a cross, with the rotating metal dome of the astronomical observatory rising above a cylindrical drum at the center. The four narrow sides of the wings were crowned with pediments adorned with relief decoration against a reddish background. When the building was completed in 1846, Hansen was so satisfied with the morphological autonomy of the elegant structure that he carved on it the inscription SERVARE INTAMINATUM (KEEP INTACT).

The contribution made by the Hansen brothers, especially Theophil, to modern Greek—and not only Athenian—architecture was undoubtedly catalytic. The Hansens brought to the native classicism of the first period the aesthetic atmosphere of mature central-European historicism. The trends that involved a stricter view of the ancient Greek models naturally continued to have their exponents; they were expressed through the personalities of architects such as Lysandros Kaftantzoglou, P. Kalkos, and others, to whom we shall turn directly. However, a number of morphological versions of a different stylistic orientation

146. Athens. Drawing by Christian Hansen in 1842 that was used as a basis for the Cathedral. It exhibits indeterminate trends of an eclectic character oriented toward medieval European models. (Source: Kunstakademie, Copenhagen.)

147. Athens. The Cathedral in its present condition, as formulated by D. Zezos. It was the first attempt to crystallize a Greek-Byzantine style for a church building. The mosaic on the facade dates from 1958. Postcard.

had also begun to appear. Of these, the most predictable in the case of Greece was, of course, the Byzantine revival in public architecture.

European experience suggested that medieval models were suitable for functional buildings, especially ecclesiastical and charitable institutions. In this direction, Christian Hansen designed the final form of the Athens Eye Hospital (1852). The Eye Hospital was the first of its kind in Europe, executed in a highly felicitous rendering of the Byzantine tradition—which was natural enough, as its creator had carefully studied the old churches of Athens and the surrounding area (figs. 143, 144). The erection of the Cathedral (1842–57) held out much promise, and the main responsibility for it was assumed by the architect Demetres Zezos. Though linked, naturally, with the Byzantine tradition, it departed from that tradition to incorporate eclectic influences. The result is now regarded as dubious, even though at the time it was dubbed Greek-Byzantine. In any event, the "Greekness" of the style of the new cathedral was superior to an unorthodox solution submitted by Theophil Hansen for a Western-style cathedral on Panepistimiou Street. The building eventually erected on this site was the Church of St.

Dionysios of the Catholics (1853–87). This was given the form of a Roman Catholic basilica, in accordance with the rather expansive morphological perception of Leo von Klenze, though it was later simplified—at least with regard to the arcaded porch on the west facade—by his Greek colleague Lysandros Kaftantzogou (1811–1885) (figs. 145–47).

Kaftantzoglou, who graduated with distinction from the San Luca Academy in Rome, represented a preeminently academic architectural personality among Greek architects of the mid-nineteenth century. His work naturally was concentrated on the reconstruction of Athens. As head of the newly founded National Technical University from 1843 to 1862, he could not fail to transmit his broad

148. Athens. The Papadopoulos High School (now the Kostis Palamas building). The proposal for the Arsakeion by the architect Stamatis Kleanthis was rejected, and this building gave him the opportunity, in 1855, to implement his own composition for a distinguished teaching institute. The building was praised by European experts. Lithograph of the time.

149. Athens. The Arsakeion Girls' School on Panepistimiou Street (1846–52). One of L. Kaftantzoglou's most important works, formulated with a mature assimilation of the morphology of austere classicism.

150. Athens. The central part of the Arsakeion. Juxtaposed with the Ionic forms of the upper story, the monumental entrance is emphasized by the pair of Doric columns framing it. At the top of the pediment is a small marble head of Athena by the sculptor Leonidas Drosis.

knowledge of architecture to many of his students, some of whom, of course, worked in other urban centers of Old Greece. The importance of his contribution to the consolidation of urban classicism was comparable to that of the Hansen brothers. Although he extensively externalized his ideas on architecture, town planning, and aesthetics in general through countless theoretical treatises and design proposals, it is only from his buildings that one can draw conclusions about his basic formal beliefs. One such building is the Arsakeion (1846–52) (owned by the Educational Society) on Panepistimiou Street. It constituted a landmark in the architect's career because, among other things, it involved him in fierce rivalry with Kleanthis, whose design was in the end rejected by the governing board of the Society (figs. 148, 149).

ΑΡΣΑΚΕΙΟΝ

The numerous well-known preliminary drawings made by Kaftantzoglou for the Arsakeion perhaps betray a certain weakness in composition and occasionally contain morphological paradoxes. The end result, however, displayed an impressive clarity in its modeling and stylistic perfection in its details. The classical character of the building, stripped of excessive ornamentation, exudes a distinctive austerity, though this is moderated on the facade, where the main entrance is strongly recessed between projecting side wings and the zone of the upper story is pleasantly broken by a row of Ionic half-columns. At the back of the internal courtyard was the school church with its unusual ground plan (now unfortunately destroyed as a result of the drastic interventions of the following century), all the interior surfaces of which were adorned with paintings of high artistic quality.

Within the confines of its scale and specific purpose, the Arsakeion signaled, with success for nineteenth-century Athens, a balanced relationship between the classical style and the official character of an urban public building (fig. 150).

The architects of modern Greek classicism envisioned the creation of a large architectural composition that would, through its faithful reference to ancient models, project a preeminently monumental result, with ideological luster. The actual realization of such a composition would assume a kind of metaphysical role in its communication with the immediate cultural environment.

The first substantial step in this direction had already been taken with the University building, but toward the end of the Othonian period two more creations realized this vision through their supreme aesthetic presence: the building complex that houses the National Technical University (1862–76) and the architectural composition of the Academy (1859–85). The former was by Kaftantzoglou and the latter by Theophil Hansen. Despite the two projects' differences in morphological character, their quality transcended the hermetically sealed world of Athens under regeneration, They were recognized as equal to the finest achievements of European classicism (fig. 91).

Although both these monumental buildings were completed in the following decade, during the reign of King George I, it should be noted that the National Technical University complex expresses the earliest and most fundamental coordinates of academic architecture, while the Academy belongs to a later stage, in which forms are perceived as more dominant—a feature of late historicism.

In the National Technical University complex, Kaftantzoglou presented Athenian classicism with its first large-scale sculptural composition set within a spacious environment and strictly organized around its axes of symmetry. The two identical ground-floor structures, flanking the main entrance on Patision Street, have tranquil Doric porticoes on their facades that welcome visitors into the forecourt. The pure white of the slender columns, with the impeccable order of their entablature, projects against the dark red background of the portico walls in a pleasant, refined play of chiaroscuro. A composition of similar inventiveness may be seen in the volumes of Kaftantzoglou's buildings in the Polytechnic and the church of Ayia Irini (figs. 151, 152).

In the background rises the imposing two-story main building, the marble staircase of which leads up to the elevated Ionic porch modeled on the Erechtheion. Its interior, which includes the large lecture theaters, is designed around a open and welcoming square courtyard with a portico around the sides. The composition as a whole renders a classical grandeur, thereby defining its ideological purpose; at the same time, it is successfully integrated into its functional mission within the Athenian historical landscape, and it reflects the distinctive features of the Attic climate.

151. Athens. The main Averoff building of the National Technical University (Metsovion Polytechnic), one of L. Kaftantzoglou's crowning achievements. The semicircular form (rotunda) of the rear of the main building (the interior of which is the official ceremonial hall) boldly displays the purely solid perception of volumes associated with the period of classicism.

152. Athens. The south concha of the church of Ayia Irini. As he did in the main Averoff building of the National Technical University (Metsovion Polytechnic) (fig. 151), here the architect, L. Kaftantzoglou, modeled the domed tri-concha church on Eolou Street with clear, intersecting volumes.

The National Technical University building was funded by Nikolaos Stournaris, Michael and Eleni Tositsas, and Georgios Averoff, all from Metsovon. It formed a bridge between the period of Otto, which was inspired by the anticipation of reconstruction, and the immediately following period of George I, in which the social and cultural coordinates, now developed to a more mature level, provided the architectural expression of the urban building with a different ideological reference point. As we shall see later, the dogmatic quality of the classical style began to retreat, and a more malleable, less symbolic, aesthetic climate began to emerge that gave renewed expressive content to the morphological tradition subservient to the academic canon (fig. 153).

153. Athens. View of the area of Neapoli and Exarchia about the 1870s. At the left can be seen the completed Averoff building of the Polytechneion, and, next to it, the original wing of the Archaeological Museum. In the left foreground is Strephi Hill. The intervening space and the plain to the west, beyond Patision Street, is still unbuilt.

The Regeneration of the Towns

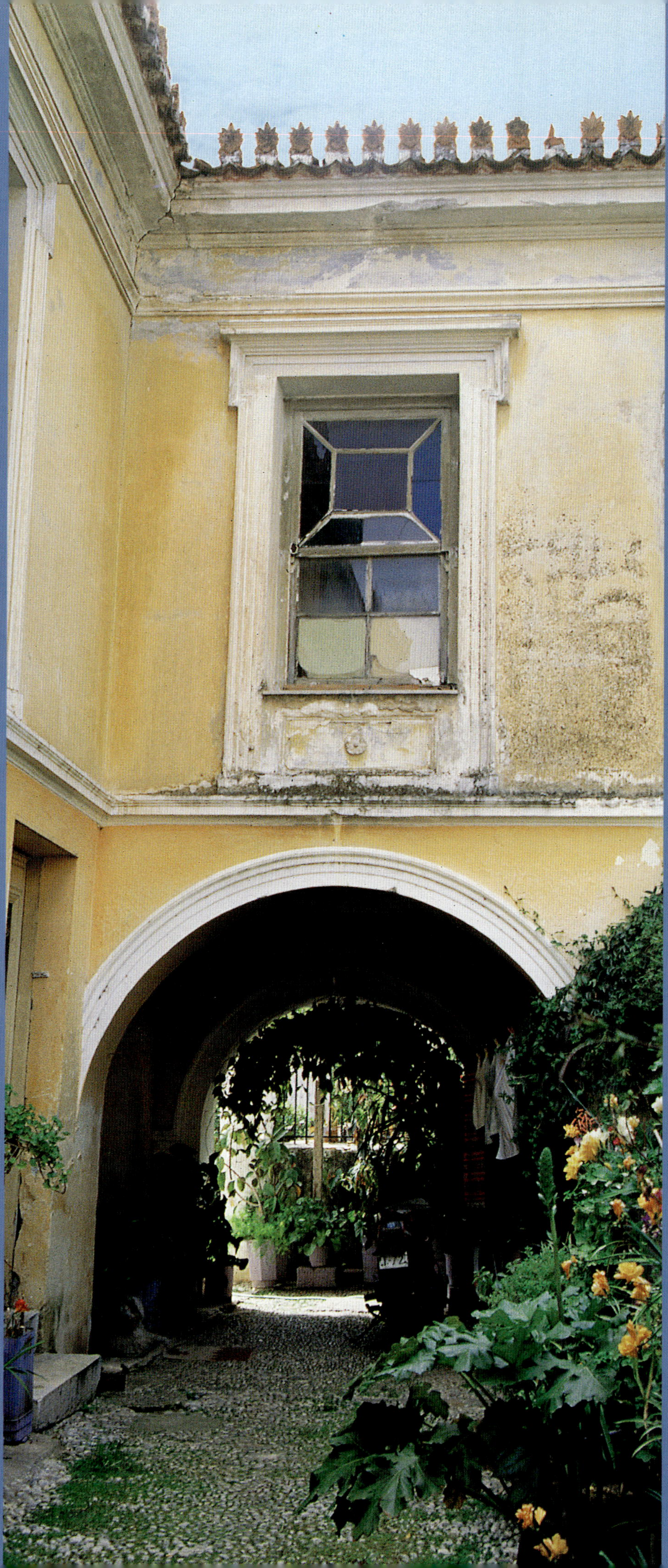

THE REGENERATION OF THE TOWNS

Social and Architectural Transformation

The reconstruction of the old towns was a pressing need. The project had begun during Kapodistrias's period and continued after his assassination, under the administrative committee that assumed the provisional government of the country until the young monarch and regent took up residence. The Bavarians followed the policy of the previous government. New town plans were drawn up by the Engineer Corps and work continued on the tracing and laying of streets, the building of bridges, and the construction of harbor works, so as to secure the development of the seaborne communications that would in turn facilitate the growth of trade.

"The royal government," wrote Frédéric von Thiersch in his book *De l'état actuel de la Grèce et des moyens d'arriver à sa restauration*, "which comes from the center of European civilization and is set firmly within this great sphere of interests, while naturally attending to the country's agriculture, will not fail quickly to grasp the significance of Greek trade and to ask what will be its basis, what the causes of its growth, what its present condition, what its future."

Syros, Nafplion, Patras, Kalamata, Galaxidi, Itea, Mesolongi, and, a little later, Piraeus were the main ports serving the import and export trade that not only satisfied the needs of Greece but also played a part in the intensive trading of merchandise between West and East.

The large commercial establishments owned by Greek expatriates, which were spread throughout the entire Ottoman Empire and could be found in Bosnia, Moldavia and Wallachia, Russia, the Austro-Hungarian empire, and Britain, and on the neighboring Mediterranean coasts of Italy, France, Spain, and Portugal, had direct connections and common interests with Greece. Similar interests were shared by those who were naturalized citizens of the countries in which they lived, while all of them looked upon Greece as their common motherland and maintained close friendly and professional ties with their relatives who still lived there.

Meanwhile, reconstruction proceeded in Argos, Tripolis, Lidoriki, Aigion, Corinth, Methoni, Pylos, and Amphissa. Plans were drawn up for the creation of new towns and, at the same time (in the general climate of admiration for ancient Greece), attempts were made to revive some of the glorious cities of the past, like Sparta, Eretria, Thebes, and Megara. The Greek and especially the foreign land-surveyors in the Architecture Department of the Secretariat of the Interior stayed very active. Their responsibilities included designing towns; constructing roads and bridges; implementing hydraulic projects; erecting, repairing, and changing the use of public buildings; locating antiquities, and so on (figs. 155–60).

The same men undertook the studies for the first private edifices in the towns. There were considerably fewer civil architect-engineers than military ones, particularly in the provincial towns. It was only natural, therefore, that the officers of the engineers who were appointed to the provinces became the main exponents of the dissemination of Neoclassicism in Greece. Under them, master craftsmen and local labor guilds learned their art. It has not yet been possible to establish the extent to which graduates of the School of Arts also rose to prominence in the provinces. Generally speaking, it seems unlikely that many would have had an impact in the provinces, because increased building activity in the capital probably kept most of them in Athens. However, some may have come to the fore in the provinces, mainly as master craftsmen for public works. Certainly, the majority of public and private projects werecarried out by local craftsmen, whose involvement

154. Sparti. Entrance vestibule of a house on Menelaou Street. This enchanting composition of classically ordered architecture includes a large vaulted passageway leading to the rear of the garden.

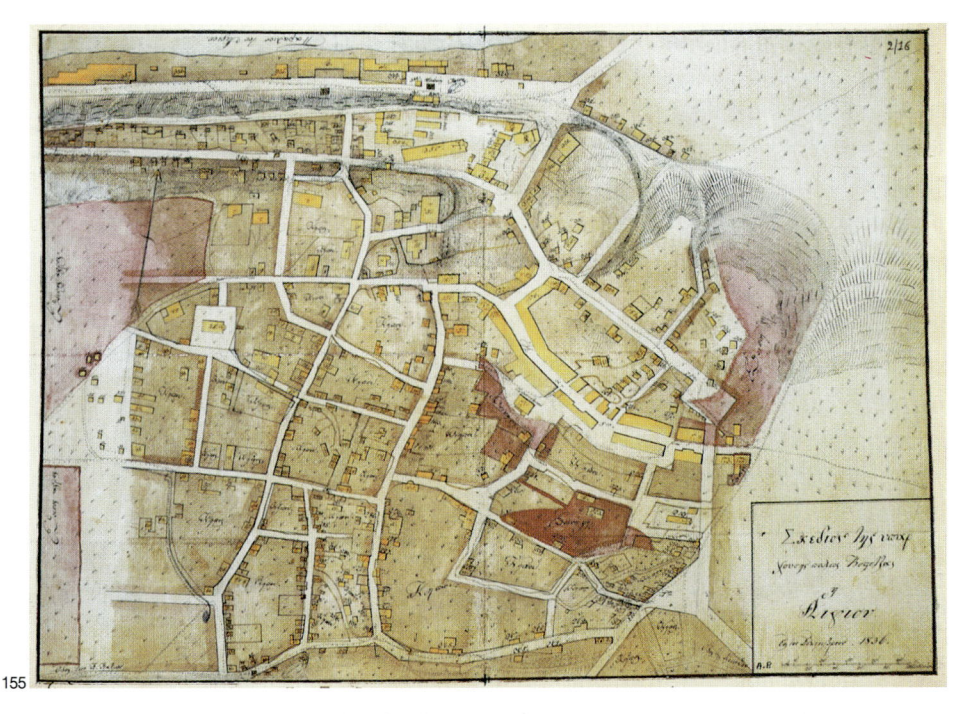

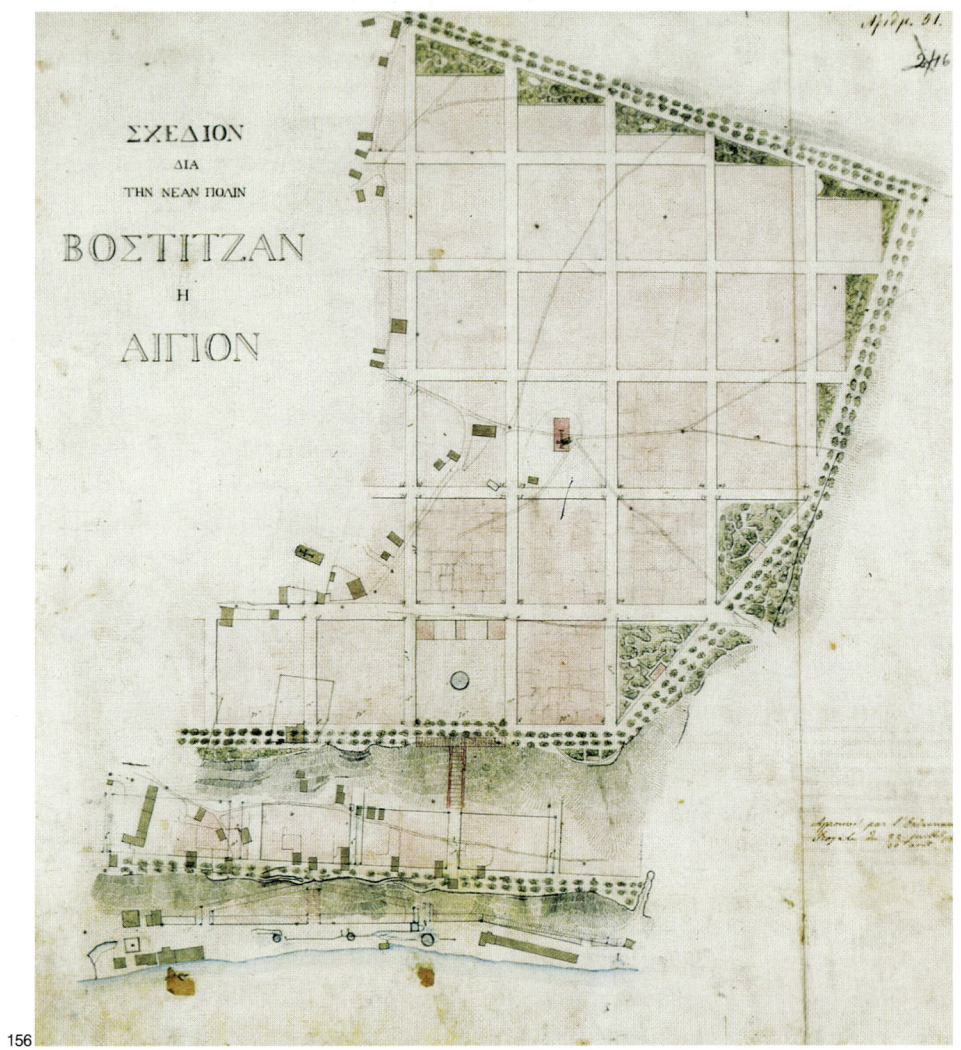

155. Aigion (Vostitza). Attempt to organize the building lines of the existing urban environment (1836). (Source: Ministry for the Environment, Town Planning and Public Works Archive.)

156. Aigion (Vostitza). The extension in the new town plan employs a rationalist design and uses a grid (1834). (Source: Ministry for the Environment, Town Planning and Public Works Archive.)

lent special local color to the spread of Neoclassicism in each region, both during this period and after Otto was exiled and George I ascended to the throne.

The two large harbor-towns of the Peloponnese, Nafplion and Patras, continued to expand at a rapid rate. Patras, in particular, experienced great demographic growth at that time, and especially after 1839, as the export trade in currants steadily increased, and imports expanded in parallel. About 1849 there was a strong immigration movement from the island of Kephallonia and from Italy, resulting from the social upheavals on Kephallonia and the political situation in Italy. Lower Patras, the new town designed by Stamatis Voulgaris, took the form of a European city. The currant warehouses were built on the avenue along the coast next to the harbor, on the first two streets parallel to the sea, and on the main streets perpendicular to them. The ground floors of the buildings, which were equipped with porticoes, were given over to commercial establishments, and the residences were located on the upper story. The traditional notables of Patras continued to retain their properties in the Upper Town.

The urban design of the town reflected life in Patras: intellectual activity, a high proportion of students attending public and also private schools (bearing witness to economic prosperity), literary soirées, performances of plays and

157. Patras. View of the most important export harbor in the Peloponnese. Depiction dating from 1863. Postcard.

158. Argos. This typical settlement was an assembly point for agricultural produce. It acquired an urban character early on in its development. Depiction dating from 1863. Postcard.

159. Nafplion. The harbor, with the historic fortifications. In the year of this depiction (1852), the harbor was in relative decline. Postcard.

160. Piraeus. The harbor during a period of rapid growth. Depiction dating from 1861. Postcard.

operas, publishing activity, and the foundation of branches of Greek and foreign banks. In this way, a new urban society was created. In the Achaian capital of the mid-nineteenth century, the picture emerged of a settlement whose urban-design atmosphere, though homogeneous, exhibited interesting variations that manifested themselves in the individual aesthetic impressions of its architecture. In the Upper Town, for example, the forms continued to have a more conservative character, in the climate of tradition and early classicism. The serene facades of the two-story houses around Ayios Georgios Square are characterized by a gentle horizontality, with their rhythmic rows of "German-type" windows (with shutters that controlled the amount of light admitted into the room), plain lintels, and straight cornices above. The continuous porticoes on the ground floors—whether arcaded or trabeated—recall the atmosphere of towns on the Ionian islands and the associated Italian and German models. It is nevertheless true that the buildings here are closer to the harmonious scale characteristic of the settlements of Old Greece and have all the hallmarks of the private architecture of the Othonian period (figs. 161–64).

This morphological conservatism seems quickly to have been overcome after the currant crisis of 1857; after local industry had taken its first steps, the wealthy society of Patras turned to more flourishing aesthetic experiences. It was now the Lower Town's turn to be embellished by residences exhibiting a more meticulous morphology, especially around its more formal cores—that is, Vasilissis Olgas and Vasileos Georgiou Protou Squares. It was evident, at least in the case of those that followed the classical aesthetic, that the structures were beginning to adopt the pure models of the Athenian school—where appropriate, of course.

A similar move toward urbanized society also occurred in Pyrgos, the economic center of the neighboring prefecture of Ilia. The bay of Katakolo was at this time transformed into a regular port and along with the beginnings of the carrying trade came the start of manufacturing and industrial production, though naturally on a smaller scale than the corresponding developments in Patras. Mainly two-story buildings went up in the commercial center of the town, with residences upstairs and shops on the ground floor. Here, too, use was made of arcades, though due to the shallow depth of the building plots they served merely as shop windows and not as porticoes (as at Patras). As in Patras, the earliest classicizing examples in Pyrgos go back to the Athenian period. Notable houses were built around Iroon Square, Avyerinou Square, and on Ermou Street. At first, in about 1840, the walls were unrelieved, the windows (with wooden shutters or louvers) were set at the level of the facade, and the outer doors usually had semicircular fanlights. After 1850 to 1860, compositions with symmetrical volumes were created, and the central part of the facade was emphasized and usually crowned with a pediment. The door frames and window frames followed the ancient orders, and balconies with carved marble corbels were common (figs. 165, 168).

161. Patras. Amalias Square (now Olgas Square) in the Lower Town. Like the main square (Vasileos Georgiou), it was retained from the Voulgaris's original design, which was later revised by C. Schaumburg. Postcard.

162. Patras. Early classical house. Despite the substantial difference between the ground floor and the upper story (due to the obligatory ground-floor portico), the facade is designed according to the academic canon, with the main axis of the composition emphasized by the balcony and the pediment.

163. Patras. Ayios Georgios Square. Homogeneous expanse of two-story urban residences, with arcaded porticoes on the ground floor.

164. Patras. Group of houses in the Upper Town (opposite the Roman Odeion). They typify the urban design and architecture of the reconstructed settlement in the area of Ayios Georgios Square.

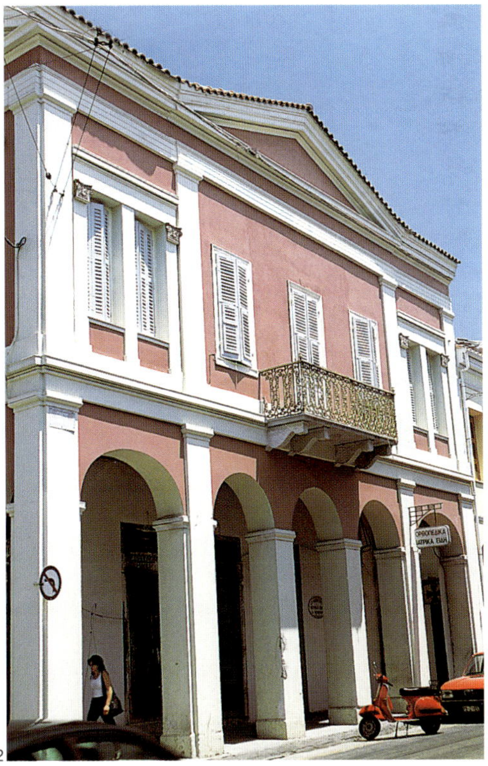
162

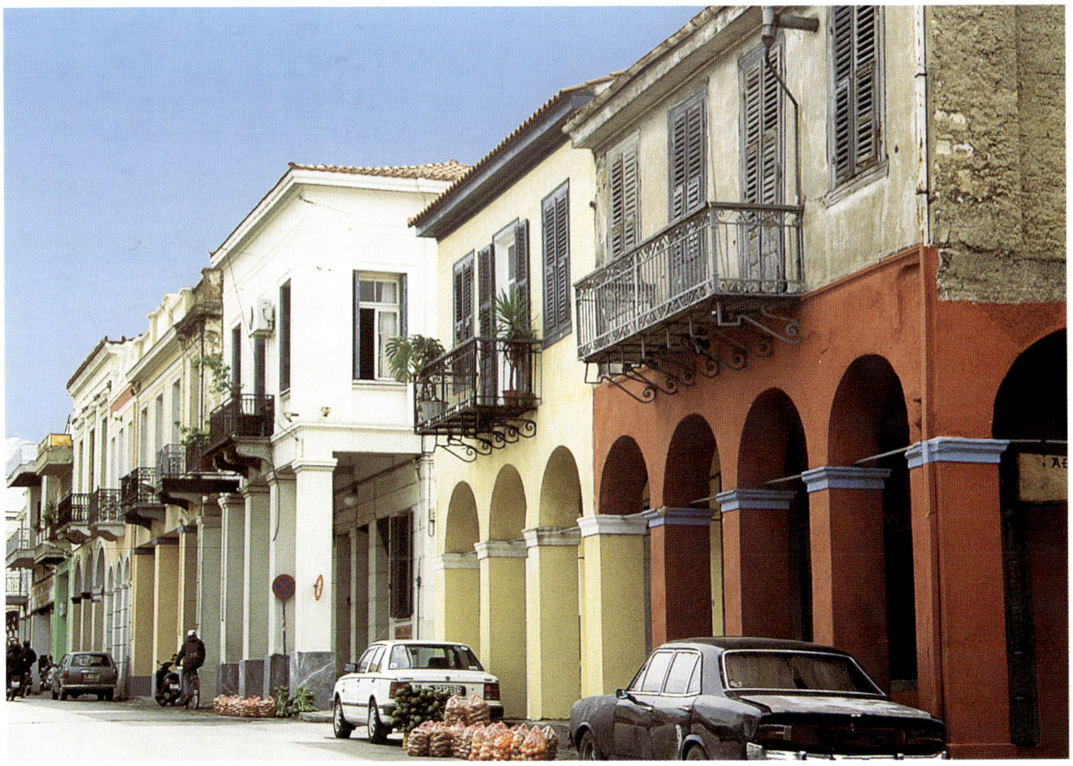
163

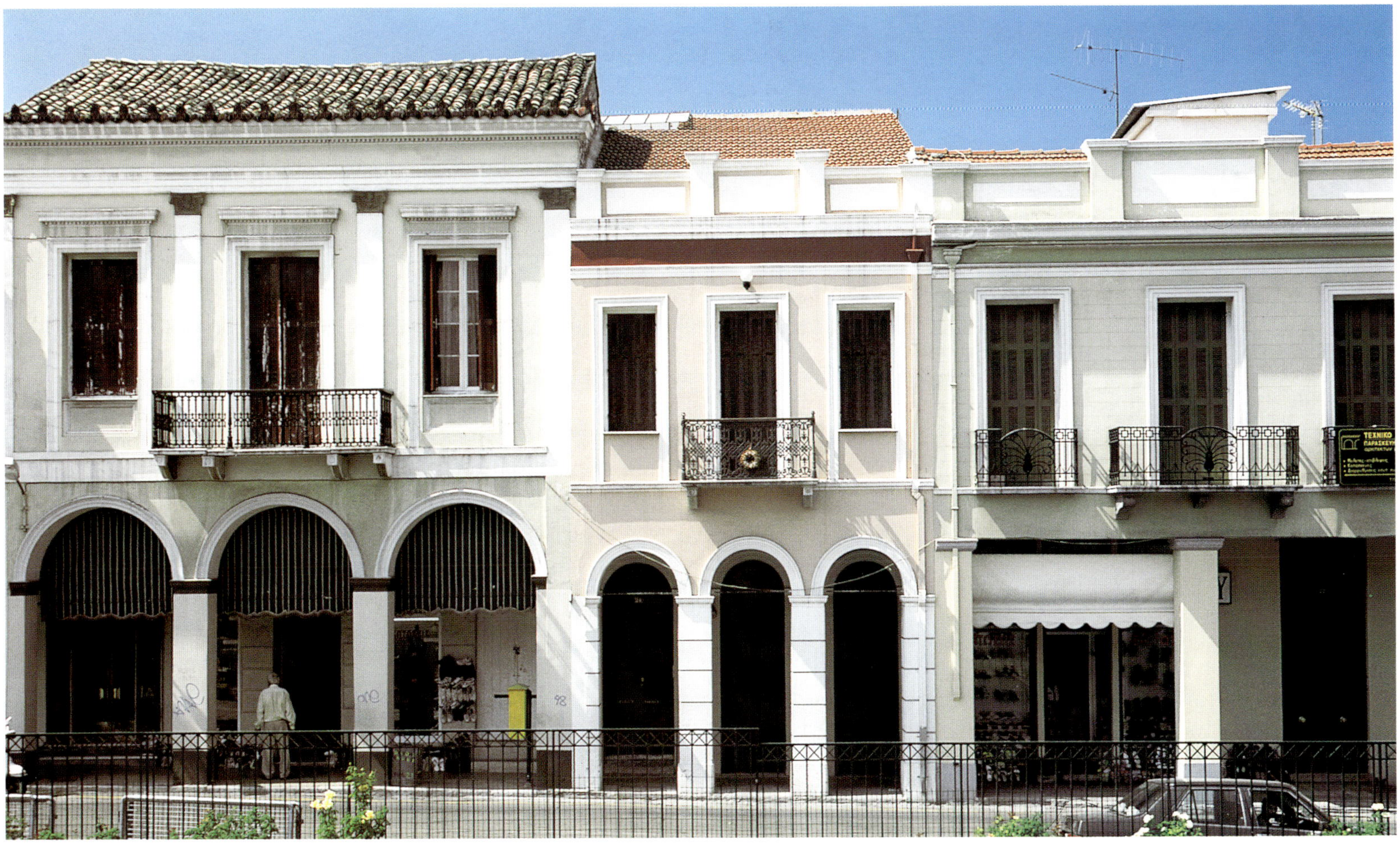
164

165. Pyrgos. The development of the town, especially after the 1870s, endowed it with the tranquil image of classical facades on newly traced streets of a commercial center. Postcard.

166. Aigion. The elegant old Town Hall building with features of the local morphological tradition. Postcard.

167. Aigion. The imposing Panayiotopoulos mansion. It is one of the most important creations of urban classicism in the Peloponnese. By the Athenian architect P. Kalkos. Postcard.

168. Pyrgos. Urban residence with shops on the ground floor. Its conservative design employs a tripartite facade, which is lent a monumental air by the pediments crowning the side axes.

At this early stage, it was unusual to see self-contained morphological elements of Athenian classicism introduced into the urban centers of the Peloponnese. One outstanding example is known in the town of Aigion: the mansion of Panayiotopoulos, built after the middle of the century by the Athenian architect P. Kalkos. In this fine three-story mansion, all the morphological elements of the facades — the window and door frames, the cornices and the lintels, as well as the corbels supporting the balconies — are carved of white marble. The interior's impressive features include the staircase vestibule supported on columns and the reception rooms, with their superb painted ceilings (figs. 166, 167).

Roughly the same is true, on a smaller scale, of Nafplion, which continued to grow, albeit at a slower rate, even after the transfer of the capital to Athens. The town remained an important port, its fortress a first-class fortification. A characteristic feature of Nafplion, unique throughout Greece, is an inherent urban image, homogeneous and dense, that incorporates the entire spectrum of the town's modern history. Buildings from the Venetian period, or from the period of Ottoman rule, underwent transformation at the time of Kapodistrias, while buildings from the reign of King Otto were added, forming a unified whole. The transmutations, though subtle, are visible to the experienced eye (figs. 169, 170).

The most interesting feature of Nafplion's architecture is that, despite the presence of classicism's severe early forms, a sense of the Italian tradition nevertheless pervades the general atmosphere, and latent Eastern elements occasionally appear. In the densely built urban environment of Nafplion, this morphological amalgam is coherent and, at the same time, acquires a revealing and truly enchanting sense of "Greekness." One is left with the impression that in Nafplion the architectural forms coexist with the very history of the Greek people — a phenomenon certainly not found in any other town in free Greece (figs. 56, 171, 172).

Piraeus, the leading port of Greece, was desolate in 1834. In 1830 only two small settlements existed there, one with four houses and four threshing floors and the other with four houses and two threshing floors. The expansion of the capital demanded the simultaneous growth of Piraeus. Accordingly, it was decided that the area, which had been abandoned for centuries, should be settled. Kleanthis and Schaubert undertook the study for the town's plan on a completely unoccupied site. As in Athens, the underlying plan clearly followed a triangle — in this case, an acute-angled triangle whose bisector was the road from Athens ending at Kantharos harbor. Along the triangle's two equal sides, rectangular grids of streets were developed.

The Chiots who had sought refuge in Ermoupolis after the destruction of their island by the Ottoman Turks in 1822 asked permission to migrate to Piraeus. A royal decree concerning the settlement of the "Chiots in Piraeus" was promulgated in 1836. According to it, all the undeveloped public plots of land on the right side of the Athens–Piraeus road were granted to the Chiots, with the view that the entire area should gradually be built up by the end of 1839. As merchants with a long tradition, beginning as early as the period of Genoese rule, the Chiots had spread by the end of the eighteenth century from Odessa, Constantinople, and Smyrna to Marseilles, Amsterdam, and London. They thus became the pioneers of modern Greek industrial development, with their main centers Ermoupolis and Piraeus. The internal migration of Chiot merchants from Syros to Piraeus was

169

170

171

112

followed, after the middle of the century, by the return of a significant number of merchants and bankers from abroad who settled in both Piraeus and Athens (fig. 173).

A second wave of internal migration to Piraeus started from Hydra; its main objective was the development of shipping. The Hydraians acquired their own settlement around the Customs House in the port, as far as the bay of Zea, and in the lower slopes of Mounichia Hill. The Chiots and Hydraians were followed by others from the rest of Greece, particularly from Crete after 1870, and by several foreigners, or at least Greeks who had acquired foreign nationality: Italians, Austrians, French, and others.

The state made land available at low prices, on the condition that it be built up quickly. Despite this, the pace of development was slow, at least initially. The rate increased gradually, however, and twenty-five years later, at the beginning of the 1860s, Piraeus was at its peak. Trade became the decisive factor in both the economic and political life of the town. At the same time, the first crafts and industries emerged, and the once small harbor began to outgrow those of Ermoupolis and Patras, ultimately winning the contest.

169. Nafplion. The contiguous archways on the ground floor indicate commercial uses, a characteristic feature of most of the houses in the central area.

170. Nafplion. Horizontally articulated facade, typical of the Othonian period, with symmetrically arranged openings.

171. Nafplion. The severe forms of early classicism in houses on Ayios Georgios Square. The uncluttered cavetto molding at the top of the corner building remains.

172. Nafplion. In the serene expanse of this classicizing facade, the central and side axes are emphasized by simple classical pediments.

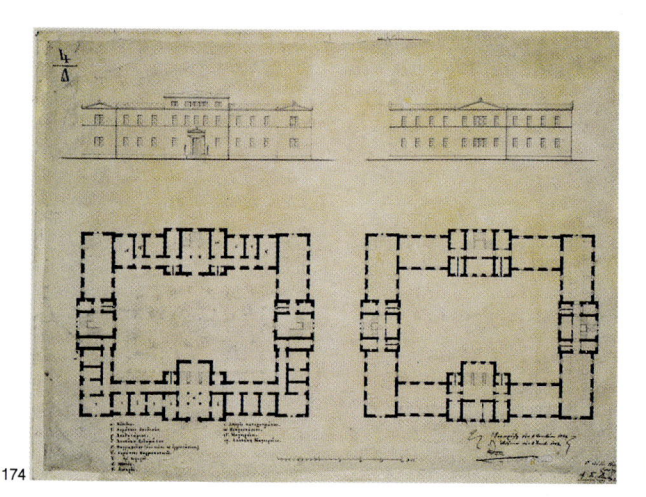

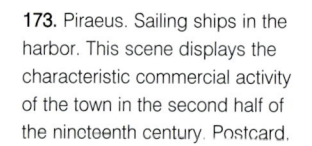

173. Piraeus. Sailing ships in the harbor. This scene displays the characteristic commercial activity of the town in the second half of the nineteenth century. Postcard.

174. Piraeus. Proposed design for the Municipal Hospital, probably by Kleanthis and Schaubert. Piraeus was better equipped than Athens with public welfare buildings, which were envisaged in the original plan. (Source: Ministry for the Environment, Town Planning and Public Works Archive.)

175. Piraeus. The gardens of Terpsithea and the avenue connecting them with the harbor. Part of the garden area was used as a training ground by the Army Cadets. The straight alignment of the original design made it possible to create public squares and green areas. Postcard.

176. Piraeus. The two historic schools on Korais Square: the earlier Ionnides School (Boys Primary School I), built in 1847, can be seen at the right. Its facade is completely plain, in the style of romantic classicism. At the left is the Ralleios School (the first Girls' School in Piraeus), by the architect Petimezas, a skilled manipulator of the dogmatic Neoclassical style. Postcard.

In the early years of Piraeus's development, Loukas Rallis, a member of the great Rallis family (based in London and active from Odessa to Marseilles), emerged as a dominant figure. The French engineer F. Feraldi, one of the first settlers in Piraeus, also played an important role. He had lived in Greece since the time of Kapodistrias; he eventually married Rallis's daughter and became a Greek citizen. Later, Feraldi's villa housed the Military Cadet School after it had been transferred twice, from Nafplion to Aigina and from Aigina to Piraeus.

A description by Fiedler is indicative of Piraeus's development: "In the autumn of 1834 I saw only a few huts on the coast at Piraeus. . . . In April 1837 I found a friendly port-town with rectangular streets, fine houses and large shops" (Fiedler K.G., *Reise durch alle Teile des Königsreichs Griechenland in den Jahren 1834 bis 1837*, Leipzig, 1840). Piraeus was a worthy rival to Athens, which it often surpassed. Most of the public works were funded by donations and bequests. The same is, of course, true of the various benevolent foundations, such as orphanages and so on. "Father," the young Dimitris Rallis asked Loukas, "you've made schools, a town hall, broad streets, pleasant gardens and other fine works here in Piraeus; what have you left me to do if ever I inherit your position?"

Alongside districts occupied by the social elite, the lower classes created their own neighborhoods, while the farmers and stock breeders remained in the margins, in terms both of the economy and of urban residence. The morphology of urban buildings, mansions of the bourgeoisie, and public buildings in general followed the style of corresponding Athenian structures. Because Athens was geographically very close, the same architects and master craftsmen and, on occasion, even the same teams that worked in Athens also worked in Piraeus (figs. 174, 175).

New architects' names rapidly emerged, however, and local teams of craftsmen formed. Although at first the parameters of Piraeus's architecture (and urban design) were associated with those of Athens, the urban character of the two neighboring towns gradually diverged from the middle of the century onward. Two essential ingredients contributed to this phenomenon. First, the people who settled in Piraeus came mainly from the most progressive groups of the Greek population of the islands. In their new homeland, they demonstrated their own dynamism and cultivated their own customs and distinctive taste. Second, the local government of the town quickly attained its independence – a privilege to which, unhappily, Athens was never able to aspire. This enabled the town plan and the construction work to be carried out effectively. Moreover, the Municipality of Piraeus also had greater opportunities for acquiring public land; a significant economic infrastructure (sustained by its dynamic production and a sizable group of benefactors); and a fine technical organization with departments that were staffed by competent engineers and architects.

Despite this, the technical experts who worked on the architecture of Piraeus for about the first two decades were drawn from the circles of King Otto. The names of well-known architects, such as Erlacher, Schaubert, and Kleanthis, are cited in connection with infrastructure projects and the first buildings. The notable Public Warehouse building (part of which is still preserved) is attributed to Kleanthis. That structure is distinguished by its combination of Greek and Italian elements, blended in an amalgam of academic sensitivity and romantic style. Other notable buildings include the Customs House, the Lazaretto, and the Municipal Market, whose forms were typical and had the distinctive functional character found in similar buildings in other Greek towns (such as Ermoupolis) erected under similar circumstances. The first residences of Piraeus (owned by Rallis, Skylitsis, Moutsopoulos, and others) were designed in the spirit of the Othonian period's austere classicism—at least as far as we can judge: the majority of the buildings themselves are now lost. Greater interest attaches to the monumental complex of residences built by Feraldi in two- and three-story units, to which reference has already been made.

Piraeus also took the lead in social welfare buildings, judging at least by the relatively early construction of schools, hospitals, and churches, usually funded by private donations. The generous benefactions made by the Rallis and Ioannides families constituted a landmark in education. The latter family was responsible for the creation of the school named after them (Ionnides School, 1847) on Korais Square, which housed the Boys Primary School I, with its uncluttered form,

177. Ermoupolis. I. Mieser residence (1841) on Protopapadaki Street. The facade was presumably designed by an architect of the Munich School, judging by the Italian quattrocento windows of the middle floor.

178. Ermoupolis. Large private building, owned by Yiasemoladas-Androulis, in the market. Shop entrances are on the ground floor; above them are two full stories with dense windows and harmoniously arranged balconies. According to a builder's inscription, this structure was erected in 1850.

179. Ermoupolis. Characteristic early classicizing facades on the main square opposite the Town Hall. The arcaded porticoes on the ground floors extend around almost the entire square.

slightly projecting side wings, and triple archway at the ground-floor entrance (fig. 176, on the right). It was a building whose plain lines stood in stark contrast with the flourishing classicizing style of the considerably later Ralleios School building next to it; this latter structure fell within the architectural perception of Lysandros Kaftantzoglou and was funded by the Rallis family (fig. 176, on the left). Similar activity can be seen in ecclesiastical buildings, in which the church of Ayia Triada (1855) was the most interesting example of a balanced composition in the so-called Greek-Byzantine style. (After many modifications, the building was replaced by the present large church.) The Catholic church of St. Paul, which is still preserved, was built by Schaubert in the form of a basilica whose facade, with its arched entrance flanked by double columns and crowned by a large pediment, owes its harmonious composition to a simplified Palladian model.

Ermoupolis followed the same course as Piraeus. Until the beginning of the nineteenth century, the settlement on Syros, like those in most of the Cyclades and the islands of the Argive and Saronic gulfs, was built on a hill overlooking the harbor, a site that offered greater protection against pirate raids. The population of the island totaled about 2,000 inhabitants, the majority of whom, though Greek-speaking, subscribed to the Catholic faith. By the beginning of the century, piracy had been significantly reduced. When the first refugees from Smyrna and Kydonies on the Asia Minor coast took refuge on the island, therefore, they initially took up residence in Ano (Upper) Syros, but as they increased daily in numbers they gradually spread down the hill to the harbor.

The number of refugees multiplied after the massacre of Chios (1822), when many Chiots settled on the island, followed by refugees from Psara. It was then that the creation began of the Lower Town (Kato Poli), with the erection of the first buildings: warehouses, the Board of Health, a few shacks, and a coffee house. These were followed by the first stone houses, most of them with two stories, the church, and the school. It is interesting to trace the Chian and Genoese influences in some of the earliest structures on the streets by the sea, where terraces of narrow-fronted buildings were constructed with high ground floors, austere forms, interior light-wells, meticulous stone masonry, and, occasionally, windows with pointed arches. However, the Neoclassicism that came to dominate Ermoupolis—and subsequently the rest of Greece, particularly after the arrival of King Otto and the Bavarians—makes it difficult to distinguish these first traces (figs. 177–80).

The population of the Lower Town, which was named Ermoupolis in honor of Hermes, god of commerce, increased in leaps and bounds, ultimately exceeding 13,000 inhabitants. At the very time that other towns in Greece were being destroyed during the Greek Uprising, horizons opened for Ermoupolis. Traffic in the port multiplied. The tacit neutrality maintained by Syros throughout almost the entire course of the War of Independence contributed to Ermoupolis's growth. Its harbor supplied both sides with munitions and corn, and it was also a center where prisoners-of-war were ransomed, ships chartered or sold, and information gathered.

180. Ermoupolis. Balcony with marble corbels and metal railings, all of a simple geometric style that points to the early phase of classicism (1851).

During the Kapodistrias period, Syros, now a free town, continued to expand rapidly. Its harbor became a center of the eastern Mediterranean carrying trade. Industry and shipping developed alongside trade, and boats of all sizes were built in its shipyard. In 1833 alone, forty-five ships were built. According to a document emanating from the Council of Elders, "There appears to be a need within the town for two main squares, and three or four lesser ones, in keeping with the size of the town, for a Bakery, a Fishmonger's, a Greengrocer's and a Butcher's. There are many other establishments, mainly (**A**) a building for the Courthouse and Jail, (**B**) a Prefecture Office building, (**C**) a barracks, (**D**) a Town Hall, (**E**) a Bourse, (**F**) a third church to the east of the town, (**G**) two primary schools at the two ends of the town, (**H**) finally, drinking fountains here and there, of which there are none at the present" (Ambelas, 1874, p. 639) (fig. 181).

The town's construction proceeded rapidly. Even though some of the Chiot community migrated to Piraeus, many remained behind in Ermoupolis, which was transformed into one of the most vigorous urban centers in Greece, with an active commercial, cultural, and social life (fig. 182).

In 1834, Ermoupolis followed the example of Athens and Nafplion and acquired a High School. There were ten functioning schools here, as well as public and private boarding schools, which were attended by large numbers of pupils, including children of expatriate Greeks from various countries. A commercial school was also founded, and there was considerable publishing activity in the town, producing newspapers, magazines, and books.

In 1836, the Hermes Club was founded, its aim being "to secure to civilized men a daily, pleasant and instructive way of passing their time, including information about trade, political news, dances at fixed seasons, permissible games and harmonious music..." (Travlos and Kokkou, 1980, p. 61). As for the ladies of Ermoupolis, these "are known for their European upbringing and above all for their simple, unaffected and cheerful manner . . . most elegantly adorned in the latest fashion." As in Syros, the ladies of Ermoupolis acquired a European appearance, not always simple and unaffected, but certainly most elegantly adorned in the latest fashion (*Ermoupolis*, 1998, p. 47) (fig. 183).

Ermoupolis, along with Patras and Nafplion, stands out from other nineteenth-century provincial towns of Greece. In the case of the first of these, in particular, it is fair to stress its preeminence with regard to the richness of its urban architecture, the sensitivity of its forms, and the gentility of its style, which have remained truly unrivaled to the present day. Although the urban modernization of Syros—based on shipping, the carrying trade, and subsequently industrial output—had some points of similarity with that of Piraeus, it was nevertheless distinguished by its own hallmarks, which helped to make Ermoupolis into one of the most flourishing towns in Greece, both economically and culturally.

The rapid and irreversible decline of the town in the last quarter of the nineteenth century, with no prospect of its being regenerated through new construction, helped preserve the urban landscape to the present day (a phenomenon also observable in Nafplion, though at a later stage). Following its new town plan (as conceived by the Bavarian W. von Weiler in 1837), the impressive harbor buildings were founded—the Warehouses, the Customs House, the imposing Lazaretto, and others. All these were designed in a romantic though at the same time functional style similar to that of the Military Hospital in Athens. Like the first public buildings in the town, the harbor buildings were the creation mainly of the Bavarian engineers Weiler and J. Erlacher. The former built the Lazaretto (1839–40), an edifice that stands out from almost all others of its kind in Greece by virtue of its size, functional composition, and flawless masonry of exposed stone blocks, with doors and windows spanned by segmental arches made of solid bricks. The same morphology had been used by the French engineer A. T. Garnot as early as the Kapodistrias period. About 1840, Erlacher also designed a number of buildings for the Food Market in Ermoupolis, while his colleague Weiler drew up the plans for the primary-school buildings with a plain, functional form. He also used the same type for the school on Mykonos (which now houses the Greek Telecommunications Company offices).

As we have already seen, construction and function were prominent in these early structures, which normally had arched doors and windows and cannot, therefore, be considered to be classicizing—at least not in the sense of using the

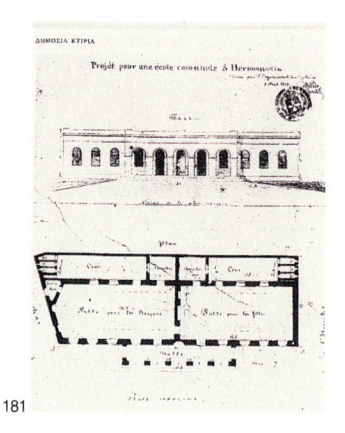

181. Ermoupolis. The Second Mutual Instruction School (a double school for boys and girls), by the engineer W. von Weiler (1838). As with most functional buildings, it deviates from classicism. The design incorporates a pronounced use of arches at the openings (*Rundbogenstil*). (Source: State General Archives, Ermoupolis Archive.)

182. Ermoupolis. Houses on the seafront in the aristocratic Vaporia district. In the larger building at the left, the horizontal expanse of the facade is in harmony with the small building on the flat roof. This projects above the parapet with its arcaded veranda and pediment.

183. Ermoupolis. The Hellas Club by the Italian architect P. Sampro. Built from 1862 to 1963 with financial support from the municipality in order to house clubs that functioned in the town on the model of English gentlemen's clubs. The building's restrained, rather cold morphology in the classical style is enriched with elements from the Palladian tradition.

184. Ermoupolis. Harbor. The Customs House, by the engineer A. Georgantas (1860). Architecture is employed here to express the function of the building, which is enriched by elements of Romanticism (mainly of Italian origins). Facade is of dressed gray marble.

185. Ermoupolis. Church of Ayios Nikolaos, by the architect G. Metaxas (1848). The self-confident, skilled handling of classical models in this monumental architectural composition is clearly distanced from the Byzantine forms of the Middle Ages.

185

186. Argos. The Market building by P. Karathanasopoulos (one of Ziller's colleagues). Large archways were widely used in buildings of this type. Here, in contrast with the earlier period in which the romantic spirit predominated, the forms are expressed in the style of Attic classicism. Postcard.

187. Argos. The Town Hall building, erected, like the Market, at a later period (1889). It preserved its monumental character in an authentic form (seen here in an old photograph) – in keeping with the expectations of the newly formed urban society of the town. Postcard.

morphology adopted by the Greek orders. In addition to their functional and constructional expression, they are much more reminiscent of a post-Romantic aesthetic mentality, enriched by elements of the Italian and, especially the Lombard, quattrocento; this was later to be assimilated not only by the Bavarians, but also by their Greek colleagues, as is revealed beyond question by the impressive facade of the Customs House in the harbor, a work designed by the military engineer A. Georgantas about 1860 (fig. 184). Interestingly, this propensity for Italian styles continued to be found down to the third quarter of the century. On the other hand, private architecture retained the familiar forms of the Othonian period, in the spirit of romantic classicism as in the Prassakis mansion, by Erlacher (1939).

Strange as it may seem, the domed basilica of Ayios Nikolaos (1848–70), a uniquely imposing structure by the architect Gerasimos Metaxas, represents the celebratory turn to the classical monumental morphology (fig. 185). Quite apart from the quality of the execution of the elements of the Greek orders (the Ionic porch on the west facade is of rare elegance), the island artistic tradition as expressed in Ermoupolis was focused on this building. The most competent marble-carvers from Tinos, the most skilled builders and carpenters of Andros, and craftsmen from other Aegean islands were attracted to Syros to contribute their art to the unrivaled aesthetic climate that set its seal on the image of the town during the period immediately that followed.

Steadily, though at a slower pace, Neoclassicism penetrated the other Cycladic islands, too. In some places it was pure; in others, it was blended with local vernacular architecture or with elements drawn from Frankish and Venetian traditions. To stroll along the narrow streets of Chora on Andros, of Tinos, of Paros, of Naxos, and of Kea, and also in the villages and the smaller islands of the Cyclades, is to encounter a large number of Neoclassical buildings.

Along with Patras, Nafplion, Piraeus, and Ermoupolis, a series of towns in the Peloponnese and Central Greece were also revitalized and rebuilt. Argos, Tripolis, Corinth, Methoni, Pylos, Nafpaktos, Agrinion, Mesolongi, Galaxidi, Itea, Amphissa, Lamia, Megara, and Thebes all gradually acquired a new form (figs. 186, 187).

These transformations were achieved either through the bold expansion of the historical seed, as in Argos during the Kapodistrias period (by Borrozin in 1831), in which case there is a fairly clear distinction between Neoclassical towns and traditional ones, or through a new town plan that structurally penetrated the historical urban fabric itself, as with the revised design for Tripolis by D. Stavridis (1836), based on the town plan drawn up by Voulgaris and Garnot at the time of Kapodistrias. The architectural modernization of this town in the nineteenth century emerged dynamically in its very center, based on straight streets. Although the houses built during the Othonian period on the relatively small building plots of the historical center were given symmetrical facades and austere elements drawn from the Greek orders, in several cases they retained the practical compositional principles of the local tradition. In general, the rationalist approach to urban design adopted by classicism showed little respect for the preexisting structure of the settlements in the architectural interventions of this period. Design

188. Tripolis. Small two-story building of the transitional period, in which the traditional scale and simple, unaffected style is combined with the basic design rules of classicism.

189. Tripolis. House on the main square, opposite the church of Ayios Vasilios. Porticoes were de rigueur on the side facing the square. The unorthodox wide span of the arches gave the conservative facades an unusual, local expression.

190. Tripolis. Two-story urban building with shops on the ground floor. Characteristic development of classicizing architecture in the provincial commercial centers of the nineteenth century.

191. Tripolis. The mansion of D. Galenos, with its severe Neoclassical design, stands out on Ethnarchou Makariou Square. It is now a school, having been donated for the purpose by the family.

192. Sparti. House on Menelaou and Agidos Streets, with a gate leading into the courtyard. This is an example of the marriage of the Peloponnesian building tradition with the plain "popular" classicism of the nineteenth century.

193. Sparti. An arched gateway on Menelaou Street (see also fig. 192) shows local morphology with characteristic sculpted impost blocks (simplified molding of Renaissance origins).

practice followed more or less the same methodology. A new, rational grid was imposed on the redesigned urban environment of the old towns, and each town was divided into neighborhoods. Where architectural features of distinctive local, historical, or artistic interest existed (remains of ancient monuments, parts of forts, and so on), these were taken into account in the town plan. It should not be forgotten, moreover, that forts and castles still played an important defensive role, though this gradually became less significant, and from about the middle of the century any fortresses that stood in the way of the expansion of the towns were partly demolished (figs. 188–91).

The view that anything that recalled the Ottoman occupation should be removed was widely prevalent during this period, resulting in the demolition of Islamic monuments, mosques, hammams, and other religious structures. There was also a widespread lack of respect for local vernacular architecture, which was erroneously thought to be Ottoman. Naturally, any buildings that did not lend themselves easily to new uses were also destroyed.

In every town, building plots were made available and funds provided by the local or national government, to make provision for suitable areas for public open spaces and buildings. Parks and ornamental and functional squares were created in which to erect administrative buildings, markets, churches, schools, and hospitals, and sites were marked out for public open spaces and buildings. At the same time, provision was made for elementary infrastructure networks, and the streets were traced, conforming to the obligation to maintain straight lines, even in the older parts of the town. This geometrical layout was due partly to the imposition of rationalist planning and partly to a new perception that urban space could be embellished by creating interesting vistas toward important landmarks, which had earlier been almost inconceivable. The minimum size of building plots was determined, as well as the first building regulations (minimum frontage, building and coverage ratios, health regulations, and so on). At the same time, government

194. Sparti. The Archaeological Museum building with its garden, in an early-twentieth-century photograph. The facade, designed according to a dogmatic view of classicism, displays the public and cultural purpose of the mansion. By the architect G. Katsaros. Postcard.

195. Sparti. The central porch of the Archaeological Museum. It displays an Ionic style with a wide architrave and pediment.

196. Sparti. Town Hall. A structure of uncluttered appearance, articulated with simple volumes arranged symmetrically. The side wings are emphasized by classical pediments. The building remains a landmark in the modern settlement of this historic town.

125

departments were created to supervise building designs and their implementation. In some cases, new types of buildings were even proposed.

These regulations, of course, were often ignored, either by the citizens or by the state itself, which was not always in a position to follow them, sometimes because it lacked suitable staff and sometimes because it could not finance the necessary expropriations. Nevertheless, most of the towns were reconstructed and gradually transformed into Neoclassical urban centers. During this same period, new towns were designed, such as Sparti by Stauffert and Eretria by Schaubert, invariably in accordance with the Neoclassical planning vocabulary (figs. 154, 192–96).

The Mediating Role of Classicism

The architecture of public buildings designed by architects, both state-employed and private, also follows the formal and stylistic demands of Neoclassicism and is of varying quality, depending on the talent and erudition of its creator. What is certain is that public buildings directly influenced the architecture of private buildings that followed the same style, either out of conviction or by imitation. The final result depended on the personal competence of the architect, contractor, or master craftsman: sometimes, it was unalloyed Neoclassicism; other times, it was a blend of Neoclassicism and local techniques and traditions. In every case, the system of Greek orders was converted into a useful and adaptable formal vocabulary, the application of which transformed the anonymous building, as though by magic, into a distinctive creation—that is, into a reference point whose presence helped to define the aesthetic of the public space (figs. 197–99).

It was relatively easy to design simple facades for one- or two-story houses by following the basic principles of style: symmetry about an axis; tripartite division of the facade into base, body, and crowning elements; maintenance of the proportions of width to height in the openings; and use of classical morphological elements, corbels, cornices, pilasters, and so on. "In order to design this facade, then, it is enough to take a guide line . . . with a plumbline . . . or better, to take the line of the threshold of the door, or of the windows, or finally, if there is one, to take the crepis, from which by using coordinates, we define the ground level and other forms needed." So writes Stamatis Kleanthis in an unpublished handwritten letter (now in the Gennadeios Library) apparently addressed to ordinary building contractors or architecture students.

These Neoclassical facades in many cases concealed a non-classical layout that continued the local tradition. The result was a series of small settlements unique in Europe, in which stylistic dogma was confined to a few public buildings while the rest retained a discreetly modified local architecture (figs. 200–207).

Neoclassicism in Greece was embraced both by craftsmen and by ordinary people, who saw in it their "glorious ancient past." This led to the "development of a popular classicism, a style used in buildings of much smaller dimensions, which is genuinely humble, naive, charming" (Mylonas, 1984, pp. 369–75).

It should not be forgotten, however, that the general prevalence of Neoclassicism contributed to the effacing, almost at a single stroke, of the local post-Byzantine architecture of the towns—though fortunately such architecture was preserved in those areas that were not liberated from Ottoman rule until later. The phenomenon was repeated with the destruction of a large number of traditional

197. Itea. Two aspects of urban classicism. The architecture of the facade on the street obeys the dictates of the classical order, while the traditional wooden *chayati* with its large window panes, stretches along the uncovered side.

198. Galaxidi. Terrace of houses on the seafront. The expanses of the classicizing facades were decisive in establishing the distinctive image of the "well-ordered picturesque quality" of this seaside settlement.

199. Galaxidi. Mansion. Though it cannot be described as Neoclassical in the sense of following the classical orders, this building reflects the balanced design of Western rationalism, which, in an early phase, influenced the regenerated settlements of free Greece.

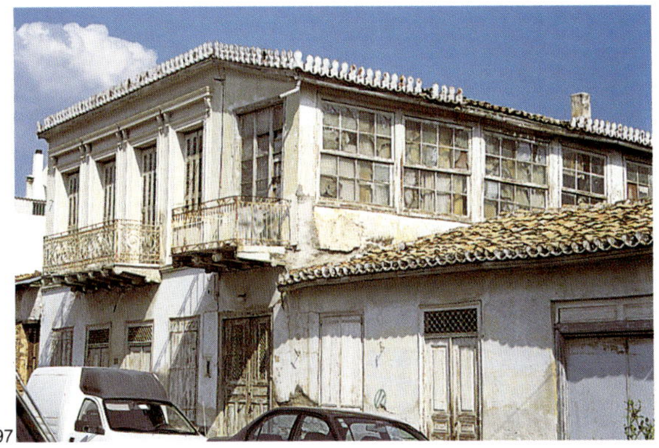

197

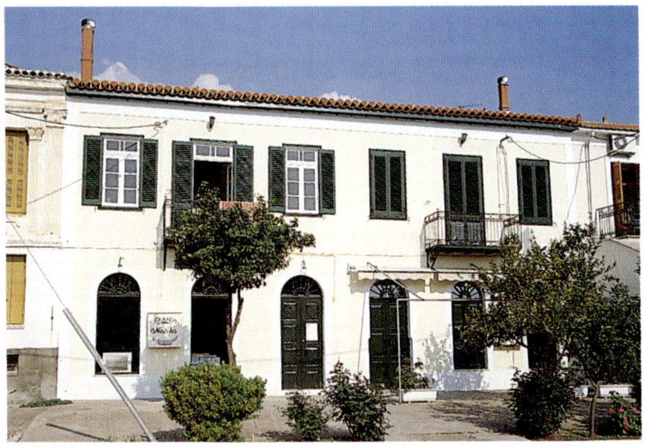

198

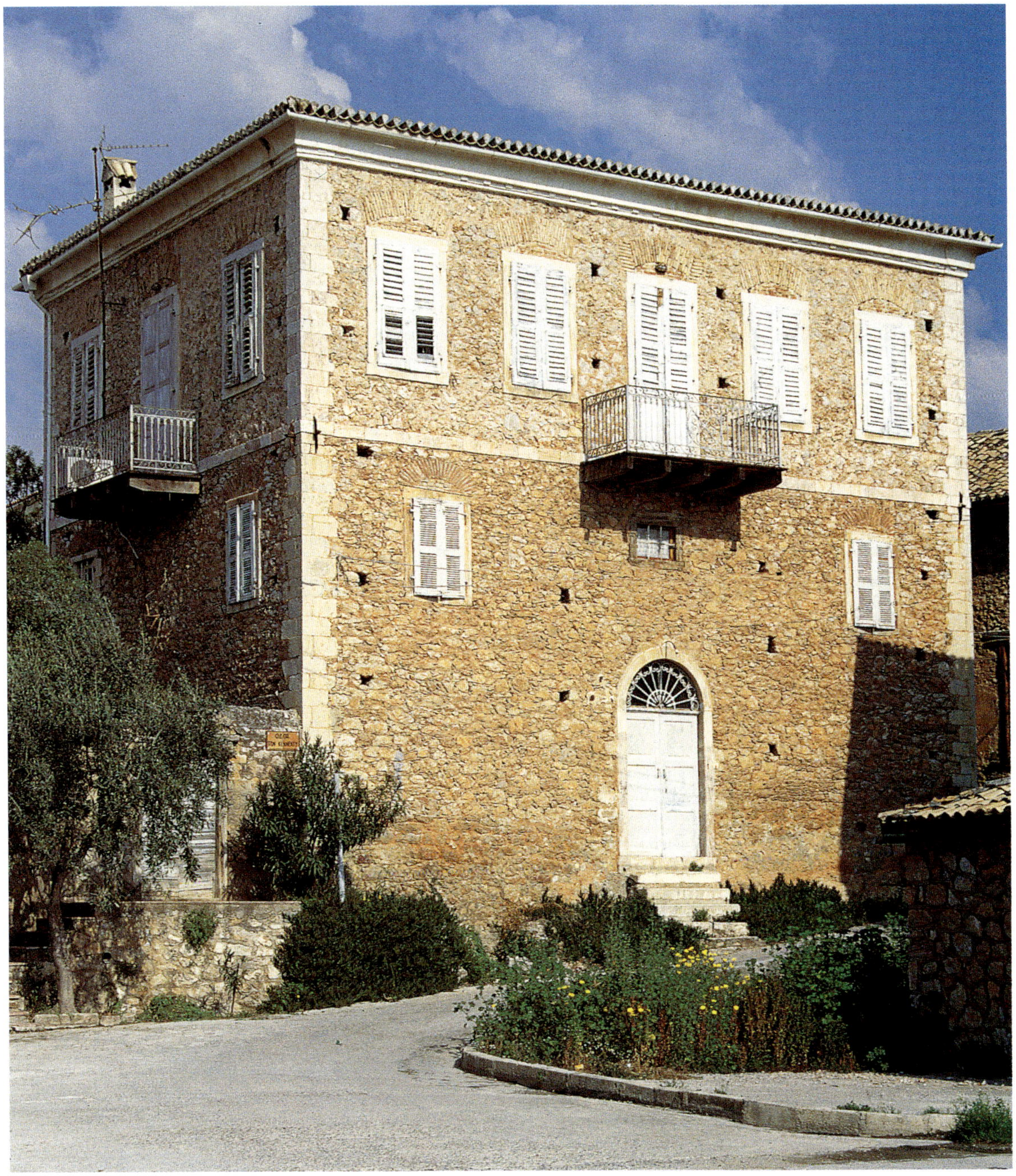

199

buildings in the towns of Macedonia, Thrace, and Thessaly. Afterward, Neoclassical buildings throughout Greece shared a similar fate in the name of a modernization that found fertile ground in the lack of culture and utilitarian attitudes of modern Greeks. In this case, too, the only settlements to survive were the ones that had, in effect, been abandoned. Here, all similarity ends. The small or large communities thus created could not, of course, be compared qualitatively or aesthetically with modern towns, possibly because, strange as it may seem, it is easier to design and achieve an aesthetically satisfying result for a small Neoclassical building than for a modern one. In the case of the latter, the lack of strict rules and principles and the abstraction of the decorative elements demand a talented architect. For the means by which "transcendence to the beautiful" is achieved are today very unclear. Despite the problems and impasses involved, the decoration,

200. Aigina. Two story-house on the seafront with a plain facade and a room on the flat roof (as in fig. 201) used to spread out the sails of boats.

201. Galaxidi. Two-story house on the seafront, with tranquilly arranged openings, a simple balcony on the first floor, and a room above at roof level.

202. Kalamata. Villa on Aristodimou Street, now the Town Hall. The composition obeys the general classical canon for a free-standing urban building: symmetrically arranged spaces, a plain porch on the ground floor, and a harmonious pediment on the roof.

203. Kalamata. Building complex housing the Port Authority and the Customs House. The form of these, on the large quay in the harbor, reflects the period of economic growth and the rise of urban life in the new coastal town.

204. Mesolongi. The entrance and overlying first-floor balcony of the building now housing the Town Hall. This rich architectural expression is executed entirely in marble.

205. Galaxidi. Large balcony of a house on the quay, with a wooden floor and corbels. The railing is a cast-steel masterpiece with references to Italian decorative models.

206. Amphilochia. Archways in a ruined building on the harbor quay. Fine rendering of the design in dressed stone.

207. Galaxidi. Central section of the facade of a house in the style of austere classicism, with the characteristic balcony railing formed of simple geometric designs.

and even more so its stylistic expression, provided certain codes by which an architect's "personality" could be stamped on his work. This gave the inanimate, practical, and useful structures an inner expression and the perfection of the beautiful. The effect was even more obvious because the inner expression was not one-sided; rather, it emphasized the essential, interventionist relationship between private and public space, which was a component of the new planning in Neoclassicism. That is, on the one hand, private architecture was influenced by the rationalist planning of the town; on the other, it was transformed into the context of a new aesthetic that imposed the discreet presence of the "anonymous" building within the urban landscape. This created a reciprocal relationship between public and private that set its conceptual seal on the image of the built environment. Here, the role of classicism did not end with the forms associated with the Greek orders, but extended to the striking aesthetic of public buildings and the associated organization of space in the towns.

208. Zakynthos. The Roma mansion, with its imposing facade built entirely of dressed stone. The monumental architecture of Italy serves as an example for the urban complexes of the Ionian islands. This building was demolished after the 1953 earthquake. Postcard.

209. Argostoli. Warehouse buildings in the harbor, during the second half of the nineteenth century. These display the ethnocentric classicism (Athenian morphological idioms that displaced the local urban architecture. Postcard.

Forms and space were restructured to the conditions dictated by urban culture. Classicism was consciously applied as a mediating aesthetic code by its anonymous users, in order to express the sense of their well-rounded relationship with the public environment, which was now an essential reference point of modern social life.

Before ending this chapter, we must mention, however briefly, the Ionian islands, where British architects transplanted a classicism more in keeping with British models. Fewer structures were built, however, because Ionian towns had been well organized ever since the Venetian period and had not suffered any destruction during the Greek War of Independence.

Nevertheless, important public buildings were erected there, particularly on Corfu, Kephallonia, and Zakynthos, and existing structures were modified in accordance with prevailing architectural trends. Corfu provides the best example of this phenomenon, because of its size and the density of the occupation, and also because it has survived to the present untouched by the devastating earthquakes of the 1950s. In this imposing town, early British classicism was harmoniously integrated into the existing buildings of the Venetian tradition. This is not surprising: the romantic survival of Palladianism in nineteenth-century Britain contained certain potential Renaissance elements, despite its strong Neoclassical component. Thus, this distinctive blend of styles gave the town a personality whose features influenced, to varying degrees, the urban centers of western Greece, especially those of the Peloponnese. This is the source of the facades that followed the Greek orders, with their meticulously worked windows and romantic balconies covered with flowers. From the Ionian islands came gateways with their carved jambs and semicircular fanlights with artful ironwork. Finally, this was the source of the luxurious interior decorations that spread to the towns of free Greece (Patras, Nafplion, and Athens itself): the painted ceilings in the salons, the fashionable sitting room with a console, and the piano — the last bringing with it the culture of music, poetry, and the spontaneous serenade sung to the accompaniment of the guitar (figs. 208–10).

210. Corfu. The Ionian Bank building, by the architect I. Chronis. The building is an example of academic models of English classicism that became established in the Ionian islands. Large pilasters articulate the facade vertically (colossal order).

The Zenith of Athenian Classicism

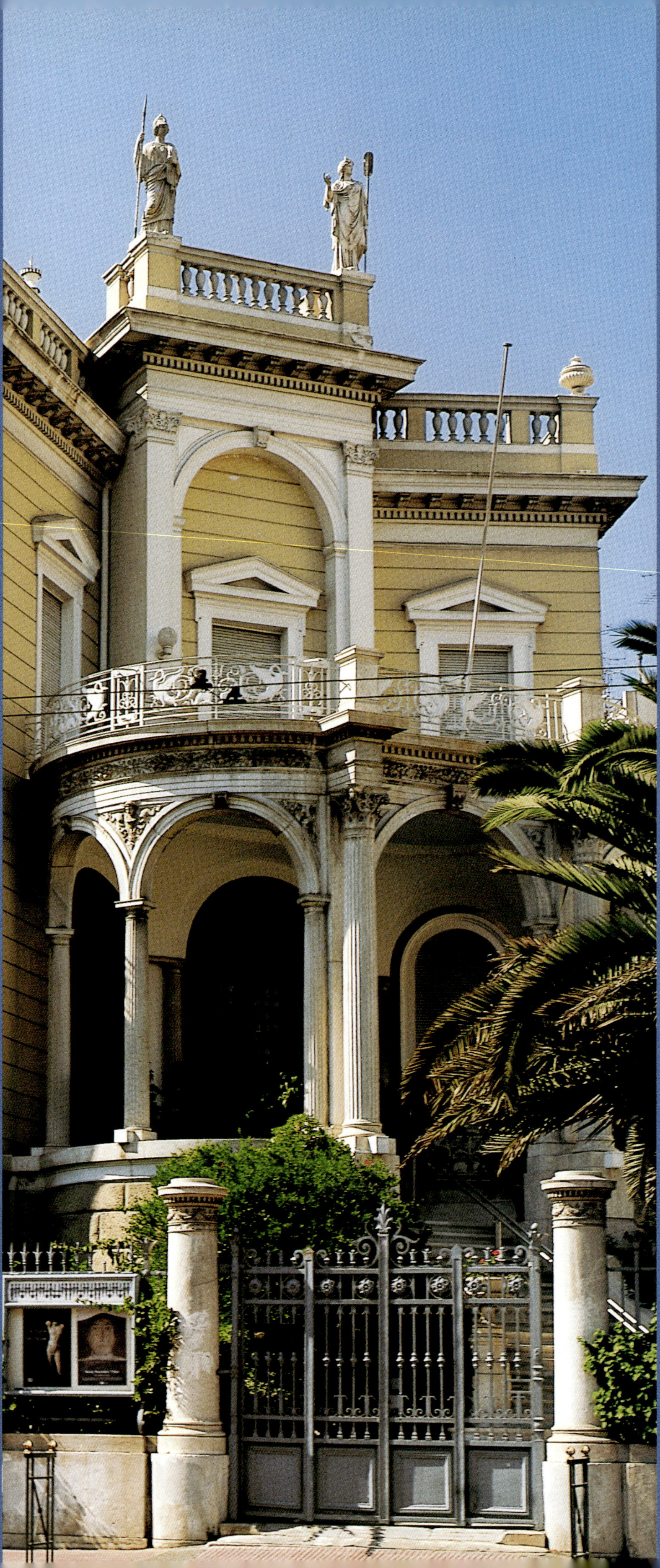

THE ZENITH OF ATHENIAN CLASSICISM

Urban Society Matures

In the course of about four decades after Athens was designated the Greek capital, its social structure had begun to become clearer and more cohesive. Under King Otto, Athens's composition was not homogeneous; non-natives of all kinds from every corner of the land jostled there in search of their fortunes. The most powerful of these were the wealthy members of Greek communities abroad, particularly the Phanariots from Constantinople. Among the newcomers were notables who had distinguished themselves during the final years of the war of liberation and foreigners, particularly those in the retinue of King Otto. Because Greece had no aristocracy, newcomers strove to secure social advancement and political advantage at all cost, creating rivalries that unfortunately dissolved social cohesion and corroded the local culture.

However, matters improved strikingly during the last third of the nineteenth century, once the men of the *ancien régime*, the ones who had been responsible for the confrontations of the past, had departed the scene. The situation continued to improve as a more cohesive social group that played an active part in public and private life arose; at the same time, the level of professional and economic activity in general steadily increased (figs. 212, 215–18).

Social progress was accompanied by substantial economic changes. It should be made clear, however, that this was true mainly in the capital and less so in other towns in free Greece. The latter, finding themselves part of a new centralized national entity, did not (with the exception of the centers of the export trade) follow an upward trajectory. Despite the creation of the National Bank of Greece in 1841, most funding came into Greece from abroad, leading to inflated loan obligations that had a restraining effect on the implementation of welfare and other public works. However, about 1860 and especially in the following decade, capital began to flow into the country from wealthy expatriate Greeks, forming an uninterrupted stream of invisible income that gradually restored the balance of the local economy. At the same time, some of the best-known names of the powerful Greeks of the diaspora (from Constantinople, Russia, Romania, Egypt, and elsewhere) came to live in Athens. Here, in addition to their benefactions and their active role in economic life, they exercised a catalytic influence on society during the reign of King George I and henceforth played an enhanced role, within a better organized productive and cultural context. The exponents of the ideological

211. Athens. Othonas Stathatos mansion, by the architect E. Ziller.

212. View of Athens in the 1879s, looking from Lykavittos toward the Acropolis. At the left is the palace, with the garden laid out and the square visible. Above the square are the dominating buildings that stood either side of Philellinon Street, the Pachys building and the Xenon hotel, the three-story Koromilas building, and the long, two-story Dimitriou mansion. At the right can be seen the royal stables (behind the cypresses), in front of which is a row of newly built residences extending roughly to the end of Akadimias Street. (Source: ELIA, Photographic Archive.)

structures of diaspora Hellenism contributed not only to economic recovery but also to the blending of the ingredients of Athenian society, and certainly shaped its urban conscience at the moral and cultural level.

This internal shift toward the full maturation of the urban mentality led to an anticipation of social development and, presumably, to a significant proportion of the population securing privileged positions that required a high level of education. Education, in fact, was a fundamental element of the new society as compared with the old. Young people aspired to higher learning, and the percentage of the population within the state studying at the university was higher in Greece than in any other country in the Balkans, and higher than in many Central European countries. The National Technical University, too, offered a broad spectrum of knowledge to Greek technicians who were to contribute to the (albeit rudimentary) reconstruction of the nation in industry and infrastructure projects, and who would help rebuild towns and design architecture of public and private buildings.

After the reforms of 1843 and the dismissal of the most important foreign professors, and after the turn to academism during Kaftantzoglou's tenure as head of the institution (1844–62), the National Technical University was revitalized as a result of measures taken by D. Skalistiris (1864–73). During the directorship of Anastasios Theophilas (1878–1901), especially, it acquired considerable authority and prestige in the sphere of technical education. With regard to architecture, the National Technical University had on its teaching staff exceptional exponents of design and pioneers of the classical tradition, such as I. Koumelis, I. Sechos, I. Lazarimos, G. Metaxas, E. Ziller, and others, whose personalities presumably exercised a profound influence on the training of architects who were active in the intensive rebuilding of Athens and other towns during the last quarter of the nineteenth and the early twentieth centuries (figs. 213, 214).

This period was marked both by development in the social and economic spheres and by the cultural progress made, mainly, among the urban population. Both public and private architecture flourished, driven by the unique impulse for regeneration at all levels during the period when Charilaos Trikoupis was prime minister.

In Athens, classicism was approaching its zenith by about 1870, the period when the most important public buildings were being or had been constructed, as we shall see below. In the urban centers of the provinces, a number of idiosyncracies continued to characterize official architecture, though even these were tending to disappear toward the end of the century, when the morphological "literature" of the capital became predominant, to a different extent in different places (except in the Peloponnese and some areas of Central Greece).

It should be emphasized, however, that Athenian classicism did not exhibit (as one might have expected) unalloyed rendering of the orders in a spirit of morphological submission to ancient models. On the contrary, formal austerity—as seen, for example, first in the Palace of King Otto and, in a later version, in the Arsakeion—was gradually transformed into a more adaptable and fertile artistic expression. As early as the 1860s, the essence of the classical style, or at least its dogmatic element, seems to be moderated and transformed into a more malleable and expressive content.

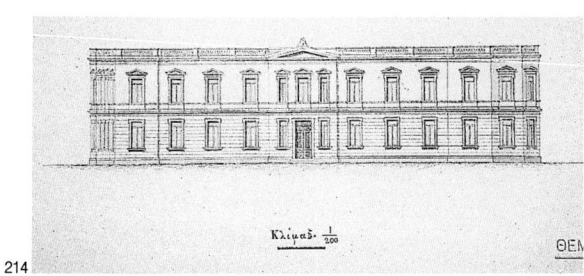

213. Design for the Patras courthouse, by students at the School of Arts.

214. Design for the facade of a public building, by students at the School of Arts. Naturally enough, the emphasis was on rendering a symmetrical, properly ordered architectural composition.

215. Athens. Omonia Square at the time of King George I. Whereas by the early years of Otto's reign Syntagma Square was a focus for the recreational activities of Athenians, Omonia Square did not follow suit until the last quarter of the nineteenth century. Postcard.

216. Athens. Aiolou Street near the church of Ayia Irini. The urban landscape of this area was formed as early as the reign of King Otto (buildings with shops, coffee houses, and restaurants on the ground floor, and residences or guest houses on the upper story). Postcard.

217. Athens. Stadiou Street at its height. The tranquil facades, with their marble balconies and symmetrical windows, usually had luxury shops or patisseries on the ground floor, which were the focal points on which Athenians based their strolls. Postcard.

218. Athens. Syntagma Square in festive mood, with a temporary triumphal arch. The campanile of the Russian church rises in the background. Engraving of the period.

215

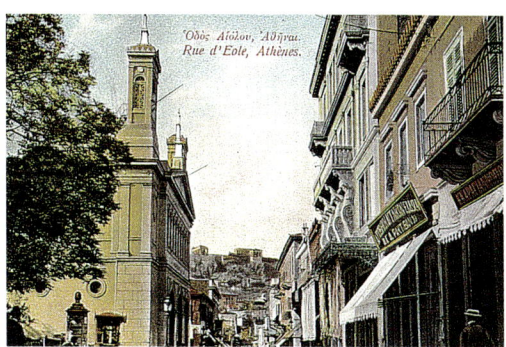

216
Ὁδὸς Αἰόλου, Ἀθῆναι.
Rue d'Eole, Athènes.

217

218

137

The academic canon is still present in the composition, of course, but it gradually begins to be enriched by an element of subjective assessment and current aesthetic critique. This is apparent in the architecture of urban buildings discussed below, whose autonomy became manifest at this period. Released from the encumbrance of its strict devotion to the historical style, Athenian architecture was brought into harmony with the blend of profoundly intellectual and progressive ideals that animated Athenian society of the time.

Public Buildings

The development of a social context was not the only factor in the maturation of urban architecture at the time of King George I: The inspired creators of major public and private architectural structures, such as the important architect Theophil Hansen, had a major impact on the urban landscape. Unlike his brother, Christian, who had left Greece, Theophil continued to supervise, albeit intermittently, the completion of the Academy building, the construction of which had begun in 1859. Since that time, he had brought his closest colleague, Ernst Ziller, to Athens, and had given Ziller full authority to supervise the work, for which he himself, as one of the most famous architects of imperial Vienna, had little time available.

Of the monumental structures in Athens that had already been built — that is, the Palace, the University, the Observatory, the Arsakeion, and the National Technical University — the Academy most strongly projected both the freedom of its aesthetic conception and modeling and its complete identification with the classical orders in a unified, self-contained structure. The brilliant edifice, built entirely of marble and completed in 1885, after a full twenty-six years, was the crowning achievement of the ambitions of intellectuals such as A. Gazis, I. Kolettis, A. Polyzoidis, G. Gennadios, and P. Omiridis-Skylitsis, all of whom had conceived the idea of founding a Prytaneum of Letters as early as the middle of the 1820s (figs. 219–23). After several delays, and after Alexandros Rangavis had drawn up the necessary charter, Simon Sinas of Vienna, the Greek Maecenas, appeared on the scene once more. At the urging of the Greek ambassador in Vienna, K. Schinas, he made available a total of 3,000,000 drachmas for the

219. Athens. The statues of Athena and Apollo being placed in position at the porch of the Academy building (1881).

220. Athens. The central Ionic porch of the Academy. This exemplary architectural composition by Theophil Hansen was modeled on the east porch of the Erechtheion.

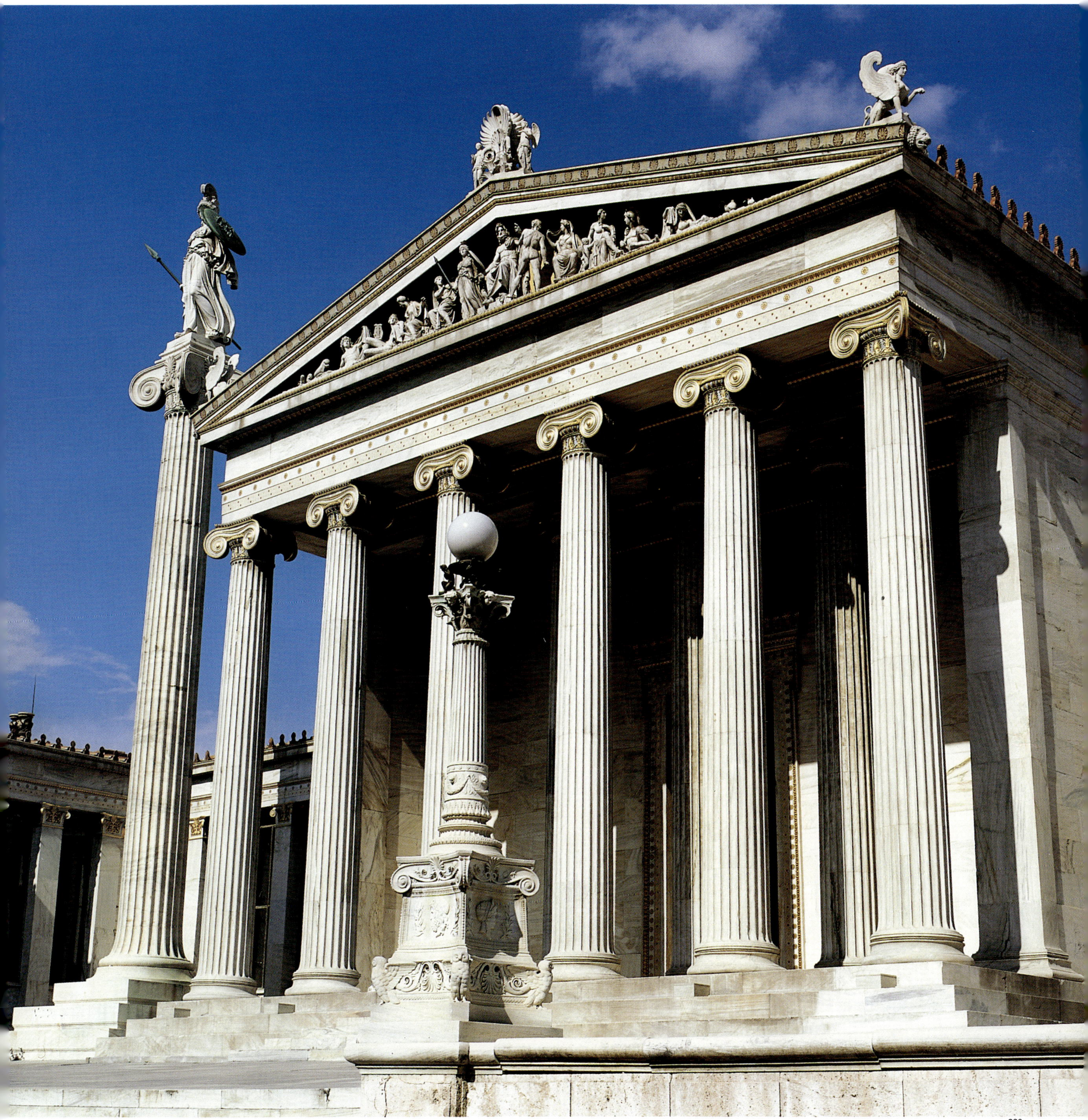

220

221. Athens. The statue of Athena at the Academy. The goddess is flawlessly executed in marble by the preeminent sculptor of classicism, Leonidas Drosis.

222. Athens. Coffered ceiling in the Academy. Ancient polychromy is fully rendered in a modern monument, attesting to the flowering of the applied arts in the nineteenth century.

223. Athens. Columns of the central porch of the Academy. This is an impressively faithful execution of the classical order in pentelic marble.

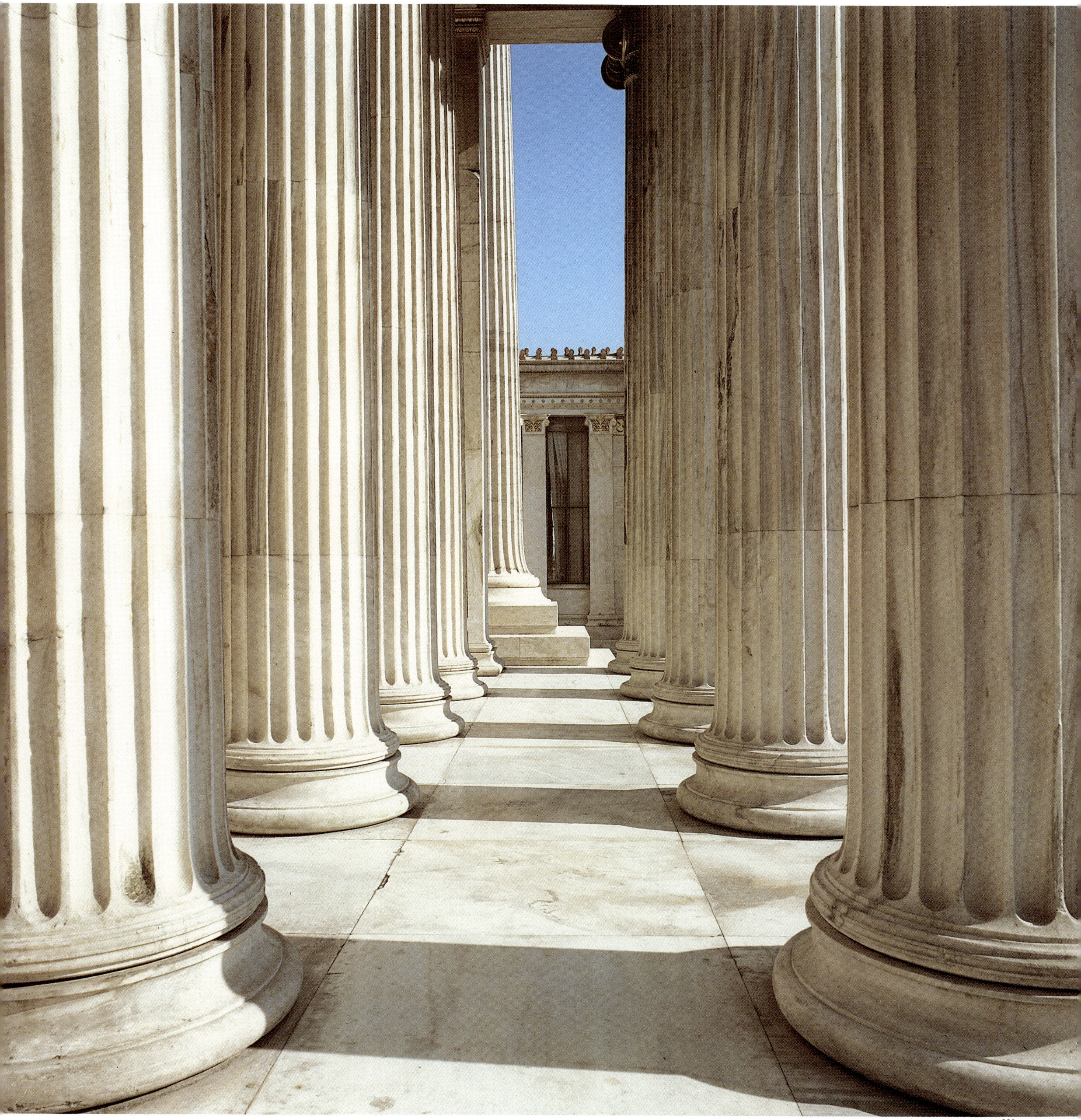

223

erection of the building and its adornment with the necessary sculptural decoration. This last was executed by Leonidas Drosis, professor of sculpture at the School of Fine Arts in the National Technical University (1834–82), while the contract work was carried out initially by B. Treiber and later (for the marble work) by N. Koumelis.

Hansen composed the tripartite arrangement of the wings of the building in a harmonious yet dynamic series of spaces. In order to give the low side wings the appearance of height, he seated them on a sturdy platform of Piraeus stone, which encircles the entire complex. The *mesodomos* (central section that houses the assembly hall) was given the eminence and elevated form of an Ionic amphiprostyle temple. The Danish architect rendered in pentelic marble, with astonishing accuracy, the *meiosis* and *entasis* of the columns and the other details of the capitals and entablature on the hexastyle facade of the central section, modeling them on the east portico of the Erechtheion. Hansen's innovation was to imitate not only his model's sculptural details but also its colors. Even though the well-known polychromy of the ancient Greeks had been discovered almost three decades earlier, very few architects of Hansen's day were incorporating it in their classicizing compositions. Color was used to decorate the taeniae of the frieze, the fronts of the cornices, the simas, and the moldings of the crowning. In a daring compositional innovation, Hansen raised two enormous Ionic columns, one on either side of the central porch-vestibule, on which Drosis set statues of two of Zeus's children: Athena, goddess of wisdom, and Apollo, god of light and harmony. A great proponent of Greek classicism, Drosis also created the central pedimental composition of the Birth of Athena, one of the finest nineteenth-century sculptural compositions on a monumental building. In addition, he executed the statue of the benefactor, Simon Sinas, and the preliminary models for the seated statues of Plato and Aristotle in the main vestibule of the Academy. The sculptures of the smaller pediments above the wings of the Academy were carved to Hansen's design in white terracotta by the Polish artist Franz Melnitzki.

In the interior of the Academy, stucco in a shade of pink was used on the walls of the large vestibule to resemble the texture of marble.

In the assembly hall, murals depicted the myth of Prometheus; these consisted of eight huge paintings by Christian Griepenkerl, one of Karl Rahl's pupils, which hung on all four sides of the hall. When it was completed, the Academy building attracted general admiration and elicited enthusiastic verdicts from Greek and foreign visitors. Hansen himself regarded it as his finest work, admitting: "I feel ineffable pleasure when I behold it." Indeed, although smaller than similar mansions in Europe, the Academy building was, in its execution, a supreme example of classicism. Its creator succeeded in evoking the spirit and delicacy of ancient Greek art.

The Academy building and the other two structures of the trilogy are not as large as corresponding public buildings in European capitals, such as the Parliament Building in Vienna or the Altesmuseum of Berlin. The buildings' smaller size, however, does not diminish them; on the contrary, it sets them on a much more human scale, more in keeping with the size of the Greek capital and, above all, with the classical models. Proximity to the ancient monuments undoubtedly had a catalytic effect on the work of the architects. Measured drawings

224. Athens. Figure of the mythical griffin on the parapet of the large stair head in the Library porch. Contributing factors to the high quality of this building were the inspired design of T. Hansen, the vast experience of his colleague, E. Ziller, and, finally, the skill of the nineteenth-century Greek sculptors.

225. Athens. National Library. The approach to the robust Doric porch of the building, by way of the exterior staircase, is flanked by fine marble lampposts.

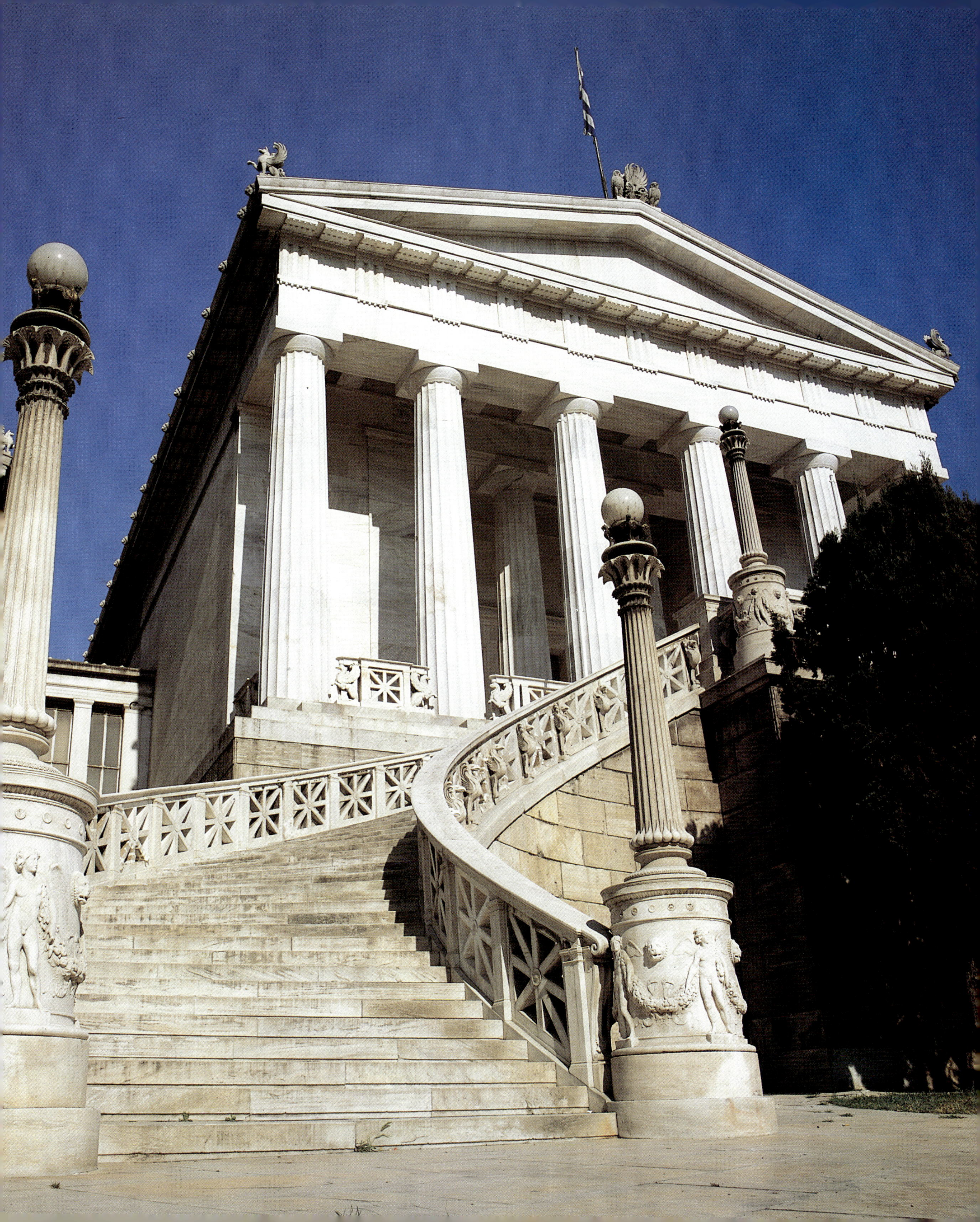

226. Athens. Partial view of the trilogy, with the library at the left and the University to the right. The harmonious relationship between the lines of the overall complex and the scale of the individual buildings integrated the complex into the built and natural environment of Athens.

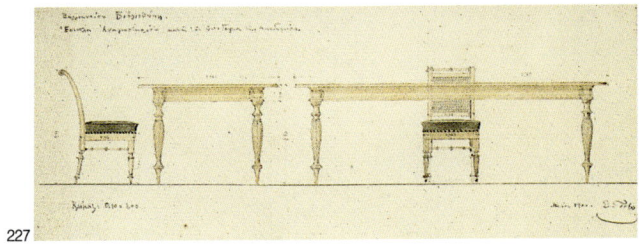

227. Design by E. Ziller for the furniture of the National Library. (Source: National Art Gallery, Athens.)

228. Athens. The reading room of the National Library, one of the finest rooms in the architecture of European classicism.

were made of every detail of the ancient architectural structures, and specific forms were transferred faithfully to the modern buildings, with varying degrees of success. Buildings based on ancient Greek models were executed on a smaller and more measured scale than those of European classicism, which were drawn mainly from Roman architecture and the Renaissance and which are accordingly heavier and more bombastic.

With the Academy now completed to the south of the University, the unit of the town plan set aside for the trilogy was taking shape precisely as its inspirer, Theophil Hansen, had imagined in 1859. The third site to the north of the University had been reserved as early as 1853 for the erection of the Archaeological Museum. It was considered the most suitable site because it was quite close to the Pnyx, the Acropolis, the Theseion, and the Areopagos, and travelers, after viewing the ancient monuments, could visit the museum "and, with a single glance, as it were, view the ruins of their ancestral glory" (State General Archives, Othonian Archive, Ministry of Religion and Public Education, file 175). In the end, the Archaeological Museum was built in 1866 on a plot on Patision Street, and the area next to the University was given over to the construction of a library.

The need for a national library had been felt soon after the War of Independence. Many rare and valuable books had accumulated, mainly through donations; these were housed in the Orphanage and afterward in the Main School on Aigina. When the latter was transferred to Athens, the books were packed in boxes and then stored in a series of unsuitable buildings (such as the bathhouse at Staropazaro, the church of Ayios Nikolaos, and the Gorgoepikoos). Using the University to house all the books was regarded, realistically, as only a temporary solution.

It is worth noting that in two early design proposals for the Archaeological Museum on the site now occupied by the National Library, both Demetres Zezos and Gerasimos Metaxas envisioned a library in addition to the exhibition galleries (figs. 230, 231). However, it has not been clearly established whether this was to be a museum library or the National Library. At the time, the word *museum* had two meanings. In the modern sense, it was a place for displaying and storing antiquities; in its ancient Greek sense, it denoted a "precinct of the Muses"—that is, a place where the arts and letters were cultivated, which might be identified with the library in question. In the end, the project was never carried out, and in 1858 Hansen was commissioned to produce a study for the National Library. In 1884 his drawings were handed over to Ziller to implement.

After a number of government initiatives, both by Prime Minister Trikoupis and by Greek ambassadors abroad, the financing of the work was undertaken by a businessman residing in Russia, Panagis Vallianos, who also represented his brothers Marinos and Andreas of the commercial house of the same name, and the work began in 1887. The building plot between the university building and Ippokratous Street was not very wide and had a distinct slope toward Panepistimiou Street. Hansen was therefore compelled to contract the typical tripartite articulation of the facade as far as possible. As a result, the imposing central core, with the Doric hexastyle porch, is noticeably less than the ideal distance from the side wings flanking it. Hansen was also obliged to set it on a high base (which formed the ground floor of the building) in order to offset the drop in height. Accordingly, two marble staircases giving access to the elevated propylon were added, with lavishly decorated parapets and elaborate lamp-posts, creating a dynamic sculptural unit with a rather eclectic style that contrasted with the tranquil self-sufficiency of the Doric order (figs. 224–26). The bare tectonic character of the marble propylon and the side wings was intensified when the pedimental sculptures and the rest of the sculptural decoration of the building, which had been undertaken by the Viennese sculptor Karl Scwertzek, had to be omitted for economic reasons. It is worth noting the accuracy of the rendering of the order in pentelic marble: in this case, Hansen used the Theseion in the Ancient Agora as his model. The most impressive feature, however, of the National Vallianeios Library (as it was called when it came into operation in 1902) is its interior. The supervisor of the work, Ziller, undoubtedly played an important part in the morphology of this interior (fig. 227). The main vestibule, the walls and ceilings of which were decorated with classical polychromy, is followed by the reading room, brightly lit by the large fanlight, and with its periphery articulated by a very elegant Ionic peristyle (fig. 228). Metal bookshelves of steel and cast-iron components made to very high structural and morphological standards line the walls at the back of the room and were placed in other rooms in the side wings.

The interior space is dominated by the distinctive atmosphere created by blending aesthetic and functional values. The result is an exemplary marriage of the monumental and the functional, which was a feature of late-nineteenth-century bourgeois architecture. This was, by extension, a basic hallmark of the urban design of the period. As can readily be seen in the Athenian trilogy, the buildings do not conform to a single canon of architecture and spatial design. On the contrary, through their differences of scale and forms, they project a contradistinction of part and whole (fig. 226).

The freedom with which architecture was incorporated within the urban design environment was typical of nineteenth-century classicism, which, in contrast with earlier periods (Renaissance, Baroque) was not bound by a predetermined interdependence between buildings and space, in the sense of a unified morphological composition. This perception is predominant in the building complex on Panepistimiou Street, though it was not repeated (at least not with the same clarity of design) elsewhere in Athens. Nevertheless, similar interest attaches to the classicizing complex on Patision Street, which began to take shape in 1870 with the gradual erection of two neighboring building complexes, the National Technical University and the Archaeological Museum. These cultural institutions, together with those of the trilogy, flanked Neapoli-Exarcheia, an important neighborhood of Athens, which has, as a result, been inhabited predominantly by professors, students, and intellectuals from that time to the present day.

The interdependence of the National Technical University and Museum complexes is a different matter from that of the group on Panepistimiou Street; the university and museum were autonomous units from the start, built in separate plots. The circumstances surrounding their creation were also independent of each other. As we have already seen, there were several earlier design proposals for an Archaeological Museum in Athens, one of them the superb composition of Klenze's proposed design (1836), and two by the county-engineer of the Cyclades, G. Metaxas, and the architect D. Zezos, experts "in the civil architecture of 1854" (State General Archives, Othonian Archive, Ministry of Religion and Public Education, file 175) (figs. 230, 231). However, the Museum was not built at that time.

Beginning a project on this scale required a correspondingly large sum of money. Fortunately, in 1856, Dimitrios Bernardakis, a diaspora Greek from St. Petersburg, offered a significant proportion of the necessary expenses (200,000 drachmas), at the urging of Alexandros Rizos Rangavis. The competition for the

229. Athens. The Archaeological Museum, by Lange, Kalkos, and Ziller. Ernst Ziller gave the edifice its imposing aspect facing the large garden that extends toward Patision Street.

230. Athens. Proposal (elevation, ground plan, and section) by D. Zezos (1854) for the Archaeological Museum. Its site was eventually occupied by the National Library. Design involving a series of wings enclosing an interior courtyard (Durand school). (Source: State General Archives, Othonian Archive.)

231. Proposal (elevation and ground plan) by G. Metaxas (1854) for the Archaeological Museum. The design involves a series of symmetrically arranged wings (Weinbrenner School) with no courtyard. (Source: State General Archives, Othonian Archive.)

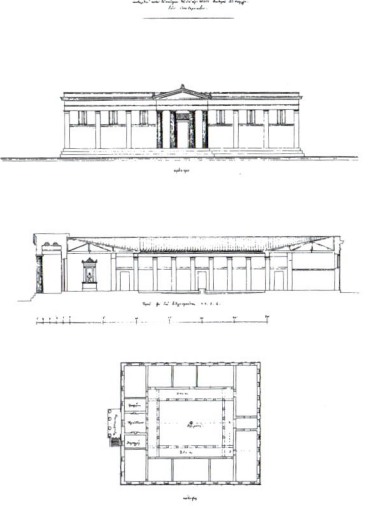

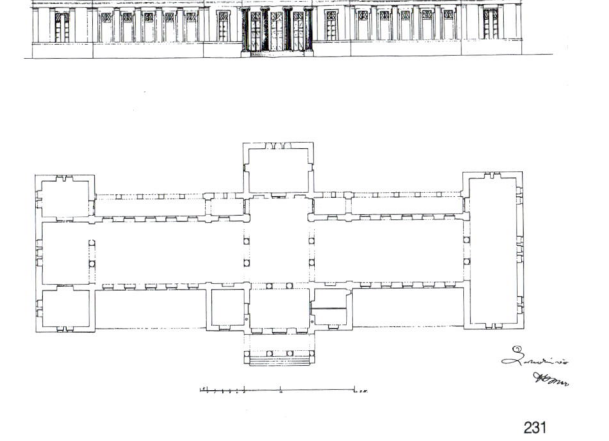

contract was then announced and fourteen design proposals were submitted by Greek and foreign architects; the adjudicating committee, however, which consisted of the professors of the Royal Academy of Munich, judged that none of them was suitable.

Two years later, Ludwig Lange, a professor at the Academy, undertook on his own initiative to produce new drawings for the Museum. The study included a closed, symmetrical complex with two interior courtyards. The chief feature of the main facade was a large Ionic portico that closely resembled corresponding examples of the classicizing school of Berlin. When the building plot on Patision Street was secured with the financial assistance of Eleni Tositsas, construction of the Museum finally began, though it was not to be completed until much later, in 1889. The project's first supervisor, Panagiotes Kalkos, was succeeded by two engineers and, toward the end, by Ziller, who implemented several changes to the original design. In particular, Ziller was responsible for the harmonious composition of the facade, with long porticoes on either side of the Ionic propylon at

232. Athens. Royal Garden (now the National Garden). This view of the garden's pleasant greenery highlights the slender trunks of the palm trees. The palace, with the stoa of Perikles, is in the background. Postcard.

the entrance. The entrance itself is a projecting element that lacks the usual classical pediment. The horizontal parapet running along the top, which was adorned with statues, gives the overall composition a sense of tranquility and spirituality. (Unfortunately, the statues had to be taken down after the earthquake in 1999.) This charming impression is displayed to even better effect by the fact that the building does not stand directly on the boundary line of Patision Street, but is set at the back of a large garden with an uninterrupted view, where it is framed by unassuming Mediterranean vegetation (fig. 229). The creation of gardens had been enthusiastically welcomed by Athenians ever since the time of King Otto, despite the shortage of water that afflicted the capital during the first decades of its existence.

Queen Amalia, with great patience and persistence, and with the advice of the botany professors T. Orphanidis and Karl Fraas, created the Royal Garden on the site set aside for the purpose by Friedrich von Gaertner. All difficulties were overcome and the shrubs and trees were brought from every part of Greece and from abroad (figs. 232, 233). This marked the beginnings of a desire among Athenians for green areas within their city. During the same period, trees were planted along the major streets and boulevards and in the first public squares, familiarizing Athenians with the aesthetic of the park. A fondness for greenery and flowers is also apparent in the first measured drawings of the city made by Kleanthis and Schaubert. "The garden has the following fruit trees: 1 vine, supported on a trellis outside the garden, above a cistern, 1 quince tree, 2 large peach trees, 3 rose bushes, 1 root of jasmine, 2 apricot trees, 5 lemon trees, 3 large and 2 small, 2 vines and other newly planted trees, cherries, etc." Similar descriptions of Athenian houses in Plaka are common in the press of the period (Kardamitsi-Adami, 1997, p. 147).

During the reign of King George I, the municipal authority first made efforts to increase the city's green areas, despite the difficulties posed by Athens's water supply. The discovery and restoration of the ancient reservoir on the lower slopes of Lykavittos Hill at the beginning of the 1870s may not have solved the problem, but it significantly improved the supply of water to the capital and contributed to the creation of new green areas. This manmade greenery formed a fine back-

233. Athens. Royal Garden. This fine example of garden design was executed under very difficult circumstances, as Athens at that time had an inadequate water supply. The plants were brought from all over Greece and abroad.

ground for the monumental classicism that was part of the urban landscape. Furthermore, the creation of green areas around the public buildings became institutionalized and was also a feature of the provincial towns, where public land was less scarce than in Athens.

In any event, the capital acquired a fine example of monumental architecture in a truly idyllic setting when, in 1886, trees were planted on the land around the Zappeion next to the river Ilissos. This land, which had been expropriated as early as 1869, was transformed a few years later, under the supervision of the French architect D. Matton, into a fine artificial landscape with an exemplary stylistic and decorative composition. The spectacular design of this garden can still be appreciated; it not only displays the Zappeion building to good effect but also opens up a vista between the Acropolis and Arditos Hill as far as the horizon of the Saronic gulf (fig. 234).

The dominant feature of the roughly 13 hectares covered by the area is the Exhibition Hall (known as the Olympia), construction of which began in 1874, financed by a bequest in the will of Evangelos Zappas from Epiros. The project was initially linked with the revival of the Olympic Games (the proposal for which goes back to the time of Otto) to an original design by F. F. Boulanger, later (1879) revised by Theophil Hansen. The latter's intervention made a decisive contribution to the composition that was finally built. This edifice differs radically from anything encountered thus far among Athenian public buildings, and no doubt largely due to the building's function as an exhibition hall. It is built on a large scale and developed horizontally, completely in keeping with the surrounding open area. As soon as one enters through the oversize Corinthian propylon, one has a feeling of an expanding space with a variety of perspective views — rather than of a closed, strictly bounded shell. Beyond the very high vestibule, with its decorated coffered ceiling, a few steps bring us to one of the finest circular courtyards of the nineteenth century. This is a two-story peristyle court with an elegant Ionic colonnade on the ground floor, and pilasters surmounted by heads of Caryatids on the upper floor (figs. 235, 236).

At some distance from this courtyard, the long, narrow exhibition room is developed in a semicircle ending in the side wings of the building and at the same time communicating with the open core of the ground plan by way of three rectangular courtyards set on the basic axes. This gives rise to interesting pathways passing through closed and open areas, and visitors to the exhibition hall experience a monumental architecture that introduces a dynamic rhythm in the procession from one exhibit to the next. Consequently, they enjoy a completely different sensation from that normally engendered by the imposing classicizing buildings of the capital, with their standard ideology and morphology.

The Zappeion was not completed until 1888, but the zenith of Athenian classicism should be assigned a somewhat earlier date — it is conventionally placed in the 1870s, and possibly even before that — because at that time the ideas of a historicism founded on the values of the system of orders were still being expressed. At this late period, morphological proposals continue to betray their rationalist dependence on historical models. With the passage of time, however, architecture evolved, especially in Europe, where it was the eclectic trends that became stronger after the middle of the century. The innate conservatism began to be overcome in Athens, too, beginning with the efforts of Theophil Hansen. As an

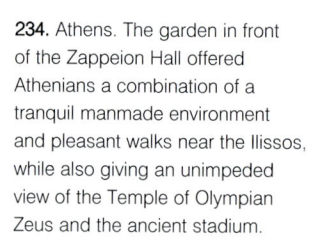

234. Athens. The garden in front of the Zappeion Hall offered Athenians a combination of a tranquil manmade environment and pleasant walks near the Ilissos, while also giving an unimpeded view of the Temple of Olympian Zeus and the ancient stadium.

235. Athens. Zappeion Hall. The imposing form of the octastyle Corinthian porch, with its large scale, is balanced with the wide reception square and extensive garden in front of it.

236. Athens. The interior circular courtyard of the Zappeion. One of Theophil Hansen's most successful compositions, with its perfect balance of the ancient orders and the monumental two-story peristyle.

exponent of a later form of classical culture, Hansen proposed, as early as the time of King Otto, an aesthetic approach different from the line laid down by the Bavarians of the Munich School. Although the architecture of the Academy followed ancient models, the building's lavish forms and colors offered a subjective interpretation of the aesthetic act. This new tendency in the expression of forms was embraced by the now mature Athenian society, reviving its innate good taste and romantic inclination—following, in short, the inexorable law of evolution.

Athenian Residences

The typical Athenian Neoclassical house was the preeminent creation of the progressive, rising social classes in the capital. By about 1865 to 1870, the Athenian residence had developed into an architectural unit fully accommodated to the conditions of urban life during the early reign of King George I; its ground plan was more functional and less bound by symmetry. Two- and three-story houses of the time included apartments occupying a complete floor, with independent, mostly interior, staircases. The courtyards and functional semi-open areas were smaller, and greenery and private gardens began to disappear from the urban scene, particularly in densely occupied areas such as Metaxourgeio and Neapoli.

A typical house from this flourishing period of urban architecture is preserved in Metaxourgeio: the "apartment building" of I. Koutsoyiannis, built just before 1870 by P. Kalkos at the junction of Agisilaou and Deliyiorgi Streets (fig. 244). The main facade on Deliyiorgi Street has a projecting central feature with pilasters on the top floor establishing the Greek orders, and is crowned by a pediment. The large central balcony on this floor and the two smaller ones placed on the side axes at the level below, with their marble floor tiles and corbels, add a sculptural quality to the overall symmetrical composition. The string courses between the stories, the cornices, based on the ancient orders, the Corinthian capitals of the pilasters, and the antefixes (all made of terracotta), sensitively underline the design's classical forms and give expression to the monumentality and constancy of the architecture, though without any excess or affectation. The morphological system here acquires its own canons: simple, horizontal indication of the stories, with plain, almost unarticulated, lower zones, while the order is rendered on the uppermost story, usually by flat pilasters surmounted by an entablature. Moreover, the taeniae, cornices, moldings at the door frames and window frames, and the entire decoration in general, adhere faithfully to original classical profiles. They are not carved in stone, however, but are worked by a special tool on the exterior plasterwork, and are known as travichta. Marble is usually found on the balconies (with their superb corbels taking the form of a pair of sculptured volutes facing in opposite directions), sometimes around the outer doors, and invariably at the base of the building, which usually coincides with the zone of the semi-basement projecting above the level of the pavement. Marbleworking reached a very high standard at this period. A series of workshops with outstanding craftsmen, and also sculptors, such as those of Kossos, the brothers Phytalis, Genovese, Malakates, and Margaritis, and even Siegel himself, undertook the completion of the "marble contract-work" (figs. 237–41).

The artwork that accompanied the building even of the most simple urban houses was taken for granted at that period and formed a kind of obligation dictated by the self-awareness of the residents rather than by any practical need imposed by occasional social expediency. It is indicative that there was no hierarchy of artistic quality. The mansions were naturally marked out by their rich decoration,

237. The most common type of marble corbel found during the height of urban classicism.

238. Athens. Typical Athenian balcony, with sculpted corbels and a metal railing.

239. Late forms of a marble corbel and a metal railing. The latter, made of cast iron, was created by Ernst Ziller and was widely found about 1900.

240. Small balcony with the window frame designed according to the ancient orders and an elegant iron railing.

241. Composite architectural frame for an outer door. The opening and the fanlight above it are designed according to the ancient orders and integrated into the overall composition of the facade. Skilled application in a petit bourgeois detached residence.

238

239

240

241

153

the expensive materials used, and their interior conveniences. However, even in simpler houses, the form of every detail was flawlessly accurate on both the exterior and the interior: outer doors with wood-carved leaves opened onto elegant wooden staircases, one for the apartment on each floor. This functional independence was a distinctive feature of Athenian private architecture that is worth emphasizing. The vestibules gave access to the rooms of each residence. Rooms that faced the street were used as reception rooms and communicated with each other by way of large multi-leafed doors (figs. 242, 243). Most important of all, the wall and ceiling surfaces were not simply painted in lime; instead, they were covered with decorative paintings. Almost every urban residence included fine, excellently executed painted ceilings. They had classical, Pompeian, Renaissance, and Mannerist subjects, all created by specialist artists, several of whom were of Italian origin.

Decorative art was one of the most important courses taught at the Athens National Technical University, where it was called *kosmematography*. This art, and those of applied decoration, marble sculpture, woodworking, and so on, were at the height of their development. The art of building itself progressed significantly when advanced vaulting systems and related mixed structures using standard iron beams began to appear alongside traditional elements involving stone masonry and timber floors. These structures, which clearly influenced the morphology of urban houses, were employed by progressive architects of the period who were at the same time professors at the National Technical University—men like A. Theophilas, I. Koumelis, I. Lazarimos, I. Sechos, and, later (about 1900), I. Kolliniatis.

The most important of these architects who had a dual capacity—that of teacher and designer—was without doubt Hansens's pupil, Ernst Ziller, who taught at the National Technical University for about a decade (1872–83). Before we turn to his multifaceted career as an architect, however, we will examine private buildings from the height of Athenian classicism known to have been designed by Greeks and their foreign colleagues. Although the majority of these no longer exist, they are still well known for the outstanding quality of their forms. At the beginning of Pireos Street, off Omonoia Square, stood the K. Mourouzis mansion (by the architect I. Sechos), a truly impressive edifice in which the two ends of the upper story project monumentally in the form of Ionic porticoes crowned by pediments. Further down the same street, at its junction with Geraniou Street, stood the unusual Tsopotos residence, in which an oversized imitation of the Lysikrates Monument forms the dominant feature of the composition (figs. 245, 246).

Close to Omonoia, in the area known as Chafteia, at Stadiou Street no. 50, stands the Evgenidis mansion, the large expanse of its facade betraying a number of eclectic trends attributed to the French architect E. Troump, who built the French Archaeological School on Sina Street and the Military Courthouse at the corner of Akadimias and Kriezotou Streets (fig. 247). Troump was also responsible for the composition of the Militiadis Negrepontis mansion at the corner of Amalias

242. Athens. Urban double residence with separate outer doors for each unit. Building in Aristotelous and Phokaias Streets, now demolished. Photograph taken in 1975.

243. Athens. Urban double residence, with a single outer door (on the side axis), with access to each apartment (entrance and staircase) opening on to the vestibule. Metaxourgeio, Agisilaou Street. Photograph taken in 1975.

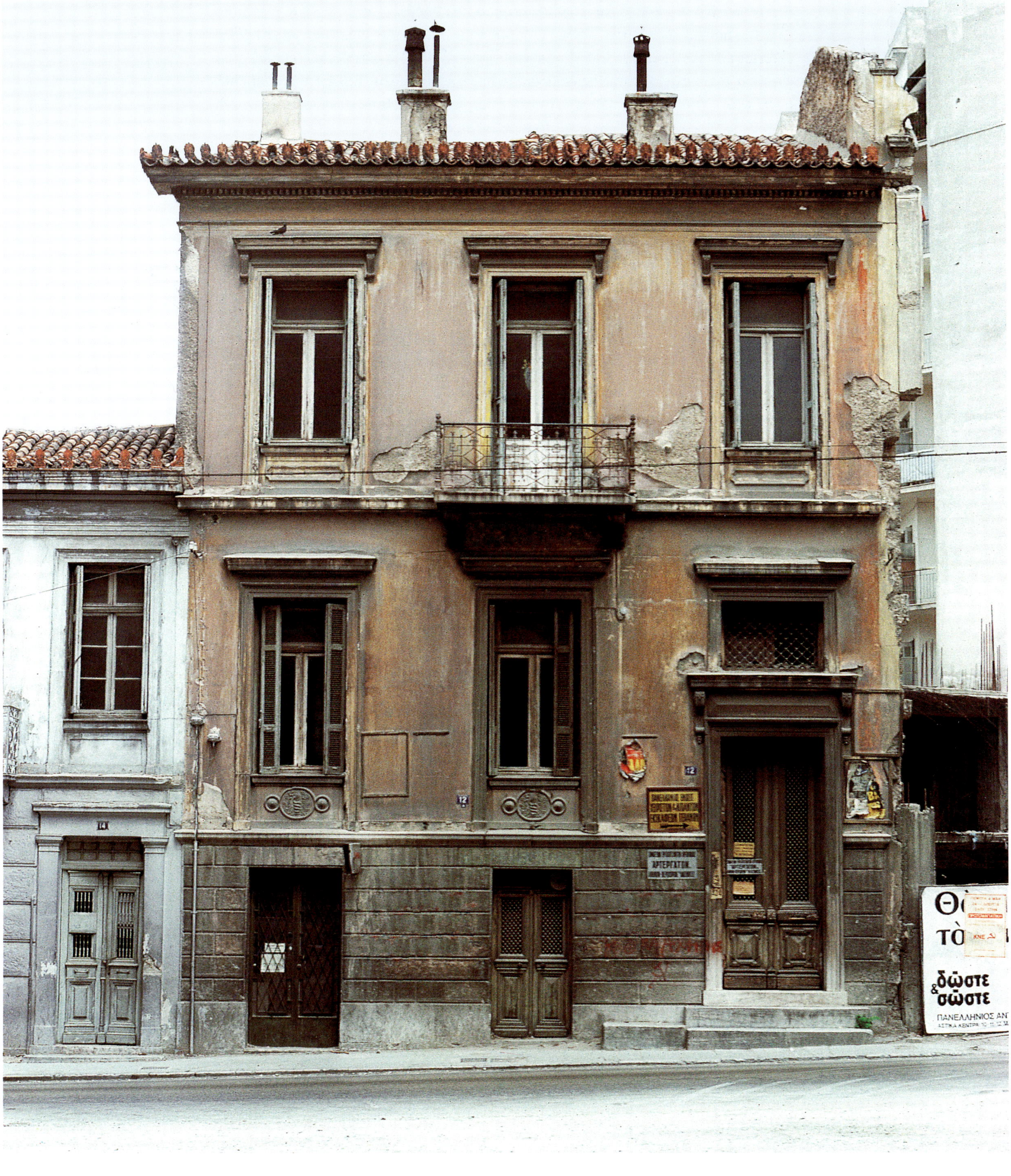

243

Avenue and Othonos Street (Syntagma Square), which was used as a palace by Crown Prince Constantine, and the monumental facade of the much later (1897) National Bank of Greece in Dimarcheiou Square (figs. 248–50). At the back of a garden on the opposite side of Stadiou Street, just before Klafthmonos Square, stood the K. Karapanos mansion, built by the famous architect of the Paris Opera House, C. Garnier, in a French Baroque revival style.

The mansion of the Italian businessman G. B. Serpieri is preserved on Panepistimiou Street, diagonally opposite the Eye Hospital; it is now a branch of the Agricultural Bank. Built about 1875 by A. Theophilas, it is composed in the tradition of the classical orders, though it incorporates elements of Italian mannerism, particularly in its interior decoration. Although stylistic deviations of this kind are rare, they do exist: one of the most distinctive contrasts with the classical spirit are found in the Gothic Revival facades of the I. N. Saripolos residence at the junction of Patision and Chalkokondyli Streets (before 1870) (figs. 251–53).

One of the most interesting groups of private mansions was that on Kifisias Avenue (the original name of Vasilissis Sophias Avenue), which started at Stadiou Street and formed a continuation of Karayiorgi Servias Street. Although this avenue had been traced as early as 1839, with a width of 30 meters and roughly as much again devoted to greenery, it was not built up until much later, at the beginning of the 1870s. The reason for the delay was that the entire side opposite the Palace

244. Athens. The Koutsoyiannis "apartment building" at the corner of Deliyiorgi and Agesilaou Streets, by P. Kalkos (about 1870). One of the finest examples of Athenian academism at its height, this building exhibits a harmonious overall composition and a rendering of the details of the ancient orders. Photograph taken in 1955.

245. Athens. The Tsopotos house at the corner of Pireos and Geraniou Streets (now demolished). The unorthodox composition of Neoclassical elements formed a source of inspiration for many modern Greek painters. Photograph taken in 1955.

246. Athens. The Mourouzis mansion at the beginning of Pireos Street (now demolished). The monumental features on the facade of this imposing private building are executed in pentelic marble. Photograph taken in 1955.

247. Athens. The Military Courthouse, by E. Troump (now demolished). The deviations from established classicism in the facade are characteristic. (Source: KTNA, P. Mylonas Archive.)

248. Athens. Negrepontis mansion in Amalias Avenue, by E. Troump. The gap between the two wings of the complex was closed by an elegant Tuscan arcade. (Source: KTNA, P. Mylonas Archive.)

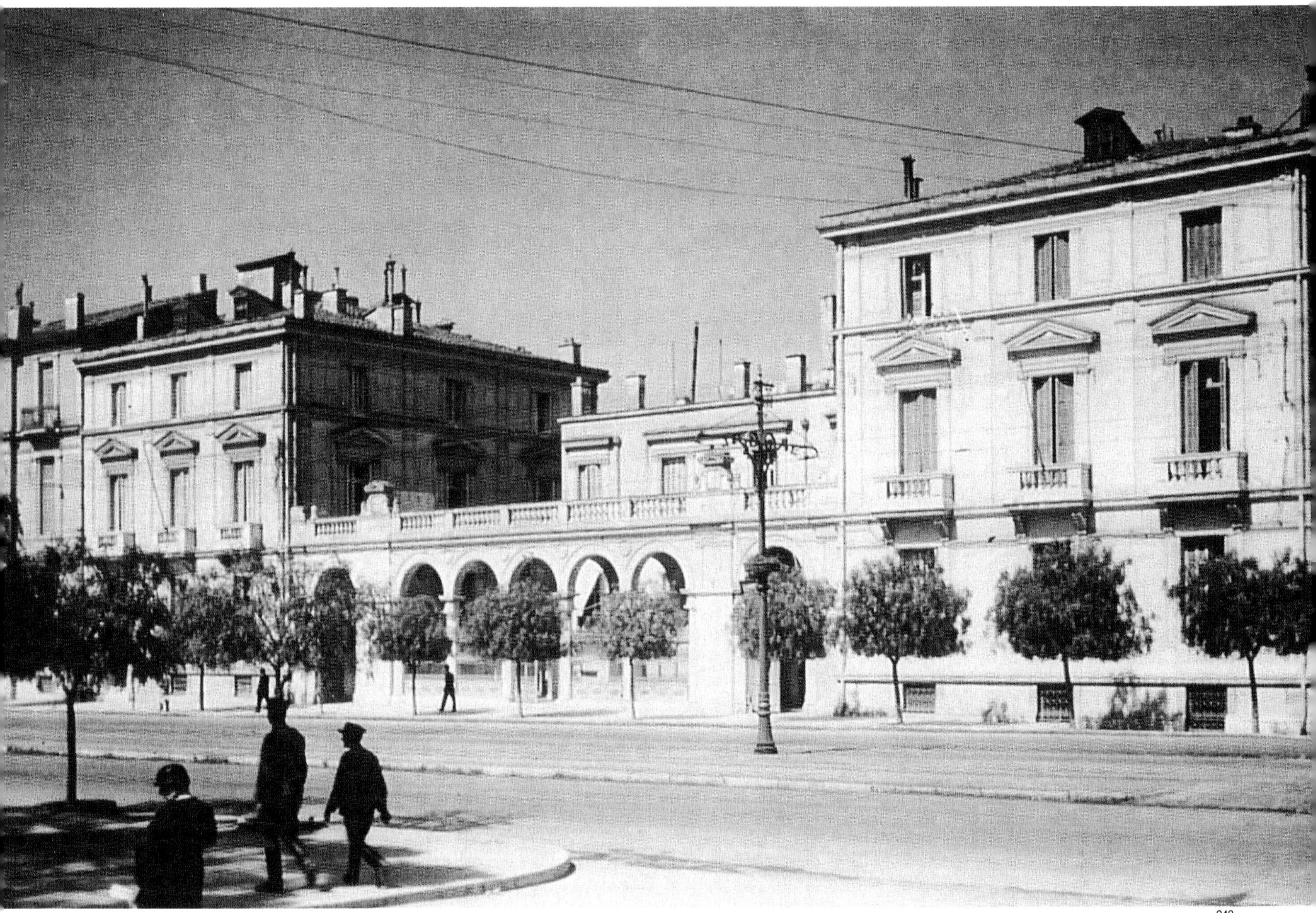

248

249. Athens. The central building of the National Bank of Greece, facing Dimarcheiou Square. Its tranquil, imposing composition is in the spirit of classicism, though overall it exudes a distinct aesthetic coldness.

250. Athens. The monumental architectural frame of the main entrance to the National Bank of Greece.

251. Athens. The Serpieri mansion on Panepistimiou Street, opposite the Eye Hospital. The architect Anastasios Theophilas employed – presumably on the instructions of the Italian contractor – an unorthodox combination of a predominantly Neoclassical facade with Italian Mannerism in a minor portion.

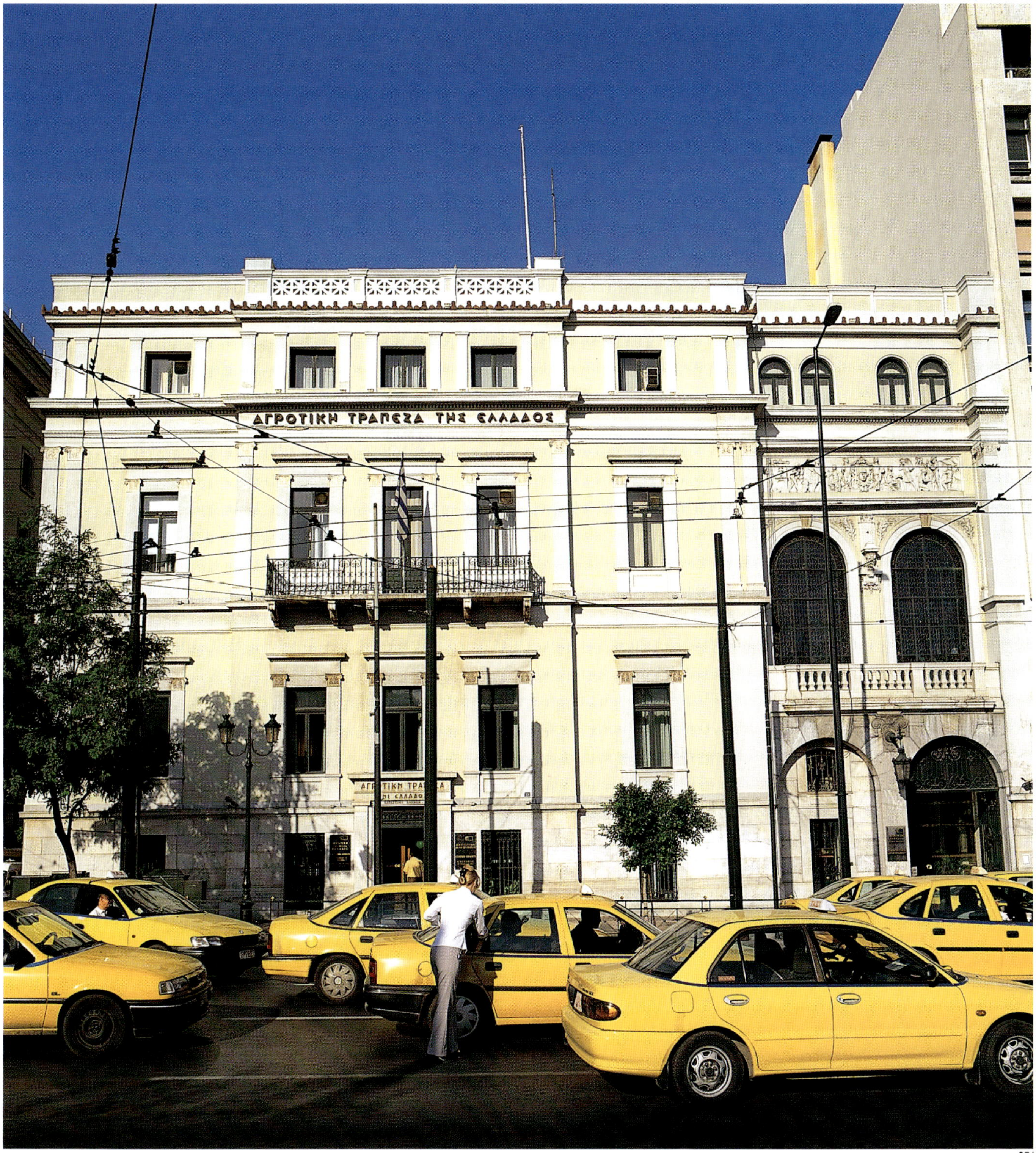

251

252. Athens. The Saripolos mansion on Patision Street (now demolished), with its Gothic Revival facade, formed the best-known divergence in Athenian urban architecture from the predominant classical canon. (Source: *Athina Saripolou-Liva* [in Greek], Athens, 1995.)

253. Athens. View of the balcony of the main vestibule of the Vergotis mansion in Vasilissis Sophias Avenue, with wood-carved decoration in late Gothic style. By contrast, the exterior of the building followed the typical design of Athenian classicism. Photograph taken in 1955.

was reserved for the erection of public offices, ministries, and the Control Council building. As a result, buildings were not permitted as far as Sekeri Street (State General Archives, Othonian archive, Ministry of the Interior, file 214).

Thus, although the Ilissia (the palace of the duchesse de Plaisance), the residence of the doctor Wern Rezer, and a number of smaller private buildings — such as the Grivas residence, the three-story building of Count Botsaris, the residence of Admiral Miaoulis, and beyond it the Rizareios School — were built on the right side (going away from Syntagma Square) of Vasilissis Sophias (formerly Kifisias) Avenue, the plots set aside for the public buildings remained vacant. The only one the state had managed to build by 1840 was that of the military pharmacy, constructed in a Byzantine style by Lysandros Kaftantzoglou. This building was later extended and housed the Ministry of Military Affairs.

Decades went by, but still the state lacked the financial means to build its ministries. Accordingly, at the beginning of the 1870s, the plots on the north side of the Palace were made available and offered for sale to private citizens. The ascent to the throne of King George I, the unification of the Ionian islands with Greece, the revival of the Great Idea, and, above all, the social and economic restructuring of the country induced many Greeks living abroad to take up permanent residence in the country. Most of these were naturally concentrated in the capital (fig. 254).

"Within three years, about four hundred large and small residences were built in Athens, some of them comfortable, well-designed and very expensive," noted the Athenian press. Among the first to have homes built were Andreas Syngros, S. Skouloudis, I. Vouros, and Papoudoff. Skouloudis and Vouros jointly assigned the designing of their mansions on Kifisias Avenue to the French architect V. E. Poitrineau; they had Troump and Piat supervise the work. Syngros commissioned his own mansion to Ziller. Competition on all sides was intense. Many elements were imported from abroad, including timber for parquet floors and door- and window-frames, windows, crystal, bathroom fittings, hearths, and bronze door and window handles, which were often gilded. By contrast, the marble elements of the facades, the columns (usually Ionic), the decorative features, the pilasters, the staircases, the railings, and the paving were all made in the Greek workshops mentioned above. Gardens with greenhouses were at the back or sides of the mansions, with carriage sheds and stables at the far back (figs. 255, 256).

The Skouloudis and Vouros residences were in a Neoclassical style with later elements drawn from the French bourgeois aesthetic; they brought a lighter, patently more modern spirit to the austere morphological canon of the Bavarian school. The Papoudoff and Syngros houses were closer to Athenian models. In the case of the Syngros mansion (now the Ministry of Foreign Affairs), the owner confessed in his memoirs that he himself had made several changes "to the design prepared by the architect Ziller," and that these had made the building "externally clumsy" (Syngros, 1908, p. 98).

These first mansions were followed by one owned by Psychas (now the Egyptian Embassy) between the residences of Papoudoff and Syngros; the Douais villa by K. Merlin (now the French Embassy) and the Charokopos mansion (now

254. Athens. View of Vasilissis Sophias Avenue near the Palace, about 1900. The Psychas mansion (now the Egyptian Embassy) can be seen at the left, with the two-and-a-half-story Syngros mansion (now the Ministry of Foreign Affairs) next to it, by Ernst Ziller. The Syngros mansion's simple form was marred by the later addition of a porch with a pediment on the upper story. (Source: ELIA, Photographic Archive.)

255. Athens. The Skouloudis and Vouros mansions (now demolished) on Syntagma Square, by the architect V. E. Poitrineau, were built in the style characteristic of the late-nineteenth-century French school of classicism. (Source: ELIA, Skouloudis Archive.)

256. Athens. The facade of the Vouros *archontiko* facing Stadiou Street. Photograph taken in 1955.

257. Athens. The Stournaris residence on Vasilissis Sophias Avenue, by Lysandros Kaftantzoglou, in which classicism's severe lines are softened by arches, rosettes, and other elements suggestive of the architect's Italian training.

258. Athens. The Syngros mansion in its present form, as the main building of the Ministry of Foreign Affairs.

259. Athens. The Charokopos mansion, now the Benaki Museum, on Vasilissis Sophias Avenue. Later expression of classicism, and one of A. Metaxas's most mature works.

257

258

259

the Benaki Museum, fig. 259) – both the work of Anastasis Metaxas – the E. Stournaris mansion, probably by Kaftantzolgou; the Psychas residence (now the Italian Embassy) and the O. Stathatos mansion, both by Ziller; the P. Kazoulis mansion, designed by the military engineer N. Schinas; and the Embirikos, P. Kalligas, Zlatanos, Voglis, and other mansions (figs. 211, 257–59).

Inside, the larger mansions followed the type of the French *hôtel privé*, while the smaller ones did not differ essentially from Athenian middle-class houses. This also holds true, more or less, for their facades: smaller homes are plainer and resemble houses from the previous period, while larger, more lavish homes reflect European influences. One of the finest such homes is the Charokopos mansion by A. Metaxas, possibly the greatest Greek architect of the end the century. When one stands before one of his works, as P. Yiannopoulos was later to write, one feels "a sense of relief, of understanding, of pleasure; you are relieved by the simplicity of line, the relative simplicity, order, harmony, nobility, delicacy" (Yiannopoulos, 1981, p. 88). Although the same cannot be said of all Metaxas's works, it is certainly true of the Charokopos mansion, which possesses the aesthetic credibility of a monumental creation. In contrast, the Stathatos mansion has the grace and elegance of a more subdued style. Its form, emphasized by elements of late historicism, exudes good taste, though it is accompanied by a bold sculptural quality that extends to the composition of the entrance, which is set on a diagonal axis and projects outward with elegant arched openings. This structure emphatically represents a supreme accomplishment by the talented Ziller. We shall deal more extensively in a later chapter with this indefatigable architect, who made a profound mark on bourgeois morphology around 1900.

The interior furnishings of the mansions on Kifisias Avenue – the furniture, chandeliers, tableware, and decorative items – were also acquired from Europe, either directly or through catalogues, with the aid of Athenian shops representing well-known foreign commercial establishments (figs. 260–62). Most of the mansions' owners belonged to a new class of Greeks who, having lived and made their wealth in Europe, began to settle in Athens. They brought with them the customs of another life, much more luxurious than that of the Athenian middle class. "In their purely Parisian salons," writes H. Bell, "you are received by fine ladies, well-educated, charming conversationalists who can discourse easily in many languages; these salons are a pole of attraction for the foreigners resident in Greece, mainly because in them they get a taste there of their remote homelands" (Bell, 1993, p. 110).

In contrast, foreigners were treated with reserve and suspicion by middle-class families, and were seldom entertained in their houses, possibly because the Greek bourgeoisie feared the foreigners would pass judgment on the austerity of their interior decoration. It is a fact that their typically spare, lightweight furniture was, among other things, very serviceable when it came time for families to move from house to house, which happened frequently, usually in the month of September.

Greek society's wealthy new bourgeoisie played a role not only in erecting luxurious private residences but also in establishing and maintaining many benevolent institutions. One important charitable contributor was Queen Olga, who served on many committees and whose presence encouraged the ladies of the Court and her wider circle to donate money to build, through collective ventures, many public welfare institutions. This led to the creation of hospitals, orphanages, prisons, poor-houses, foundations for the protection and education of destitute women and children, and so on.

260–262. Athens. Decorative items from the Skouloudis residence, ordered and designed by Claudien of the J. Graux establishment in Paris, show the French decorative tradition in all its glory.

Large gilded bronze bowl.

Table candlestick in the same style as a clock for S. Skouloudis's office.

Table clock of marble and gold, 70 cm high, in the style of Louis VII, decorated with garlands and bows. (Source: ELIA, Skouloudis Archive.)

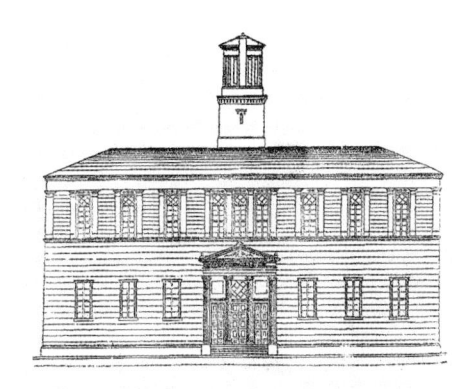

Πρόσοψις τοῦ Βαρβακείου Λυκείου.

263. Athens. The Varvakeios School, by P. Kalkos (demolished in 1956). Its austere, solid form was probably designed to balance the light tetrastyle Ionic porch at the entrance to the building. Lithograph of the period.

264. Athens. The Ionic porch of the Varvakeios School. Its use of orders and proportions are in the spirit of "archaeological" classicism. (Source: KTNA, P. Mylonas Archive.)

265. Athens. The Second Primary School on Adrianou Street, by Panagiotes Kalkos (1875–76). Despite its small size, the building exudes a harmony and monumental style appropriate to the intellectual character of an educational building.

266. Athens. The porch of the Athens Town Hall, illuminated at night.

ΔΗΜΑΡΧΕΙΟΝ

Most of the benevolent institutions were housed in buildings erected for the purpose on a collective basis; they included the Evangelismos Hospital, by A. Metaxas, the Asylum for the Incurable, the Parnassos Literary Society, which founded and ran a night school and hospital for working children, and the Workshop for Destitute Women. Others, like the Syngrou Prison, the Women's Prison, the Averoff Prison, the Dromokaition Mental Hospital, and the Chatzikonstas Orphanage, were built using donations from a single wealthy benefactor. There were, of course, examples of institutions that, whether the recipients of donations or not, were erected thanks to the initiative of the Municipal Authority, among them the Infant Orphanage, built to designs by G. Metaxas; the Municipal Theater, by Ziller; the Municipal Market, by I. Koumelis; and the Varvakeios School (figs. 263, 264), Second Primary School, and Town Hall building, all designed by P. Kalkos (figs. 263–68).

Unlike their European counterparts, most of the public buildings in Greece followed the Neoclassical style with varying degrees of fidelity and success. In Europe it had become an established practice to differentiate functional buildings, especially those intended for public welfare use, by a rather eclectic morphological style, one that alluded to their distinctive specific function. An exception, in the case of Athens, is formed by prison buildings, which were constructed in a more austere, fortress-like style.

267. Athens. The Town Hall building. The original two-story design exhibits proper proportions, despite the robust appearance of the Doric porch at the entrance. Postcard.

268. Athens. The Town Hall building after the addition of the upper story. The overall effect disturbed the authentic proportions of the building.

The Unredeemed Territories

Γ΄ ΣΩΜΑ ΣΤΡΑΤΟΥ

THE UNREDEEMED TERRITORIES

The Period of Modernization

Toward the end of the nineteenth century, Old Greece, with the boundaries created after the arrival of King George I, had begun to take form. Athens was now the preeminent political, administrative, intellectual, cultural, commercial, and consumer center in the land. Athenians' way of life, their dress, and the architecture of their houses were all models to be imitated. Although the economy continued to be based on farming and stock raising and the population of the towns accounted for less than one quarter of Greece's total population, urban types of residences rapidly spread throughout the country. Larger and smaller Neoclassical houses, which have come to be known as popular Neoclassical buildings, exist in both large urban centers and tiny villages. Athenian Neoclassicism is even found on the Ionian islands, though only as a small proportion of the local architecture. The unification of the Ionian islands with Greece did not change the social life of the capital cities on the three largest islands, Corfu, Zakynthos, and Kephallonia, which was based on the models of the rest of Europe.

Generally speaking, Greece strove, sometimes authentically and sometimes through simple imitation, to become part of Europe and to shake off its Eastern past. Although this was the case in the newly founded Greek state, which had experienced almost half a century of independent life, the Eastern element was kept alive and frequently flourished in the unredeemed territories. In Epiros, Thessaly, Macedonia, Thrace, the north Aegean islands, the Dodecanese, and Crete, the situation differed hardly at all from that of Greece in the period before the Uprising—there Greece maintained its distinctive and characteristic local features, though it also frequently deteriorated.

Greece did not always maintain the best diplomatic relations with the Sublime Porte (the Ottoman court in Constantinople), and this understandably affected the quality of life in the unredeemed territories. New living conditions emerged as a result of the political reforms—the Tanzimat—instituted in 1839, which offered some guarantees of fundamental rights to all subjects of the Ottoman Empire, regardless of their religious convictions. An important contribution was also made by the Charter that followed the Crimean War in 1856, known as the Hatti Humayun, which gave Christians the right to be represented both in the Supreme Judicial Council in Constantinople and in provincial administrative councils. Although Christian representation was something of a facade and certainly was not proportionate to their numerical superiority, Christians were able to demand certain rights and privileges, such as the right to own land and to engage in commercial and shipping activities. The Ottoman Empire's economic and commercial relations with the West, which were mainly in the hands of Christians, reinforced these privileges. At the same time, a strong trend toward urbanization emerged, aided by a movement of the population from the mountainous, less secure regions to the larger villages and towns.

The urban centers of unredeemed Greece, as we have seen, preserved the characteristic structure of traditional Ottoman towns, with irregular, narrow, labyrinthine streets that did not follow any predetermined plan but were defined largely by the terrain, the security of the settlement, the climate, and social needs. A town was divided into neighborhoods, called *machalades*, centered on a religious building, whether mosque or church. Small open areas, crossroads, resting places, fountains, bathhouses, markets, inns—all these, in their randomness and variety, struggled, so to speak, against the urban identity of these centers, without actually obliterating it. On the contrary, they lent great vitality and charm to the urban environment.

269. Thessaloniki. The entrance to the Stratarcheio.

270. Constantinople. Greeks in Phanar (end of nineteenth century). Occupants of the historic quarter on a street in Constantinople, some wearing traditional costume and others European dress. In the background, the dense rows of *sachnisia* create a highly picturesque atmosphere. Engraving of the period.

The introspective character of social life, which was organized by ethnic group, accounts for the absence of large public buildings. The architecture of the residences followed the traditional morphology of the Balkan towns: large mansions with masonry walls at the lower level and timber structures on the upper stories, projections (*sachnisia*), painted fanlights, lattice windows; smaller single- or two-story buildings, sometimes made of brick, though more often constructed of timber (stone structures are much more expensive than wooden ones — and there was in any case the risk that a more luxurious, modern structure would attract the attention of the authorities).

From about the middle of the century onward, the situation began to change. Ottoman towns were gradually reformed by new, progressive governors and legislators. Old neighborhoods were redesigned. Frequent fires spread rapidly through neighborhoods built with timbered houses, completely destroying them — and leaving areas free for rebuilding. Sometimes fires were deliberately set by the

271. Constantinople. Western and Eastern elements are combined with an eclectic intent. The excessive jostling together of heterogeneous forms is characteristic. (Source: National Technical University, Morphology Archive.)

272. Constantinople. Neoclassical three-story building in the Pera neighborhood. In some cases, the Greek population assimilated pure forms of classicism. (Source: National Technical University, Morphology Archive.)

governors themselves (like Rasim Pasha in Ioannina) when their attempts to modernize the towns met with resistance.

Western European architecture was introduced into the Greek territories under Ottoman rule in two ways. On the one hand, Greek merchants who were subjects of the Ottoman Empire traded with the great commercial houses of Trieste, initially, and then with those of the Balkan countries, Russia, Austria, Italy, and France; the merchants traveled frequently to Europe and to free Greece, bringing back the new architectural currents predominant in these lands. On the other hand, the Ottoman government itself intervened, introducing modernizing reforms, redesigning towns, erecting new administrative buildings, hospitals, schools, and so on, and enacting new town-planning legislation and building regulations (fig. 269).

In these large public buildings we encounter what might be called a new style, clearly influenced by European Baroque and French Neoclassicism, with excessively rich morphological decoration and strong use of pointed arches. This style

175

was to become predominant in modern Constantinople and served as a model for all the towns under Ottoman rule, particularly Thessaloniki. Its influence was still evident in the first eclectic examples at the beginning of the twentieth century. The influences of the new style might even be said to be found in the first Neoclassical buildings erected by the Greek Christians and Jews, although in that case the models are often drawn directly from the Western world and, of course, from Greece (figs. 270–72).

For Greeks, in particular, Neoclassicism was more than an architectural style; it was one of the ways they could associate themselves directly with the free motherland and the ancient past. As has been repeatedly emphasized, it therefore acquired particular symbolical significance. It is also typical that the first large educational or benevolent institutions, which were funded by donations from wealthy benefactors, mainly followed a Neoclassical style not only in the last decades of the nineteenth century but down almost to the interwar period, when the corresponding forms had finally been abandoned in Athens and Old Greece.

Epiros   Although it is easy to identify many common features among Greek urban centers of the unredeemed territories, it would be inappropriate to generalize, because local societies exhibit important differences. In Epiros, for example, where the ratio of the Greek to the Turkish population was almost 3 to 1, the economy was based largely on farming, stock raising, and craft industries. Beginning as early as the first half of the nineteenth century, first Arta and then Ioannina were transformed into major economic centers of the region. In 1878, three years before the liberation of Arta, the population of Ioannina had reached 110,000 inhabitants and that of Arta, 36,000. Ioannina was the administrative, military, commercial, and intellectual center of the region, a node in the network of major commercial routes linking the Ionian and Adriatic coasts with Albania, Thessaloniki, and Macedonia, and the most important center of the carrying trade in the area. Nevertheless, significant groups of the population continued to possess the retrogressive, conservative mentality characteristic of the past (figs. 273–78).

In 1869 Rasim Pasha, the modernizing governor of Epiros who had studied engineering in Berlin, sought to embellish and upgrade the old market of Ioannina, but his efforts met with great resistance from Greek, Turkish, and Jewish owners of craft industries and merchants. Convinced that no one was prepared to implement his ideas, he set in motion a plan to set fire to the area. As in Thessaloniki, this was a deliberate act, the ultimate aim of which was to facilitate the redesigning of the town. Hundreds of properties, workshops, shops, inns, and bakeries were reduced to ashes. On the day after the disaster, European engineers began to draw up a new plan, on which the town's reconstruction was based. The new buildings abandoned the traditional architecture either wholly or in part. The burgeoning class of wealthy merchants and scholars who had traveled and lived in Europe now imported a new way of life, in which the hallmarks of prosperity were evident. The ground plan of the residences changed to conform to European models.

273. Ioannina. Characteristic transformation of corbels: these Western-style learned forms are carved in stone, though they recall earlier wooden structures.

274. Ioannina. Transformation of the corbel into a classical form carved in marble.

275. Arta. One of the earliest "urban" houses in the center of town. The traditional element recedes and gives way to an imported rationalist aesthetic.

276. Ioannina. Local architectural tradition displays substantial transformations in the direction of early classicism.

277. Arta. Urban architecture enriched by more mature elements of the classical orders, such as the window- and door-frames on the upper story. The balcony's corbels adhere to the simplified geometry of traditional technique.

278. Preveza. The forms preserve influences of Western origins, at least in their details: the simple profile of the corbels, the learned balcony railing, and the cross-section of the horizontal cornices.

The Jewish community made an important contribution to the development of the new town. (Four-fifths of the residences destroyed in the fire belonged to Jews.) The Jews of Ioannina, who were wealthy merchants and scholars receptive to new and progressive trends, built their mansions in accordance with the dictates of contemporary architecture (fig. 280). Initially, a limited number of Neoclassical features (balconies, a few outer doors) appeared; gradually, those features increased. The design of several of buildings clearly reflects the contributions of educated architects, among them S. Mineiko of Poland, Bernasconi of Italy, P. Sakellariou, and, later, P. Melirrytos, who worked on the town plan and particularly influenced local architecture. The scion of a wealthy Ioannina family, Periklis Melirrytos returned to his native town in 1893, having completed his studies at the National Technical University in Athens, and built a large

279. Ioannina. The Pasha's residence, which now houses the Commercial School. The Ottoman rulers embraced the unsullied aesthetic of urban progressivism.

280. Ioannina. The Levis mansion. The aesthetic effect of rationalist design is fully realized in the tranquil horizontal facade with symmetrically organized elements.

number of important public and private buildings, most of them following the Neoclassical morphology. One of the first buildings constructed in the 1870s was the residence of the governor. Known as the Pasha's *konaki*, it was surrounded by an extensive verdant garden adorned with springs and fountains. After several changes of use, the most important being to house the Commercial School, it is now a school building (fig. 279).

In his efforts to Europeanize the town, the governor, Rasim Pasha, had begun to build a large new stone structure to serve as a government house and barracks, and also a building for an orphanage. Known as the Georgios Stavros Orphanage, after the man who provided the building plot, the building's design is attributed to S. Mineiko. While they cannot be considered to express Greek styles, both buildings, as well as that of the Eighth Army Division (known as the *konaki* and also begun by Rasim), nevertheless have several individual Neoclassical elements, such as columns, door frames, and window frames (figs. 281, 282).

These first public buildings were followed by a series of others, such as the Haritie Municipal Hospital, the Chatzikonstas Hospital, the Ottoman Girls' School (now the Post Office), the Papazogleios Weaving School for Girls, the new Zosimaia School, and others. The last three, designed by P. Melirrytos, exhibit all the elements of Neoclassicism. The two educational institutions, in particular (the Zosimaia School and the Papazogleios School), exemplify, in morphological terms, a pure formulation of the "national" style in northern Greece: The Zosimaia School is a single-story building designed with characteristic porticoes on wings placed either side of an Ionic propylon. It is based on the University in Athens by Christian Hansen. The Papazogleios School is designed on the same principles: a two-story structure symmetrical about the main axis, with Corinthian columns on the upper story. In its general lines it recalls educational buildings contemporary with it built in the type commonly employed by the architect Kallias about 1900 for the provincial towns of Greece (figs. 282, 284). Such schools not only were widespread in Greece (the Greek state first contributed to the constructions of a large number of educational institutions after the Kapodistrias period) but also made an impression on European experts when they were presented at an international conference on the construction of buildings held in Paris in 1906.

Naturally enough, the architecture of public buildings and *archontika* influenced that of middle-class houses. The Epirot craftsmen began to add to their traditional stone buildings a number of more or less austere Neoclassical elements.

281. Ioannina. The Post Office building. In the multicultural society of the town after liberation, Neoclassical morphology was regarded as the obvious solution for a public building. This one originally housed the Ottoman Girls' School.

282. Ioannina. The Georgios Stavros Orphanage, in the still-unredeemed town, displays the standard morphology of the "national" architecture.

283. Arta. Architectural frame of an external door in a house in the commercial center. The historic order is applied to a private building in the spirit of the authentic form of the models.

284. Ioannina. The Zosimaia School. Exhibits complete identification with the monumental models of Athenian classicism.

285. Ioannina. Monumental composition of the doorway of the Georgios Stavros Orphanage.

286. Arta. The museum of the town's historic stone bridge. This elegant architectural composition is integrated into the environment and combines morphological rationalism with a picturesque overall effect.

This produced a mixed morphology involving elements drawn from both local traditional architecture and Neoclassicism (figs. 285, 286).

Central and Northern Greece

Like Epiros, Thessaly was for the most part an agricultural region where the Moslem population formed a minority. In the plains, the Turkish pashas shared between them the rich estates (*chifliks*) on which Christians worked as tenant farmers, while in the mountain regions the free, self-governing communities known as head villages consisted exclusively of Greeks. From the middle of the nineteenth century onward, the population steadily moved to the nearest towns, resulting both from a change in Ottoman policy and from frequent looting raids by Albanian irregulars. The opportunity afforded by the Hatti Humayun for non-Ottoman citizens to acquire landed property enabled several Thessalian merchants living abroad to purchase land. Particularly in the years just before the annexation of the area to Greece, the Ottomans, foreseeing political change, sold their *chifliks* at derisory prices and left Thessaly, thereby enabling even ordinary farmers to acquire their own land.

There were two large towns in Thessaly in the first half of the century: Larisa, with a population of about 30,000 inhabitants, and Trikala, with 12,000. None of the other townships exceeded 5,000 inhabitants — not even Ambelakia, Tyrnavos, or Ayia, in which craft-industrial units had begun to develop alongside farming and stock raising.

Volos, the only import and export harbor in the region, began to expand about 1830. A number of warehouses and shops began to appear in the area between the fortification walls of the old castle and the coast. The Greeks of Thessaly were the first to grasp the significance of the town's expansion toward the sea and of the creation of a new settlement. In 1850 they asked the sultan to send a special engineer to draw up a plan for a new town to rival those of Europe. Despite the opposition of the Ottoman beys of the area, the town expanded continuously. Five years later, the first Christian church, of Ayios Nikolaos, began to function, followed shortly afterward by the first boys' school and then the girls' school. The new town of Volos was, in effect, the first Thessalian town to be designed according to Western models. The street grid is perfectly rectangular and the new buildings follow Neoclassicism.

The mansion of the land-owning Chatzilazaros family is one of the first built in Volos. King George I, who stayed in it when he arrived in the town with his retinue a few days after Volos's liberation, is said to have expressed his admiration for the beauty, richness, and conveniences his lodgings offered. A three-story building with a central axis of symmetry, the mansion's ground-floor side wings, and its second story, in the shape of a cross with pergolas covering the spaces left by the arms, recall an early romantic classicism of the beginning of the nineteenth century. So, too, do the two low ancillary buildings with porticoes on their facades to the right and left of the door leading to the courtyard; these structures served as accommodation for the doorkeeper and the carriage driver.

The growth of Volos was followed, on a smaller scale, by that of Karditsa, a new town built during the final years of Ottoman domination. In contrast, Larisa and Trikala did not flourish. In 1875 Larisa was described as a "large mud-field" by the Frenchman De Vogue, who added that rarely did a town create such a lamentable impression. There is a similar description of Trikala in 1884 — in a local newspaper, moreover. "Trikala, an inland town, bearing the Ottoman stamp in

287, 288. Preveza. Details of arched doorways in houses of the town. Their decorative expression reveals heterogeneous trends: popularizing, traditional, Venetian, and classicizing.

289. Trikala. The Dorothea School (1875). The arrangement of three wings in a U shape is commonly found in educational buildings. Stripped of decorative elements, the school's appearance is austere.

290. Trikala. Typical two-story facade on the main square. At the top, window openings are separated by Corinthian pilasters; at the bottom, a row of shop-doors are surmounted with arches.

291. Larisa. Two-story single residence. This home represents the type of mature classicism prevalent in the provinces.

292. Larisa. Corner building in the market with shops. A conservative, though essential, decoration of commercial establishments occurred in accordance with the classical orders.

289

290

291

292

293. Larisa. General view of the town center toward the end of the nineteenth century. Classicism and later aesthetic trends have stamped their quality on the urban landscape of the provincial towns. Postcard.

294. Trikala. General view of the town center toward the end of the nineteenth century. The urban image is displayed both in the classically ordered facades of the buildings and in the expansive design of the open public areas. Postcard.

295. Volos. The Athanasakeion Archaeological Museum. Its severe morphology is based on the National Archaeological Museum in Athens. Postcard.

296. Volos. Ionic porch of the main entrance to the Athanasakeion Archaeological Museum.

297. Ambelakia. The Mantareios School. This imposing structure reflects the social activity of an economically flourishing little settlement. Postcard.

298. Volos. The Achillopouleion Hospital (end of the nineteenth century). Postcard.

299. Kavala. The villa of the Hungarian tobacco merchant P. Herzog (about 1890), which now houses the Town Hall. It impressively displays the aesthetic trends of European eclecticism (in this case, the castellated style).

everything, is today a center of all kinds of filth and a sea of putrid water." Earlier descriptions of both towns, however, were different (newspaper *Oi Ergatai*, January 24, 1884). In the case of Trikala, in particular, Greek and foreign travelers describe the fine municipal market shaded by large plane trees, the *archontika* of Turkish agas and beys and Christian merchants, the old castle, the mosques, churches, inns, schools (Turkish and Greek), the *tekedes* (religious meeting places), hammams, fountains, stone bridges, and the river (figs. 289, 290).

In the last years before liberation, both towns had fallen into decline. Ottoman oppression and fear of raids by Albanian Turks, who attacked the Christian neighborhoods, pillaging, ravaging, and destroying, naturally inhibited the development of the Thessalian towns. The description by H. Holland, who toured Greece in the early nineteenth century, is indicative: "Although the relation between the two peoples was that of master and slave, it is easy to see that all the external signs of decline are to be found to a greater extent amongst the former. The Greek towns generally give the impression of active, useful life, apart from those in which the population found itself locally oppressed." (Holland, 1989, pp. 90–98, 120–21). The annexation of Thessaly to the modern Greek state found the town inhabited by a fair number of rich Turks, a majority of Greeks (about 60 percent), including several wealthy merchants, and a few Jews, who held the retail trade.

After liberation, the rehabilitation and reconstruction of towns began. The fires that occurred in 1881 in Karditsa and in 1882 in Larisa, where almost the entire central market was reduced to ashes, decisively contributed to the change of forms and to Europeanization (figs. 291–93).

Here too, the architecture of urban buildings from the Ottoman period followed the model of the traditional urban residence in Ottoman towns. In contrast with Epiros, where, as we have seen, Neoclassical elements appeared by the middle of the century, in the Thessalian plain (which was a more agricultural area), older, traditional forms of architecture continued to be found, such as organically articulated building spaces, covered balconies (*chayatia*), projecting *sachnisia*, and the like.

With the exception of a few isolated examples in Volos, Neoclassicism did not emerge in the towns of Thessaly until the last two decades of the century, after the area's annexation to the Greek state. Although some buildings exhibit the simple morphology of Athenian classicism of the Othonian period, most structures exhibit all the features of the late period of the style, in the form predominant in free Greece and analyzed in the previous chapter. It seems, therefore, that primarily Greek engineers from Old Greece worked here, bringing Athenian models with them.

Alongside urban houses and mansions, public buildings were erected, mostly educational institutions and hospitals, but also courthouses, town halls, museums, banks, churches, theaters, hotels, and stations for the newly created railway. The first industrial units also appeared: flour mills, iron industries, tobacco factories, tobacco warehouses, food and drink industries, and so on. Toward the end of the century, a truly impressive economic change is observable in these basically agricultural centers, especially in Trikala, Karditsa, and, of course, Volos, where the rising manufacturing industries, particularly tobacco production, attracted some

300. Kavala. D. Tokkos mansion (1879). This building's imposing appearance, though expressed in accordance with European morphological examples, overtly retains the general lines of the local tradition.

members of society into capitalistic activities and fostered the corresponding mentality (figs. 294–98).

Alongside the purely Neoclassical buildings, structures soon appeared with ostentatious elements of eclecticism; later, it was modernism's turn, with the expressive formations of Art Nouveau and Art Deco appearing. At this time, these styles made their appearance in Athens and above all in Thessaloniki, in buildings usually designed by architects who had graduated from French and German polytechnic institutions. Neoclassicism, however, continued to be the predominant form of architecture in the early decades of the twentieth century, too, despite the fact that it began to be abandoned in Athens, where it gave way to eclecticism and, shortly afterward, to the modern movement.

The situation in the northern Aegean islands and Macedonia, which were liberated in 1912 to 1913, is characterized by many common features as well as several differences. Generally speaking, the towns of Macedonia (Kastoria, Florina, Kozani, Edessa, Veria, and Serres) followed the path of the other towns of northern Greece. Kavala, which was, in effect, created at the end of the nineteenth century, and Thessaloniki were special cases.

The important changes and reforms made by the Ottoman administration and the influx of rural dwellers to the towns, as people sought security and financial opportunities, applied as much to Macedonia as to Epiros and Thessaly. The nineteenth century saw the triumph of urban ideas and, of course, important transformations in the structures and functions of urban centers. Concomitantly, existing towns expanded and new ones were created on sites where the growth of significant economic activity was predicted. The strong voices of Central Europe were not long in making themselves heard in the Ottoman Empire, even if only as a distant reverberation.

The creation of Kavala and Alexandroupolis is evidence of the new trends. Confined within the fortification walls of their castle, the Greeks of Kavala received permission in 1864 to venture outside and create the first settlement of their own next to the harbor. From the beginning of the nineteenth century, the harbor of Kavala had contributed to a modest business activity, which increased perceptibly within a few decades, when foreign commercial establishments began to build warehouses and offices there, transferring from Drama the administrative headquarters of their commercial activities. Up to then, as the birthplace of Mohamed Ali, the regent of Egypt, Kavala had enjoyed many advantages, and these had affected both the Turkish and the Greek populations, which were on as good terms with each other as could be expected (figs. 300, 301).

301. Kavala. Complex of tobacco warehouses in the town center. Large-scale functional buildings that are unique testimony to the flourishing production and export of tobacco in the nineteenth century.

After the creation of the new Christian neighborhood outside the walls of the Panayia area, there was an influx of Greek merchants seeking to settle in the town. The economic situation that developed led to the rapid evolution of the neighborhood into a strong harbor-town, the second largest in northern Greece after Thessaloniki. Foreign merchants and diplomats representing Britain, France, Italy, Austria, Russia, and, later, America and Egypt, transformed the town into a

European urban center, bringing to it the customs and way of life of their distant homes. Naturally enough, Western influences also extended to architecture (figs. 269, 299).

Just before 1900, *archontika* of all types could be seen on the seafront at Kavala: large stone houses with *sachnisia* on the upper stories, owned by rich Turkish merchants; two- and three-story *archontika* with elements borrowed from eclecticism, owned by foreign representatives and Greek businessmen. The most prevalent type, however, seems to have been the modern *archontiko* found in the Ottoman Empire, with curved pediments and strongly emphasized lintels above the windows coexisting with Neoclassical corbels, cornices, and pilasters. This is a type of mixed elements, though it is not without its own charm. Among these *archontika* are some in which the dominant feature is the pediment typical of central Macedonia, with its relatively steeply sloping sides and a base without a horizontal cornice. The large public buildings, boys' school, girls' school, and the first tobacco warehouses are much more austere. The major flowering of Kavala, however, when its characteristic architectural personality emerged, came at the end of the nineteenth century and the first two decades of the twentieth century.

Thessaloniki, the "mother of all Macedonia" from as early as pre-Christian times, is a case unique in the whole of Greece. Throughout the history of the Byzantine empire, it was the second city, the "co-capital." Although Thessaloniki went into decline, particularly under Ottoman occupation, it never ceased to be a Balkan metropolitan center, especially from the seventeenth century onward.

The pressure brought to bear by European consuls on the Ottoman administration at the beginning of the nineteenth century led to the reorganization of Thessaloniki so that it could play a new, upgraded role in international economic developments. The interventions carried out in the town plan, particularly in the second half of the century, transformed and embellished the city. These changes, of course, are directly associated with the enhanced economic role played by Thessaloniki in the surrounding area. The sea walls, which had been rendered obsolete by developments in warfare, were demolished, to be replaced by the quay and the avenue along the seafront parallel with it. Istira, an area of vital commercial importance, was redesigned, and new neighborhoods were created to the west and east of the settlement outside the walls. Thessaloniki was transformed into a European metropolis, and the life of its inhabitants followed suit: a new urban class emerged, living on Chamidie Avenue and in the neighborhoods of Pyrgoi and Exochoi (fig. 302).

Following the style of European boulevards, a series of identical buildings was erected on Chamidie Avenue, which began at the White Tower (the last remnant of the demolished Ottoman fortifications and a landmark of Thessaloniki) and ended in Sintrivaniou Square. These buildings, the property of the sultan, were let to foreign consuls and wealthy bourgeois tenants for high rents. The facades of these two-story, detached houses followed the morphology of a late, but nonetheless austere, Neoclassicism. Chamidie Avenue is perhaps the only example in Greece of the organized construction of high-quality urban houses. In contrast, the

302. Thessaloniki. Repeated facades of urban houses in the Chamidie quarter. This picture captures a high-quality urban ensemble that disappeared forever with the expansion of the city to the east of the White Tower. Postcard.

303. Thessaloniki. The Papapheion Orphanage. This large-scale architectural composition gives expression to declining European historicism (such as French eclecticism and classicism), conveying an authoritative, imposing aesthetic.

304. Thessaloniki. The entrance to the Papapheion Orphanage.

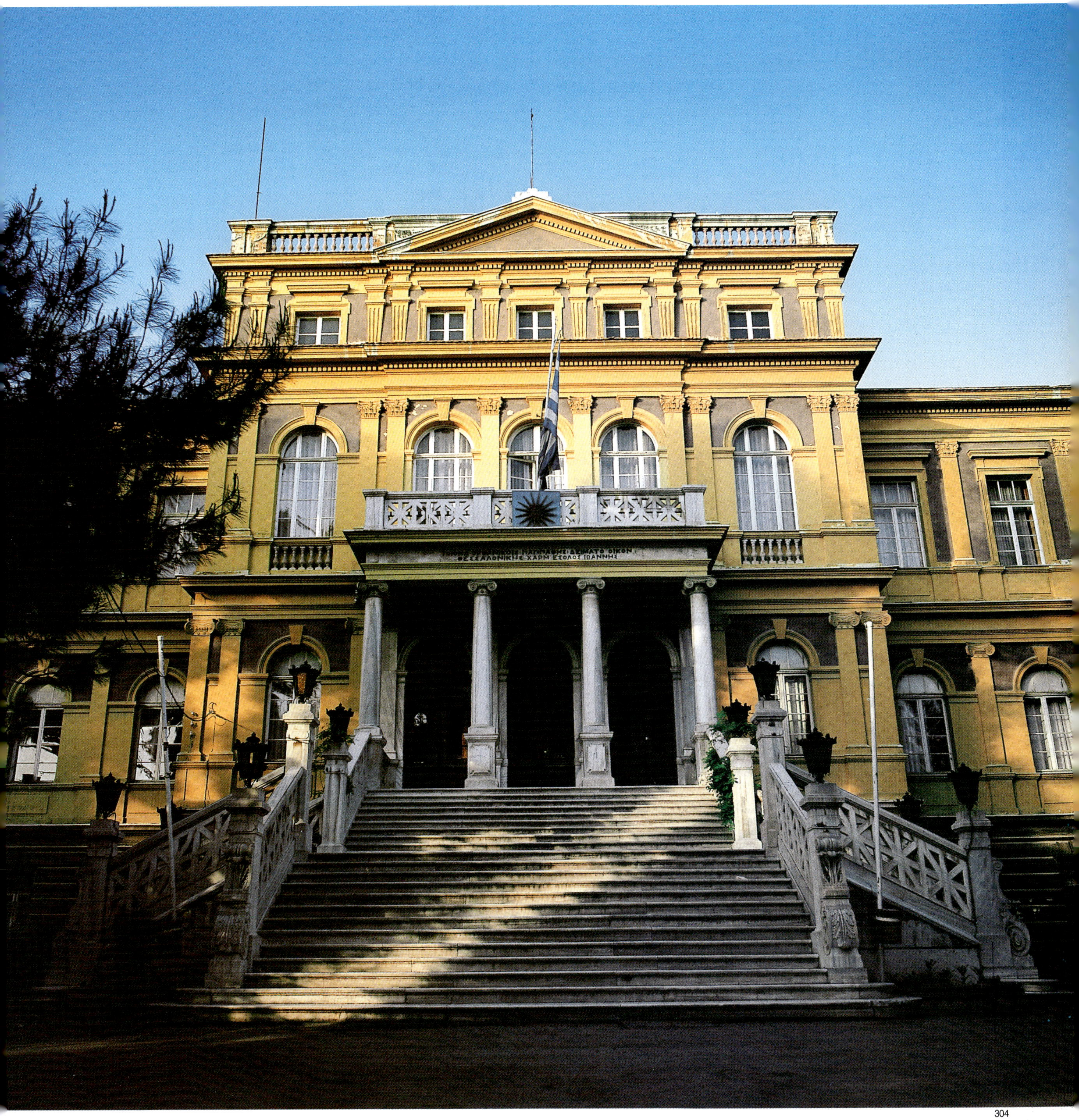

304

phenomenon is common in other European cities. It should be noted that this was not a Greek initiative, and that the houses on Chamidie Avenue were not intended for Greeks — or at least not exclusively for Greeks. Attempts to build pre-designed types of houses in newly created suburbs in other Greek towns, about 1900, were a complete failure, even though those houses were not completely identical with each other.

In a few cases, two or three similar houses occur one after the other in Thessaloniki. These are usually family complexes owned by two or three siblings that were built not by the owners themselves but by their parents. It is interesting to compare the buildings on Chamidie Avenue with those on Vasilissis Sophias Avenue in Athens, which were erected at about the same time. Here, as we have seen elsewhere, owners competed with one another to build the finest, the richest, the largest mansion. The result was an avenue lined with small and large high-quality edifices, each different from the rest, reflecting the personality not only of the architect but also of the owner, and all of them bound together in a unified aesthetic whole.

During this period, important public buildings were erected in Thessaloniki (figs. 269, 303–311). The Government House, the Imperial Lyceum, and the barracks gave new form to the city's image and became its new landmarks. They exhibit a striking morphological unity that combines eclecticism with Baroque elements. Their models can be found in Europe rather than Constantinople, where the familiar Baroque-influenced Turkish style was predominant, with its excessive use of pointed arches and an abundance of decorative elements. All three buildings

305. Thessaloniki. The remodeling of the central element of the University building in a Neoclassical style with characteristic pilasters, window frames, and pediment.

306. Thessaloniki. The Imperial High School, later the first building of Aristotle University, in its original form. Postcard.

Large-scale public buildings reflect the priority given by the Ottoman authorities to the creation of an infrastructure of buildings to serve the needs of the developed societies of the towns. Characteristic here is the remodeling of certain morphological elements of the previous period in the classicizing style imposed by the new progressive mentality after the city was united with Greece.

307. Thessaloniki. The Government House in a photograph (about 1900). Postcard.

308. Thessaloniki. The Government House in its present form, with the cornice converted into a pediment.

309. Thessaloniki. The Army General Headquarters in a photograph (about 1900). Postcard.

310. Thessaloniki. The Army General Headquarters today.

191

were by the Italian architect V. Poselli, who worked for several years in Constantinople before 1886, when he made his permanent home in Thessaloniki in order to construct a series of public buildings for the Turkish authorities. "The public buildings owed to Ottoman initiative," wrote G. F. Abbot in 1903 (Kolonas and Papamatthaiakis, 1980, p. 22) (figs. 312, 314).

Despite their eclectic character, these buildings are severe and plain; in fact, they closely reflect compositional principles of classicism, as became even more evident when, after liberation, the curved Baroque pediments were replaced by triangular classical ones. The objective of this was to "Hellenize" the buildings without detracting from or seriously conflicting with their morphology (see also figs. 307, 308).

In contrast with the public buildings, there are many examples of private structures—urban residences, villas, and country houses—that clearly exhibit influences of the school of Constantinople and other modern trends current in the rest of Europe. In such cases, the personal preferences, and undoubtedly also the social roots, of the owner played an important role (fig. 315).

At the end of the century, Thessaloniki numbered about 120,000 inhabitants. Ottoman Turks, Greeks, Jews, Bulgarians, West Europeans, merchants, and diplomats gave the town its unique color. Their residences reflect their different cultures, social status, and origins. Banks, commercial buildings, and workshops supplemented the picture of a European city that was brought to completion in the

311. Thessaloniki. The Civil Hospital in a photograph (about 1900). Postcard.

312. Serres. The Government House, its architectural morphology similar to that of the Civil Hospital of Thessaloniki (see fig. 311). Postcard.

313. Bursa. The Cadet School. Postcard.

314. Mytilini. The Turkish Idadiè School. Postcard.

first decades of the twentieth century. Pure Neoclassical architecture is found only rarely in Thessaloniki (fig. 316). One of the most characteristic surviving examples is the Greek Consulate on Proxenou Koromila Street, built by Ziller in 1890 and financed by Andreas Syngros (fig. 317).

The region of Thrace also has its own distinctive features. In modern times it was sorely tried both by raids by devotees of Bulgarian expansionism and by Young Turk zealots until, in 1919, its western portion was united with Greece. It may be noted that the Bulgarian occupation was among the harshest ever experienced by Greece. There was a merciless attempt to "Bulgarianize" the area, destroying every trace of its Greek identity. After offering strong resistance, the inhabitants of the flourishing Greek communities were obliged to emigrate. According to statistics available in the Patriarchate, it is estimated that in the year 1914 alone 115,000 refugees left Thrace and settled in free Greece. Despite this, the Greek population continued to form a majority in the towns, and a significant number of Greek merchants remained. In Xanthi and Komotini, Greek bankers and scholars overwhelmingly outnumbered their Turkish, Jewish, and Bulgarian counterparts (figs. 318–20).

The personality of the oldest important town in Thrace, Komotini (the "Koumoutzina" of Byzantine times), altered significantly over the centuries, as society was transformed by the mass settlement of Moslems from the East and the conversion of the Pomaks to Islam. Living conditions were very difficult for the

315. Thessaloniki. Expanse of buildings on the quay. The twin effects can be seen of European Belle Époque taste and influences from the East (late urban architecture of Constantinople). Postcard.

Christians. However, the gradual weakening of Ottoman might in the nineteenth century paved the way for new growth. In the last quarter of the century, the Greek community of Komotini had taken over virtually all the import trade, which was now carried on the railway. The great wealth thus amassed enabled Greek merchants to buy large estates (*chifliks*) and create the first industries: flour mills and, above all, tobacco-processing workshops. Urbanization here followed a path parallel with that of the tobacco-producing centers of Thessaly. Xanthi also developed at the same period. The first well-documented evidence for the social and economic life of the town dates from the middle of the nineteenth century and relates directly to the processing and trading of tobacco.

The majority of the large mansions of both towns were built in this period and followed the typology of Balkan architecture. Many of them belonged to Ottoman

316. Thessaloniki. House at 59 Egnatias Street, about 1900. Here, Greek style has been introduced to private architecture.

317. Thessaloniki. "National" classicism as represented in the Greek Consulate, by the architect Ernst Ziller.

Turks. Even today, a significant number of inhabitants form what is known as the Ottoman minority, which retains its own customs and practices. Several inns and tobacco warehouses were built at the same period, as were important educational institutions, financed by donations and bequests from members of the Greek community. Their architecture recalls that of Thessaloniki rather than of Athens. It is possible, moreover, that the same architects also worked here (figs. 321–26).

The new town of Dedeagach (modern Alexandroupolis) was created and expanded in the 1870s. Designed by the Austrian company owned by Baron Hirsch, which had undertaken to construct and run the Constantinople-Thessaloniki railway line, the port of Dedeagach was intended to serve the company's immediate needs. The town rapidly developed into the most important port of Thrace, gathering in the export trade of the region. The first buildings erected in the area of the port were the railway station, warehouses, a customs house, and residences for the administrative officials and workers. Afterward, the town expanded when Greek merchants and foreign diplomats settled there. During the Russo-Turkish war of 1876 to 1878, the area was occupied by the Russians, who extended the town plan "in the new European style, with straight, wide streets and avenues, and squares." New buildings were in the European style (Karadimou-Yerolymbou, 1997, p. 72).

Neoclassicism came late to Thrace, mainly in a number of public and educational buildings and, to a lesser extent, in urban residences, and it never became the dominant architectural ideology. Wherever it is found, it contains elements of eclecticism, Baroque-influenced Turkish forms, and Art Deco. It followed Greek models only rarely, because the style had begun to be abandoned not only in Europe but also in free Greece. The change is particularly apparent in Athens, which, in contrast with previous periods, was now in the vanguard and more open to new influences.

Thessaloniki was subject to similar influences. As we have already seen, it was transformed into a cosmopolitan city in which new trends were much more intense. Most of the architects who were designing during this period were graduates of the Constantinople School of Fine Arts, which usually followed in the steps of the French Beaux-Arts and other foreign polytechnic schools.

318. Komotini. House on Tsanakli Street. Its forms indicate the bourgeois sensibility, now at a more than local level.

319. Komotini. House on Tsanakli Street. The transition from the local tradition to classicism can be seen: the plain facade is organized symmetrically and divided horizontally; however, the *sachnisi* above the arched entrance continues to be an indispensable feature.

320. Komotini. Fully designed three-and-a-half-story urban mansion. The morphological subservience to a classical design overshadows the curved cornices above the windows.

321. Xanthi. Harmonious facade of a three-story mansion. Here, the "urban" morphology engages in a dialogue with the aesthetic tradition of Turkish Baroque.

322. Xanthi. Three-story mansion. Despite the "classical" character of the facade, the general picture does not efface the elements of a local aesthetic tradition.

323. Xanthi. Twin facades in a residential complex next to the Kouyioumtzoglou *archontiko*. Mannerist features executed in red brick are projected against the generally classicizing appearance of the facade, giving the whole a picturesque quality.

324. Xanthi. The old Garrison building. This large structure, whose imposing composition emphasizes tectonic elements of the facades, is executed in red brick.

325. Xanthi. Kouyioumtzoglou mansion. Westernizing forms and decoration are not completely disengaged from the traditional style of an Eastern cosmopolitanism.

326. Xanthi. Symbolic depiction of an eagle above the founder's inscription of a house.

The Islands

The conditions prevailing on each of the islands were unique, and their distinctive features are reflected in the local architecture.

The architecture of Samos seems to be closer to the models of the Greek mainland. From 1837, the island enjoyed independent status under Ottoman suzerainty, an unusual regime that resulted in the development of a form of social and political life different from that of the other Aegean islands. In the second half of the nineteenth century, the Samians founded small craft-industrial units producing wine, tobacco, cigarettes, and tanneries, leading directly to the growth of the economy of the island. This was followed by considerable building activity. The new urban residences that were erected largely followed Athenian Neoclassicism, though naturally with influences from the coast of Asia Minor (fig. 329).

Chios and Lesvos, unlike Samos, remained Ottoman possessions until the beginning of the twentieth century. Chios, in particular, was desolated after the massacre of 1822, in which some 20,000 Chiots lost their lives. Many inhabitants abandoned the island and settled on Syros, where they founded Ermoupolis, and elsewhere.

After the proclamation of Athens as the capital of the new state, a Chiot neighborhood was founded in Piraeus, where refugees from that island were highly active. During roughly the same period, some of them began to return to their native island, which began to recover its former way of life.

About the middle of the nineteenth century, there was a new attempt at economic and cultural reconstruction, but the earthquake of 1881 interrupted its progress for a time, compounding the effects of the 1822 massacre. Nothing remained of the eighteenth-century town, other than the general layout of the streets. The new town was swiftly built, its model being nearby Smyrna. Although Neoclassical influences can be seen both in the public buildings and urban houses of Chora and in the large urban houses of the plain, which were reconstructed on the ground floors of earlier buildings, the majority of these buildings were by no means pure types with clear morphological features. The bourgeois houses of Chios are more subdued and conservative than those of neighboring Mytilini, as we shall see directly. At the end of the nineteenth century, a new quay was added to the port of Chios, and developed into an area for strolling and social intercourse, complete with a new club and the Quay Theater (figs. 327, 328, 330, 331).

Lesvos was a different case. Before liberation, the island had three large towns, Mytilini, Mithymna, and Plomari (the headquarters of the corresponding *kazades*, or provinces), as well as eighty-six smaller townships and villages. Olives, the main product of the island, and its derivative products, oil and soap, formed the primary source of the island's wealth, along with fishing and other agricultural produce. The population, a mere 25,000 in 1830, was approaching 120,000 by the end of the 1870s.

The great majority of Lesvos's inhabitants were Greek, there being no more than 15,000 Ottoman Turks. After the reforms of the Tanzimat, and especially after the Hatti Humayun, which granted Greek subjects the right to own land, the rebuilding began of Mytilini and the entire island in general. The great earthquake of 1867, which nearly destroyed the town (1,500 of the 2,500 houses were demolished), left Greek properties virtually untouched. "A circumstance that

327. Chios. The Korais Library. Modification of the proportions of the building as a result of the annex dictated by the modern functional needs of the institution.

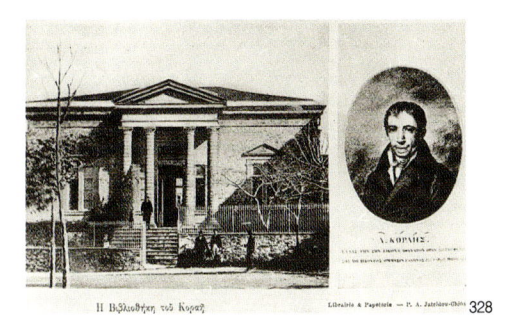

328. Chios. The Korais Library. The intellectual style of the Greek order directly references the building's purpose. Old photograph taken before the recent addition to the superstructure. Postcard.

329. Samos. The architectural ensemble on the quay, about 1900. Its monumental character and conservative aesthetic are in keeping with the island's social and cultural atmosphere. Postcard.

330. Chios. The High School. The excellently executed bare masonry enriches the harmony of the style by lending a charming picturesque quality to the expression. Unfortunately, recent plastering detracts from the building's authentic style. Postcard.

331. Chios. The High School. The modern aesthetic impression, created after the facades were covered with plaster.

made a lively impression on me," observed the French geologist M. Fouqué, who visited the island to collect data, "is that, while all the other circumstances were the same, the villages inhabited by Turks suffered incomparably more than those inhabited by Greeks; even in mixed villages, this same difference could be observed between the houses that belonged to the two peoples. This is due, I believe, to the fact that the houses of the Turks are old and poorly maintained, while those of the Christians are mainly newly built and repaired."

The earthquake was followed by a fresh wave of rebuilding. A few years later, in 1873, another European, the Austro-Hungarian vice-consul on the island, Dr. Bargigli, noted: "The Castle, Mytilini, with its new buildings, has become one of the finest provincial towns of second rank in the empire." The British traveler Mary Walker also refers to the beautiful villas of Mytilini (see Sherzeri, 1873). The town acquired a European form: large urban residences with shops on the ground floor, coffee houses on the seafront, and country houses in the suburbs. The influence of the new architecture extended to the smaller towns and even the villages (figs. 332–37).

Education was provided free on the island, and the schools were maintained by the communities and housed in structures built with donations from wealthy Greeks abroad or with financial contributions from the communities. In contrast with private architecture, the majority of these buildings followed Neoclassicism (figs. 340, 341). The same held true for many welfare institutions and public buildings. In the case of residences, however, references to the classical orders are less clear. Residential buildings exhibit elements of a neo-Renaissance style intermingled with Neoclassical features and the expansive expression of a restless Mannerism; they indiscriminately use affected decorative elements drawn from the corresponding Italian or French traditions, the main objective being the display of wealth and social status.

The interior decor of homes and mansions is particularly interesting, influenced variously by the vernacular tradition, the Baroque-influenced Turkish decoration of Constantinople and the coast of Asia Minor, and European tastes. Similar influences can be found in some of the exterior morphological elements, which were probably directly associated with the origins of the craftsmen. The characteristic Macedonian type of pediment often appears, for example, as do the rich,

332. Mytilini. Georgiadis villa (about 1885) built on the edge of the town. The building is effectively liberated from the Greek orders and integrated into the restless forms of French eclecticism.

333. Mytilini. Private residence (about 1890). Despite the late date of the building, it exhibits a distinctive form of classicism.

334. Mytilini. Private residence (now the property of the University of the Aegean). In the facade's harmonious composition, a sequence of orders is successfully used in the pilasters articulating the stories. An elegant Tuscan porch is on the ground floor.

335. Mytilini. Vournazos villa (end of the 1880s) at Vareia. The late classicizing composition has dynamically formed individual facades and rich decorative brickwork.

336. Mytilini. Vournazos villa. The elegant belvedere on the south side of the entrance facade.

337. Mytilini. Vournazos villa. Painted ceiling with an allegorical subject in a circular reception room on the ground floor.

curved forms and decorative elements of Constantinople. On the other hand, the intervention of an educated or an empirical architect is frequently apparent. A. Adalis unequivocally made his mark on the last decades of the nineteenth century. A native of Mytilini, Adalis rapidly established a network of contacts with prominent families and undertook the construction of many public and private buildings. Having studied in Athens and Bavaria, Adalis may have proposed very austere morphological expressions, closer to Athenian Neoclassicism, but the owners' models, like their way of life, were much nearer to those of Constantinople and Thessaloniki. Thus, the end product rarely displays extreme severity or austerity.

In an interesting twist, an unusual capital is incorporated into the Neoclassical style, frequently replacing the Ionic or Corinthian capital (figs. 338, 339). Probably carved after the Ionic model of the temple at Phigaleia, sometimes in marble and sometimes in stone, it is a unique phenomenon in the Greek Neoclassical tradition. The houses of the lower classes were simpler, and the marble features were replaced by wooden ones, but they still showed a tendency toward ostentation. This characteristic distinguished the morphological solutions found in Mytilini from the milder forms encountered elsewhere — for example, on Chios, Samos, Rhodes, and Kalymnos.

We have left the case of Crete till last, because it differs significantly from the other regions. Crete was not included by the London Protocol of 1830 in the newly founded Greek state, despite its long struggles against the Ottoman Turks. On the contrary, one year later it was presented by the sultan to Mohamed Ali, the regent of Egypt, in return for his assistance during the 1831 uprising on the island. Crete remained an Egyptian possession until 1841, when it reverted to the Ottomans. A number of important changes took place during the period of Egyptian rule, including the disarming of both the Christian and the Moslem populations. Equality was also restored between the two communities in the freedom to manage their property and the payment of taxes.

These measures led to a gradual movement of Ottoman Turks into the urban centers and the corresponding settlement of Greeks in the countryside. Although there were more than three times as many Christians as Ottoman Turks in the population of the island as a whole, the Christian population of the three large towns, Chania, Heraklion, and Rethymnon, was less than a quarter of the total. Clearly, the few Greeks in the towns were not in a position to influence building activity there. As the Greek consul in Chania, N. Sakopoulos, wrote in 1867: "It is true that large sums are spent each year on the erection of buildings, but these are the sultan's palaces or other buildings of use only to the ruling race, such as mosques, Ottoman schools, barracks, shipyards, etc., and apart from other public welfare buildings for non-Moslems, no concern has been shown" (Tsivis, 1993) (figs. 342, 343).

Generally speaking, the morphology of buildings on Crete followed that of the Ottoman public buildings erected throughout the Empire. Some reflect the influence of local architecture or the reuse of elements taken from earlier structures; Neoclassical features appear only toward the end of the period.

Through the Halepa Pact of November 1878, which followed the European Conference in June of the same year, the sultan ceded significant privileges to the Greek population, along with a degree of political independence, which, though limited, was certainly more than symbolic. Several wealthy Cretan émigrés returned to the island. The ratio of Ottomans to Christians in the towns began gradually to change and was eventually reversed. The life of the town dwellers was

338. Mytilini. Ionic impost block of expressive form in the church of Ayios Therapon. This type, with its stylized elements, is often found in the settlements of Lesvos.

339. Mytilini. The distinctive campanile of the church of Ayios Therapon (designed by A. Adalis, about 1900), with Mannerist elements typical of the period in the provinces.

significantly influenced by the European way of life enjoyed by the Christian Phanariot pashas of Crete, Europeans, people of Near Eastern origins who lived permanently on the island, foreign consuls, and, above all, by Cretan émigrés who settled there.

Changes are also evident in the architecture of the first houses built during this period, which have features clearly influenced by Western architecture. It may be an exaggeration to call the architectural style Neoclassicism; nevertheless, certain designs involving the classical orders and academic approaches appear in the architecture of the towns, mainly on buildings erected outside of the old urban environment. In Chania, examples include the houses of the Markantonakis family, Baron Schwartz, Themistoklis Mitsotakis, and Valerios Kaloutsis.

Chania was the only Cretan town in which the mansions' renewed, purely urban style compared favorably with the formal variety and picturesque quality of the Venetian past. In the modern town's straight streets, flanked by greenery and trees, a number of Neoclassical detached houses are still preserved, among them those of Phoumis, Karavelakis-Agazades, and Koundouros. Despite their late morphology, these are not characterized by decorative excess or stylistic aspiration

340

pursued in the interests of superficial ostentation and self-promotion (as on Mytilini, for example). Chania society was distinguished by a mature urban culture and a fairly conservative mentality, which has to some extent been preserved to the present day (figs. 344–46).

In Heraklion, in contrast, after the devastating earthquake of 1856 and particularly after the massacre and the torching of the town at the hands of the Ottoman Turks on August 25, 1898, the balanced development of private architecture was lost. Moreover, the restless local society of entrepreneurs was not at all amenable to a fertile assimilation of the classicizing aesthetic. In Heraklion, therefore, mainly eclectic forms, whether classicizing or not, are found—and in only a few examples, thanks to heedless modern building activity. Despite the introduction of tranquil classical lines into the forms, the earliest preserved buildings retain interesting stylistic links with the Venetian and Ottoman past (figs. 347, 348).

The forms used in educational institutions usually reflect classical models. This strong urge to promote "Greekness" was characteristic of the urban societies in the unredeemed provinces.

340. Eresos, Lesvos. The Theophrasteios School. Its harmonious composition incorporates an Ionic propylon with a reception porch at the main entrance.

341. Ayia Paraskevi, Lesvos. The wings of this imposing school complex extend over the green gardens.

This strong blend of tradition and Italianate elements has a very cohesive presence, with a notable projection of Renaissance morphology, particularly in the neighboring town of Rethymnon. To a greater extent in this town than in the old harbor of Chania or in Heraklion, one finds urban houses with skillfully rendered decoration of the classically ordered window frames and outer doors. Carved in local sandstone, this type of decoration is a feature of anonymous architecture down to about 1900. In contrast, public architecture displays a tendency toward its own "academic" rules of design, which are far removed from the lively amalgams of the styles of the past. Their creators were the Greek and foreign engineers who staffed the public works departments; they carried out studies for and erected private structures, mainly houses, in the time not devoted to their obligations to the municipalities. Most were civil engineers rather than architects, as is readily apparent in the quality of the facades.

At the end of 1898, Prince George, the second-born son of King George I, was appointed High Commissioner of the Great Powers in Crete and took up residence on the island, thereby starting the process of unification with Greece. Just before

342. Rethymnon. The silhouette of a towering Turkish minaret dominates an alleyway on Crete.

343. Heraklion. Kazantzaki Street. Rationalization of traditional architecture in the late Turkish period.

the arrival of Prince George on the island, however, there was a massacre in Heraklion and Chania, and substantial portions of the Greek neighborhoods were burned down. The situation in Rethymnon was rather different: after an ill-fated uprising in 1889, the Halepa Pact had been revoked. The Ottoman population continued to exceed the Greek, even at the beginning of the twentieth century.

After ten years of the protectorate, Crete was united with Greece in 1909, and the urban centers were remodeled. In many new buildings, the principles and morphological elements of Neoclassicism can easily be recognized: axes of symmetry; organization of spaces; and ordered articulation of the facades, pediments, pilasters, corbels, cornices, and statues. Outside the Ottoman centers, Crete was less affected. Neoclassicism on the island resembles that found in Old Greece. Many of the engineers who worked on Crete graduated from the Greek National Technical University, though there were also, of course, graduates of foreign architecture schools, and some foreign engineers. A few elements of Renaissance and Mannerist decoration found in some buildings probably should be attributed to the local learned architectural tradition.

344. Chania. Mitsotakis house in the Chalepa district. Clear cubic form emphasized by the three axes of the windows and the central balcony, which is supported on slender Ionic columns.

345. Chania. Karavelakis-Agazades house. Conservative modeling of the facade with a distyle reception porch, a typical feature of the luxury single residences in the town.

346. Chania. Phoumis house. The morphology of the two-story facade is in accord with the late trends of Athenian classicism.

It should not be forgotten, of course, that during the years of the long Venetian occupation (1204–1669 A.D.), the Cretan towns were designed according to the principles of Venetian town planning and architecture—fortified within their city walls, they boasted an organized street grid, large squares, and grandiose public and private buildings. Some of the buildings, such as the Government House in Chania (which also served as the residence of the rector) were demolished by the Ottoman Turks to make room for new buildings. Most of them, however, remained intact to modern times, only to be destroyed in 1941 by the bombs of German planes during the battle of Crete, and thereafter by Greeks themselves in the name of an ill-conceived "development." (Fortunately, the structures that have survived are now listed by the state as historical monuments.) The architecture of Crete differs significantly from that of other towns we have examined in Thessaly, Thrace, Epiros, and Macedonia (figs. 349, 350). It is only in Chora on Chios and Mytilini that a number of interesting elements can be identified. By the period

347. Heraklion. Public building on Evans Street, from the final period of Ottoman occupation. The building's forms point to the trend toward Europeanization.

under examination, however, both these towns had deteriorated so badly under the effects of natural disasters and human intervention (earthquakes, fires, and other calamaties) that elements of the Genoese period were barely visible and no longer exerted a decisive influence on their architecture.

To sum up, Neoclassicism was introduced to the unredeemed territories in the final decades of the nineteenth century and spread during the early twentieth century, at a time when it had already begun to decline throughout Europe and even the large urban centers of Old Greece, where architects were turning to new styles. The reasons are purely ideological: the Greeks of the unredeemed territories embraced Neoclassicism with a passion equal to that shown by the citizens of the new Greek state from 1828 onward. It was the style that linked them with their glorious past, with ancient Greece. It was the architecture that confirmed their Greek identity: except that now the models were not the ancient monuments, nor the works of the great European masters (though these did not

348. Heraklion. Two-story mansion on the seafront. Late classicism is mixed with Mannerist elements. Successive niches are flanked by columns and crowned by a curved pediment.

349. Chania. The dense settlement with its public and religious buildings in the old harbor. Engraving of 1867.

350. Heraklion. The old High School. Venetian, Ottoman, and eclectic influences, assimilated toward the end of the nineteenth century into a unified architectural expression, coexist with (very rare) classicism. Postcard.

cease to be the finest examples of design, whatever objections may be raised to some of them).

Instead, the models were specific contemporary buildings in modern Greece, though they were not always noteworthy and frequently included modern (rather Mannerist) elements. As we have seen several times in this chapter, the forms in question were those of the Neoclassicism that made its appearance in the capital of the Ottoman Empire, Constantinople, where it was enriched by elements drawn from the East and from Baroque-influenced Turkish forms. Finally, the eclecticism that had begun to conquer the Western world not only strengthened these trends but acted as a catalyst for them.

Mass Classicism

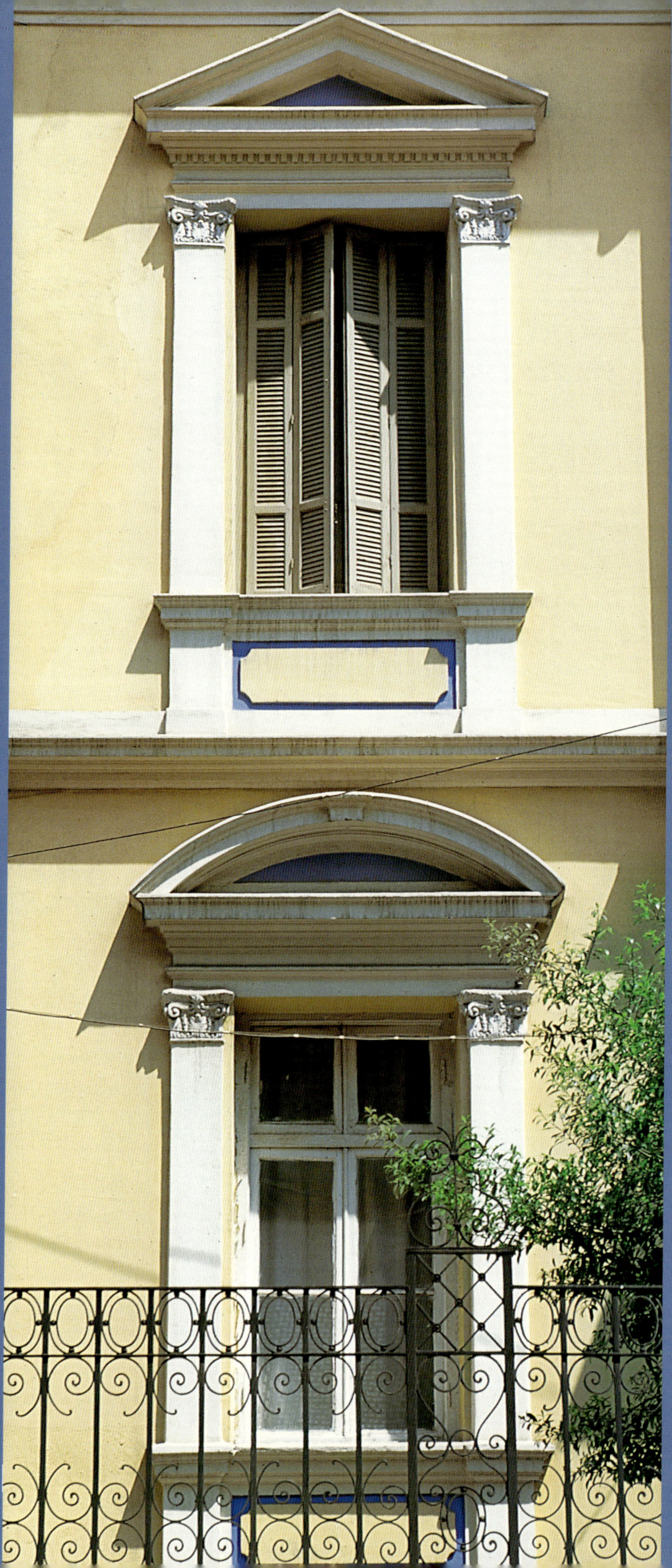

MASS CLASSICISM

The Late-Nineteenth-Century Aesthetic

Three factors in the history of the modern Greek state from 1870 to about 1910 shaped the fundamental features of the productive and cultural structures of its society. The first was the annexation of Thessaly and an—albeit small—part of Epiros to Greece in 1881, under Prime Minister Koumoundouros. This was an event of very great importance because it strengthened the credibility and self-confidence of the Greeks. It was the second major foreign policy success under King George I, the first being the unification of the Ionian islands with Greece in 1864 (fig. 352).

The second factor was the implementation of a substantial policy of state modernization under the government of Charilaos Trikoupis from 1874 onward, especially in the decade from 1885 to 1895. It involved a large number of infrastructure projects in the towns and countryside, which were realized by attracting foreign capital—and which also led to the orientation of production to a capitalist economy. More specifically, a number of short-term economic measures were implemented (foreign loans to support bank capital, the inflow of money from Greeks of the diaspora, and the attendant activation of the commercial, entrepreneurial market, as well as usury). These measures gave an impulse to a transient private prosperity and flowering of the urban centers, but adversely affected the small landholders and small farmers of the countryside. The new commercial system drove a large part of the weaker agricultural classes to the towns, where the population quickly burgeoned. This economic and political crisis intensified during the 1890s, was exacerbated by the defeat suffered in 1897 in the Greco-Turkish War in Thessaly, and led ultimately to the dominance of conservative political groups until the uprising of 1900.

The third important factor in the new order in late-nineteenth-century Greece was the relative uniformity and independence of flourishing bourgeois society's cultural behavior. We have already commented on the changes in structures and sensibilities that occurred during the first period of King George I's reign. The expansion of the national territory, developments in production, strengthening of the urban centers, and, finally, pervasive ideological fermentation, which was focused exclusively on the realization of national visions (subjugated regions in northern Greece, bloody revolutions in Crete, and others), all helped form a picture with distinctive features.

Unredeemed Hellenism developed culturally during this period. Its position was strong: it retained its influence undiminished in the flourishing commercial towns of the Ottoman Empire, to a lesser extent in the Danubian provinces, and much more so in the southern Balkans, Asia Minor, and Egypt. At the same time, it developed, on the one hand, a competitive response to foreign entrepreneurial interests and, on the other, strong links with various European cities. This led not only to economic prosperity but also to a distinctive Greek-centered culture with a strong sense of community. Greek benefactors were very active in public welfare institutions, educational institutions, orphanages, and hospitals; more significantly, however, there was increased cultural penetration of this wider region, not only by Constantinople but also by Athens herself (fig. 351). From the flourishing capital came clubs and associations that supported education and promoted social and moral institutions that strengthened the intellectual and national development of Greeks under Ottoman rule.

This idiosyncratic cultural entity, which comprised free Greece on the one hand and the unredeemed territories on the other, makes it genuinely difficult— especially regarding the late nineteenth century—to draw conclusions about the

351. Kavala. Influences of Athenian classicism. Part of a facade enriched by elements of the ancient orders: at the bottom, a window crowned by a curved pediment; at the top, a window with a triangular pediment.

352. The realization of the dream and the unfulfilled visions.

aesthetic ideologies and responses of the new bourgeoisie. However, as far as classicizing architecture is concerned, the Athenian model steadily gained ground and was promoted in urban centers in the rest of Greece as an ingredient of the urban population's cultural as well as political maturity. There is no doubt that Athenian classicism in both public and private buildings exerted a restraining (and possibly also aggressive) influence on the political chimera of the Great Idea, which associated the progress of Hellenism with the recapture of Constantinople as its capital.

The Athens of the Trikoupis period undoubtedly had overcome its inferiority complex with regard to the much-debated theory of the "second capital." This was exemplified by its urban planning and architecture: Athens represented a sovereign example of expressive architecture set within an unrivaled historical landscape—an image of homogeneous aesthetic behavior, in which classically ordered composition and "classical" spirituality won mass acceptance and played a distinctive unifying role. This role allowed explorations of "naturalistic" architectural experiments during the late period of Neoclassicism, though without lapsing into the ostentatious devices of eclecticism and a barren mannerism, which occurred in the urban centers of unredeemed Greece. In short, the architecture of Athenian urban buildings had consolidated an independent, self-contained basis and had, in effect, liberated itself from the vacillating tendencies of late European historicism. Most importantly, private, not public, architecture was prominent in mass expression—that is, at the creative level of the lower social classes (figs. 353–56).

On the other hand, private buildings naturally borrowed the morphological features associated with their official appearance from certain outstanding buildings which, through their quality, signaled this turn by mature Athenian architecture to a fertile expressive field (figs. 357–59).

The Academy building by Theophil Hansen (figs. 219–23), discussed at length earlier, stands at crossroads of this development. Although the Academy dates to the Othonian period, its dynamic morphology was indisputably ahead of its time. While the structure's distinctive quality utilized the authentic system of the ancient Greek orders, its composition as a whole expressed a renewed, "rhetorical" approach to the aesthetic assimilation of individual features of these orders.

The Work of Ernst Ziller

The next step involved diverging stylistically from the classical models and, consequently, the clear transcending of morphology by the given stylistic canon. Although the influence of French architects from about 1870 to 1880, mainly on private buildings (the Evgenidis, Vouros, and Skouloudis residences, and others; see figs. 255, 256), should not be underestimated, the lead in this was undoubtedly taken by Ernst Ziller and his multifaceted creative activity, which covered virtually the entire building spectrum of his period. Through his extensive professional work, Ernst-Maurice Ziller (1837–1923), who was from Silesia in Germany, rendered the most aesthetically homogeneous and stylistically faithful version of late modern Greek bourgeois architecture in the last quarter of the nineteenth and first years of the twentieth centuries.

Ziller took up residence in Athens in 1861 and lived there until his death. At the same time as he supervised Theophil Hansen's Academy, he also devoted himself to archaeological excavations—especially in the Theater of Dionysos, the Panathenaic Stadium (fig. 360), the Parthenon, and other sites. Thanks to these ex-

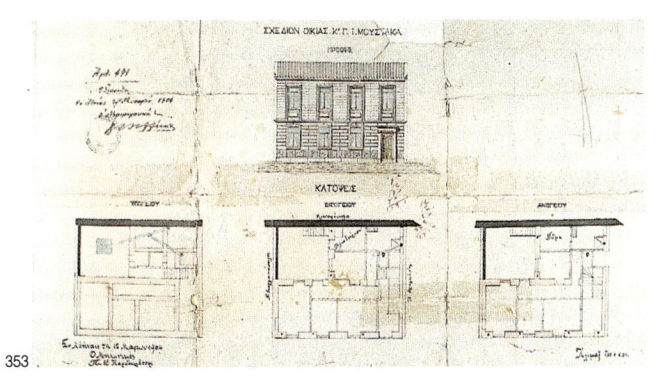

353, 354. Athens. Building permits for urban residences in the first decade of the twentieth century.

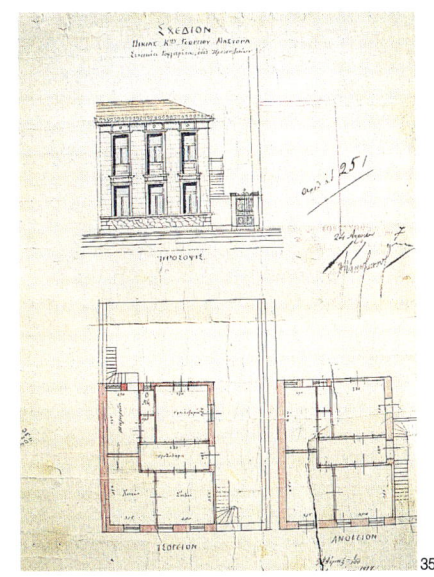

355. Lefkada. Single residence. Original, expressive arrangement of the volumes.

356. Lavrio. Single residence. Monumental ostentation with a successful application of the ancient orders on the facade.

357. Athens. 24 Nikis Street, first floor. Advanced plastic composition adorns the top of the building, which presumably alludes to the ancient repertoire.

358. Athens. 24 Nikis Street, ground floor. Richly decorated window frames, using forms and material derived from late classicism.

359. Athens. House of John F. Smith (next to the Alexandros Vourlis house) at the corner of Voukourestiou and A. Soutsou Streets (now demolished).

359

360. Athens. The Panathenaic Stadium. Reconstruction drawing by E. Ziller (1869). The excavation of the monument had just begun at that time. (Source: KTNA.)

361. Zakynthos. The Municipal Theater (now destroyed). The facade is articulated with classical and Renaissance elements. By E. Ziller. Postcard.

362. Zakynthos. Drawing of the Municipal Theater. By E. Ziller.

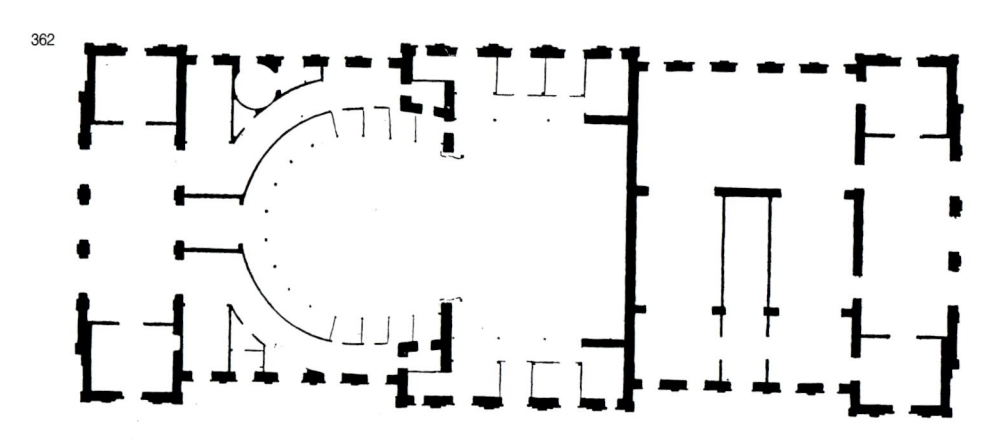

cavations, he acquired a firmly grounded knowledge of the detailed application of the models of the classical orders. Ziller also espoused and assimilated the aesthetic approach of his master, Hansen, which had been cultivated in the spirit of the so-called Greek Renaissance. As the great Viennese architect explained, this was a fertile development of the classicizing school of Schinkel, enriched by refined features drawn from the revival of Roman architecture in the Italian Renaissance. With this background, Ziller was a conscientious devotee of the Viennese direction taken by late Greco-Roman historicism, which he personally transformed into a more functional formal vocabulary, submissive to the scale, harmony, and sculptural values of the classical Greek models. Moreover, his excellent handling of design and style enabled him to combine the Athenian morphological tradition with the most distinctive aesthetic trends of late-nineteenth-century European architecture to produce an organic unity. His contribution, though regarded by some as marking the decline of Athenian classicism, in fact represented the creative maturing of an already flourishing aesthetic phenomenon, which, in the end, escaped the stage of degeneration and repeated stylization. Ziller employed eclecticism only rarely, when he had to deal with buildings with special functions, such as churches, country villas, and the like.

Ziller's compositional style was revealed fully developed in his first works, the Zakynthos Theater (1871) and the Patras Theater (1871–72) (figs. 361–63). In both, he employed two-story arcaded facades of Renaissance style. The aesthetic result was heavier in the case of Zakynthos, however, where the architect made use only of pillars and flat pilasters to organize the facades. In Patras, the composition acquired harmony and elegance from the slender Ionic columns that supported the arcades. From the point of view of proportions and the flawless application of the orders, however, Ziller's most characteristic response to urban architecture came a few years later in the Basil Melas mansion in Athens (1874) and the major composition of the Town Hall of Ermoupolis on Syros (1876) (see photograph p. 233, fig. 387).

The Melas mansion, in particular (fig. 364), which stands on Dimarcheiou Square and now houses offices of the neighboring Bank of Greece, is a simplified, smaller-scale version of the corresponding wealthy commercial building complexes in Vienna, such as the Heinrichhof apartment building (1861–65), built by Theophil Hansen. The Melas mansion displays the following characteristic features: the tower-like elements at the corners of the building, the use of rusticated blocks (in fact made of plaster) in the lower zones and at the corners, the classically ordered window frames, the archways on the ground floor, the door frame accentuated by columns at the main entrance, the emphasis on the *piano nobile* (the main story) achieved by large balconies, the pseudo-caryatids at the doors of the outer balcony, and, finally, the balustrade with decorative flowerpots at the top of the building.

All these Italian ingredients gave the building a distinctive metropolitan character that accommodated the changed aesthetic demands of the Greek grand bourgeoisie of the period.

Ziller's morphological perception was a dynamic factor in the attainment of a new aesthetic expression. The power of this factor emerged most forcefully in what was undoubtedly the architect's masterpiece: the residence of Heinrich Schliemann, the Iliou Melathron (1879) on Panepistimiou Street (figs. 367, 368). The compositional clarity with which the internal rooms and the facades are designed and the exemplary application of the sculptural and painted decoration elevate this

363. Patras. The Municipal Theater. Highly expressive example of the architect's approach to composition. By E. Ziller.

364. Athens. The Melas mansion on Dimarcheiou Square. This monumental example of private architecture shows the clear influence of late-nineteenth-century Viennese classicism. By E. Ziller.

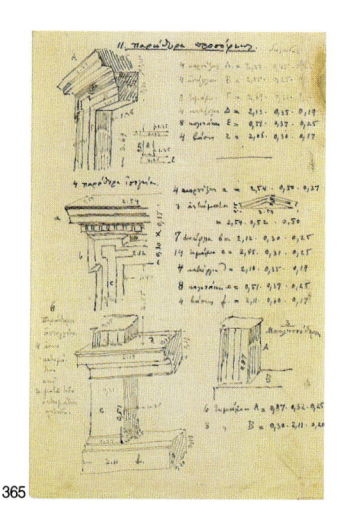

building to the highest level of quality on a European scale. Here, again, we find the central motif of the two-story arched loggia with marble Ionic columns. The side sections of the main facade, moreover, have arched and rectangular windows and marble balconies, pairs of Ionic (bottom) and Corinthian (top) pilasters, a cornice, and, above the cornice, a balustrade and statues. The horizontal components of the composition (a base with several courses of rusticated blocks, string courses between the stories, arcades, main cornice, and balustrade) are skillfully balanced with the vertical axes (vertically aligned windows, and pilasters, bases, and statues) in a perfectly harmonious whole. Inside this little palace, the walls were painted by the Slovenian artist Yuri Subic about 1880 with superb scenes based mainly on the Third Style of Pompeian painting. In sum, the architectural and artistic virtues of the building create a perfectly harmonious and balanced morphology that reveals Ziller's talent, Subic's skill, and, of course, the genius and personality of the great investigator of Aegean prehistory, Heinrich Schliemann.

The rather fulsome image of this building, diverging as it did from classicism, elicited a number of isolated, but perfectly understandable, objections from some Athenians. Future developments, however, were on the side of Ziller, who, over the following years, built a vast number of private and public edifices and churches in various parts of Greece. In addition to the Stathatos mansion (see fig. 211), which we have already encountered, he created other, similar buildings toward the end of the century, among them the residences of Deliyiorgis (Akadimias and Kanaris Streets), Kasdonis (Philellinon Street), Voglis (Ermou Street), Koupas (Panepistimiou and Voukourestiou Streets), and Varvaressos, Patsiadis, Metaxas (in Piraeus), as well as the two hotels owned by the benefactor Bangas on Omonoia Square, at the beginning of Athinas Street. Over the entire spectrum of his public and private architectural output, Ziller was able effortlessly to apply his morphological systems and deftly incorporate them into each individual case — in a manner that might be regarded as a kind of rationalist design. (figs. 365, 366, 369, 370).

The public buildings designed by Ziller that perhaps best illustrate the architect's development with regard to his stylistic choices are two that had the same function: the Municipal Theater (fig. 373) and the Royal (now National) Theater (fig. 371), work on which began in 1873 and 1895 respectively. The Olympia Theater by Stavros Christidis adopted a different approach (fig. 372). The Municipal Theater, opposite Town Hall, was one of the finest theater complexes in Europe. Its demolition in 1939 signaled the beginning of a biblical destruction of Neoclassical buildings in the capital that lasted for at least three decades. Ziller gave the structure its final form after a number of experiments with the design, during which building work was suspended. Finally, after Andreas Syngros had undertaken the project's financing, some time after 1887, Ziller settled on a composition distinguished by the clarity of its spaces, the conservative use of decorative elements, and an imposing tranquility, which emphasized the building's bourgeois character. The harmonious blending of independent features assigned the building, despite its late date, to the classicizing approach. By contrast, the considerably later Royal Theater on Ayiou Konstantinou Street, with its succession of juxtaposed projecting Corinthian columns on the facade that draw out the entablature above them into a series of dentilations, and with the distinctly sculptured quality of the pedestals on the stylobate and the multiple frames of the windows, indicates a divergence from the classical style, despite its derivation from a Roman model. It was created in the same way that a sculptor chisels his forms from the uniform mass of his material, revealing his artistic aim with the immediacy

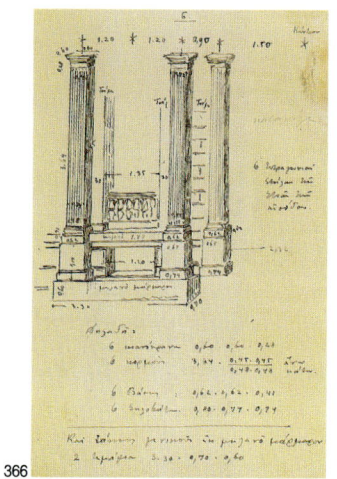

365, 366. Athens. Sketch by E. Ziller of structural details for the facade and entrance staircase of the palace of the crown prince on Irodou Attikou Street (now the Presidential Palace). (Source: Kunstakademie, Copenhagen.)

367. Athens. Iliou Melathron. Part of the facade on Panepistimiou Street. The building's dense, strongly modeled composition incorporates elements of the ancient orders, resulting in a masterpiece of design aimed at the unity of the monumental style. By E. Ziller.

368. Athens. Iliou Melathron. Painted decoration in the large dining room, by Yuri Subic. Elegant figures in a Pompeian style hover against the blue background. (At the bottom can be seen display cases of the Numismatic Museum, which now occupies the building.) By E. Ziller.

369. Piraeus. The Patsiadis house on the quay at Zea. Felicitous development of the volumes of the building on the curving line of the street. The rows of arches on the ground floor and upper story offer an unimpeded view over the Saronic Gulf from the rooms behind them. The ground floor was designed from the beginning for commercial exploitation. By E. Ziller.

370. Piraeus. The Patsiadis house and the neighboring urban building, in the style characteristic of the early twentieth century.

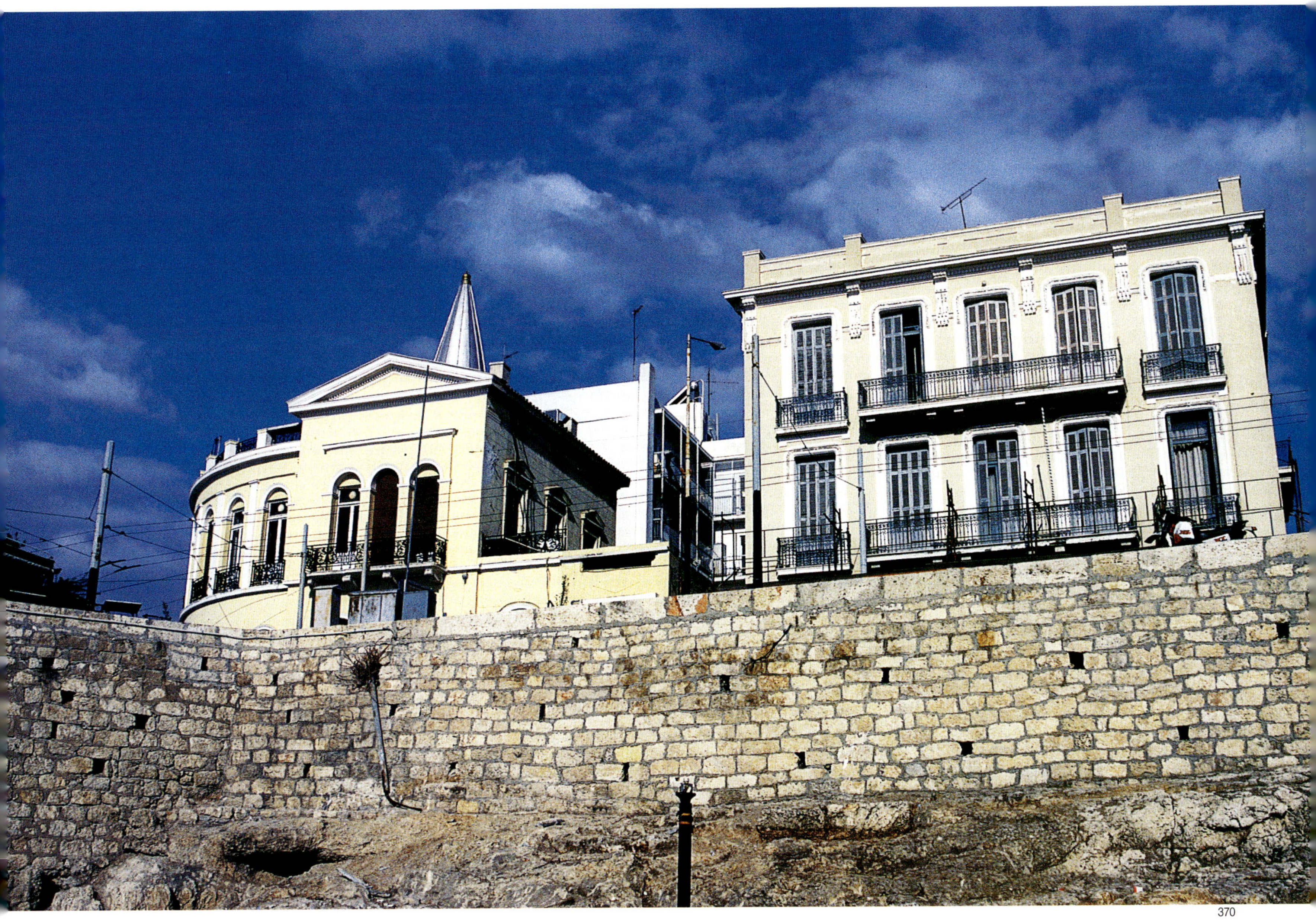

370

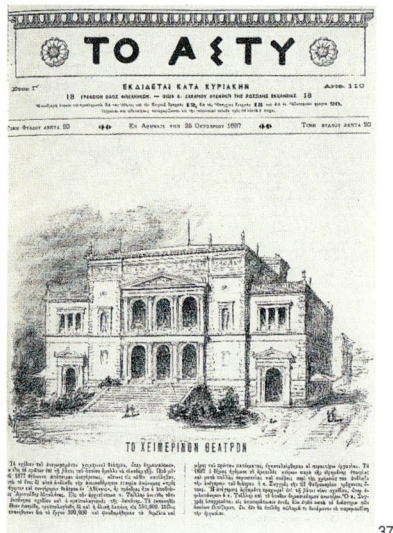

371. Athens. Royal Theater on Ayiou Konstantinou Street. The model for its functional design was the Royal Theater in Copenhagen. Here, the facade is articulated by a dense row of Corinthian columns that stand on the "pedestal" formed by the ground floor and support an indented entablature based on Hadrian's library. By E. Ziller.

372. Athens. The Olympia Theater, by the architect Stavros Christidis, about 1910. Late application of classicism with rather unorthodox proportions between the elements of the orders, and with a "stage-design" approach. The greatest figures in Greek melodrama performed in this theater. The site is now occupied by a new opera building. (Source: KTNA, P. Mylonas Archive.)

373. Athens. The Municipal Theater on Dimarcheiou Square. Full-page illustration in the newspaper *To Asty* (October 25, 1887). Although of moderate scale, it was one of the most notable buildings of its kind, of a European quality.

It was inaugurated with operettas performed by French companies. It staged both plays and operas until 1916, when the first opera house, the Olympia, was built on Akadimias Street. The Municipal Theater was demolished in 1939.

of the modeler. The form of the building does not derive, as do those of earlier buildings, from a telling assembly of classical elements that determine the symbolic value of architecture. Rather, it emerges as a work of art whose aim is to transmit directly its aesthetic and functional qualities.

This fundamental shift also became clear in the morphological choices made by Ziller in his ecclesiastical architecture. In this, he did not completely espouse either the Greco-Roman or the Byzantine style, except in a few cases, such as Ayios Georgios on Lykavittos Hill and Ayios Athanasios at Pyrgos (classicizing perception in the former, Greek-Byzantine references in the latter), built in 1885 and 1891 respectively, and also in the earlier church of Vello (1880), in which the bonds between the forms and Byzantine morphology were even stronger.

In his other churches, however, such as that of the Chatzikonstas Orphanage (1900) and Ayia Triada on Piraeus Street; Ayios Loukas on Patision Street, Athens; the Phaneromeni in Aigion (1890); the church of Villia, Attica (1893); and others, Ziller deliberately entered the realm of historical orders to embrace the morphological idiom of his mentor, Theophil Hansen (design-proposal for the Athens Cathedral). He combined Byzantine, Romanesque, Renaissance, Italo-Lombard, and even Arab elements in a single aesthetic system and further enriched his forms with pointed turrets and a variety of decorative brickwork motifs that mark the culmination of his design skill (fig. 375).

At this point a pressing question arises: did the product of Ziller's ecclesiastical architecture, Greek classicism, and the endeavor to revive a Greek-Byzantine style become no more than marginal trends as a result of the neo-Romantic and eclectic spirit of the German master's aesthetic aspirations? The answer is no. In precisely the same way, the accomplished classicizing aspirations of L. Kaftantzoglou that are manifest in the churches of Ayia Irini and Ayios Konstantinos, and the harmonious Byzantine-revival design of the Chrysospiliotissa by D. Zezos, remained simply interesting experiments that did not lead to substantial changes (fig. 374). Church building in Greece continued, for the most part, to repeat the conventional perception embodied by the Athens Cathedral. Precisely because it failed to provide a convincing answer to the problem, the form of this building expressed an incompetence and conservatism that perhaps reflected the unsteady course of religious ideology characteristic of Greek society (see fig. 147).

Irrespective of the innate contradictions and the attendant morphological impasses that indeed distinguished ecclesiastical architecture, in late-nineteenth-century Greece, all other kinds of urban buildings, both private and public, had turned decisively toward the new aesthetic expression. Private architecture, of course, was more receptive to transitional stylistic changes and particularly to the tendency to broaden the stylistic spectrum, following Ziller's example. From about 1880 onward, this tendency became apparent in the large and small urban centers of Greece, especially in Central Greece and the Peloponnese, though also on some of the islands. The same is true to an even greater extent in the capital's neighbor, Piraeus, where, despite the emphasis on classical expression, it can be found in the earlier public buildings of this town, such as the High School on Korai Square and other, similar school buildings erected between about 1860 to 1870,

374. Athens. View of the dome of the church of the Chrysospiliotissa on Aiolou Street. The Byzantine-revival architecture, though rather stylized, is not inferior to the spiritual style of the models of the Greek Christian tradition. By D. Zezos and E. Ziller.

375. Athens. The church of Ayios Loukas on Patision Street. View from the southeast. The building expresses the architect's emancipation from the established styles, though it nonetheless renders a unified aesthetic approach. By E. Ziller.

the Tzanneion Hospital, the elegant Stock Exchange Building that served as the Town Hall (with the well-known Clock Tower, now demolished), and, of course, the monumental Municipal Theater built by Ioannis Lazarimos, architect to the Piraeus Municipality and professor at the Athens National Technical University. When work began on this last building in 1884, it was at least ten or twelve years later than the corresponding buildings on Zakynthos and at Patras, and roughly contemporary with the Municipal Theater in Athens, all projects by Ziller. Yet it represented to the letter the unsullied classical tradition, clearly influenced by the German morphological school. I. Lazarimos was similarly successful in the church of Ayios Nikolaos in Piraeus, which was roughly contemporary with the theater. Despite the rather academic coldness of its appearance, this building has the virtues of good proportions and harmonious forms, and of a very fine interior decoration, both painted and carved in the technique of nineteenth-century marble (figs. 379, 380).

376. Piraeus. Architecture of private urban houses on the main street, Vasileos Georgiou Protou Street. The rather plain building at the right exemplifies the modest morphology of the mid-nineteenth century. The larger structure at the left, with the strongly modeled elements, is clearly later.

377. Piraeus. Two-and-a-half-story residence on Bouboulinas Street in the town center. Mature execution of an urban building with an excellent application of classical elements on the facade. Different colors (ocher and white) show off the tectonic elements, particularly those associated with the ancient orders.

378. Piraeus. Single residence on Kountouriotou Street. Richly (perhaps excessively) articulated facade, with pilasters of two different sizes: large ones establishing the order on the upper story, smaller ones for the openings.

However, the most characteristic features of the architecture of Piraeus at this period were its lively modeling of forms and its monumental scale, found even in private buildings and especially in detached residences. These features derived in part from the progressive temperament of settlers from the islands, who, despite their disparate origins, strove to promote their new urban culture. More so than in Athens, this type of promotion affected all aspects of Piraeus society and was particularly evident in the form of urban buildings (figs. 376–78, 381).

The same idiom appears, though with greater emphasis, in Ermoupolis on Syros, which had similar social and cultural parameters to Piraeus. The port of the capital city, however, enjoyed the advantage of a dynamic Municipal Authority, with which fine engineers collaborated, either directly or indirectly: men such as G. Metaxas, G. Petimezas, I. Lazarimos, G. Zizilas, A. Theophilas, and others. The public buildings include the imposing Chatzikyriakeion Orphanage, the Tzanneion Hospital, the eclectic Post Office building, the picturesque facilities of the

379. Piraeus. Municipal Theater. The tranquil, rather conservative appearance of the facade is emphasized by the elegant Corinthian porch of the main entrance at the center. Its monumental scale makes the building the finest surviving nineteenth-century theater building in Greece. By I. Lazarimos.

380. Piraeus. The Town Hall on the quay with the Market building on the left in the background. The freestanding Neoclassical mansion (known as the Clock Tower), with its original composition of volumes, was the most popular meeting place for the people of Piraeus. It originally served as a stock exchange, and was demolished about 1970. Postcard.

381. Piraeus. The flourishing aspect of private architecture in the town center about 1900. The style is enriched by expressive modeled forms, niches containing statues, balustrades, and other embellishments. The ground floor was given over to commercial uses, usually some form of recreation.

382. Piraeus. The Chatzikyriakeion Girls' Orphanage, shown in an old photograph taken while it was still functioning. Plain rows of arched windows in a Renaissance style on the upper story are characteristic of the general rationalist style of the historic benevolent foundation.

383. Neo Phaliro. The Grand Hotel owned by the Railway Company, built to attract visitors to the new bathing facilities. Postcard.

384. Neo Phaliro. The Aktaion Hotel dominating the coast at Phaliro. Its architecture strongly displays features of late historicism, a style that was flourishing in Vienna at the time. Postcard.

Municipal Bathhouse at Phreattyda, and the cosmopolitan recreation center at Zea and Neo Phaliro, which was embellished at the beginning of the following century by the Aktaion Hotel, a building of metropolitan luster built by P. Karathanasopoulos (figs. 382–84). All these buildings seduced the forms adopted by the residences and villas into a similar wealth of expression, to be seen in the coastal mansions of Pheraldis, Koumoundouros, Meletopoulos, Vernikos, Skouloudis, and others. In this fin de siècle aesthetic atmosphere, however, Ziller exercised a catalytic influence on Piraeus. Not only did he build fine detached residences characteristic of his perception, among them those of Metaxas, Patsiadis, Varvaressos, and others, but he also created, on the slopes of Kastella, an entire neighborhood of country houses in picturesque style, with dressed walls and restless three-dimensional forms.

The rhetorical aesthetic of Ziller's works was completely in keeping with the cultural trends and upper-class ambitions of modern Greek businessmen; it is not surprising, therefore, that the energetic German architect was invited by the people of Ermoupolis to create their Town Hall building. Its foundations were laid in 1876, and it remains to this day the most magnificent example of its kind (fig. 387). Dominating the beautiful town, it takes visitors by surprise as they see it from the harbor. However, the emphatic monumental aspect of the building should not lead us to an erroneous estimation of the islanders' aesthetic sensitivity. For this, possibly the most impressive Neoclassical town in Greece, was not so much complacent, but had considerable depth in the ingredients of its urban culture. From these ingredients emerged the notable social and intellectual life of the town, that had earlier been expressed through the Italian-style Palladian "Club" building and the Apollo Theater, both by the architect P. Sampo (beginning of the 1860s) (figs. 385, 386).

Down to the last third of the nineteenth century, indeed, the architecture of the houses of Ermoupolis combined the grace and delicacy of the Italian school in their interior decoration with the sensitivity of line and the noble monumentality of Greek classicism in the exterior forms—a unique blend of aesthetic values that has been preserved intact to the present day, carved in gray marble (fig. 388). The facades—frequently joined—are articulate details based on the classical orders, such as window frames and strongly emphasized luxurious entrance doors, lintels, pilasters, undulating cornices, and, occasionally, large pediments. The marble balconies, with their elaborate corbels (whose types may reflect chronological phases), reveal a transition from, in their earliest forms, the Corfiot approach to, at a late phase, the classical Athenian school (figs. 389, 390). Most important of all, the mansion's luxurious interiors, such as those of Velissaropoulos, Kois, Negrepontis, Vapheiadakis, and many others, reveal an unprecedented repertoire of forms and colors in the decoration of ceilings in the reception rooms and common areas (figs. 391–94). In drawing on the (mainly) Italian artistic tradition and the carving skills of the island craftsmen (the stone carvers of Andros and especially the sculptors of Tinos), Ermoupolis developed a visual aspect that distinguished it from other towns, like Nafplion, Corfu, Patras, and even Athens. The Kambielo neighborhood on the coast of Corfu may be compared with the district of Vaporia in Ermoupolis, but, for obvious reasons, the latter projects a more distinctively Greek air, with the white pediments of its houses gazing out over the deep blue Aegean.

After the unification of the Ionian islands with Greece in 1864, the town of Corfu exhibited typical forms of Greek classicism and eclecticism that were

385. Ermoupolis. The Apollo Theater. Facade with a highly conservative rendering of Italian stylistic features. The central element, articulated by large pilasters, reflects the Palladian school. By P. Sampo.

386. Ermoupolis. The auditorium of the Apollo Theater with its decorated ceiling. Original arrangement of the painted motifs. The large rosettes contain depictions of famous European composers.

387. Ermoupolis. Town Hall. Of surprising scale and morphological quality, this imposing edifice, built by Ziller, is inextricably linked with the town's then-flourishing society.

388. Ermoupolis. View of the impressive architectural environment in which the nineteenth-century town's image is crystallized.

389. Ermoupolis. Balcony in an urban residence. The quadrant at either side is characteristic and is also found in the Ionian islands. The geometric rendering of a lyre on the railing was common in the earliest phase of classicism.

390. Ermoupolis. Part of a residence facade. The windows, with their plain frames, and the balcony, with the elaborate railing, stand out against the dressed isodomic masonry of the wall.

distinct from the local morphology, which was based on Venetian and British models. Examples of Greek classicism and eclecticism form a minority, however, and have a fairly discreet presence; most represent the influence of Athenian examples, and they have little effect on the coherent local character of this fine urban complex of the Ionian islands.

It should be noted, moreover, that Western classicism, that is, the classicism that passed through the strong filter of the Italian Renaissance, influenced other towns in Old Greece, and not only in the early period. Despite the steadily increasing dissemination of late Athenian morphological models to the major centers of the Peloponnese (Aigion, Patras, Tripolis, Nafplion, Kalamata, Sparti, and others) and Central Greece (Mesolongi, Nafpaktos, Amphissa, Itea, and even the picturesque Galaxidi) (figs. 395–98), these towns continued, in varying degrees, to project their own individual personalities. It would be a mistake to identify these differences based solely on the morphology of their architecture; we must also take into account other factors that influence the urban landscape, whether directly or indirectly. Patras, Aigion, and even Pyrgos share an architectural approach, because they belong to the same geographic area. Differences can be distinguished, however, among each town's urban-planning scales and regulations; in each case, unique local variations derive from the creative spirit and cultural identity of the individual urban populations.

In contrast with Patras, Pyrgos, for example, although it can boast some notable Neoclassical houses and the monumental market in the commercial quarter, has an urban image that projects an indeterminacy and introspection more appropriate to societies that have endeavored to open up to a Western cultural style only recently. It would be no exaggeration to identify a more conservative atmosphere, even in the large town of Tripolis itself. Here we find the style of a capital city, with private mansions; squares and parks; the church of Ayios Vasilios, built entirely of dressed stone, with its imposing, soaring campaniles; and an interesting blend of Neoclassical units (like those on Ethnomartyron Street), though in these it is not easy to define a predominant morphological character. A transitional spirit can be detected in the urban structure—a relatively slow turn to the new cultural conditions (fig. 399).

Conservative rural-commercial society rather diffidently opened up to urban models. This society was making economic progress and broadening its cultural horizons, but it continued to be conditioned by the centripetal forces of locality. This was especially true of the Greek towns that were not on the sea, and therefore did not enjoy the active, modernizing force of a busy port. In the case of Pyrgos, at least, there is a clear connection between the harbor at Katakolo and the significant change in the circumstances of its urbanization. The port was not merely a guarantee of the carrying trade: in the nineteenth century, it contributed to industrialization and, through agencies, to the organized disposal of goods in other ports—in short, to the acquisition of prosperity and cosmopolitanism.

During the last quarter of the nineteenth and in the early twentieth centuries, Patras had the privilege of experiencing—perhaps more than any other town—the force of progress, based on the parameters mentioned above. Despite retaining certain features of Italian origin, to which reference has already been made, its urban image rapidly turned to a more homogeneous style, with elements borrowed from late Athenian classicism. The residential complexes around the impressive Vasileos Georgiou Protou Square, for example, and those along the straight arteries, such as Korinthou, Kalavryton, Ayiou Nikolaou, and Mezonos, were

391. Ermoupolis. Painted decoration on the formal staircase of the Velissaropoulos residence. On the wall in the background is an impressive illusionist rendering of an imaginary landscape inspired by ancient Greece.

392. Ermoupolis. View of a sitting room in an upper-class residence. It reflects the atmosphere of luxury and warmth typical of the daily life of the town's bourgeoisie.

393. Ermoupolis. Painted ceiling in the Velissaropoulos residence. An allegorical subject is flanked by decorative motifs drawn from late classicism.

394. Syros. Chrousa. Painted ceiling in the Vapheiadakis villa. Stylistically, it indicates a clear departure from Neoclassicism in the direction of the fluid forms of Rococo. Within the oval frame, an Attic village woman wearing traditional costume is depicted in a naïve realistic style (see also fig. 507).

395. Pyrgos. The Municipal Market building. Large-scale edifice with a monumental style. In its general lines, it reflects the "school" of Ziller, the architect to whom it is usually attributed.

396. Aigion. The Market building, by E. Ziller. The relatively small structure, with its expressive morphology and asymmetrical features, displays a romantic intent characteristic of the compositional preferences of its creator.

397. Pyrgos. The porch of the Municipal Market, with a typical composition of arches supported on elegant Ionic columns.

398. Pyrgos. The Town Hall mansion. Its richly decorated facades display an expression close to Palladian models: clear organization with pilasters; alternating arches and pediments above the windows; and a strong crowning element for the building as a whole, with garlands, a parapet, and a row of terracotta statues. Postcard.

399. Tripolis. Church of Ayios Vasileios. The imposing domed basilica, erected in the late nineteenth century, combines two important creative elements: the outstanding design of the monument, both overall and in detail, and the masterful execution of the dressed stonework by local craftsmen.

400. Patras. Painted decoration of a ground-floor ceiling in the building shown in fig. 401. Typical classicizing motif, revealing an academic approach; flawlessly executed.

401. Patras. Monumental composition in a two-story urban building. The robust architecture of the upper story is balanced with the open portico on the ground floor, which is supported on slender Ionic columns.

comparable in all respects with their counterparts in Athens. Indeed, at that time, architects were summoned to the capital of Achaia from Athens—among them Ernst Ziller, the creator of the town theater, whose influence on some of the private houses is undisputed (figs. 400–4).

Patras, of course, also benefited from a large-scale town plan that offered a number of fine prospects for the construction of Neoclassical buildings in its squares and streets. The modern expansion of Kalamata gave similar prominence (though on a smaller scale) to the complexes along the straight lines of Aristomenous, Pharon, and other streets and around Ypapandi Square and Street. The rapid industrialization of the town during the end of the nineteenth century promoted the expansion of the settlement in the direction of the sea and the harbor, where its prosperous society built detached residences, some of them in the restless style of eclecticism or even modernism (*Jugenstil*). In nearby Sparti, however, a fairly conservative version of classicism developed. This phenomenon was possibly a result of the town's historical past; it was also associated with the initially classicizing structure of the town plan, and, finally, with the mentality of the society itself, which was typical of the conservative tradition and the rural-commercial urban population (figs. 405–8).

Indeed, the fact that the society of some towns encompassed a fully formed collective consciousness, a distinguished historical past, as explicitly attested in the case of Sparti, Mesolongi, Nafplion, and, of course, Athens, needs to be taken into account as a substantial factor in both the selection of and the adherence to the classical architectural idiom. Local history was not identical, of course, for all towns, and in several places in Central Greece and Thessaly, and also in the Cyclades, local vernacular architecture was very strong and the connection with the glorious historical tradition, therefore, was rather tenuous. Nevertheless, the urban centers of Central Greece and some of the Cyclades, which belonged to the free territories from as early as 1832, had assimilated the classicizing tradition as part of a historical process, and they were more advanced in this than other towns to the north, which were incorporated into the nation state at a later date (figs. 409–11).

402. Patras. The National Bank of Greece, next to the Municipal Theater. The harmonious composition of the symmetrical two-story facade presents the tranquil expanse of the arcade on the ground floor and the felicitous disposition of the niches containing statues in the zone with the upper-story windows.

403, 404. Patras. Late eclectic style in the urban architecture of the capital of Achaia. A pronounced decorative character is distinguished by the quality of the design's execution.

403

404

405. Kalamata. The Zoumboulis mansion. In an expressive treatment, elements of the facades are modeled according to Mannerism. The arches above the openings are semicircular on the ground floor and segmental on the upper story. Beneath the cornice is a frieze, interrupted by the unusual corbels of the little room on the roof.

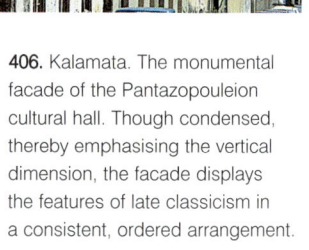

406. Kalamata. The monumental facade of the Pantazopouleion cultural hall. Though condensed, thereby emphasising the vertical dimension, the facade displays the features of late classicism in a consistent, ordered arrangement.

407. Sparti. View of Menelaou Street. Gentle forms, human scale, and balanced urban style contribute to an ensemble that still retains the features characteristic of the period of its creation.

408. Tripolis. The Town Hall. With its uncluttered application of the ancient orders, this building expresses the conservative character of the Athenian school in its symmetrically organized elements.

409. Paros. Expressive rendering of mature urban architecture in a two-story house of the island settlement. It tends toward a monumental style, though without shunning the picturesque quality of the building as a whole.

410. Patmos. Monumental classicizing composition of a door frame, styled after Italian models.

411. Andros. Urban villa with the elements of the facade organized according to the dictates of classicism. Its aesthetic style reflects the cultural ingredients of island society in the nineteenth and early twentieth centuries.

Decentralized Classicism

The modern Greek state's formation was nearly complete by the first decades of the twentieth century. Only the Dodecanese remained under foreign rule—a situation that would persist until mid-century.

Unification was neither easy nor automatic. Time and energy were required by both the local population and state diplomats. However, despite the difficulties that naturally arose from the doubling of the country's area and population, and from the differences and local features of the various regions, the annexation of the New Territories and the resolution of the related social and economic problems proceeded smoothly. Unification with Greece awoke ideals similar to those that had emerged in Old Greece during the early years after liberation. Neoclassicism spread everywhere (though selectively, as we shall see below) as the style that symbolized unity, roots, and ancient Greece. Hopes that the country would expand to include Constantinople and Smyrna had been extinguished. Athens was now the undisputed national center and its aesthetic radiated outward (figs. 412–14).

The architecture of new urban formations was clearly influenced by that of the capital. Since the final years before unification, classicism had penetrated the territories ruled by the Ottoman Turks, as we have seen. The Thessalian towns (Larisa, Volos, Karditsa, and Trikala) and Arta in Epiros (the only town of the province that was to be annexed to Greece by the Treaty of Berlin) gradually adopted the same form as other urban centers of Central Greece (figs. 415–19). Remote from Constantinople and closer to Old Greece, they were naturally influenced by the latter. They were transformed from small Ottoman towns into urban European-style centers. Alongside the wealthy mansions and urban houses there now appeared commercial establishments such as banks and hotels. An important role in the formation of these towns was played by open spaces (parks and squares) and, of course, by public buildings: government offices, courthouses, museums, hospitals, railway stations, and educational institutions.

On the other hand, some towns, under the indirect influence of historical and national criteria, exhibited a local and certainly earlier trend toward urbanization that followed a more "natural" course. In other words, a society with a high level of culture and a cohesive upper class is more likely to embrace urban

412. Lamia. View of the large square with the main hotel. Newly built houses line the hill on which the castle stands. This expressive picture captures the urban style assumed by the town after its liberation. Postcard.

413. Lamia. View of the main square. In the left foreground is the official hotel, its ground floor given over, in typical fashion, to coffee houses and restaurants. In the background, two-story houses display the distinctly conservative classicizing aesthetic of Old Greece. Postcard.

414. Volos. Characteristic view of a town about 1900, at the height of its social prosperity and cultural growth. The Bank of Athens building (by P. Karathanasopoulos, now demolished) displays the eclectic approach predominant in the architecture of New Greece. Postcard.

415. Larisa. Two-story house on the new lines of the town plan, with the essential greenery on the side facing the street. The elements of the facade are symmetrically arranged, with a spare application of established morphological models.

416. Lamia. Upper story in a building in the new town center (R. Pheraiou Street). The architecture of the town after liberation was directly influenced by the capital, with buildings constructed in the style of Athenian classicism.

417. Agrinion. Papastratos complex, in which the residence (at the right) is formulated in a more Mannerist style, with Renaissance and other elements, revealing a transitional approach.

418. Arta. The Michalis house on the main square. The gentle expanse of the facade is densely set with windows, and the dressed facing of the ground-floor zone displays strong morphological features (note the alternating white and dark blocks of stone in the arched lintels above the doorways).

419. Mesolongi. The Razikotsikas apartment building. Its scale is impressive for a provincial building, and its style follows the morphological directions of late Athenian classicism.

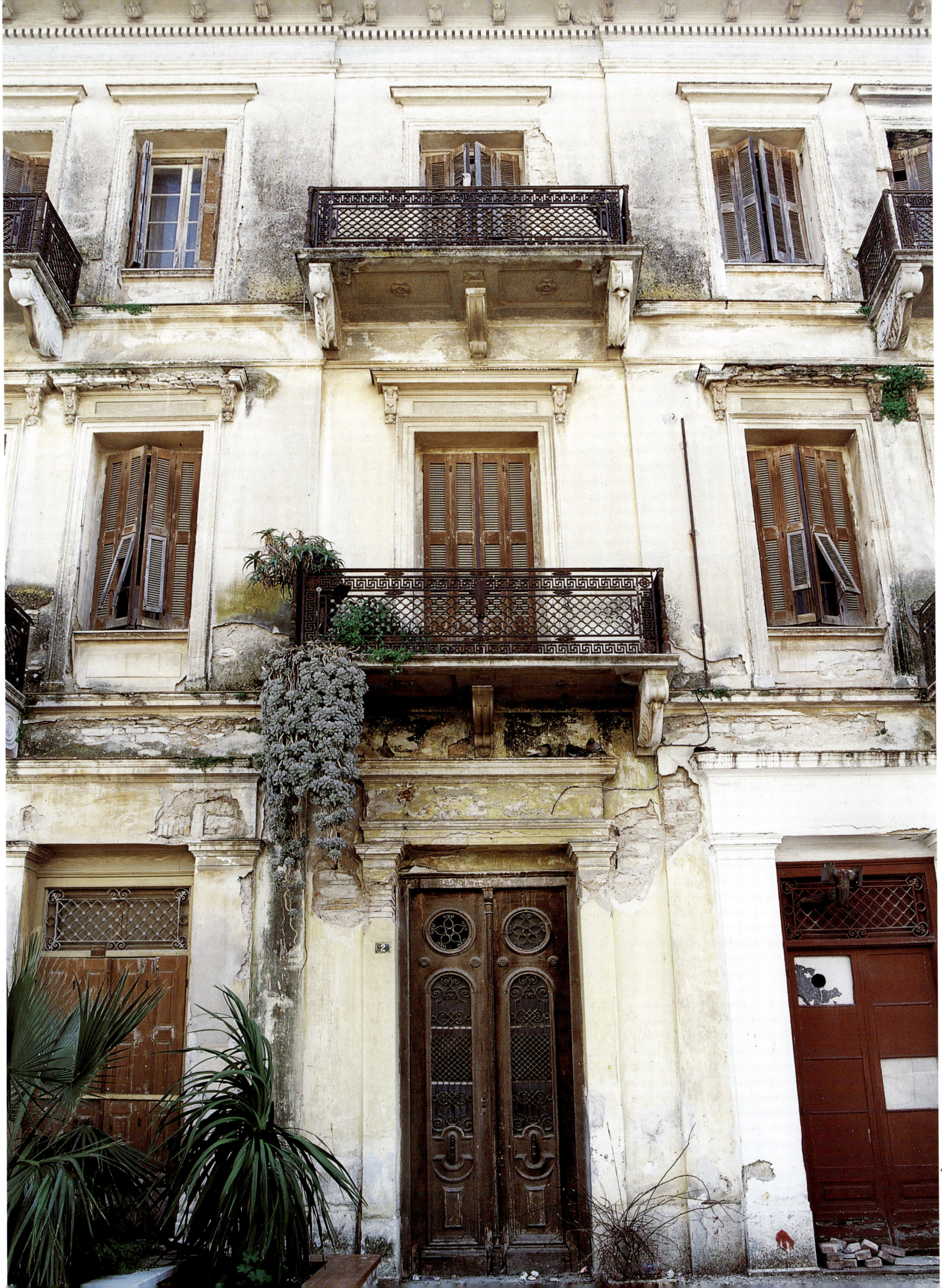

420. Heraklion. Monumental design of a mansion on the corner of Eikostis Pemptis Avgoustou and Epimenidou Streets. Despite its generally classicizing style, the restless design of the volumes and the morphological richness of the facades express the pluralist aesthetic approach predominant in the town about 1920.

classicism. This was the case in Chania about 1900. It is the phenomenon described earlier, which is also associated with the historical connections between Crete and the West. Here the eclectic approach to the given forms was evident, though it cannot be detected quite as easily in neighboring Rethymnon, where the classical idiom seems to spring from its Venetian roots and tends to exhibit the "natural" changes the style underwent in later years. And on many of the central Aegean islands, change occurred only when the Athenian models were disseminated unmodified in all directions. Until this particular phase, nothing more than a type of local classicism can be found anywhere in Greece (figs. 420–22).

The case of the Dodecanese is characteristic in this respect: the impressive growth of mercantile activities and reciprocal business and cultural relations with towns in Asia Minor contributed to the flowering of a distinctive form of urban classicism. This occurred to a lesser extent on Rhodes, much more so on Kalymnos and Symi, and with impressive uniformity on Kastelorizo.

421. Chania. Municipal Market, entrance facade. Inaugurated in 1913, this monumental structure displays a felicitous wealth of morphological elements appropriate to its function.

422. Chania. N. Bistolakis house. The Ionic porch at the entrance is a feature characteristic of urban mansions of Crete's upper-class inhabitants.

The mass expression of classicism should not, therefore, be ascribed only to the influence of Athenian typology; rather, it indicates the full diffusion of the classical idiom, about 1900, to a large number of settlements in Greece and—most importantly—to its spontaneous adoption by the whole of society in each place. Interpreting this process of adoption in association with local morphological idioms leads us inevitably into a labyrinth of individual case studies. Reference has already been made, in general terms, to the phenomenon's initial essential components, with respect to design and ideology: to questions relating to the national and urban consciousness, to the commitment to the historical models of current taste, and so on (figs. 423–29).

However, the phenomenon does not always arise from such complex parameters. Particularly toward the end of the nineteenth century and in the early twentieth century, the law of supply and demand affected the stylistic choices made by various local social groups. Any local demand for urban architecture could be met by offering, in place of classicism, either modified stylistic models that sprang from potentially eclectic schools (such as the School of Fine Arts in

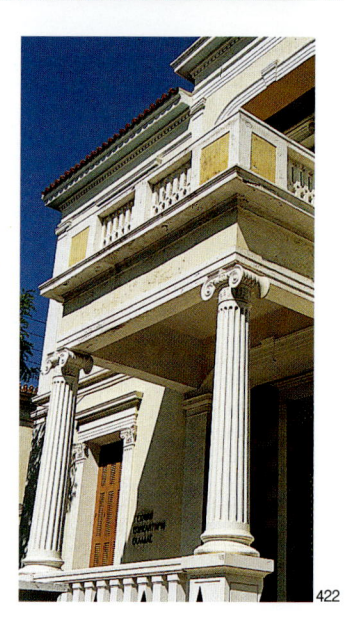

423. Rhodes. Venetoklis villa. Built by the master craftsman Theocharis, the well-designed appearance of its luxurious architecture reflects the cosmopolitan sensibility of its Egyptian owners.

424. Rhodes. Interior of the Kakavas country residence. A richly decorated reception room by Theocharis indicates the prosperity of the home's industrialist owners.

425. Karpathos. Item of furniture with a mirror in the A. Theologos house. This kind of furniture was imported to the island mainly from Smyrna.

426. Chios. An urban house. Its heterogeneous morphological elements convey a rather restless, romantic character—in contrast with the ordered, harmonious outline of the facade. Unfortunately, part of the ground floor is marred by a modern intervention.

427. Chios. Kalvokoresis mansion. Within the facade's tranquil lines, elements of local origin appear, especially in the dressed zone of the ground floor and the monumental, Italian-influenced courtyard gate..

249

428. Symi. View of the settlement showing the imposing beauty of a succession of classical elements. This presumably reflects the collective aesthetic demands of the local society of the day. The forms are implemented in an empirical manner and echo the urban architecture of Smyrna and other centers in the surrounding area.

429. Karpathos. General view. The character of the settlement expresses the bourgeois sensibility of its inhabitants, whose economic interests had brought them into contact with the developed centers of the eastern Mediterranean.

429

430. Komotini. House in Tsanakli Street. Typical example of the urban expression of private architecture. The facade, however, includes a distinctive local feature: the large recess on the ground floor creates a kind of open vestibule, which was no doubt advantageous given the area's climate.

431. Kavala. The Conservatory. This building was originally a private mansion, after which it was converted into a bank. The imposing classical pediment, with its decorated tympanum, establishes the building's architectural style and aesthetically dominates the two-story facade's (morphologically late) composition.

432. Thessaloniki. Themelis-Michailidis mansion, on Vasilissis Olgas Street. This building from the late period of classicism exhibits a conservative use of forms drawn from different styles, such as the central cartouche above the first-floor veranda.

433. Thessaloniki. The old Melissa Orphanage, on Vasilissis Olgas Street. Formerly the residence of Osman Ali Bey (late nineteenth century). Its imposing appearance incorporates heterogeneous elements more appropriate to the aesthetic approach of Beaux-Arts.

434. Xanthi. Projection in the upper story of a house on Ayiou Vlasiou Street. Although the decoration of the facade follows the approach of mass classicism, the bay window supported on corbels reflects Eastern influences, from Constantinople or Smyrna.

Constantinople) or, as in the case of the classicism of Symi, self-contained examples. Differences between towns, of course, are related to a specific community's receptivity and the historical conditions under which it formed. This accounts, for example, for the obvious differences between the forms of urban architecture found in Samos, Chios, and Mytilini. This is even more evident among the towns of Old Greece and the corresponding centers of the Greek territories that remained under foreign occupation until 1912.

In fact, Macedonia and Thrace, which were annexed to the main body of the Greek state in the twentieth century, projected their own personalities through the morphological idioms of their urban buildings. They are fairly surprising to conservatives, who believe that there is an inevitable connection between form and idea. After the liberation of these towns from Ottoman rule and their unification with Greece, classicism made a late appearance there, too, strengthening and emphasizing this unification. However, it never became the predominant architectural style. New architectural movements had arrived, just as on Chios and Lesvos, leading to the creation of an unusual eclectic urban architecture (figs. 430–34).

In some types of buildings, such as educational institutions, government buildings, and banks, classicism continued to predominate. As we have already seen, a significant number of educational buildings were erected throughout Greece even before liberation, because education and culture had always been a means of keeping the national consciousness alive and sustaining hopes of a better future.

The Symbolism of Style

As early as the late eighteenth century, Kosmas of Aitolia was advising the people, "It is better, my brother, to have a Greek school than to have fountains and rivers." He also exhorted Christians to "give of their ability and their goodwill for the school," either "of their own toil" or "jointly from the village" or "from monasteries." This was an attempt to adjust to the local, natural, and social circumstances, observing the principle that public buildings should be "monumental" (fig. 439).

The success of these buildings led to favorable comments by the inspectors of primary education. "Young children, who formerly detested school, and rightly so, now, out of love for their teaching institutions, cannot wait for the light of day, when they can be in school." So says the inspector of the Cyclades, A. Valassis, while G. Vlamos notes in his treatise on school construction: "Not only has a special style evolved for schools, which is applied everywhere and reveals the sacred purpose of the foundation from the outside, but special architects have also emerged." He goes on to describe the buildings: "let the facade of the school be simple and composed of the Greek orders, because in the simple is to be found beauty and order, since it affects the soul of the child who gazes on it twice a day (let every school be of harmonious shape and colors, since the school is the child's second home)" (Vlamos, 1904, p. 30) (figs. 441, 442).

435. Chalkida. The Palirria Hotel, with its characteristic circular belvedere above the main entrance at the junction of the building's facades.

436. Chania. Villa with a circular veranda in the Ionic order, surmounted by a tower at the corner of the building.

437. Chania. House with a circular veranda on the upper story.

438. Mytilini. Chatzichristophas villa. Richly decorated three-story tower, located at the junction of the two volumes of the building.

In 1912, in an article in the journal *Archimedes*, E. Kriezis considered that buildings of this kind were alien to the landscape and would remain alien — to the environment and also to the child, who would compare them with the simple local forms and shapes. Nevertheless, these schools were not only popular, they became models that were followed in many of the subjugated areas of Macedonia, Epiros, Lesvos, and elsewhere (figs. 440, 443, 444). At the same time, they naturally influenced the local architecture by introducing classical elements, albeit belatedly. It is interesting to note that wherever an educational building of this kind exists, it is still in use, as a school or as a cultural or exhibition center for the region.

A similar influence was exercised by local government offices, town halls, courthouses, and so on, and also by the branches of banks built directly after liberation in every town in northern Greece and in the capitals of the larger islands. The bank buildings symbolized local economic prosperity in the most convincing manner. More specifically, the National Bank and the Bank of Greece opened a series of branches in the 1930s, most of them designed in Athens by the organizations' respective Technical Services. The architects associated with them are N. Zoumboulidis and K. Papadakis. The buildings' modern forms, often constructed of reinforced concrete, represented personal expressions of the period's academic architecture. They clearly display all the hallmarks of modern classicism that emerged at the same time in Europe and the Soviet Union. It was a type of classicism favored mainly by totalitarian regimes characterized by a reversion to Doric columns, pediments, symmetry, and sober, inflexible forms. Fortunately for Greece, the buildings were on a scale small enough that they never attained the provocative style of their "fascist" models, though on occasion they came dangerously close (fig. 445).

Once again, ancient Greece was pressed into service to emphasize "Greekness," particularly in the newly liberated areas. Alongside the public buildings arose an admittedly modest number of late-Neoclassical private structures. These were mainly houses, in which traditional materials were frequently replaced by modern ones, especially for the load-bearing structure, which would often be made of cement. The new towns were given a certain archaizing, though rather superficial, style. It was, however, too late. These buildings remained isolated examples; they may have set their stamp on the time, but their influence did not extend to the surrounding area or bestow a more catholic aesthetic perception on local communities. The movements of renewal that penetrated northern Greece, especially Thrace, Macedonia, and Lesvos, had been consolidated, and they created a dominating architectural spirit.

439. Galaxidi. The Girls School. One of the earliest examples of Neoclassical style in a public building in free Greece.

440. Drawing for the school at Skalochori on Lesvos (Source: KTNA.)

441, 442. Colored lithographs that circulated in the late nineteenth century and served as typological and morphological models for a vast number of schools in the Greek provinces. One is a design for a school with two grades, the other for a school with four grades. Architect: D. Kallias. (Source: Ministry of Education Archive.)

443, 444. The Alexandroupoli High School and the Xanthi Primary School. Despite detailed deviations of typology and the application of the orders, educational buildings throughout Greece followed a single style, inspired by the classical spirit. Their construction was usually funded by donations from wealthy expatriate Greeks. Postcards.

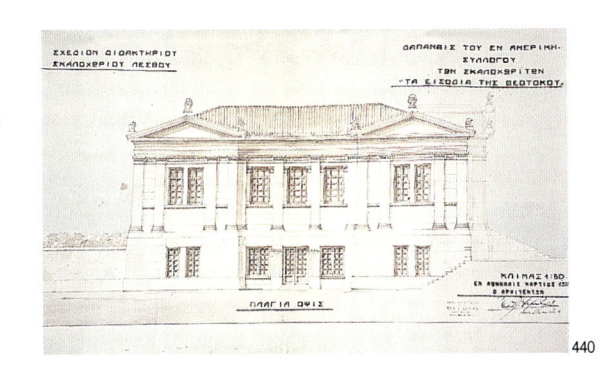

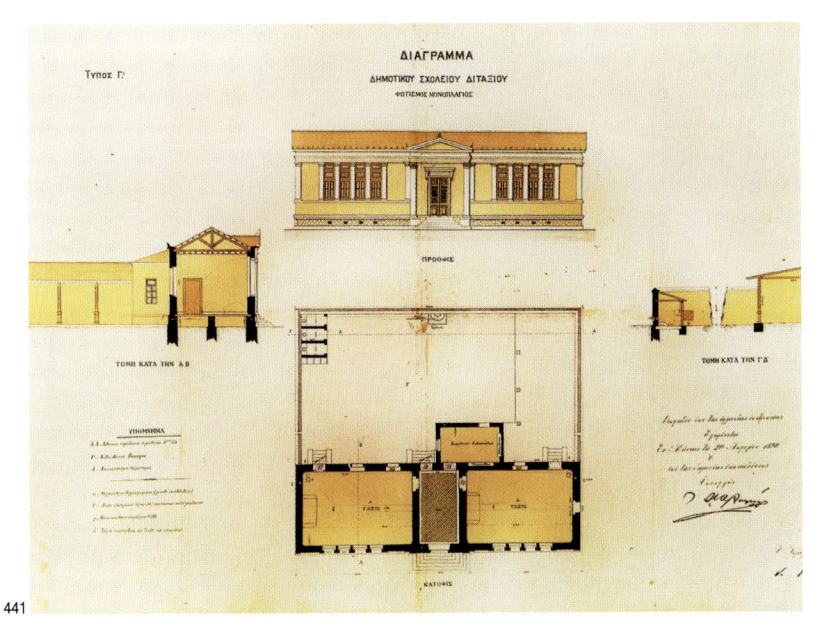

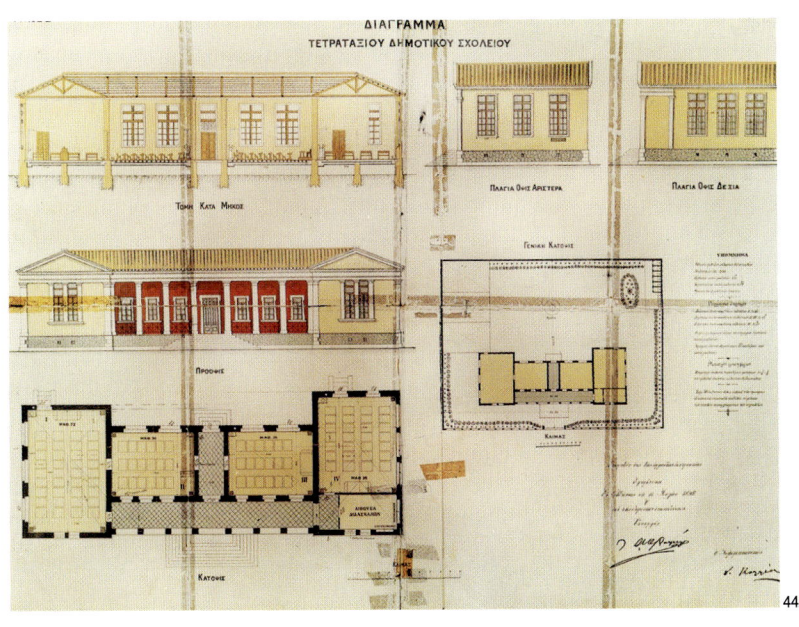

The Byzantine Revival

In Thessaloniki, the capital of northern Greece, the fire of 1917 marked the beginning of a new period. "From the ashes of Thessaloniki will be born a new city, the like of which is not to be found in the Mediterranean," declared E. Venizelos to the Greek Parliament (13th session, December 6, 1919).

The issue of Greekness also arose in this case, but the solution was different. Whereas, at the beginning of the nineteenth century, Athens had revived the vision of ancient Greece, a century later, Thessaloniki was to revive the vision of Byzantium. Its new town plan called for Byzantine monuments, and the new morphology that was proposed and largely implemented also drew its models from Byzantium. On this occasion, too, just as a century earlier, Greeks and foreigners formed a unified workforce with shared views. On the international town-planning committee formed at that time, the names of T. Mawson and E. Hébrard are to be found alongside those of K. Kitsikis and A. Zachos.

"There can be no question but that the new city should be accommodated to its inherited character. When I say accommodated, I mean that both the new

445. Serres. The National Bank of Greece, a rather unorthodox composition utilizing the classical orders. It displays a persistent adherence to the symbolic coupling of form and content, especially in the expression of the credit institution's authority and reliability.

monuments of the city, that is, its public buildings, and also the private buildings, must not only satisfy modern needs, but also form an appropriate environment for these old buildings" (Kitsikis, 1919, p. 13). These lines, written by K. Kitsikis, are strongly reminiscent of Kleanthis's views regarding Athens.

Byzantine-revival architecture, however, failed to gain the same acceptance as Neoclassicism. Although examples occur not only in Thessaloniki but also in Ioannina, Preveza, and even Athens, they are all isolated buildings, except of course in the center of the Macedonian capital, where Byzantine-revival architecture was employed on the scale of an urban-design unit (figs. 446, 447). The social process, the political environment, and the development of new technology did not, in the end, prove capable of creating a climate like the one that had permitted the formation of Neoclassicism and its dissemination to almost every corner of Greece for almost an entire century.

As noted above, the new styles that had been consolidated in the rest of Europe displaced conservative classicism there. With the exception of a brief revival just before the Second World War, conservative classicism was abandoned as early as the middle of the nineteenth century, apart, perhaps, from buildings in a few special categories, such as museums or courthouses. Elsewhere, revived classicism was identified with totalitarian regimes, providing another reason for its rejection – and its replacement by modern aspirations based on the radical movement of morphological renewal.

446. Ioannina. The Town Hall building, it was originally a branch of the National Bank of Greece. The harmonious Byzantine-revival morphology expressed its integration into the local medieval culture. It is thus one of the few examples in which this kind of building deviates from the classical tradition.

447. Thessaloniki. Mediterranean Palace Hotel. Although it is built in the general spirit of Byzantine-revival morphology, its aesthetic is strongly modified in the direction of Arabic decorative forms. This complex on the quay achieves a romantic style that is not devoid of an exotic, picturesque quality.

The Transition to Modernism

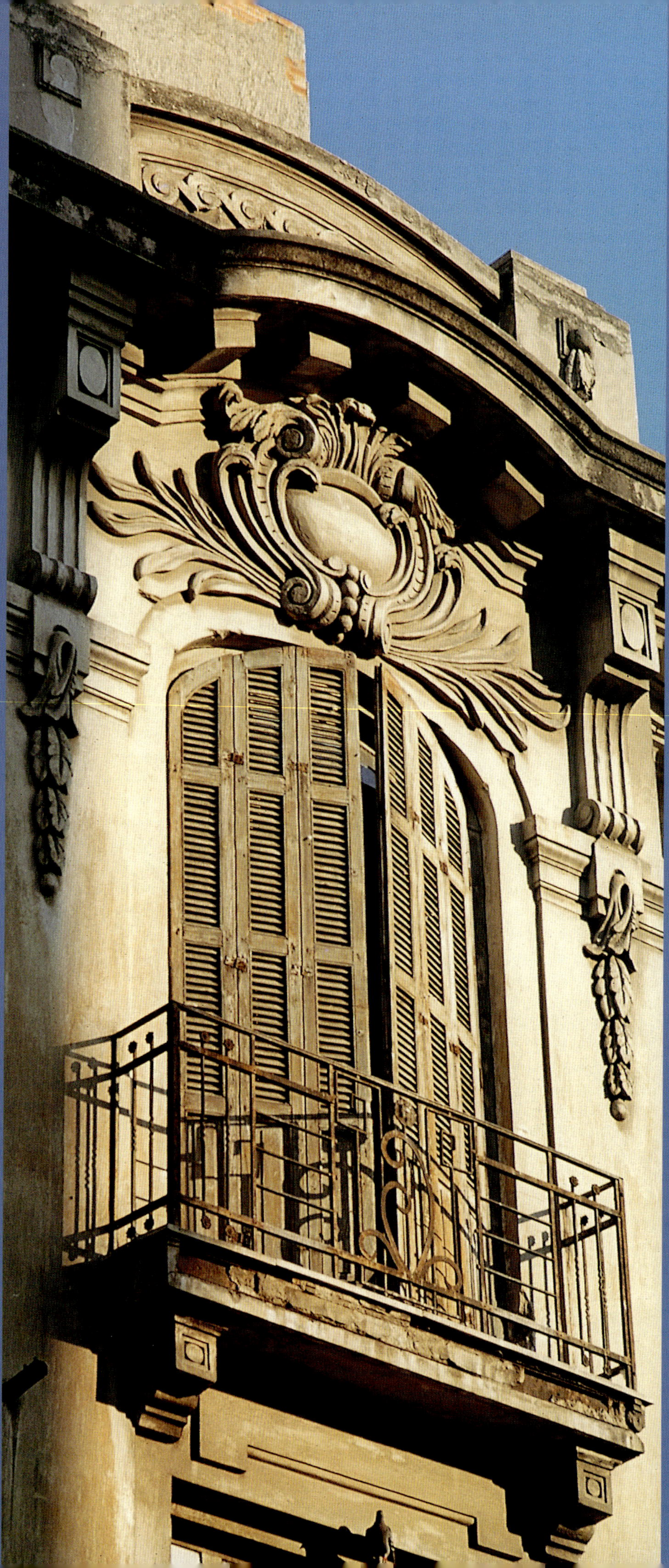

THE TRANSITION TO MODERNISM

The Centers That Received the New Styles

From about the middle of the nineteenth century, eclecticism made its appearance in Europe as a successor to classicism and, more generally, historicism; eclecticism was an architecture that borrowed elements and stylistic motifs from various periods and combined them in one building. Although eclecticism was founded on interesting theoretical views, it quickly degenerated into a superficial approach to the designing of facades. The use of a vast number of decorative elements often resulted in a rather tasteless morphological supplement. Moreover, Neoclassicism itself had, in its final phase, abandoned its initial austerity and plainness in favor of a richer vocabulary.

France, with Paris of the Second Empire (1852–70) at its center, played an important role in the formation of eclecticism. The major remodeling carried out in the French capital under Napolean III by the civic planner Baron Haussmann signaled a new period. Perceptions of the beautiful changed, with building facades employed to display wealth and, by extension, power. The École des Beaux-Arts, which was placed under state control in 1864, was the leading institute to reproduce the aesthetic of urban opulence combined with an academic approach to design. Eclecticism, which differed from country to country, was to make its mark on European architecture in the second half of the nineteenth century.

After a short time lag, owed mainly to the fact that classicism was regarded by Greeks as their national architecture, eclecticism also came to Greece. Its exponents were Greek graduates of the École des Beaux-Arts in Paris and the School of Fine Arts in Constantinople. The new currents swiftly attracted a section of the public, especially in the two large urban centers, Athens and Thessaloniki (fig. 449). In the former, the new style was adopted with little or no resistance, displacing existing Neoclassical morphology in a transformation that was gentle and conservative. However, the result is considered to be not so much the pure spirit of eclecticism, but rather a stage of conscious reevaluation (within the aesthetic climate of the Beaux-Arts) of classicism's morphological values (figs. 450–56).

At the beginning of the twentieth century, classicism continued to be the prevalent architecture of Athenian middle-class single- and double-story

448. Thessaloniki. Decorative element above a window in an urban residence (at the corner of Katouni and Vasileos Irkaleiou Streets) suggests the general spirit of Beaux-Arts, though it also incorporates a restless Art Nouveau morphology.

449. Thessaloniki. Decorative element at the top of the building and a strongly modeled window frame in an urban residence (Egnatia Street 109) that dates to the period of the Second French Empire.

450. Athens. Decorative details of the Law Court Building (by Raoul Brandon). Greek models are expressed through the Beaux-Arts aesthetic. (Source: KTNA.)

451. Athens. Design proposal for the Law Court Building (by Raoul Brandon). Return to the monumental expression of classicism. (Source: KTNA.)

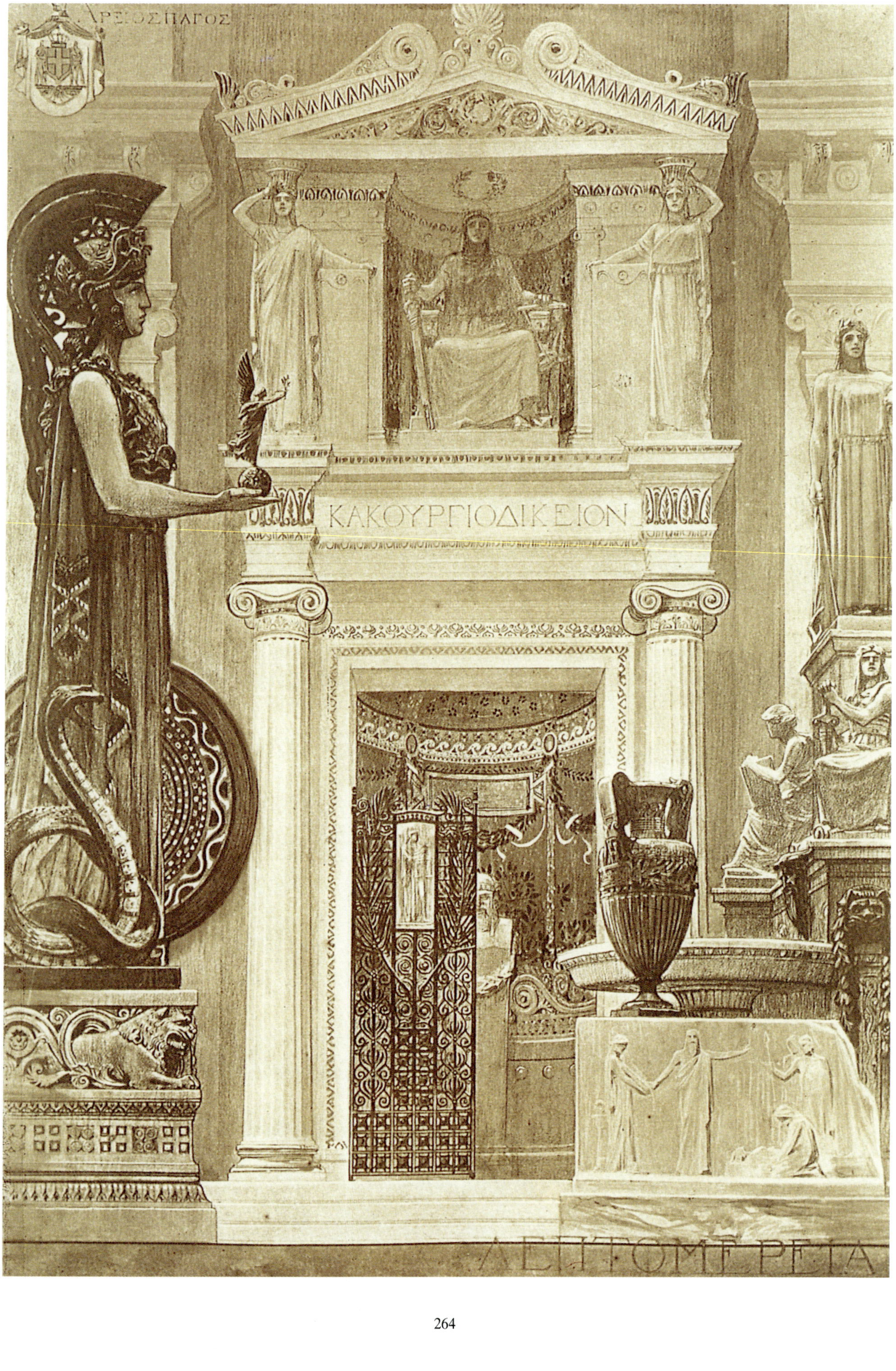

450

ΑΘΗΝΩΝ

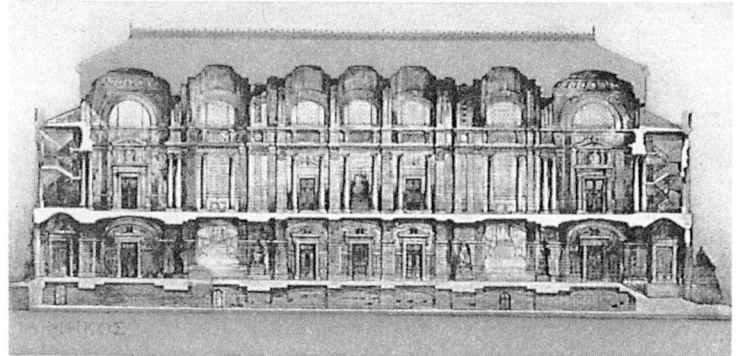

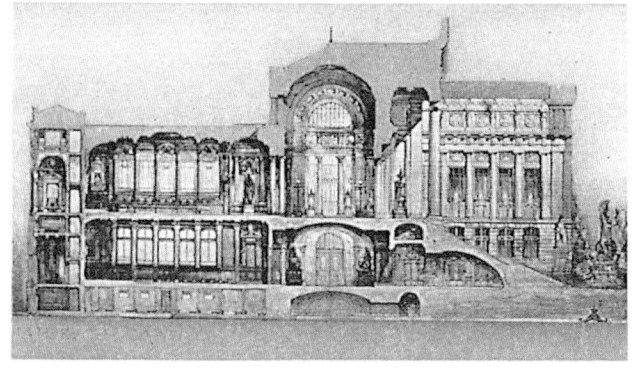

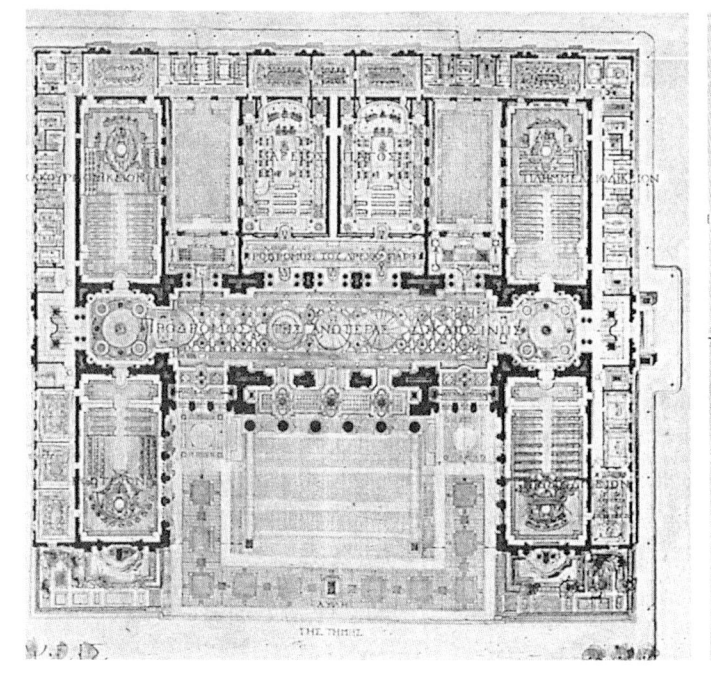

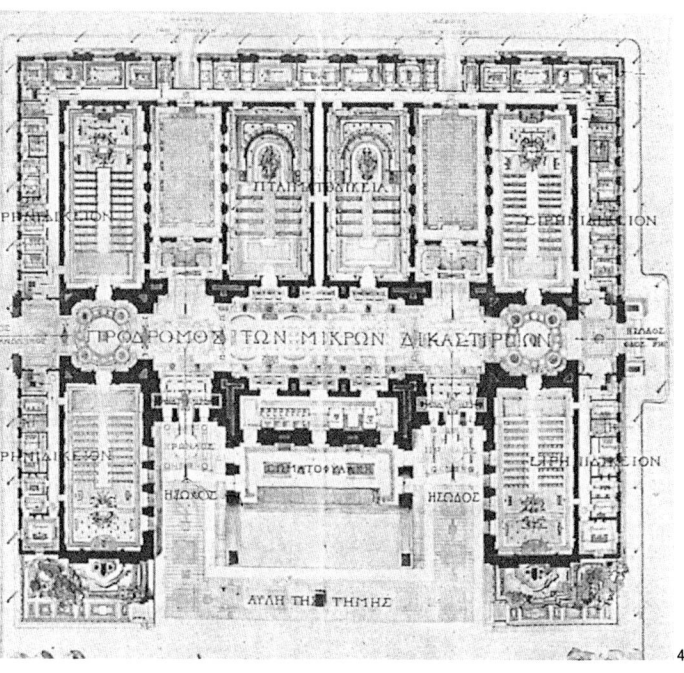

ΠΡΟΟΠΤΙΚΗ ΟΨΙΣ ΤΟΥ Μ...

452. Athens. Design proposal for the Law Court Building (corner of Vasilissis Sophias Avenue and Rigillis Street) by the architect Alexandros Nikoloudis. Awarded first prize in a competition in 1912. Despite classicizing features drawn from the Roman repertoire, the building's overall style is informed by the spirit of Beaux-Arts. (Source: ELIA, Photographic Archive.)

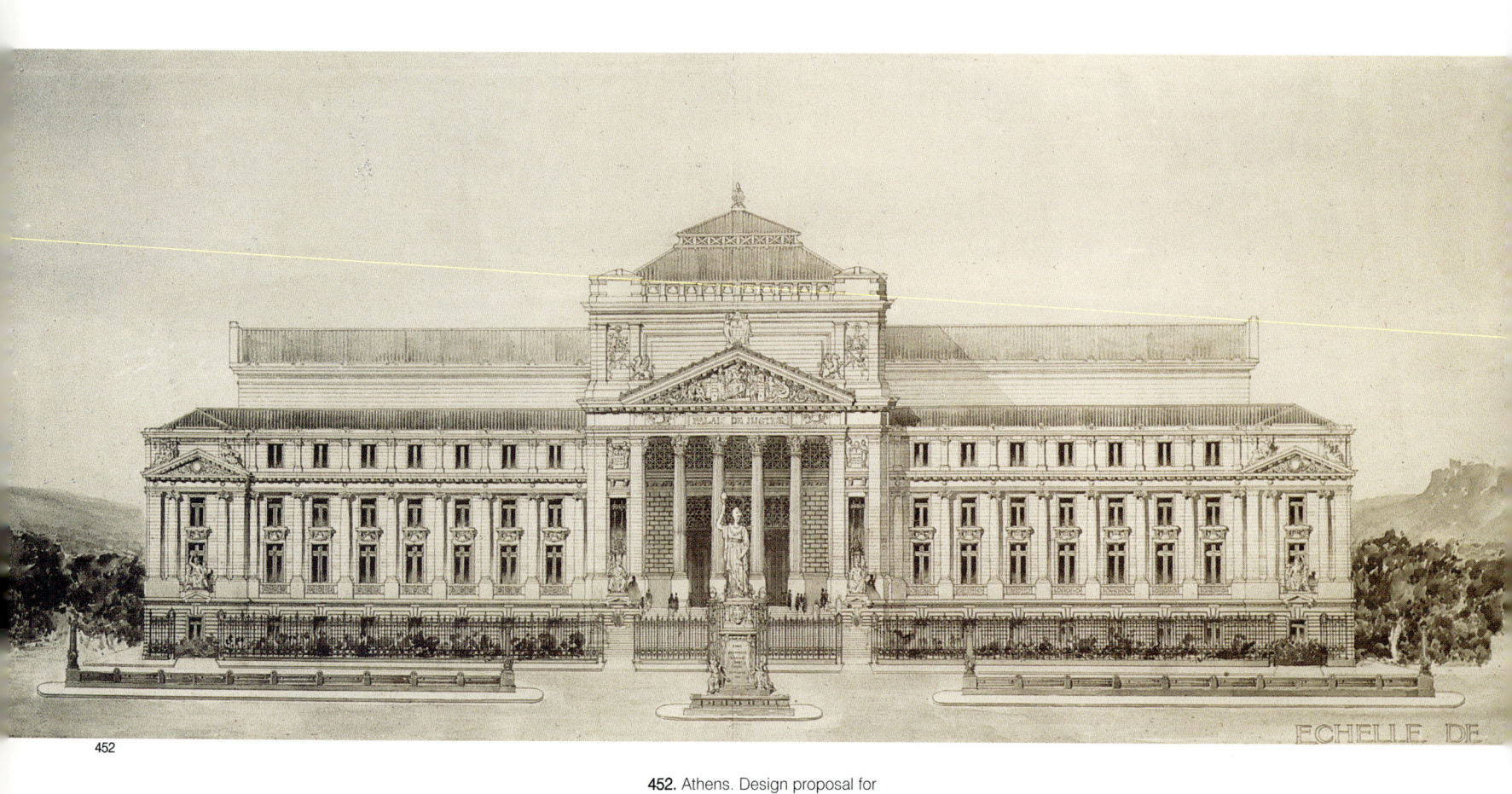

453. Athens. Cross-section of the Law Court Building, as proposed by Alexandros Nikoloudis. The building's excessively large scale and decorative elements are expressed with unrivaled design skill. (Source: ELIA, Photographic Archive.)

454. Piraeus. The Vatis mansion by the architect Alexandros Nikoloudis. When it was erected at the beginning of the twentieth century, its metropolitan character dominated the quay of Greece's leading port.

455. Piraeus. Mansions at Kastella with a view of the sea.

456. Athens. The Sarogleion Building of the Officers' Club (on the site intended for the Law Court Building). By Alexandros Nikoloudis (1924). It exhibits the monumental morphology in the style of the Second French Empire, though, characteristically, it transcends aesthetic moderation.

456

residences. In urban mansions and apartment buildings, however, a new form of building steadily took hold, and new trends of morphological ostentation came to the fore as the population of the city increased by the day. After the restrained eclecticism of the previous century, the appearance of which, though gentle and conservative, had shaken the severe discipline of Athenian Neoclassicism and opened the way for new aesthetic perceptions, the margins for choice were now considerably widened. Renaissance Mannerism and French Baroque now made a greater mark on late classicism. The introduction of neo-Baroque into Athens at a fairly late date (figs. 453, 458) contributed to the dissemination, alongside the more recent Art Nouveau style, of versions of the *Jugendstil-Secession* and, later, of Art Deco, despite the great differences between them (figs. 448, 459–64). Moreover, Ziller, with his characteristic country villas in the Athenian suburbs (described in the previous chapter), had prepared Athenians to accept features that were foreign to austere classicism. Indeed, the picturesque style that he frequently used had

457. Karditsa. The Arni Hotel. Bold application of the fulsome expression of French Beaux-Arts. A tall dome intensifies the vertical aspect of the corner elements.

458. Patras. Luxury urban house in the style of late classicism, on Trion Navarchon Square. A hemispherical dome lends prominence to the corner element.

270

many features in common with the architecture of Art Nouveau, which was emancipated from the classical orders (figs. 465–73).

None of these new trends, however, managed to prevail in the modern Greek capital. They coexisted with Neoclassicism in the early decades of the twentieth century but never displaced it completely. It is characteristic that they are found mainly in upper-class neighborhoods, where, apart from the architects, the owners of the houses either came from Greek communities abroad—mainly in Egypt and Turkey—or were well traveled and maintained contacts with the rest of Europe. In middle-class neighborhoods, however, small single- or two-story houses continued to be built with clear classicizing features, while more modern motifs were found only rarely and were invariably of a much poorer quality.

In 1929, when E. Venizelos decided, after marrying Elena Skylitsi, to build his own mansion on Vasilissis Sophias Avenue, he assigned the project to A. Metaxas, an established architect at the royal court. Venizelos requested a Neoclassical

459. Nafplion. Artificial modernism (Art Nouveau) in a facade that still retains its classicizing features.

460. Heraklion. Narrow-fronted two-story facade with a tentative composition incorporating heterogeneous elements.

461. Kalamata. Decorated facade on the axis of the outer door and the window above it. Refined taste in the direction of the French aesthetic school.

462. Athens. Balcony in the neighborhood of Kypseli (Mytilinis Street). The design of the railing, with its succession of volutes, is descended directly from the Viennese *Jugendstil.* The same motif is often used in the urban architecture of Athens about 1920 to 1930.

463. Athens. Balcony of a house in Kypseli (Kelainous Street). Linear rendering of the decorative motifs expressed in the spirit of Art Deco.

464. Athens. Entrance of a house in Kypseli (Ithakis Street). Abstraction and a bold geometric expression are integrated into the aesthetic of Art Deco.

465. Design study by E. Ziller for a country villa. Although the organization and articulation of space are conservative, they are appropriate to the unfettered expression typical of late Romanticism.
(Source: National Art Gallery.)

466. Drawing of a villa integrated into the urban landscape, by E. Ziller. (Source: National Art Gallery.)

467. Kastri, Attiki. Building by I. Antoniadis. The structure's characteristic arrangement includes vertical windows and a projecting roof. The design exemplifies the search for expressivity at the transition from Art Nouveau to modernism.

468. Kalamata. Gothic Revival two-story house. Empirical rendering of decadent European models.

469. Kalamata. Detail of a house on the seafront. Complacent decorative expression of picturesque architecture, about 1900.

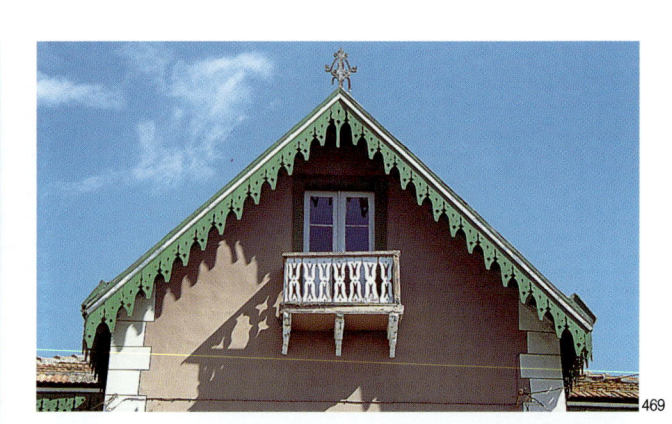

470. Volos. The railway station. Its boldly picturesque architectural expression contrasts with the conservative form of the urban mansion in the background. Similar railway stations were built about 1900 in many parts of Greece. Postcard.

471. Kifisia. Villa. Details from north of the Alps were transferred to the upper-class suburb of Athens, where they were excellently rendered.

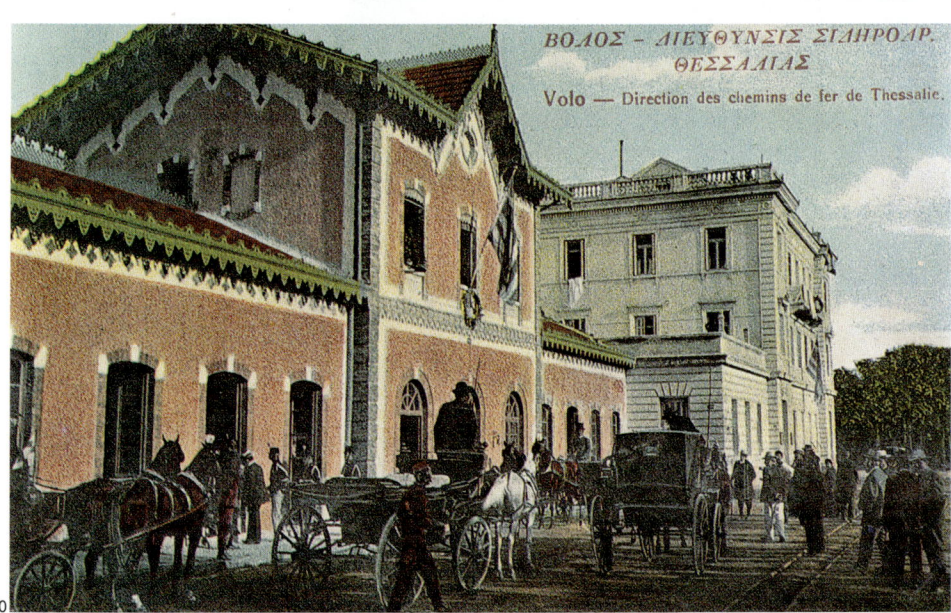

472. Syros. Country villa with a form inspired by Romanticism.

473. Athens. The Margarita villa at Ambelokipi on Kifisias Avenue. Unexpected application of the English castellated style, at the final decline of classicism.

474. Piraeus. Mansion on Vasileos Georgiou Street in the center of the town, by the architect V. Tsagris. Represents an attempt to incorporate the spirit of classicism in the stylized morphology of the *Jugendstil*.

475. Athens. Apartment building on Ioulianou Street (Aigyptou Square), probably by V. Tsagris. Modernist abstraction is mixed with eclectic motifs, and the vertical features are projected in unified zones.

476. Athens. Pallis mansion in Syntagma Square, by A. Metaxas.

ΙΕΚ ΩΜΕΓΑ
ΩΜΕΓΑ
ΜΑΚΕΔΟΝΙΑΣ ΘΡΑΚΗΣ
everest
HOTEL ACHILLEAS

476

building, despite the fact that Metaxas had abandoned Neoclassicism and moved on to newer architectural trends.

The situation began to change about the middle of the 1930s, when the first buildings following the modern movement made their appearance in Greece (figs. 474–76). No examples of Athenian architecture prior to that can claim distinctive or outstanding features that reveal the assimilation and reworking of the styles—that is, a local Baroque, Art Nouveau, or Art Deco architecture. In the case of the modern movement, by contrast, Greek architects, although at first naturally coming under the influence of Europe, went on to formulate what might be called their own school. Contributing factors may have been Le Corbusier's writings on the relationship between modernism and the Cyclades, on the one hand, and, on the other, the fact that functionality and austere forms created the appropriate conditions for a new "Greekness," for which architects were passionately and persistently searching.

A similar picture emerges in the urban centers of Old Greece. The new styles appeared in those towns as a reverberation of the capital and, more rarely, the foreign centers of Europe, with the result that their influence is much less profound.

As discussed in previous chapters, the situation in northern Greece is much different. In towns such as Kavala, Mytilini, and Thessaloniki, the influence of the

477. Mytilini. A. Efstratios villa. The asymmetrical composition of the volumes and the emphasis on the vertical lend this Gothic Revival building a romantic style and great dynamism.

Asia Minor coast and, above all, of Constantinople had opened the way for reforming influences at an early date (figs. 477, 478).

About 1900, Thessaloniki presented a multicultural image. Its population had greatly increased. The development of trade and industry was accompanied by the appearance of banks, businesses, and large import and export companies, both local and foreign. The way of life combined the modernism of the West with the carefree existence and opulence of the East.

Eclecticism invaded both the public and the private space of Thessaloniki. Here, it was not the architect who sought to persuade his client to accept new trends; on the contrary, the client was the one demanding new styles, for reasons of personal promotion and ostentation. Alongside public buildings, the first large business premises, equally imposing bank buildings, majestic hotels, theaters and, a little later, cinemas, and multiple recreation centers all emerged. From Baroque-influenced Turkish architecture and eclecticism (rich in decorative elements that differed from Athenian eclecticism, and frequently influenced by French colonial architecture), Thessaloniki easily made the transition to Art Nouveau. Thessaloniki was the city in which this particular artistic expression flowered and was vindicated in Greece. The architects, and also the owners, were usually foreigners, mostly

478. Kavala. Villa of Baron A. de Zolnay Vix. The building's abstract design takes a Gothic Revival approach.

479. Thessaloniki. Mansion of Ahmet and Mehmet Kapatzis on Vasilissis Olgas Street. Detail of the facade reveals the cohesion of style, with a well-rounded use of form and color.

480. Thessaloniki. Mansion of Ahmet and Mehmet Kapatzis. The building's composition, in the style of Viennese Art Nouveau, takes a high-quality aesthetic approach to both parts and whole.

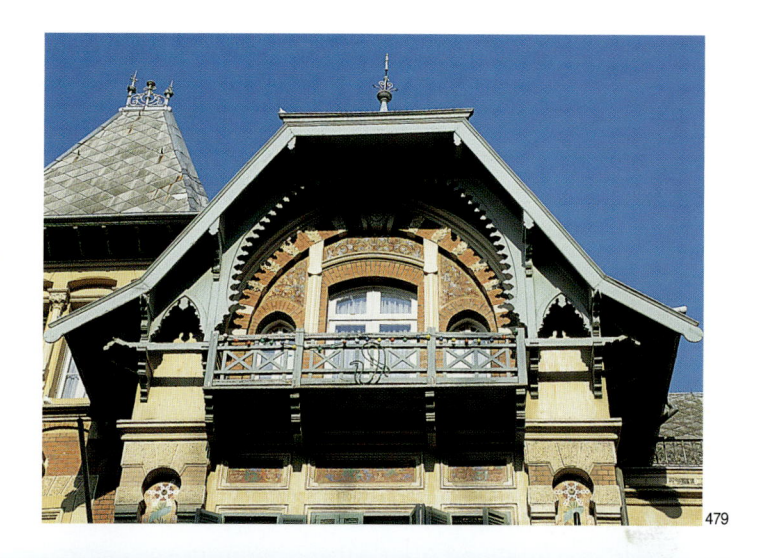

481. Thessaloniki. Bianca villa. Detail of the facade shows the balcony door's unorthodox geometric design and the broken lines of the roof above it.

482. Thessaloniki. Bianca villa. Residence of the Jewish businessman Dino Fernandez, designed by P. Arigoni (1912). One of the few buildings in urban architecture of the time (about 1900) that offered an aesthetically well-rounded image of central European nouveau.

483

Italians and Jews. A large number of urban residences, commercial establishments, and, above all, elegant country villas appeared in the city and the suburbs. Many of them are noteworthy examples of architecture, even in European terms. However, unification with Greece and the fire of 1917, with the consequent redesigning of the town, gradually transformed the urban landscape (figs. 479–87).

The reaction of the newspaper *Estia* in November 1912, a few days after the liberation of Thessaloniki, is revealing: "Villas to the right and left," writes the correspondent, describing the neighborhood of the country houses, "shut off the view of the sea and are themselves shut off by large gardens, catching the eye not so much for their beauty as for their style. I should say their styles. Or better, the absence of any style. For indeed there is no style in these architectural fabrications" (Kolonas, 2000, p. 296).

Although the inhabitants of Old Greece may have looked down on the architecture of Thessaloniki, the same was not true of the inhabitants of other towns in northern Greece, for which Thessaloniki, along with Constantinople and the other large urban centers of the Ottoman Empire, continued to serve as a model. Moreover, in several of these towns, such as Xanthi, Komotini, Florina (figs. 488, 489), and, especially, Kavala, the foreign companies (who dealt mainly in the stocks of tobacco in the region) often used their own architects. The results are not always remarkable, of course. The engineers who arrived to meet the needs of foreign commercial houses usually had no experience with urban architecture and were not particularly talented in this sphere. Their handling of the new architectural vocabulary was not always very successful. This is evident in Kavala, both in smaller petit bourgeois or bourgeois residences and in mansions, such as the modern Town Hall, built at the end of the 1890s, which was formerly the property of the Hungarian tobacco merchant Baron Pierre Herzog, or the modern Conservatory of Kavala, also once owned by Baron Herzog, with its lavish, but rather inelegant Gothic Revival features (figs. 490–94). Similar architectural forms can be seen in the large tobacco warehouses, though here the results are better, because the decoration was more austere. The Municipal Tobacco Warehouse, probably built in the early twentieth century for the Turkish tobacco merchant Kizi Mimin, is an exception, with its imposing facade surmounted by an overly lavish decorative element heavily burdened with floral and geometric motifs, suns, coats-of-arms, Corinthian imposts, and more: a characteristic example of the late urban architecture of the Ottoman Empire. The earliest buildings of the Greek community of Kavala had a similar architecture, except that they were often dominated by Neoclassical elements. In contrast, the influence of the local vernacular architecture, as in the old *archontiko* on Tembon Street, with its characteristic Macedonian pediment and simply designed facade, is seldom found.

One encounters more local memories, perhaps, in Xanthi, where the old urban style successfully coexists in harmony with the newly adopted forms of architecture preferred by the rising bourgeois class. It should not be forgotten, however, that the area of Kavala outside the castle is a completely new town that seeks consciously to distinguish itself from the old. At Xanthi, the corresponding distinction is gentler and less obvious.

Particular interest attaches to the bourgeois residences of this same period in Mytilini, especially the country villas in the suburbs, which have already been mentioned. In later villas, eclectic aspirations are apparent, along with strong influences from neighboring Smyrna. Moreover, architects from the mainland frequently helped design buildings on the island. In addition, countless examples

483. Thessaloniki. Mansion of Ahmet Kapatzis on Vasilissis Olgas Street. It exhibits asymmetrical composition, color differentiation in the decoration, and variety in the forms of the roofs—all features that indicate a departure from the academic forms of the past.

484. Thessaloniki. Bordeaux villa, by X. Paionidis. An onion dome surmounts the little tower.

485. Thessaloniki. The Red House opposite the church of Ayia Sophia. Detail of a facade. Original handling of medieval styles and different materials achieve a unified romantic expression.

486. Thessaloniki. Detail of a facade of the Customs House, by the architect E. Modiano. Its excessive decoration is in the spirit of late eclecticism.

487. Thessaloniki. Commercial building at the corner of Vasilissis Sophias and Tzimiski Streets. Large scale and emphasis on the vertical characterize this metropolitan structure.

AL HALIL
Χειροποίητα χαλιά
AL HALIL
Χειροποίητα χαλιά
ΕΛΛΗΝΙΚΗ ΦΙΛΟΞΕΝΙΑ
ΚΡΑΤΗΣΕΙΣ ΞΕΝΟΔΟΧΕΙΩΝ Α.Ε.
Goody's

487

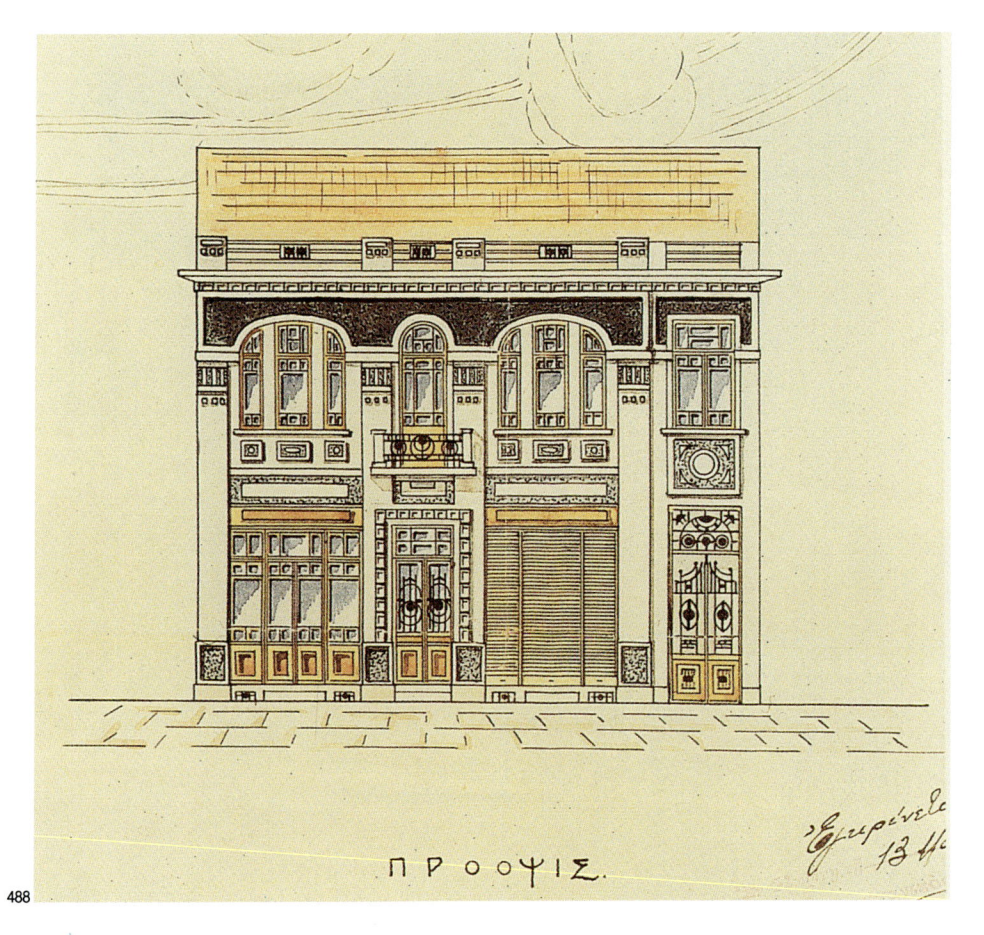

488. Florina. Design for the facade of a two-story building, by N. Papanousis.

489. Florina. Design for an urban residence in accordance with early-twentieth-century sensibilities.

490. Kavala. K. Krantonellis mansion on Venizelou Street. The rich decoration in the taste of late French eclecticism gives the building an imposing, though anachronistic, character.

491. Kavala. Two-and-a-half story residence at the corner of Skra and Komninon Streets. The distinctive forms of the Viennese *Jugendstil* are authentically designed and skillfully applied in the external plastering.

of expansive morphological compositions for urban villas were published in luxurious albums showing their implementation in the suburbs of Vienna, Paris, Berlin, and other cities. With these "recipes" at hand, it was no doubt easier for architects of the period to come to an agreement with their patrons (fig. 495).

The interior decoration of most of these buildings, such as painted ceilings and wall paintings, is of a similar quality and aesthetic (figs. 496–98). However, the interior decoration of a house or public building does not always follow the style of the facades. (This is true throughout Greece, not just for the region under examination.) The reasons are many: Sometimes there are no suitable craftsmen in the area, or those that are to be found retain elements of a more vernacular local tradition. Sometimes the craftsmen in the area come from a culture foreign to the architecture of the place and the style of the building. It is also often the case that, for purely economic reasons, a building's interior is completed at a later stage, or it is updated some time later in a more modern decorative approach. The results vary.

492. Kavala. Terrace of small two-story houses in the commercial center. The buildings reveal an identical repetition on the large scale coupled with a variety of decorative embellishments on the small. This charming complex dates to the 1920s.

493. Kavala. Municipal Tobacco Warehouse. Detail of the facade. Its decorative excess seeks to use heterogeneous morphological elements to produce a sculptural effect.

494. Kavala. Municipal Tobacco Warehouse. This functional building is aesthetically integrated into the urban environment.

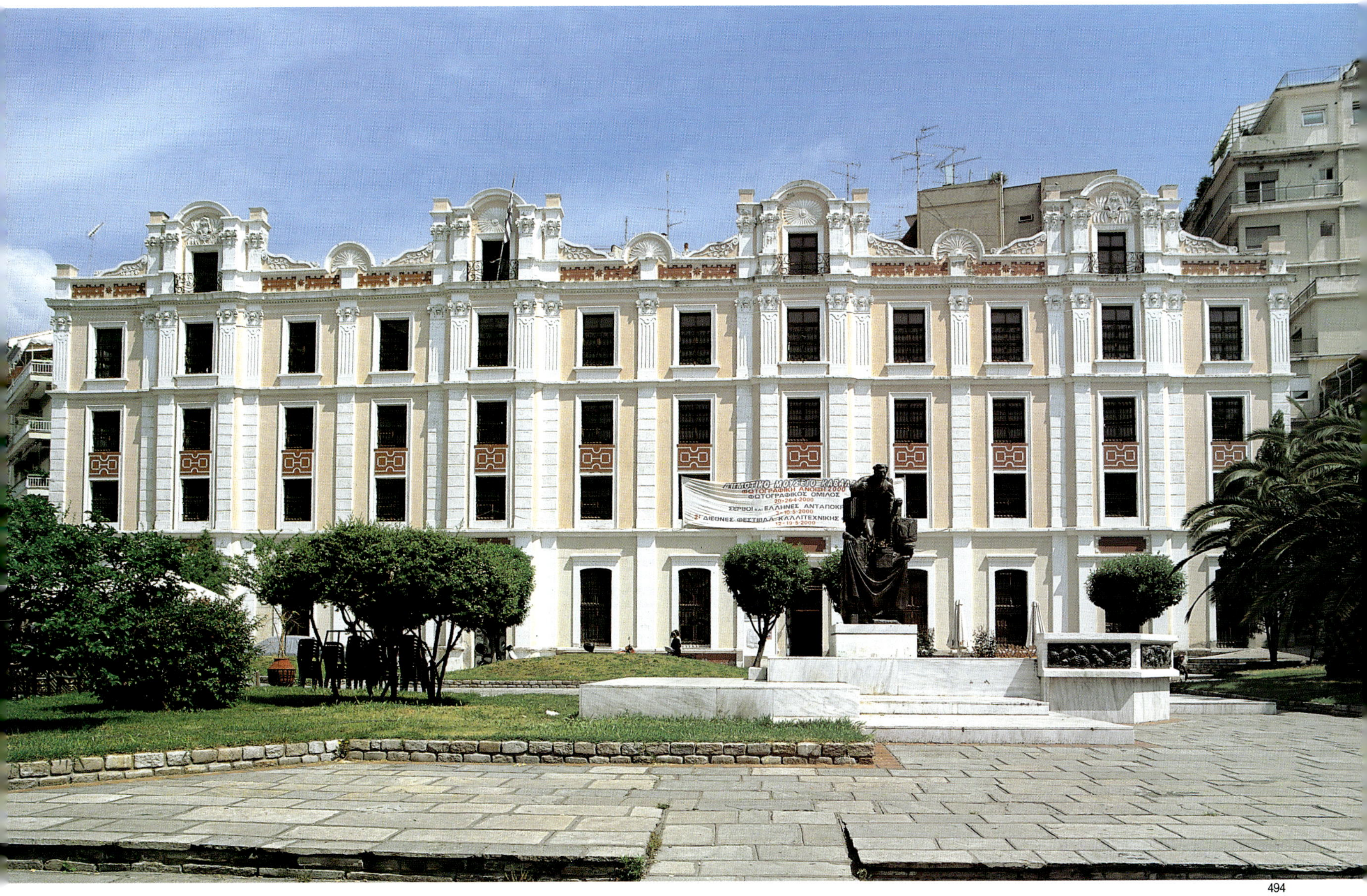

494

495. Mytilini. Building on the quay. Part of the facade. Blend of styles and decorative motifs in a composition reflecting the predominant aesthetic trends of the local urban society.

496. Mytilini. Painted ceiling in an urban house. This decorative detail is executed in an expressive *Jugendstil* motif.

497, 498. Mytilini. Details of wall paintings in the interior of an upper-class house. Both paintings are in the style of Italian Mannerism, and their allegorical subjects are borrowed from ancient mythology.

Between Academism and "Greekness"

There was a final turn to Neoclassicism in the middle of the 1930s. A fresh outburst and revival of nationalism was cultivated in Greece against a background of similar ideas and aesthetic trends in Europe. A modern classicism was born, a classicism that, without any prejudice, made use of cement. The influences of the fascist architecture of Italy and Germany and the revolutionary architecture of Russia are perceptible. However, the foundations and ideology of this new movement are not clear. There can be no doubt that the dictatorship of Ioannis Metaxas, who ruled Greece from 1936 to 1941, played a role, but the Greek government certainly cannot be identified with that of Mussolini, far less with that of Hitler. The Greek structures that represent this return to classicism are not characterized by the empty arrogance and excessive bombast of the corresponding buildings in Rome, Munich, or Berlin (figs. 499–504).

In the 1930s, a vast number of public works buildings (schools, banks, memorial monuments, exhibition stands) were designed in Greece in which the classicizing elements were obvious, as architects endeavored to create a "new Greek style." A treatise on this subject, by D. E. Tsipouras, professor in the School of Fine Arts of the Athens National Technical University, expounds the theory that Greeks "are the descendants of the great Greeks," and that their architecture should abandon "French, English, and generally speaking foreign tones" and return to its sources, the ancient and Byzantine civilizations (Tsipouras, 1921, p. 4).

Symmetry, monumentality, the classical orders, pediments, and antefixes all made their appearance once more. Sometimes the associations go much further back — for example, in the branch of the National Bank by the architect Zoumboulidis in Preveza, in a Byzantine-revival style, or the bank in Nafplion, with elements borrowed from the decorative forms of Mycenaean monuments. Similar buildings exist in the Greek towns of both Old and new Greece. Their architecture has common features, because their creators were drawn from the central services in Athens and rarely from among provincial engineers.

The tendency to return to the Neoclassical forms of the previous century reached its height in 1937, when the Municipal Council of Thessaloniki decided to make a plot of land available to build the memorial designed in 1830 by Kaftantzoglou. "It is undoubtedly a historical event that it has fallen to our Municipal Council to discuss the work of a Macedonian and Thessalonikian who had the colossal inspiration, approaching the inspiration of those who created the Parthenons and their pediments; it is, I say, our honour and fortune that we have been called upon to discuss such a matter of supra-national inspiration. Take care, for the Memorial will be taken from you by Athens. Athens may have an Acropolis, but it cannot also take the Memorial from the man who devised it and has a Macedonian soul" (Kardamitsi-Adami, 1999–2000, p. 196). War intervened, of course, and the municipality's plan was never carried out. The decision, however, is indicative of the ideology and atmosphere of the time.

The architectural world attempted to provide an answer to morphological questions in order to rediscover a Greek style of moderation and harmony.

The pioneers of the modern movement themselves were concerned with the true meaning of classical architecture, though they reacted against the mere imitation of selected elements.

499. Tripolis. The Malliaropouleion Theater, by A. Metaxas (1909). Organic composition following the classical canon. Decorative style approaching Art Nouveau.

500. Thessaloniki. National Bank of Greece. This multi-story building with a robust square volume has an entrance emphasized by an imposing Doric porch.

501. Thessaloniki. Ionian Bank. The facades are harmoniously articulated, and a pedimented porch dominates the axis of symmetry.

For Greek architects, the fascist architecture of the interwar period was a trap. It would be superficial to believe that they were serving an absolutist ideology through their work. What happened at this time was precisely what had happened a century earlier: they believed that through modern classicism they had rediscovered the connection with the glorious past. The Asia Minor disaster, which marked the end of a dream, was still fresh. People needed to feel proud again. This may have been one of the reasons that the return to classical models came to an end after the Second World War. It became obvious that in order to satisfy national pride it was not necessary to utilize morphological symbols and obsolete stage designs in order to discover ideological references. Moreover, the social process, political reforms, new technological developments, and an increased sensitivity to economy and rationalism in meeting the housing needs of the weaker classes (as well as the refugees from the Asia Minor disaster) were circumstances strong enough to encourage all efforts to redefine a "Greek-based" stylistic repertoire capable of replacing classicism.

502. Tripolis. Law Court Building. Classicism makes a late appearance in this public building, whose function is emphasized by the design's imposing style.

Nonetheless, the urban architecture of the 1920s continued, in most cases, to proceed along the easy road of employing the fake motifs of an imported modernism. Meanwhile, its architects placed their hopes in the radical revision of their models: self-sufficiency and clarity in form, rationality and credibility in function and construction. It was thus clear that the last approaches to the "Greek Middle Ages," and even more so the optimistic investigation of the unexplored forms of the popular tradition, did not go beyond the level of a theoretical substructure disproportionate to the meager numbers of truly successful applications. And it was precisely then that ardent devotees of the dream of a "return to the roots" launched their arrows for the first time against the sterile academism of the classical tradition—distancing themselves, of course, from the similar aesthetic debates that had been conducted some twenty years earlier by the devotees of the Beaux-Arts. Whereas the criteria used by the latter were purely aesthetic, the former had on their side the undoubtedly realistic dictates of the movement of renewal. The hour then arrived for the (albeit isolated) forces of reaction, and men

503. Xanthi. National Bank of Greece. The ancient orders are used emphatically in the disproportionately sized entrance porch.

of restless intellect with a passion for investigation set out on what was almost a crusade to document and defend the crudely captured body of the aesthetic values of classicism. Beginning in 1933, Kostas Biris has presented in his writings a historical and critical review of the Athenian dimension of this phenomenon. He also contributed to the organization in 1938 of the first exhibition devoted to the architecture of classicism, at the very time when, by unhappy coincidence, the Municipal Theater, one of Ziller's works, was being demolished.

Nevertheless, the majority of the public buildings bequeathed by the nineteenth century to the Greek towns have survived, thanks to their functionality. What was, in the end, lost was the connecting tissue of anonymous Neoclassical architecture — the morphological ingredient that, by general consent, expressed human behavior as an aesthetic condition at the individual and social level. This was a code of "aesthetic memory," which was unique in the history of nineteenth-century European architecture in terms of its mass acceptance, its objective qualitative existence, and its deterministic relationship with its historical, social, and ideological content.

504. Nafplion. Law Court Building. The architectural style functions as an intermediary between the building and its use.

Epilogue

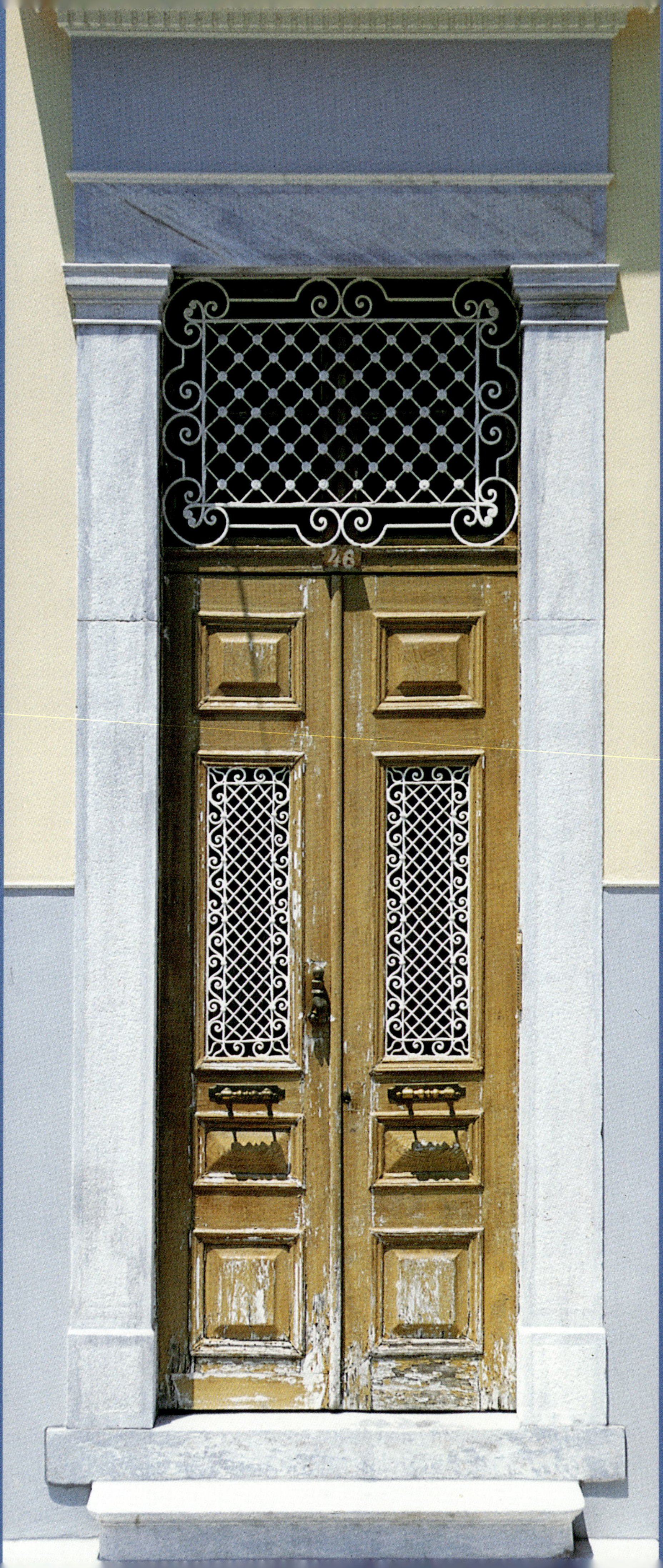

EPILOGUE

Revisiting the Aesthetics of Classicizing Logic

As historians of architecture confront the challenge of unraveling well-established aesthetic perceptions of the evolution of building types and forms in a given geographical and historical space, they must, in their conclusions, maintain an objective and essentially ethical stance with regard to related views of the past. Among other things, this means they should address those substantive issues that have either been overlooked or misinterpreted by earlier scholars.

The phenomenon of classicism in modern Greek architecture, however, obliges the scholar to review and, on occasion, radically revise the formal associations of a critical theory. For the very people who contributed to this architecture (patrons and architects), which lasted for at least eight decades, must have consciously broken with the local evolution of post-Byzantine tradition, disdaining, in particular, its vernacular basis.

An equally serious break had already taken place in Europe in the eighteenth century, with the emergence of the Romantic movement. One of the concomitants of this was the ideological return to the models of antiquity. There was an essential difference here, however. European art distanced itself at that time, at least in theory, from the established academic canons, which were inextricably linked with the waning historical styles (Renaissance and Baroque). Proponents of Hellenism, in contrast, in the heady climate of national rebirth and given the spectacular opening up of Greece's economic, intellectual, and cultural horizons, unhesitatingly opted for the canon of the monumental model (turning toward classical antiquity), subjecting romantic creative expression to the rules of rational design.

The present study has repeatedly stressed the essential factors in this turn toward classicism, the aesthetic trend that made its mark on the culture of Greece in the nineteenth century. It has emphasized less, perhaps, that the promotion of urban culture among the wider Greek population helped strengthen the esteem in which people held the arts in general. In the past, a phenomenon of this kind might have been connected more with a religious judgment than with a conceptual one. The theory that a work of architecture was a work of art accommodated to the logic of aesthetic appreciation was something truly unprecedented. This theory, born of a newly created sense of social freedom, dictated the treatment of even private buildings — that is, houses — in a spirit that mirrored the public, and official, aesthetic.

This mirroring of the morphology revealed the role of nineteenth-century architecture as intermediary between the public and the private spheres of life in the towns. In many cases, the mediation was made with the greatest skill — the result of a profound and multidimensional assimilation of ideological and aesthetic experiences, as cultivated preeminently in Athenian classicism. Sometimes, however, it remained shallow and allusive, as, for example in the application of a uniform classicizing veneer applied to the houses of the remote island of Symi.

At the opposite end of the scale from this last example lies the architecture of the Ionian islands. Its aesthetic, which was formulated far from ideological associations and the role of intermediary, exhibited the undisguised self-confidence of a distinguished and continuous urban culture. In this case, indeed, one can speak of a "popular" classicism, not precisely in the class sense of the word, but in the sense of the wide popular acceptance of the forms (clearly academic) that were assimilated in the inheritance of the locally imposed tradition. Something like this happened in Athens, though in a clearly defined chronological phase and under specific historical, social, and political circumstances. The acceptance of the classical order system in the urban architecture of Greece did not involve identical, or

505. Patras. Typical design of a Neoclassical entrance: two-leaf door with a fixed fanlight on the ground floor of an urban house (see also: photo p. 12).

506.

506. Syros. Painted ceiling of a formal room in a residence. Although it is a conservative expression, it clearly has been influenced by the Italian school.

507. Syros. Chrousa. Painted ceiling in the Vapheiadakis villa. This example shows a clear divergence from classicism toward naturalistic decoration.

even similar, processes. From the passages cited above and the descriptions in this book, it is evident that the aesthetic demands of individual population groups diverged substantially—sometimes in opposite directions.

For example, the distinctive cultural background and education characteristic of the urban communities of the New Territories (northern Greece, islands of the eastern Aegean, and others) mainly gave classicism the special national-symbolic content appropriate to public welfare buildings. In contrast, these communities unhesitatingly chose for their private architecture the aesthetic originality of invention and the visual wealth of metaphorical decoration. The dominant role was played by Beaux-Arts, Mannerism, and formal experimentation, which could only superficially be described as eclecticism.

Finally, the unexpected acceptance in these regions of the fluid formations of the *Jugendstil*, which appear, for example, on the elegant villas of Thessaloniki, Kavala, Mytilini, and elsewhere, undoubtedly betrays the pioneering intent characteristic of the buildings' users, though it perhaps also reveals an excessive projection of the "good life" as well as contradictions between the residents' aesthetic criteria and their cultural experiences. For the truth is that classicism was not imposed on the communities of northern Greece in order to make them forget the terrible intellectual leveling of the period of Ottoman occupation by offering them pleasant images and delightful visions. Quite the reverse. Classicism, with its disciplined harmonies and its precise, delicate system of orders, corresponding with the masterpieces that were its historical models, came in the form of cultural capital. Its aim was to invest in the functions of the intellect, to disclose the power of reflection, and, finally, to recall the latent ideas of historical memory. Consequently, the rendering of this style, with its austere vocabulary of patterns, made greater demands on its exponents. Its incorporation into an environment that had a related morphological tradition, such as in areas with strong Italian influences like the urban centers in western Greece and the Aegean islands, was entirely predictable (figs. 505–27). Here it imposed its aesthetic quality, tolerating details drawn from the Renaissance and, occasionally, local morphological compromises.

To close, it may be said that for Hellenism after the national uprising, with the cultural dynamism of its newly constituted pluralistic society, classicism offered—to a different extent in each place—an aesthetic cohesion, or at least the most reliable means of achieving it. Classicism embodied, as a means of aesthetic perfection, the logical development of a historical, ideological, and morphological amalgam. For this reason, its implementation never proffered a superficial satisfaction through a false decorative role. Though Greek classicism attained its zenith and then its maturity, it never presented the image of decline. It always kept alive the ingredient of memory, and for this reason it may perhaps be considered, even with its undeniably local quality, the last historical style of European architecture.

Bibliography

Index

Sources of Illustrations

Abbreviations

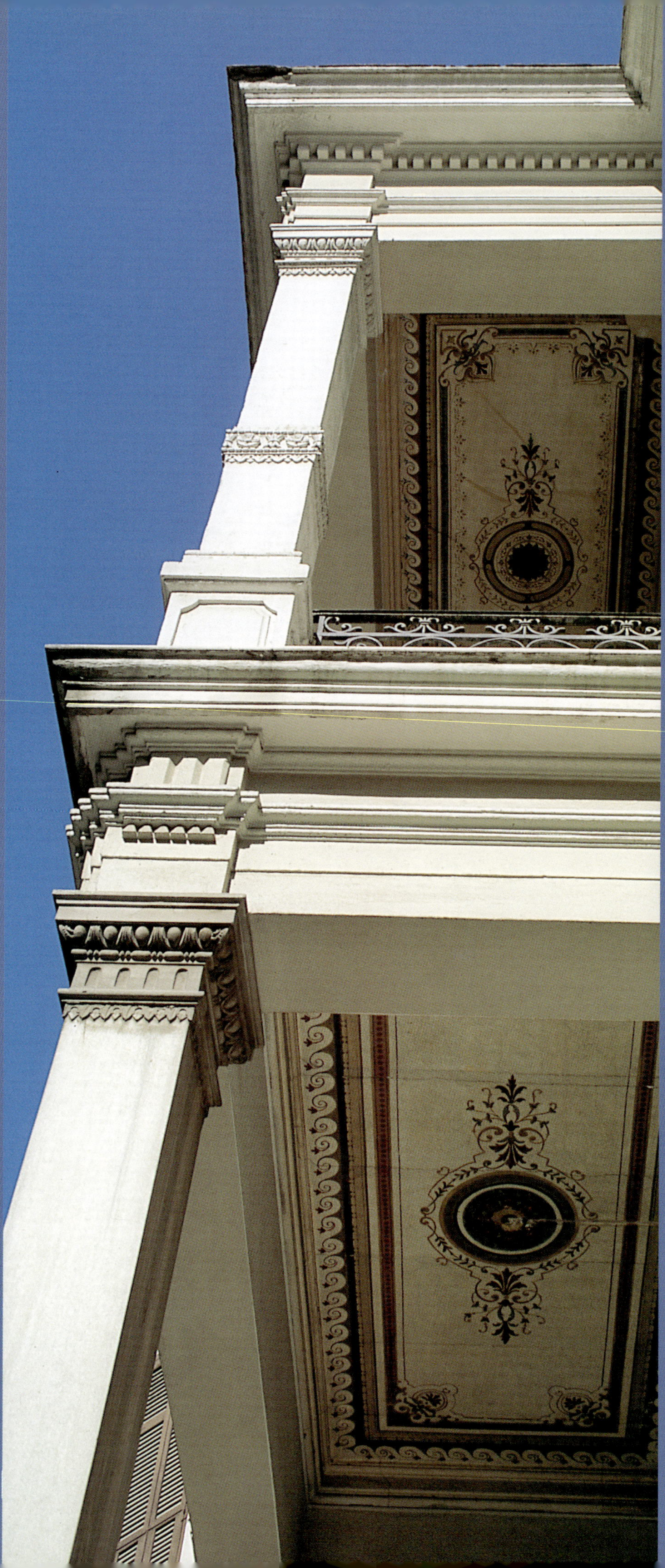

BIBLIOGRAPHY

Agathos S., *Κέρκυρα. Ιστορία–μνημεία–μουσεία,* Athens 1985.

—, *Αχίλλειο. Η ιστορία και ο θρύλος,* 1992.

—, *Αναμνήσεις από την Κέρκυρα. Τ' απομνημονεύματα του Κάιζερ Γουλιέλμου ΙΙ,* n.d.

Agoropoulou-Birbili A., *Τριαντάπεντε σχέδια του Αναστασίου Σάρτζιντ από τη Ζάκυνθο του 1841–1862,* Solomos and Distinguished Zakynthians Museum, Athens 1972.

—, *Η αρχιτεκτονική της πόλεως της Κέρκυρας κατά την περίοδο της Ενετοκρατίας,* Athens 1977.

—, 'Η αστική κατοικία στην αγγλοκρατούμενη Κέρκυρα και οι επτανησιακοί όροι δομήσεως,' *Κερκυραϊκά Χρονικά,* vol. 26, Corfu 1982.

—, *Ιωάννης Χρόνης,* exhibition catalogue, TEE, Corfu 1997.

Agriandoni C. – Fenerli A. – Karakoulidis I., *Ερμούπολη–Σύρος. Ιστορικό οδοιπορικό,* Ermoupoli Municipal Development Company, Athens 1999.

Ambelas T., *Ιστορία της νήσου Σύρου,* Syros 1998 (first edition 1874).

Anairousi F. – Mylonadis L., *Ο Κάμπος της Χίου,* n.p. 1995.

Anastasiou T., *Σύρα. Ιστορική μνήμη, περιήγηση,* Syros 1998.

Andreadaki-Vlazaki M., *Ο νομός Χανίων μέσα από τα μνημεία του,* Hellenic Ministry of Culture, Athens 1996.

Andrianakis M., *Η παλιά πόλη των Χανίων,* Athens 1997.

—, *Χίος, Οινούσες, Ψαρά. Ιστορία, παράδοση, σύγχρονη πόλη,* Athens 1997.

Angelomatis G., *Ελληνικά ρομαντικά χρόνια,* Athens 1965.

Antypas P., *Αναμνήσεις και προοπτικές τ' Αργοστολίου,* Kephallonia Historical and Laographic Museum, Athens 1986.

Argyrou K. – Lefkokilos S. – Philippa M., *Η αρχιτεκτονική της Λευκάδας,* Society for Lefkada Studies 1971.

Avgerinou K. – Tsotsorou E., 'Οι δημοτικές αγορές της Ελλάδας 1830–1940,' lecture to the Department of Architecture, National Technical University, Athens 1986 (typescript).

Avramopoulou M. – Voutsila V., *Λάρισα,* n.p. 1962.

Αθηναϊκός Κλασικισμός, Municipality of Athens – Cultural Centre, Athens 1996.

Αστικό Ελληνικό Σπίτι Θεσσαλονίκης 1880–1912, Macedonia Laographic and Ethnological Museum, Thessaloniki 1985.

Bakounakis N., *Πάτρα 1828–1886,* Athens 1988.

Belitsos T., *Η Λήμνος και τα χωριά της,* Athens 1994.

Bell H., *Ταξείδι στην Ελλάδα,* vol. Α΄, Neo-Hellenic Historical Library, n.p. 1993.

Bickford-Smith P. A. H., *Greece under King George,* Athens 1893.

—, *Βιομηχανικά κτίρια στη Λέσβο, 19ος και αρχές 20ού αιώνα. Ελαιοτριβεία, σαπωνοποιεία,* Prefectory of Lesbos, 1986 (reprint).

Biris K., 'Τα πρώτα σχέδια των Αθηνών,' in *Αθηναϊκαί Μελέται,* vol. I, Athens 1933.

—, 'Εκατό χρόνια αθηναϊκής αρχιτεκτονικής,' in *Αθηναϊκαί Μελέται,* vol. II, Athens 1939.

—, *Αι Αθήναι από του 19ου εις τον 20όν αιώνα,* Athens 1966, Athens 1995 (reprint).

Biris M., *Η οικία Κουτσογιάννη και ο αρχιτέκτων της Π. Κάλκος,* Athens 1972.

—, *Μισός αιώνας αθηναϊκής αρχιτεκτονικής,* Athens 1978.

—, 'From late neo-classicism to the emergence of modernism 1900–1930,' in *Greece – 20th-century Architecture,* Deutches Architektur Museum, Frankfurt 1999.

Boukas M., *Οδηγός των πλείστων και κυριωτέρων πόλεων της Ελλάδος,* Athens 1875.

Bountzouvi-Bania A., 'Το Ναύπλιο στα χρόνια 1828–1833,' *Eranistis,* vol. Β΄, Athens 1986.

Bouras C., *Χίος,* National Bank of Greece, Athens 1974.

Burnouf E., 'La Grèce en 1886,' *Revue des deux mondes,* Paris 1887.

Charalambopoulou C., *Ιστοριολαογραφικά Ναυπακτίας,* Athens 1985.

Christodoulou C., 'Η ιστορία της νήσου Ύδρας από την αρχαιότητα μέχρι σήμερα,' *Φωνή της Ύδρας,* Hydra 1989.

Christou C., *Το αρχοντικό της Αγροτικής Τράπεζας,* Athens 1985.

Dandis X., *Η αρχαία και σύγχρονη Αίγινα,* Athens 1967.

Davos V., *Στον Πύργο και στην Ηλεία του 1821–1930,* Athens 1996.

Demacopulos J., *Ανθολογία ελληνικής αρχιτεκτονικής,* Hellenic Ministry of Culture, Athens 1981.

—, *Η κατοικία στην Κρήτη κατά την τελευταία περίοδο της Βενετοκρατίας,* Goulandris-Horn Foundation, Athens 1997.

Demenegi-Virivaki A., *Παλαιά Ανάκτορα Αθηνών 1836–1986,* Athens 1994.

Deschamps G., 'La Grèce d'aujourd'hui,' *Revue des deux mondes,* Paris 1892.

Dimitropoulos A., *Σύρος. Οδηγός για τον επισκέπτη,* Athens 1993.

Dodwell Ed., *Περιηγήσεις στην Ελλάδα* (first edition London 1819), vol. Α΄: *Σάλωνα, Φωκικά Χρονικά,* vol. Β/2, 1990.

Dorizas N., *Τα κτίρια του Πειραιά κατά τον 19ο αιώνα,* Society of Friends of the Municipal Theatre of Piraeus, Athens 1997.

Dountsi A., *Κέρκυρα, το νησί των χρωμάτων,* Athens 1996.

Ergolavos S. – Celebi, Evl. *Ταξίδι στην Ήπειρο,* Epiros 1996 (second edition).

Evelpidis C., *Οικονομική και κοινωνική ιστορία της Ελλάδος,* Athens 1950.

Exarchos Th., *Κέρκυρα, καρτ-ποστάλ. Έλληνες και ξένοι εκδότες,* Athens 1997.

—, *Ξάνθη. Ματιά στο χτες της πόλης μέσα από φωτογραφίες,* Thrace Cultural Development Centre, 1997.

—, *Τα αρχοντικά της οδού Ελευθ. Βενιζέλου,* Xanthi 1999.

Fessa-Emmanouil E., *Η αρχιτεκτονική του νεοελληνικού θεάτρου,* Αθήνα 1994.

Fieder K. G., *Reise durch alle Teile des Koenigsreichs Griechenland in den Jahren 1834–1837,* Leipzig 1840–41.

Fountoulaki O., *Stamatios Kleanthes (1802–1862),* doctoral dissertation, Munich 1979 (typescript).

Georgandopoulos Ep., *Τηνιακά. Αρχαία και νεωτέρα γεωγραφία και ιστορία της Τήνου,* Palamidis, Athens 1889.

◀ Thessaloniki. Morphological detail: superimposed balconies in a late classicizing urban residence.

Golombias G., *Οι καρτ-ποστάλ της Κοζάνης 1904–1925*, Hellenic Ministry of Culture – Municipality of Kozani, Kozani 1996.

Grigorakos N., *Μαλλιαροπούλειο Θέατρο*, Athens 1980.

Holevas N., *Αρχιτεκτονική του Μεσοπολέμου στα Βαλκάνια*, Athens 1994.

Holland H., *Ταξίδι στη Μακεδονία και Θεσσαλία (1812–1813)*, Athens 1989 (reprint).

Ikonomou K., *Ναύπακτος. Ιστορικός και τουριστικός οδηγός*, Athens 1980.

Ioannidis S., *Ξάνθη 1870–1940. Εικόνες και μαρτυρίες από την ιστορία της*, Xanthi 1990.

Johannes H. – Biris K., *Αι Αθήναι του Κλασσικισμού*, Athens 1939.

Kafkoula K. – Papamichos N. – Chastaoglou V., *Σχέδια πόλεων στην Ελλάδα του 19ου αιώνα*, Aristotle University of Thessaloniki, Thessaloniki 1990.

Kaflikourdi G. – Alexiou S., *Αίγινα. Οδηγός για την ιστορία και τα μνημεία της*, n.p., n.d.

Kaïka-Mandanika G., *Πάτρα 1870–1900. Η καθημερινή ζωή της Πάτρας στην αυγή της Μπελ επόκ*, Patra 1998.

Kairophylakas K., 'Η Ζάκυνθος όπως την είδαν οι περιηγηταί,' *Ημερολόγιον της Μεγάλης Ελλάδος*, n.p. 1930–1931.

Kakakiou K., *Ρόδος. Αστική αρχιτεκτονική και επαύλεις στο γύρισμα του αιώνα*, National Technical University, February 1996 (typescript).

Kaloyeropoulos D., *Επτανησιακά σημειώματα*, Athens 1930.

Kaloyirou N., *Αρχιτεκτονική και πολεοδομία στη μεταπολεμική Θεσσαλονίκη*, Centre of the History of Thessaloniki, Municipality of Thessaloniki, n.d.

Kambouri-Vamvakou M., *Το art-nouveau στην αρχιτεκτονική της Θεσσαλονίκης* (Festschrift for Professor N. K. Moutsopoulos), Aristotle University of Thessaloniki, Thessaloniki, n.d.

Kambouroglou P., *Ιστορία του Πειραιώς από του 1833–1882 έτους*, Athens 1883.

Karadimou-Yerolymbou Al., *Η ανοικοδόμηση της Θεσσαλονίκης μετά την πυρκαγιά του 1917*, Municipality of Thessaloniki, Thessaloniki 1985–1986.

–, *Μεταξύ Ανατολής και Δύσης*, Athens 1997.

Kardamitsi-Adami M. – Papanikolaou-Christensen A., *Το Οφθαλμιατρείο Αθηνών 1843–1993. Εκατόν πενήντα χρόνια από την ίδρυσή του*, Athens 1993.

Kardamitsi-Adami M., *Οι πρώτοι Έλληνες μηχανικοί*, Τεχνικά Χρονικά, vol. 8/4, Oct.-Dec. 1988.

–, 'Το Αρχαιολογικό Μουσείο της Αθήνας. Δύο άγνωστα σχέδια των Δ. Ζέζου και Α. Μεταξά,' *The World of Buildings*, vol. 12, Feb. 1997.

–, 'Το αθηναϊκό σπίτι στα πρώτα μετά την απελευθέρωση χρόνια,' in *Αρχιτεκτονική και πολεοδομία από την αρχαιότητα έως σήμερα. Η περίπτωση της Αθήνας*, Athens 1997.

–, *Ernst Ziller. Αναμνήσεις*, Athens 1997.

–, 'Η στέγαση των πρώτων δημοτικών σχολείων της Αθήνας,' in T. Papakonstandinou (ed.) *Αι Αθήναι ως εκπαιδευτική πόλις από τον 19ον προς τον 20ό αιώνα*, Athens University (Museum of the History of Education), Athens 1999.

–, 'Οι περιπέτειες του παλαιού Βαρβακείου' in T. Papakonstandinou (ed.) *Αι Αθήναι ως εκπαιδευτική πόλις...*, op. cit.

–, 'Τα διαδοχικά κτίρια της Σχολής Χιλλ,' in *Αι Αθήναι ως εκπαιδευτική πόλις...*, op. cit.

–, 'Τα διδακτήρια της Φιλεκπαιδευτικής Εταιρείας,' in *Αι Αθήναι ως εκπαιδευτική πόλις...*, op. cit.

–, 'Το Α΄ εν Αθήναις Γυμνάσιο, ένα σχολείο σε αναζήτηση στέγης,' in *Αι Αθήναι ως εκπαιδευτική πόλις...*, op. cit.

–, 'Τα σχέδια του Λύσανδρου Καυταντζόγλου για το ηρώον των πεσόντων στην πολιορκία του Μεσολογγίου,' *Χρονικά Αισθητικής*, vol. 39–40, 1999–2000.

Karouzos C. *Ρόδος*, Athens 1949.

Karouzou S., *Το Ναύπλιο*, Commercial Bank of Greece, Athens 1979.

Karydis M., *Η ιστορία της Αίγινας*, Athens 1979.

Kasimatis I., *Από την παλαιά και σύγχρονη κυθηραϊκή ζωή*, Athens 1937.

Katsoyiannos N., *Τα Τρίκαλα και οι συνοικισμοί τους*, Larissa 1992.

Kimoulakis G., *Σύμη, με τα μάτια της ψυχής*, Athens 1998.

Kitsikis K., *Η κτιριολογική άποψις του νέου σχεδίου της Θεσσαλονίκης*, Athens 1919.

Kladou-Bletsa A., *Τα Χανιά έξω από τα τείχη*, TEE, Chania 1978.

Kokkou A., 'Τα πρώτα αθηναϊκά σπίτια,' *Αρχαιολογία*, vol. 2, 1982.

Kokosoulas G., *Βενετσιάνικα μνημεία του νομού Ρεθύμνου*, University of Crete, Rethymno 1980.

–, *Μεσολόγγι 1830–1990*, n.p., n.d.

Kolonas V. – Papamatthaiaki L., *Ο αρχιτέκτονας Vitaliano Poselli*, Thessaloniki 1980.

Kolonas V., *Η εκτός των τειχών επέκταση της Θεσσαλονίκης. Εικονογραφία της συνοικίας Χαμηδιέ (1885–1912)*, doctoral dissertation, University of Thessaloniki 1991 (typescript).

–, *Θεσσαλονίκη 1912–1992. Οκτώ δεκαετίες νεοελληνικής αρχιτεκτονικής*, Macedonian Museum of Modern Art, Hellenic Ministry of Culture – Municipality of Thessaloniki, Thessaloniki 1993.

–, 'Αρχιτεκτονική του art déco. Η εμφάνισή της στη Θεσσαλονίκη,' *The World of Buildings*, vol. 5, 1994.

–, 'Μεταπολεμική αρχιτεκτονική στη Θεσσαλονίκη,' *The World of Buildings*, vol. 7, 1997.

–, 'Η αρχιτεκτονική δημιουργία στην Ελλάδα κατά την περίοδο 1900–1912,' in C. Chatzijosiph (ed.) *Ιστορία της Ελλάδας στον 20ό αιώνα*, vol. Α΄, Athens 1999.

–, *Αρχιτεκτονική Ιστορία της Ελλάδας του 20ού αιώνα, 1900–1922*. vol. Α΄, *Οι απαρχές*, Athens 2000.

Konstandinopoulos C., *Η Αίγινα στα χρόνια του Καποδίστρια*, Athens 1968.

Kounadi-Papadatou M., *Παλιά σπίτια στην Κεφαλλονιά*, Athens 1998.

Kydoniatis S., *Αθήνα. Παρελθόν και μέλλον*, Athens 1985.

Kyriakidis K. – Malikouti T., *Ναύπλιο. Αναγνώριση και ανάλυση ιστορικού κέντρου*, National Technical University, Athens 1984.

Kyriazis P. – Nikolinakos M. (ed.), *Οι πρώτοι έλληνες τεχνικοί επιστήμονες της περιόδου της Απελευθέρωσης*, TEE, Athens 1976.

Lagouros S., *Τουριστικός οδηγός Τήνου*, Athens 1983.

Lambrynidis M., *Η Ναυπλία*, Athens 1950.

Leotsakos S., *Ρόδος, το σμαραγδένιο νησί*, Athens 1949.

Liapis A., *Η Κομοτηνή και η περιφέρειά της. Ιστορική, περιηγητική, αρχαιολογική σκιαγραφία*, Komotini 1996.

Loyer F., *Architecture de la Grèce contemporaine*, doctoral dissertation, Paris 1966 (typescript).

Lygizos G., *Παλιά αντριώτικα σπίτια*, Athens 1983.

Machairas K., *Λευκάς και Λευκάδιοι επί αγγλικής προστασίας (1810–1864)*, Corfu 1940, Athens 1979 (reprint).

Malagari L. – Stratidakis C., *Ρέθυμνο. Οδηγός για την πόλη*, Athens 1995.

Malikouti T., *Λειτουργική συγκρότηση και αρχιτεκτονική εξέλιξη του ιστορικού κέντρου του Πειραιά 1835–1912*, doctoral dissertation, Athens 1999 (typescript).

Meletopoulos I., *Πειραϊκά*, Athens 1945.

Micheli L., *Πειραιάς, από το Πόρτο Λεόνε στη Μαγχεστρία της Ανατολής*, Athens 1988.

Molochas N., *Οι χάρτες της Πάτρας*, Athens 1985.

—, *Το Λιμάνι της Πάτρας*, Athens 1991.

—, *Ο Φάρος της Πάτρας*, Athens 1997.

Monioudi-Gavala D., *Η πόλη της Χίου. Κοινωνία, πολεοδομία, αρχιτεκτονική*, Prefecture of Chios, 1995.

Moschopoulos N. G., *Ιστορία της Κεφαλλονιάς*, Athens 1985.

Mousson Alb., *Κέρκυρα και Κεφαλλονιά. Μία περιήγησις το 1858*, Neo-Hellenic Historical Library, n.p. 1955.

Moutsopoulos N., *Μακεδονική αρχιτεκτονική. Συμβολή εις την μελέτην της ελληνικής οικίας*, Thessaloniki 1971.

—, *Θεσσαλονίκη 1900–1917*, Thessaloniki 1980.

Mylonas P., 'Μια αδημοσίευτη συλλογή αρχιτεκτονικών σχεδίων της κλασσικιστικής Αθήνας,' *Νέα Εστία*, 1984.

Mylonas S., *Ζάκυνθος. Καλλιτεχνικός τουριστικός οδηγός*, n.p., n.d.

Myriklis I., *Ταξείδι στην Ύδρα*, n.p., n.d.

Natsios D. – Davanellos N., 'Η Παλιά Λαμία. Ιστορικό και φωτογραφικό λεύκωμα,' *Φθιωτικά Χρονικά*, Lamia 1982.

Natsios D., *Οι δρόμοι και οι πλατείες της Λαμίας. Συμβολή στην τοπική ιστορία*, n.p. 1998.

Nenedakis A., *Ρέθεμνος. Τριάντα αιώνες πολιτεία*, Athens 1983.

Νεοκλασική Ερμούπολη, Mortage Bank, Athens 1998.

Νεοκλασική αρχιτεκτονική στην Ελλάδα, intr. J. Travlos, Commercial Bank of Greece, Athens 1967.

Νεώτερα μνημεία της Θεσσαλονίκης, Hellenic Ministry of Culture – Ministry of Northern Greece, Thessaloniki 1985–1986.

Orlandos A., *Περί της νήσου Πέτσας ή Σπετσών*, Piraeus 1877.

Panayiotopoulos V., *Πληθυσμός και οικισμοί της Πελοποννήσου, 13ος–18ος αιώνας*, Historical Archive of the Commercial Bank of Greece, Athens 1985.

Pandis M., *Κέρκυρα, το Βαϊλάτο του Αλευχικού και το Πεντάχωρο*, n.p. 1986.

Papadatou-Yiannopoulou C., *Εξέλιξη του σχεδίου πόλεως των Πατρών, 1829–1989*, Patra 1991.

Papageorgiou-Venetas Al., *Εδουάρδος Σάουμπερτ 1804–1860*, Athens 1999.

—, *Ο Leo von Klenze στην Ελλάδα*, Athens 2000.

Papageorgiou-Venetas Al., *Hauptstadt Athen*, Munich – Berlin 1994.

Papamichail S., *Ας γνωρίσουμε την Κάρυστο*, Karystos 1993.

Papanikolaou P., *Ιστορία της Φιλαρμονικής Εταιρείας Πύργου 'Απόλλων,' 1881–1993*, Pyrgos 1995.

Papanikolaou-Christensen A., *Αθήνα 1818–1853. Έργα δανών καλλιτεχνών*, Athens 1985.

Papanikolaou-Christensen A., *Χριστιανός Χάνσεν*, Athens 1993.

Papastamos D., *Ε. Τσίλλερ. Προσπάθεια μονογραφίας*, Hellenic Ministry of Culture and Science, Athens 1973.

Papastavros A., *Ιωαννίνων Εγκώμιον*, Ioannina 1998.

Paraskevaidis P., *Λέσβος. Ιστορία, λαογραφία, αρχαιολογία, περιήγηση*, Athens 1989.

—, *Οι περιηγητές για τη Λέσβο*, 3rd edition, Mytilini 1996.

Perilla F., *Hydra, Spetsae, Psara*, Athens 1950.

Philippides D., *Νεοελληνική αρχιτεκτονική*, Athens 1984.

—, *Λύσανδρος Καυταντζόγλου*, Hellenic Ministry of Culture – ETBA Cultural Foundation, Athens 1995.

Polemis D., *Η ιστορία της Άνδρου* [*Πέταλον*, παράρτ. 1], Andros 1981.

Πρακτικά Α΄ Διεθνούς Συνεδρίου Χίου για την ιστορία και τον πολιτισμό του νησιού, Prefecture of Chios, 1988.

Russack H. H., *Deutsche bauen in Athen*, Berlin 1942.

Sambanopoulos K., *Ο νομός Κοζάνης στο χώρο και στο χρόνο. Φύση, ιστορία, παράδοση*, Arts and Letters Association of the Prefecture of Kozani, Kozani 1993.

Sarandis A. – Salvador L., *Πρελούντια για τη Ζάκυνθο. Φωτογραφίες από τη Ζάκυνθο του 1900*, Athens 1988.

Sargin R., 'Νεοκλασικές επαύλεις της Ζακύνθου,' *Περίπλους*, vol. 13–14, 1987.

Sathas K., *Το εν Ζακύνθω αρχοντολόγιον και οι ποπολάροι*, Athens 1962 (reprint).

Sherzeri C., *Η επαρχία της Σμύρνης*, Vienna 1873.

Skarpia Hoipel X., *Η μορφολογία του γερμανικού κλασσικισμού (1789–1848) και η δημιουργική αφομοίωσή του από την ελληνική αρχιτεκτονική (1833–1897)*, doctoral dissertation, Thessaloniki 1976 (typescript).

Skopelitis S., *Πύργοι Μυτιλήνης*, Athens 1975.

—, *Αρχοντικά της Λέσβου*, Athens 1977.

Skoutelis N. – Zanon P., *Η αρχιτεκτονική κληρονομιά των Οινουσών*, Oinousai Naval Museum, 1999.

Synadinos P., *Πάτρα. Πολιτισμός, ανάπτυξη, πολεοδομία*, Patra.

Syngros A., *Απομνημονεύματα*, vol. Γ΄, Αθήνα 1908.

Thomopoulos S., *Ιστορία της πόλεως των Πατρών*, Patra 1950.

Tloupas T. – Kliapha M. – Tsapala-Vardouli P., *Στο Βαρούσι*, Gnosi, Athens 1988.

Travlos J. – Kokkou A., *Ερμούπολη*, Commercial Bank of Greece, Athens 1980.

Triandou E., *Ο Βόλος μέσα από την ομίχλη του χρόνου*, n.p. 1994.

Tsandaridis G., *Mon Repos*, Athens 1985.

Tsipouras D. E., *Αρχιτεκτονικαί βάσεις προς δημιουργίαν νέου Ελληνικού ρυθμού*, Athens 1921.

Tsitsas A., *Κέρκυρα. Νοσταλγικές αναδρομές*, Society for Corfiote Studies, Corfu 1992.

Tsivis G., *Χανιά 1252–1940*, Athens 1993.

Tsokopoulos V., *Πειραιάς 1835–1870*, Athens 1984.

Θεσσαλονίκη. Οι πρώτες έγχρωμες φωτογραφίες, 1913 και 1918, Athens 1999.

Vernardakis A., *Το μέλλον των Αθηνών*, Athens 1902.

Vlamos G., *Η Υγιεινή του Σχολείου*, Athens 1904.

Vlassopoulos I., *Το νησί Τήνος*, Athens 1992.

von Thiersch F., *De l'état actuel de la Grèce et des moyens d'arriver à sa restauration*, F. A. Brockhaus, Leipzig 1833.

Whitton-Paipeti H., *Corfu. Pictures from the Past*, Corfu 1990.

Yannoulis A., *Aigina*, n.p. 1986.

Yiannopoulos P., *Η ελληνική γραμμή*, Athens 1981.

Ziogas R., *Παραδοσιακά κτίρια της νεότερης Καβάλας*, Kavala 1982.

Zivas D., *Η αρχιτεκτονική της Ζακύνθου από τον ΙΣΤ΄ μέχρι τον ΙΘ΄ αιώνα*, Athens 1970.

INDEX

(page numbers in italics refer to captions)

Abbot, G. F. 192
Adalis, A. 203, *203*
Adam, Robert 53
Adriatic 176
Aegean *42, 201,* 222, 231, 302
Aegean islands 29, 40, *42,* 49, 122, 173, 187, 199, 248, 302
Agrinion 122, *246*
Aigina 58, *59, 60,* 62, 63, *67,* 71, 115, *128,* 145
Aigion 105, *106, 110,* 111, 227, 236
    Aigion market *238*
    Panayiotopoulos mansion *110,* 111
    Phaneromeni (church) 227
    Town Hall building *110*
Albania 176
Alexandroupoli High School *257*
Alexandroupolis 187, 194
Ambelakia *46, 47,* 182, *184*
America 71, 83, 187
Amphissa 105, 122, 236
Amsterdam 111
Andros *40,* 122, *244*
Antonio Villa 53
Apollo Epikourios (temple) *17*
Arabs 36
Ardittos Hill 149
Areopagos 145
Argive and Saronic gulfs (islands) 116
Argos 56, 58, 63, 105, *107,* 122, *122*
Argostoli 33, 53, *54, 131*
Arkadia 49
Art Deco 187, 194, 270, *272, 278*
Art Nouveau 187, *263,* 270, 271, *271, 273,* 278, *279, 280, 292*
Arta *45,* 176, *177, 180, 181,* 244, *246*
Asia Minor 29, 48, 117, 199, 200, 213, 248, 279, 294
Asia Minor disaster 294
Athens 10, 21, 22, 23, 25, 32, 36, 58, 71, *71,* 72, *72,* 73, *73,* 74, *74,* 75, *75,* 77, *77,* 78, *79,* 80, *81,* 82, 83, *83, 84, 85,* 86, *86,* 88, 89, *89, 90,* 92, *94,* 96, *96,* 97, *97,* 98, *98,* 100, *101,* 102, 105, 111, 113, *114,* 115, 119, 132, 135, *135,* 136, *136,* 138, *138, 140,* 142, *144,* 145, 146, *147, 148,* 149, *149,* 150, *150, 151,* 152, *154, 156, 157, 158, 160,* 162, *162, 163, 164,* 166, *167, 168,* 170, *170,* 173, 176, 178, 179, 186, 187, 190, 194, 195, 199, 203, 213, 214, *215, 216, 218,* 219, *221, 222, 223, 226,* 227, *227,* 228, 229, 231, 240, 244, *245,* 256, 258, 263, *263, 266, 267, 268,* 270, *272, 274, 275, 276,* 292, 299
    Academy *10, 35,* 100, 138, *138, 140,* 142, 145, 152, 214
    Acropolis *17, 25,* 74, 75, *81,* 85, 88, 92, *135,* 145, 149, 292
    Agricultural Bank 156
    Ancient Agora 71, 146
    Arsakeion 92, 98, *98,* 100, 136, 138
    Asylum for the Incurable 170
    Averoff Prison 170
    Ayia Irini (church) 100, *101, 136,* 227
    Ayia Triada (church) 116, 227
    Ayios Konstantinos (church) 227
    Ayios Loukas (church) 227, *227*
    Bangas hotels 222
    bathhouse at Staropazaro 145
    Botsaris, Count residence 80, 162
    Britain 105, 131, 187
    Byzantine and Christian Museum *90,* 92
    Cathedral 97, *97*
    Charokopos mansion (now the Benaki Museum) 162, *164,* 166
    Chatzikonstas Orphanage 170, 227
    Chrysospiliotissa church 227, *227*
    Church tower 75
    Dekozis-Vouros, Stamatios house 89, *89, 90,* 92
    Deliyiorgi house 222
    Dimitriou, A. mansion *86, 94,* 96, *135*
    Dromokaition Mental Hospital 170
    Embirikos mansion 166
    Evangelismos Hospital 170
    Evgenidis mansion 154, 214
    Exhibition Hall (known as the Olympia) 149
    Eye Hospital *94, 96,* 97, 156, *160*
    Feraldi's market 77
    Finlay residence 80
    First Primary School *84*
    French Archaeological School 154
    Gorgoepikoos (church) 145
    Greek Parliament (Palace of King Otto) 86, *86,* 258
    Grivas residence 162
    Hill School 72
    Iliou Melathron 219, *222, 223*
    Ilissia mansion *90,* 92
    Infant Orphanage 170
    Kalligas, P. mansion 166
    Karapanos, K. mansion 156
    Kasdonis 222
    Kerameikos 86
    King Otto's Palace 72, 86, *86,* 136
    Kontostavlos residence 71, *72,* 89, *89*
    Koupas mansion 222
    Koutsoyiannis, I. "apartment building" 152, *156*
    Lykavittos *86,* 88
    Lysikrates Monument *21*
    Maisonette mansion 92
    Melas, Basil mansion 219, *221*
    Merlin, K. mansion (now the French Embassy) 162
    Metaxourgeio 152, *154*
    Miaoulis, Admiral residence 162
    Military Courthouse 154, *158*
    Military hospital 88, *89,* 119
    Mourouzis, K. mansion 154, *157*
    Municipal Market 115, 170
    Municipal Theater 170, 222, *226,* 228, 296
    National Archaeological Museum 102, 145, 146, *147,* 184
    National Library 142, *144,* 145, *147*
    National Technical University (Metsovion Polytechnic) 71, 85, 98, 100, *101,* 102, 136, 138, 142, 146, 154, *175,* 178, 206, 228, 292
    Negrepontis, Militiadis mansion 154, *158,* 231
    Observatory 97, 138
    Old Parliament Building 71, *72*
    Olympia Theater 222, *226*
    palace of the crown prince (now the Presidential Palace) 222
    Papadopoulos High School (now the Kostis Palamas building) *98*
    Papoudoff residences 162
    Parnassos Literary Society 170
    Plaka 71, *74, 75, 79,* 149
    Pnyx 145
    Psychas mansion (now the Egyptian Embassy) 162, *163*
    Psychas residence (now the Italian Embassy) 166
    Rallis, A. house *90,* 92
    Rezer, Wern house 162
    Rizareios School 162
    Rododaphne villa *90,* 92
    Roman Forum 72, *73, 78*
    Royal (now National) Theater 222, *226*
    Royal Garden 148, *148, 149*
    Royal Mint 88
    Royal Press and Lithographic Workshop 88
    Saripolos, I. N. mansion 156, *162*
    Second Primary School *168,* 170
    Serpieri mansion 156, *160*
    Skouloudis mansion 162, *164, 166,* 214, 231
    St. Dionysios of the Catholics (church) *96,* 97
    Stathatos, Othonas mansion *135,* 166, 222
    Syngros mansion 162, *163, 164*
    Syngrou Prison 170
    Temple of Wingless Victory *21*
    Tourelle residence 92
    Tower of the Winds 23, *24, 25*
    Town Hall *168,* 170, *170,* 222, 228
    town plan of Athens 74, 77, *77,* 83, 86
    trilogy 62, 142, *144,* 145, 146
    Tsopotos residence 154, *157*
    University *79,* 92, *92,* 100, 138, *144,* 145, 179
    Varvakeios School *167,* 170
    Venizelos, E. 258, 271
    Vlachoutsis house *78,* 80
    Voglis residence 222
    Vouros, I. mansion 162, *164*
    Vourou-Eftaxia Museum *89*
    Women's Prison 170
    Workshop for Destitute Women 170
    Zappeion 149, 150, *150, 151*
    Zlatanos mansion 166
Attica 71, 227
Audoy 55
Austria 55, 175, 187

Austrians 113
Austro-Hungarian 105, 200
Averoff, Georgios 102
Ayia 182

Balkan architecture 194
Balkans 213
Bargigli Dr. 200
Baroque 29, 32, *32, 33,* 34, 40, *42,* 48, 49, 80, 146, 156, 175, 190, 192, 194, *196,* 200, 210, 270, 278, 279, 299
Bavaria 75, 86, *96,* 203
Bavarian(s) 53, *56, 57,* 61, 82, 85, 86, *89, 94,* 105, 118, 119, 122, 152, 162
Beaux-Arts 195, *253,* 263, *263, 266, 270,* 294, 302
Belgium 72
Bell, H. 166
Berlin *22,* 61, 72, 81, 82, *84,* 86, 96, 142, 148, 176, 244, 288, 292
   Altesmuseum 142
Benaki Museum *86, 164,* 166
Bernardakis, Dimitrios 96, 146
Bernasconi 178
Biris, Kostas 296
Bonirote, Pierre 85
Borrozin 122
Bosnia 105
Boulanger, F. F. 150
Brussels 72
Bulgarian(s) 192, 193
Bursa *192*
Byzantine empire 188
Byzantine style 162, 227
Byzantine-revival architecture 97, *259*
Byzantium 258

caryatids 219
Ceccoli, Rafaello 85
central Europe 48, 81, 187
central Greece 122, 136, 227, 236, 240, 244
Chalkida 255
Chania 30, *38,* 39, 203, 204, 206, *207,* 208, *210,* 248, *248, 255*
   Government House 208
   Kaloutsis, Valerios house 204
   Karavelakis-Agazades house 204, *207*
   Koundouros house 204
   Markantonakis family house 204
   Mitsotakis house 204, *207*
   Phoumis house 204, *207*
   Schwartz, Baron house 204

Chios 39, 40, *42,* 117, 199, *199, 200,* 203, 208, *249,* 254
   Chora 199, 208
   club 199
   Quay Theater 199
Chiots 111, 113, 117, 199
Chronis, Ioannis 53, *53, 132*
Constantinople 49, 85, 111, 135, 173, *174, 175,* 176, 190, 192, *193,* 194, 195, 200, 203, 210, 213, 214, 244, 254, *254,* 263, 279, 283
Corfu 30, *31,* 32, 34, *35,* 48, 53, *53, 54, 55,* 58, 68, *68,* 131, *132,* 173, 231
   Kambielo neighborhood 236
   Kapodistrias mansion 53
   Liston 53
   Mon Repos 53, *54*
   School of Architecture 53
   School of Fine Arts 53
   Spianada 53, *54*
Corinth 58, 63, 105, 122
Council of Elders 74, 118
Cretan(s) 29, 32, 36, 39, 203, 204, 208
Crete 29, 36, 39, 40, 113, 173, 203, 204, 206, *206,* 208, 213, 248, *248*
Crimean War 173
Crown Prince Constantine 156
Cyclades 39, 116, 122, 146, 240, 254, 278

Danubian Principalities 71
Danubian provinces 213
Danubian regions 48
De Bosset 53, *54*
De Vogue 182
Dedeagach 194
Devaud, A. 55, *56*
Dodecanese islands 40, 173, 244, 248
Drama 187
Drosis, Leonidas *98, 140,* 142
duchesse de Plaisance 85, *90, 92,* 162
Durand, J. N. L. 81

eclectic 97, *97,* 145, 150, 170, *175,* 176, 192, 204, *210,* 227, 229, *240, 245,* 248, 254, *276,* 283
eclecticism 13, 82, *185,* 187, 188, *188,* 190, 194, *201,* 210, 214, 219, 231, 236, 240, 263, 270, 279, *284, 287,* 302
École des Beaux-Arts 263
École Polytechnique 81
Edessa 187
Egypt 135, 187, 203, 213, 271
Embirikos mansion 166

Enlightenment 17, *17,* 48, 49
Epiros, 29, 173, 176, 182, 186, 208, 256
Erechtheion *138,* 142
Eretria 105, 126
Erlacher, J. 115, 119, 122
Ermoupolis (see also Syros) *10, 67,* 89, 111, 113, 116, *116,* 118, *118,* 119, *120,* 122, 199, 219, 229, 231, *232, 233, 234, 235,* 237
   Apollo Theater 231, *232*
   Ayios Nikolaos (church) *120,* 122
   Customs House 115, 119, *120,* 122
   Food Market 119
   Hellas Club *120*
   Hermes Club 119
   Kois mansion 231
   Lazaretto *67,* 119
   Negrepontis mansion 231
   Prassakis mansion 122
   Town Hall *10, 116,* 219, 231, *233*
   Vapheiadakis villa 231, *237, 301*
   Vaporia district 231
   Velissaropoulos residence 231, *237*
   warehouses 117, 119

Feraldi, F. *77,* 115, 116
Florina 187, 283, *286*
Fouqué, M. 200
Fraas, Karl 148
Franks 40
French occupation 53
French Revolution 49, 50, 58

Gaertner, Friedrich von 77, 86, *86,* 88, 89, 148
Galaxidi 105, 122, *126, 128, 130,* 236, *256*
Garnier, C. 156
Garnot, A. T. 55, *57, 67,* 119, 122
Gasparis-Kalandros, Andreas 55
Gazis, A. 138
Gennadios, G. 138
Genovese 152
Georgantas, A. 96, *120,* 122
Georgiadis villa *201*
Georgiadis, M. 85
German idealism 81
Germany 81, 89, 214, 292
Goethe 22, 82
Gothic Revival 156, *162, 274, 278, 279,* 283
Great Idea 214
Greek renaissance style 219
Greek War of Independence 83, 131

Greek-Byzantine style 97
Griepenkerl, Christian 142

Halepa Pact 203, 206
Hallerstein, Haller von 74
Hansen brothers 62, 86, 97, 98
Hansen, Christian 59, *72,* 88, 89, *89, 92, 92,* 96, *96,* 97, *97,* 179
Hansen, Theophil 85, *94,* 96, 97, 100, 138, *138,* 142, *142,* 145, 146, 150, *151,* 152, 154, 214, 219, 227
Hatti Humayun 173, 182, 199
Hébrard, E. 258
Hegel, W. E. 82
Heideck, Karl Wilhelm Freiherr von 61
Heller, Karl 85
Heraklion 39, 203, 204, 206, *206, 208, 209,* 210, *248, 271*
Herder, Johann Gottfried von 22
Hill school 72
Hill, I. 71
historicism 18, 26, 97, 100, 150, 166, *188,* 214, 219, *230,* 263
Hitler 292
Hoch 86
Hoffer, J. 88, 89
Holland 72
Holland, H. 186
humanism 49
Hydra 113

Ilia 108
interwar period 176
Ioannides family 116
Ioannina *45,* 49, 175, 176, *176, 177, 178, 178, 179, 180, 181,* 258, *259*
   Chatzikonstas Hospital 179
   Commercial School 178, *178*
   Eighth Army Division building 178
   Georgios Stavros Orphanage 178, *179, 181*
   Girls' School (now the Post Office) 179, *179*
   government house 178
   Municipal Hospital 179
   Papazogleios Weaving School for Girls 179
   Pasha's *konaki* 178
   Zosimaia School 179, *180*
Ionian Academy *35*
Ionian Bank 53
Ionian islands 29, 30, 32, *33,* 36, 39, 40, 49, 53, 55, *55,* 63, 131, *132, 132,* 162, 173, 213, 231, *235,* 236

Ionian Parliament Building 53
Ippoliti, P. 55
Isaias, S. 55
Italian Renaissance 17, 22, 36, *40*, 219, 236
Italy 53, 55, 61, 63, 72, 105, 107, *131*, 175, 178, 187, 292
Itea 58, 105, 122, *126*, 236

Jefferson, Thomas 53
Jewish (Jews) 176, 178, 186, 192, 193, *281*, 283
Jugendstil 270, *272*, *276*, *287*, *291*, 302

Kaftantzoglou, Lysandros 71, 85, *94*, 96, *96*, 97, 98, *98*, 100, *101*, 116, 136, 162, *164*, 227, 292
Kalamata 105, *128*, *129*, 236, 240, *242*, *271*, 274
Kalkos, Panagiotes (Βρεττός) 97, *110*, 111, *147*, 148, 152, *156*, *167*, 168, 170
Kallergis, I. 55
Kallias, D. 179, *257*
Kalliroi fountain 75
Kalymnos 203, 248
Kapodistrias period 58, *59*, *60*, 61, 62, 82, 118, 119, 122, 179
Kapodistrias, Ioannis 17, 53, *53*, 58, 61, 62, 71, 82
Karapanos, K. mansion 156
Karathanasopoulos, P. *122*, 231, *245*
Karditsa 182, 186, 244, *270*
Karlsruhe 81
Karpathos *249*, *250*
Kastella 231, *268*
Kastelorizo 248
Kastoria 187
Katakolo 108
Kavala *185*, *186*, 187, *187*, 188, *213*, *252*, 278, *279*, 283, *287*, *288*, 302
  Baron Pierre Herzog 283
  boys' school 188
  castle 187
  Conservatory *252*, 283
  girls' school 188
  Municipal Tobacco Warehouse 283, *288*
  Panayia area 187
  tobacco warehouses 186, *187*, 194, 283
  Tokkos, D. mansion *186*
  Town Hall *185*
Kea 122
Kennedy, P. H. 53, *54*
Kephallonia 32, *33*, *35*, 36, *36*, 53, *54*, 58, 107, *131*, 173

Kifisia *274*
King George I 100, 135, *136*, 138, 149, 152, 162, 173, 182, 206, 213
King Otto 16, 53, *56*, 62, *72*, 75, 86, *86*, 88, 89, 92, 102, 107, 111, 115, 118, 135, 136, *136*, 148, 150, 152
Kiphisos 75
Kitsikis, K. 258
Kleanthis, Stamatis 55, 58, 61, 62, 71, *71*, 74, 75, 77, *77*, 78, 80, *83*, 86, 88, *90*, 92, 98, 111, *114*, 115, 126, 149, 258
Klenze, Leo von 75, 77, *77*, 80, *81*, 82, 86, *96*, 98, 146
Koliopoulos residences 62
Kolliniatis, I. 154
Komninos, T. 85
Komotini 193, 194, *195*, *252*, 283
Koraïs, Adamantios 17
Kosmas of Aitolia 254
Kossos 152
Koumelis, I. 136, 154, 170
Koumelis, N. 142
Koumoundouros 213, 231
Kozani *44*, 187
Kriezis, Andreas 88
Kriezis, E. 256
Kydonies 117
Kythira 32

Lamia 122, *245*, *246*
Lange, Ludwig *84*, 148
Larisa 182, *182*, *184*, 186, 244, *246*
Laurent, C. 85
Lavrio *215*
Lazarimos, Ioannis 136, 154, 228, *229*, *229*
Le Corbusier 278
Le Roy, Julien-David 22, *24*
Lefkada 55, *215*
Lesvos *40*, 199, *203*, *205*, 254, 256, *257*
liberation 17, 29, 36, 39, *44*, 49, 53, 135, 176, *179*, 182, 186, 192, 199, 244, *245*, *246*, 254, 256, 283
Lidoriki 58, 105
Lixouri 53, *54*
London 22, *23*, *25*, 71, *73*, 111, 115, 203
London Protocol 71, 203
Ludwig I 75, *80*, 82, 86
Lueders, G. 89
Lykoudis, Stylianos 58
Macedonia 29, 48, 128, 173, 176, 187, 188, 200, 208, 254, 256, 258, 283, 292

Maitland, Thomas 53, *54*
Malakates 152
Mani 49
Maniots 32
Manitakis, E. 55
Mannerism 156, *160*, 200, 214, *242*, 270, *291*, 302
Margaritis 152
Marseilles 111, 115
Materialstil 89, *89*
Matton, D. 149
Mawson, T. 258
Maximilian 86
Megara 105, 122
Melirrytos, P. 178, 179
Melnitzki, Franz 142
Mesolongi 105, 122, *130*, 236, 240, *246*
Metaxas, Anastasis *164*, 166, 170, *271*, *276*, 278, 292
Metaxas, Gerasimos 58, *94*, *120*, 122, 136, 145, 146, *147*, 170, 229
Metaxas, Ioannis 292
Methoni 32, 105, 122
Mimin, Kizi 283
Mineiko, S. 178
Mithymna 199
modern movement 278, 292
modernism 187, 261, 263, *271*, *273*, 278, 279, 294
Mohamed Ali 187, 203
Moldavia and Wallachia 71, 105
Monemvasia 32, 49
Mounichia 113
Moustoxydis, Andreas 61, 62
Munich *80*, 81, 82, 86, 89, 92, *116*, 148, 152, 292
  Glyptothek 82
  Propylaia *80*
  Royal Academy 148
  School 92, *116*, 152
Mussolini 292
Mykonos 119
Mylonas, P. *94*, *126*, *158*, *167*, 226
Mytilini *42*, *192*, 199, 200, *201*, *202*, 203, *203*, 204, 208, 254, *255*, *272*, 278, *278*, 283, *290*, *291*, 302

Nafpaktos 122, 236
Nafplion 30, 32, *48*, 49, *53*, *56*, 58, 61, 62, 63, *63*, *64*, *66*, 71, 82, 105, 107, *107*, 111, *113*, 115, 119, 122, 132, 231, 236, 240, *271*, 292, *296*
  Armansberg residence *63*
  Kallergis residence 62
  Koliopoulos residence 62

Law Court Building *296*
Mauer residence 62
Military Cadet School 82, 115
National Bank 292
Town Hall *64*
National Bank of Greece 79, 135, 156, *160*, *240*, 256, *258*, *259*, 292, *293*, *295*
National Technical University (Metsovion Polytechnic) *71*, 85, 98, 100, *101*, 102, 136, 138, 142, 146, 154, *175*, 178, 206, 228, 292
Naxos *40*, 122
Neapoli *102*, 146, *152*
Neo Phaliro *230*, 231
  Aktaion Hotel *230*
neo-Romantic and eclectic spirit 227
New Territories 244
Nikoloudis, Alexandros *266*, *267*, 268
Nointel, marquis de *71*

Odessa 111, 115
Old Greece 36, 98, 108, 173, 176, 186, 206, 209, 236, 244, *245*, 254, 278, 283
Olympic Games 150
Omiridis-Skylitsis, P. 138
Ottoman Empire 29, 30, 105, 173, 175, 187, 188, 210, 213, 283
Ottoman Girls' School 179, *179*
Ottoman period 24, *64*, *73*, 75, 186
Ottomans 32, 39, 182, 203

palace of St. Michael and St. George 53, *55*
Panathenaic Stadium 214, *218*
Papadakis, K. 256
Papazogleios Weaving School for Girls 179
Paris 24, 29, 53, *57*, 82, 156, *166*, 179, 263, 288
Paros *243*
Patmos *39*, *243*
Patras *10*, *57*, 58, 63, *67*, 68, *68*, 105, 107, *107*, 108, *108*, 113, 119, 122, 132, *136*, 219, *220*, 231, 236, *239*, 240, *240*, *270*, *299*
  Avyerinou Square 108
  Iroon Square 108
  Lower Town *57*, 68, *68*, 108, *108*, 117, 118
  Municipal Theater *220*
  Upper Town 107, 108, *108*
  Vasileos Georgiou Protou Square 108, *108*, *113*
  Vasilissis Olgas Square 108, *108*

310

Patriarchate 193
Pauzié 55
Peloponnese 32, 39, 48, 49, 107, *107, 110*, 111, 122, 131, 136, 227, 236
pentelic marble *21*, 88, *140*, 142, 146, *157*
Percier, Charles 53
Perrault, Claude *19*
Petimezas, G. *114*, 229
Peytier, E. 55
Phanariots 135
Phreattyda, Municipal Bathhouse 231
Phytalis brothers 152
picturesque style *72, 92, 126, 174, 181, 198, 200*, 204, *229*, 231, 236, *243, 260, 270, 274*
Piraeus 104, *107*, 111, 113, *114*, 115, 116, 118, 119, 122, 142, 199, 222, *224*, 227, 228, *228*, 229, *229, 230*, 231, *268, 276*
  Ayia Triada 116, 227
  Ayios Nikolaos 228
  Catholic church of St. Paul 116
  Chatzikonstas Hospital 179
  Chatzikyriakeion Girls' Orphanage 229, *230*
  Chiot neighborhood 199
  Customs House 113, 115, 119, 122
  High School 227
  Hydraians settlement 113
  Kantharos harbor 111
  Koumoundouros mansion 231
  Lazaretto 115
  Meletopoulos mansion 231
  Metaxas residence 222, 231
  Moutsopoulos residence 116
  Municipal Market 115
  Municipal Theater 228, *229*
  Municipality 228
  Patsiadis house 222, *224*
  Pheraldis mansion 231
  Post Office 229
  Rallis, A. house *90, 92*, 116
  Skylitsis residence 116
  Stock Exchange Building 228
  Town Hall 228, *229*
  Tzanneion Hospital 227, 229
  Valerios Kaloutsis house 204
  Varvaressos residence 222, 231
  Vernikos mansion 231
Pisamanos, Gerasimos 53
Plomari 199
Poitrineau, V. E. 162, *164*
Polyzoidis, A. 138
Pomaks 193

Portaria *44*
Portugal 105
post-Romantic schools 81, 82
Preveza *177, 182*, 258, 292
Provveditore Generale of the East 30
Pylos 105, 122
Pyrgos 108, *110*, 227, 236, *238*
  Ayios Athanasios 227
  Municipal Market *238*

Rahl, Karl 96, 142
Rallis, Dimitris 115
Rallis, Loukas 115
Rasim Pasha 175, 176, 178
rationalism 58, *64*, 82, *126, 181*, 294
Renaissance 17, 18, 22, 29, *30*, 32, 34, 36, *37*, 40, *40, 53, 64*, 88, 89, *124*, 131, 145, 146, 154, 200, 206, *218*, 219, 227, *230*, 236, *246*, 270, 299, 302
Rethymnon *29, 37, 38*, 39, 203, 206, *206*, 248
"return to the roots" 294
Revett, Nicholas 22, *22, 23*, 25
Rhodes 203, 248, *249*
Rizos Rangavis, Alexandros 146
Rococo 48, 49, 80, *237*
Romanesque elements 227
Romania 135
Romanticism 17, 18, 26, 82, *120, 273, 275*
Rome 53, 72, 98, 292
Royal (now National) Theater 222, *226*
rue de Rivoli 53
Rundbogenstil 89, *120*
Russia 48, 61, 105, 135, 145, 175, 187, 292
Russo-Turkish war 194

Sakellariou, P. 178
Sakopoulos, N. 203
Samos 199, *199*, 203, 254
Sampo, P. 231, *232*
San Luca Academy 98
Sante Hanuk 71
Schaubert, Eduard 58, 61, 62, 71, *71*, 74, 75, 77, *77, 84*, 85, 86, 88, 111, *114*, 115, 116, 126, 149
Schaumbourg, Baron Charles de 55, 63, *68*
Schelling 82
Schiller, Johann Christoph Friedrich von 22
Schinas, K. 138

Schinas, N. 166
Schinkel, Karl Friedrich von 61, 62, 82, *85*, 86, 96, 219
Schliemann, Heinrich 219
School of Architecture 53, 85
School of Arts *83*, 85, 86, 96, 105, *136*
Scwertzek, Karl 146
Secession 270
Sechos, I. 136, 154
Second Empire period 263
Second World War 259, 294
Septinsular Republic 53
Serres 187, *192*, 258
Siegel, C. 85, 152
Silesia 214
Sinas, Baron Georgios 96
Sinas, Simon 96, 138, 142
Siphnos 42
Siteia *39*
Skalistiris, D. 136
Skylitsi, Elena 271
Skylitsis 116
Smyrna 49, 111, 117, 199, 244, *249, 250, 254*, 283
Soutsos, Panayiotis 75
Spain 105
Sparti *105, 124*, 126, 236, 240, *242*
  Archaeological Museum *124*
Spiliadis, N. 61
St. Petersburg 58, 146
Stauffert, Fr. *84*, 88, 126
Stavridis, D. 55, 122
Stavros, Georgios 178, *179, 181*
Stier, Wilhelm 61
Stournaris, Nikolaos 102
Stuart, James 22
Subic, Yuri 222, *223*
Switzerland 55
Symi 248, *250*, 254, 299
Syngros, Andreas 162, 193, 222
Syros (see also Ermoupolis) 67, 89, 105, 111, 116, 117, 118, 119, 122, 199, 219, 229, *237, 275, 300, 301*
  Ano (Upper) Syros 117
  Lower Town (Kato Poli) 117

Tanzimat 173, 199
temple at Phigaleia 203
Theater of Dionysos 214
Thebes 105, 122
Theophilas, Anastasios 96, 136, 154, 156, *160*, 229
Theseion 145, 146

Thessaloniki *173*, 176, 187, 188, *188*, 190, *190, 191*, 192, *192*, 193, *193*, 194, *194*, 195, 203, *253*, 258, *260*, 263, *263*, 278, 279, *280, 281*, 283, *283, 284*, 292, *293*, 302
  barracks 190
  Chamidie Avenue 188, *188*
  Civil Hospital *192*
  Government House 190, *191, 192*
  Greek Consulate 193, *194*
  Imperial High School (Lyceum) 190, *190*
  Ionian Bank *293*
  Memorial 292
  National Bank of Greece *293*
  Papapheion Orphanage *188*
  White Tower 188, *188*
Thessaly *44, 46, 47*, 128, 173, 182, 186, 187, 194, 208, 213, 240
Thiersch, Frédéric von 85
Thiersch, Ludwig 62, 85
Thrace 29, 48, 173, 193, 194, 208, 254, 256
Tinos *40*, 122, 231
Tositsas, Eleni 102, 148
Tositsas, Michael 102
Treiber, B. 142
Triantaphyllos, Agathangelos 85
Trieste 49, 175
Trikala 182, *182, 184*, 186, 244
Trikoupis, Charilaos 136, 145, 213, 214
Tripolis *57*, 58, 63, 105, 122, *123*, 236, *239, 242*, 292, 294
  Ayios Vasileios *239*
  Ethnomartyron Street 236
  Law Court Building *294*
  town plan *57*
Troump, E. 154, *158*
Tseroulis, Antonios 55, *67*
Tsipouras, D. E. 292
Turkish Baroque *196*
Tyrnavos 182

Unredeemed territories 62, 171, 173, 176, *179*, 209, 213

Valassis, A. 254
Vallianos, Andreas 145
Vallianos, Marinos 145
Vallianos, Panagis 145
Vallianos, Theodoros 55, 58, *59, 60*, 61, *67*
Valsamakis, Dionysis 58

Vasilissis Olgas Street 108, *253, 280, 283*
Venetian period 36, *38, 39, 64*, 111, 131
Venetian tradition *31, 37, 66,* 122, 131, *182*
Venetian(s) 29, 30, *31*, 32, 34, *35*, 36, *37, 38,* 39, *39,* 40, *40,* 49, 53, 62, *63, 64, 66,* 111, 122, 131, *182*, 204, 208, *210*, 236, 248
Venizelos, E. 258, 271
Venizelou Street *287*
Veria 187
Vienna 82, 86, 96, 138, 142, 219, *230*, 288
    Heinrichhof 219

Parliament Building 142
Villia, Attica (church) 227
Vlamos, G. 254
Volos 182, *184*, 186, 244, *245, 274*
    Ayios Nikolaos (church) 182
    Chatzilazaros mansion 182
Vostitza (Aigion) 58, *106*
Voukourestiou Street (school) 75
Voulgaris, Stamatis 55, *56, 57, 68,* 107, *108*, 122

Walker, Mary 200
War in 1897 (Greco-Turkish in Thessaly) 213

Weiler, W. von *67*, 88, *89*, 119, *120*
Winckelmann, Johann Joachim 22, *22*, 82

Xanthi 193, 194, *196*, *197*, *198*, 254, *257*, 283, *295*

Yiannopoulos, P. 166
Young Turk zealots 193

Zachos, Aristotelis 48, 258
Zakynthos *29, 31*, 32, *32*, 34, 36, 131, *131*, 173, *218*, 219, 228
Zappas, Evangelos 149
Zavos, Lambros 55

Zea (bay) 113, *224,* 231
Zentner, Friedrich von 85
Zezos, Demetres *83*, 97, *97,* 145, 146, *147*, 227, *227*
Ziller, Ernst *10, 122, 135*, 136, 138, *142, 144,* 145, 146, *147,* 148, *152,* 154, 162, *163*, 166, 170, 193, *194, 214, 218,* 219, *220, 221, 222, 222, 223, 224, 226,* 227, *227,* 228, 231, *233, 238,* 240, 270, *273,* 296
Zizilas, G. 229
Zlatanos 166
Zoumboulidis, N. 256, 292

SOURCES OF ILLUSTRATIONS

Birbilli Aphr. 19

Biris M. photographic archive. 29, 30, 33, 34, 35, 36, 37, 38, 39, 53, 54, 70, 71, 72, 73, 74, 75, 76, 77, 135, 152, 154, 168, 169, 170, 172, 177, 178, 196, 197, 198, 199, 200, 201, 205, 207, 213, 214, 215, 216, 217, 218, 240, 241, 242, 243, 244, 245, 246, 253, 256, 258, 259, 273, 274, 275, 287, 288, 289, 290, 291, 292, 300, 326, 327, 331, 332, 333, 334, 335, 336, 337, 338, 339, 340, 341, 342, 343, 344, 345, 346, 347, 348, 355, 356, 408, 411, 420, 421, 422, 423, 424, 425, 426, 427, 436, 437, 438, 439, 454, 460, 468, 469, 471, 473, 477, 495, 496, 497, 498, 503

Georgouleas I. 204, 206, 276, 277, 278, 279, 280, 281, 282, 283, 284, 285, 286, 299, 301, 304, 305, 308, 310, 318, 319, 320, 321, 322, 323, 324, 325, 415, 416, 417, 418, 419, 430, 431, 432, 433, 434, 446, 478, 490, 491, 492, 493, 494

Kakakiou K. 423, 424

Kardamitsi-Adami M. photographic archive. 1, 3, 4, 5, 6, 7, 8, 20, 21, 31, 55, 59, 60, 61, 69, 87, 88, 96, 127, 130, 131, 132, 145, 148, 153, 157, 158, 159, 160, 161, 165, 166, 167, 173, 175, 176, 186, 187, 194, 208, 209, 232, 233, 234, 263, 267, 270, 293, 294, 295, 297, 298, 302, 303, 306, 307, 309, 311, 312, 313, 314, 315, 328, 329, 330, 349, 350, 352, 353, 354, 361, 373, 380, 381, 382, 383, 384, 398, 412, 413, 414, 435, 443, 444, 445, 447, 457, 470

MELISSA Publishing House photographic archive. 40, 42, 103, 104, 140, 185, 219, 266, 357, 358, 359, 368, 409, 410, 428, 429

Papaioannou P. 370, 455

Vournous E. 426, 427

Voutsas V. 16, 56, 62, 89, 90, 162, 163, 164, 171, 179, 180, 182, 183, 184, 188, 189, 190, 191, 192, 193, 195, 202, 203, 210, 237, 238, 239, 363, 385, 386, 387, 388, 389, 390, 391, 392, 393, 394, 395, 396, 397, 399, 400, 401, 402, 403, 404, 405, 406, 407, 458, 459, 461, 462, 463, 464, 472, 499, 502, 504, 505, 506, 507

Yerolymbos G. 91, 108, 109, 110, 129, 136, 137, 139, 143, 149, 150, 151, 211, 220, 221, 222, 223, 224, 225, 226, 228, 229, 235, 236, 249, 250, 251, 265, 268, 269, 316, 317, 364, 367, 369, 376, 377, 378, 379, 448, 449, 456, 474, 475, 476, 479, 480, 481, 482, 483, 484, 485, 486, 487, 500, 501

ABBREVIATIONS

ELIA   Hellenic Literary and Historical Archive
KTNA   Documentation Centre for Neo-Hellenic Architecture, Benaki Museum

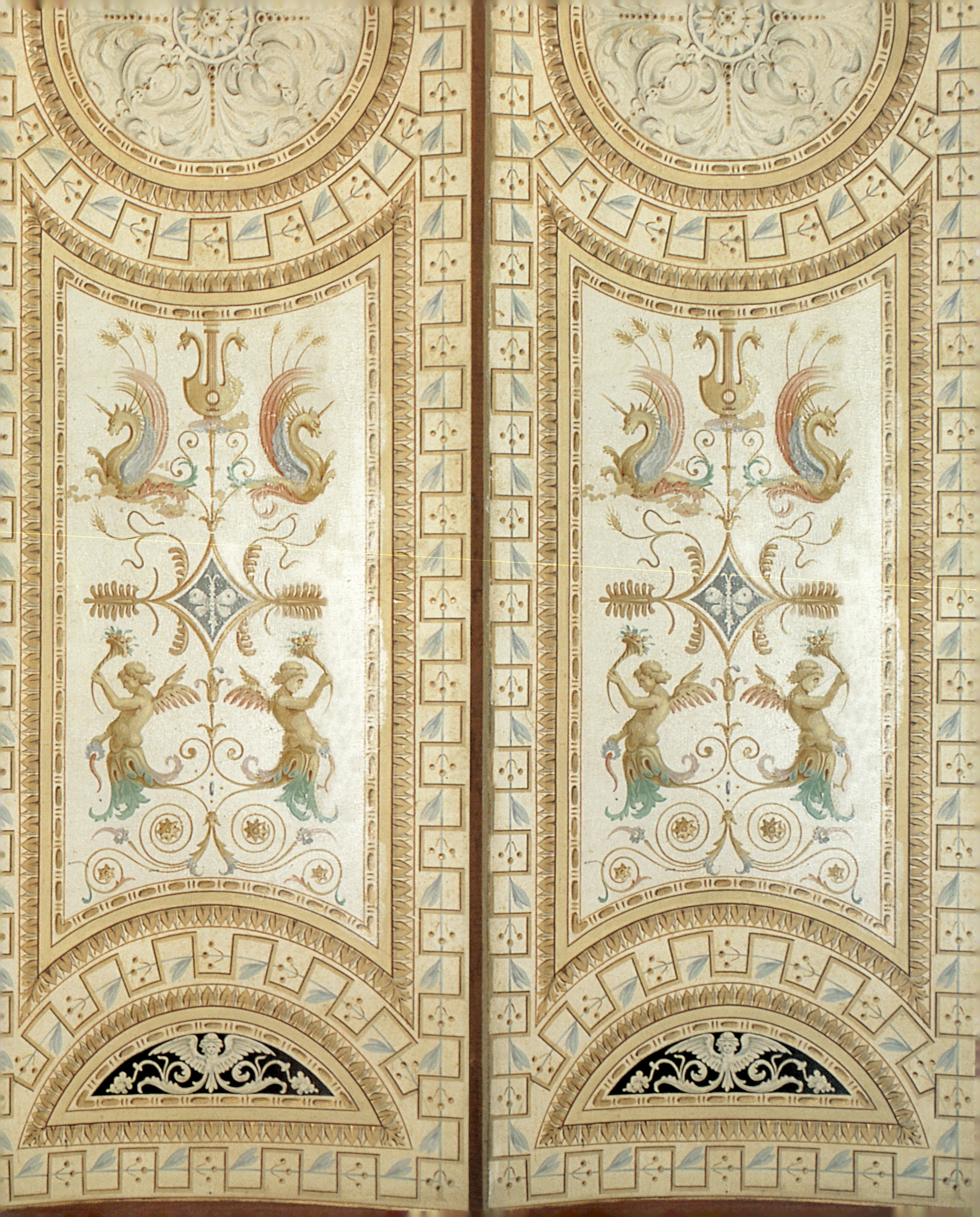